# The Cambridge Companion to Science Fiction

Science fiction is at the intersection of numerous fields. It is a literature which draws on popular culture, and which engages in speculation about science, history and all types of social relations. This volume brings together essays by scholars and practitioners of science fiction, which look at the genre from these different angles. After an introduction to the nature of science fiction, historical chapters trace science fiction from Thomas More to the present day, including a chapter on film and television. The second section introduces four important critical approaches to science fiction drawing their theoretical inspiration from Marxism, postmodernism, feminism and queer theory. The final and largest section of the book looks at various themes and sub-genres of science fiction. A number of well-known science fiction writers contribute to this volume, including Gwyneth Jones, Ken MacLeod, Brian Stableford, Andy Duncan, James Gunn, Joan Slonczewski and Damien Broderick.

# THE CAMBRIDGE
# COMPANION TO
# SCIENCE FICTION

EDITED BY
## EDWARD JAMES
AND
## FARAH MENDLESOHN

CAMBRIDGE
UNIVERSITY PRESS

CAMBRIDGE UNIVERSITY PRESS
Cambridge, New York, Melbourne, Madrid, Cape Town, Singapore, São Paulo, Delhi

Cambridge University Press
The Edinburgh Building, Cambridge CB2 8RU, UK

Published in the United States of America by Cambridge University Press, New York

www.cambridge.org
Information on this title: www.cambridge.org/9780521816267

First published 2003
Fifth printing 2008

Printed in the United Kingdom at the University Press, Cambridge

*A catalogue record for this book is available from the British Library*

*Library of Congress Cataloguing in Publication data*
The Cambridge companion to science fiction / edited by Edward James and
Farah Mendlesohn.
p.   cm.
Includes bibliographical references and index.
ISBN 0 521 81626 2 – ISBN 0 521 01657 6 (pb.)
1. Science fiction – History and criticism.   1. Title: Companion to science fiction.
11. James, Edward, 1947 –   111. Mendlesohn, Farah.
PN 3377.5.S3C36   2003
809.3'8762 – dc21        2003043808

ISBN 978-0-521-81626-7 hardback
ISBN 978-0-521-01657-5 paperback

# CONTENTS

## Part 2. Critical approaches

## Part 3. Sub-genres and themes

List of contents

CONTRIBUTORS

BRIAN ATTEBERY'S latest book is *Decoding Gender in Science Fiction* (2002). He has also published two studies of fantasy literature, and is co-editor with Ursula K. Le Guin of *The Norton Book of Science Fiction* (1993). He won the IAFA Distinguished Scholarship Award in 1991 and the Mythopoeic Scholarship Award in Myth and Fantasy Studies, 1992. He directs the graduate programme in English at Idaho State University.

MARK BOULD is a Senior Lecturer in Film Studies at the University of the West of England, Bristol. His reviews and articles have appeared in *FEMSPEC, Foundation, Intensities, Public Understanding of Science* and *Science Fiction Studies*. A major contributor to the Wallflower Critical Guides to Contemporary Directors, he is the author of *Reading Science Fiction* (http://www.bloomsburymagazine.com), *A Lone Star: The Cinema of John Sayles* (2003), and *Film Noir: From Fritz Lang to Fight Club* (2004).

DAMIEN BRODERICK is a Senior Fellow in the Department of English with Cultural Studies in the University of Melbourne, Australia, and holds a PhD from Deakin University. His publications include novels, popular science, radio drama and literary theory, including *Reading by Starlight: Postmodern Science Fiction* (1995) and *Transrealist Fiction* (2000); see bibliography at http://www.panterraweb.com/the_spike.htm.

ANDREW M. BUTLER is Field Chair in Film Studies at Buckinghamshire Chilterns University College, where he also teaches Media Studies and Creative Writing. Since 1995 he has been features editor of *Vector: The Critical Journal of the British Science Fiction Association*. He is the author of Pocket Essentials on *Philip K. Dick* (2000), *Cyberpunk* (2000), *Terry Pratchett* (2001) and *Film Studies* (2002), as well as being the co-editor, with Farah Mendlesohn and Edward James, of *Terry Pratchett: Guilty of Literature* (2001).

JOHN CLUTE was born in Toronto in 1940 and moved to London, England, in 1968. Novelist, writer, poet, editor and above all critic and reviewer, there is not much in science fiction that he has not been involved in. He has won three Hugo Awards for Best Related Work, for *The Encyclopedia of Science Fiction* (with co-editor Peter Nicholls) in 1994, *Science Fiction: The Illustrated Encyclopedia* in 1996 and *The Encyclopedia of Fantasy* (with co-editor John Grant) in 1998. He also won a World Fantasy Award in 1998 for *The Encyclopedia of Fantasy*, and has won the Eaton Award, the SFRA's Pilgrim Award and the IAFA's Distinguished Scholar Award. Two volumes of his collected reviews have been published. His latest works are *The Book of End Times*, *Tesseracts 8* (with co-editor Candas Jane Dorsey), and his first science fiction novel, *Appleseed*, published in 2001.

KATHRYN CRAMER is a writer, critic and anthologist presently co-editing the *Year's Best Fantasy* and *Year's Best SF* series with her husband David G. Hartwell. She recently completed *The Hard SF Renaissance* (2002), an anthology co-edited also with Hartwell; their previous hard science fiction anthology was *The Ascent of Wonder* (1994). She won a World Fantasy Award for best anthology for *The Architecture of Fear* (1987), co-edited with Peter Pautz; and she was nominated for a World Fantasy Award for her anthology, *Walls of Fear* (1990). She is on the editorial board of *The New York Review of Science Fiction*, and lives in Pleasantville, New York.

ISTVAN CSICSERY-RONAY, JR is Professor of English and World Literature at DePauw University, and a co-editor of *Science Fiction Studies*. He has published widely on international science fiction, and his book, *The Seven Beauties of Science Fiction*, is forthcoming from Wesleyan University Press. He won the Science Fiction Research Association's Pioneer Award for best critical article in 1992, for his essay 'The SF of Theory: Baudrillard and Haraway'.

ANDY DUNCAN won a Sturgeon Award for the novella 'The Chief Designer' (2001), a World Fantasy Award for the story 'The Pottawatomie Giant' (2000) and another World Fantasy Award for the collection *Beluthahatchie and Other Stories* (2000). His stories have appeared in *Asimov's*, *Realms of Fantasy*, *SciFiction*, *Starlight 1*, *Starlight 3*, *Weird Tales* and various year's-best anthologies, while his critical articles have appeared in *Foundation*, *The New York Review of Science Fiction* and the *SFRA Review*. With F. Brett Cox, he edited the anthology *Crossroads: Southern Stories of the Fantastic*. He lives in Northport, Alabama.

JAMES GUNN is Emeritus Professor of English at the University of Kansas and the author of a dozen novels, including *The Listeners* (1972), and *The*

*Immortals* (1962) (which was adapted into a TV movie and a series, 'The Immortal'), and half a dozen collections of short stories. His most recent novel is *The Millennium Blues* (2000) and his most recent collection is *Human Voices* (2002). He also has written extensively about science fiction, including the Hugo-Award-winning *Isaac Asimov: The Foundations of Science Fiction* (1982); *Alternate Worlds: The Illustrated History of Science Fiction* (1975); and *The Science of Science-Fiction Writing* (2000). He is the editor of many books, including the six-volume anthology series *The Road to Science Fiction* (1977–88). He has been president of the Science Fiction Writers of America and the Science Fiction Research Association, and has won the Pilgrim Award and the Eaton Award.

VERONICA HOLLINGER is Associate Professor of Cultural Studies at Trent University in Ontario, Canada. She co-edits the journal *Science Fiction Studies* and is co-editor, with Joan Gordon, of *Blood Read: The Vampire as Metaphor in Contemporary Culture* (1997) and *Edging into the Future: Science Fiction and Contemporary Cultural Transformation* (2002). She was the first winner (in 1990) of the annual SFRA Pioneer Award for best critical essay on science fiction.

EDWARD JAMES is Professor of History at the University of Reading, although he spent the academic years 2001–3 in the Department of History at Rutgers University, New Jersey. He has published numerous studies on early medieval France and Britain, most recently *Britain in the First Millennium* (2001), as well as articles on the history of science fiction. He won the Eaton Award for best critical work on science fiction for *Science Fiction in the Twentieth Century* (1994), and has co-edited three books of essays on science fiction. Between 1986 and 2001 he was editor of *Foundation: The International Review of Science Fiction*; he continues as its production editor.

GWYNETH JONES writes science fiction and fantasy for both adults and young people. She has been nominated for the Arthur C. Clarke Award five times, the fourth time for her novel *North Wind* (1995), the second in the Aleutian series. The first novel in the same series, *White Queen* (1991), was co-winner of the James Tiptree Award, for science fiction exploring gender roles. In 2002 she won the Clarke Award for *Bold as Love* (2001). Her fairy-tale collection *Seven Tales and a Fable* (1995) won two World Fantasy Awards. She writes for teenagers under the name Ann Halam; *The Fear Man*, by Halam (1995), won the Dracula Society's Children of the Night award. She lives in Brighton, UK.

ELISABETH ANNE LEONARD received her PhD from Kent State University, Ohio and her MFA from the University of Pittsburgh. She is the editor of *Into Darkness Peering: Race and Color in the Fantastic* (1997). She currently lives in northern California with her family.

MICHAEL LEVY is Professor of English at the University of Wisconsin-Stout. He has published two books, numerous scholarly articles and innumerable reference book entries and book reviews in the fields of science fiction and children's literature. He is currently working on a critical edition of A. Merritt's *The Moon Pool*. On 1 January 2002 he became Past President of the Science Fiction Research Association and Vice President of the International Association for the Fantastic in the Arts. He was recently named to the editorial board of the journal *Extrapolation*.

KEN MACLEOD was born in Stornoway, Isle of Lewis in 1954. He studied zoology at Glasgow University and researched biomechanics at Brunel University, where he became involved in socialist politics. After working for ten years in the information technology industry he became a full-time writer in 1997. He has written eight novels, several short stories and some articles and reviews. He won the 1996 Prometheus Award for *The Star Fraction* (1995), the 1998 Prometheus Award for *The Stone Canal* (1996) and also won the British Science Fiction Association Award for *The Sky Road* (1999). He lives in West Lothian, Scotland.

FARAH MENDLESOHN is Senior Lecturer in American Studies at Middlesex University. Between 1997 and 2003 she was Chair of the Science Fiction Foundation, and in 2001 she became Editor of the SFF's journal, *Foundation: The International Review of Science Fiction*. She has co-edited books of essays on *Babylon 5* and on Terry Pratchett, and published articles and reviews of science fiction. Her book *Quaker Relief Work in the Spanish Civil War* was published in 2001.

HELEN MERRICK is co-editor with Tess Williams of *Women of Other Worlds: Excursions through Science Fiction and Feminism* (1999), which received the Australian 'William Atheling Jr' award for science fiction criticism. She is author of a number of articles on feminist science fiction and science fiction fandom, and is working on a book called *Feminist/Science/Fictions*. Currently, Dr Merrick lectures in Internet Studies at Curtin University of Technology in Western Australia, where her research interests include cyberculture, virtual communities and comparative histories of the Internet and the science fiction community.

WENDY PEARSON is currently a PhD student in English Studies at the University of Wollongong in Australia. She has an MA in English from McGill University in Canada and taught for fifteen years in Cultural Studies and English at Trent University before returning to doctoral studies. She has published a number of articles, including 'Alien Cryptographies: The View from Queer', which won the Science Fiction Research Association's Pioneer Award in 2000 for the best critical article of the year. She is also the recipient of the Science Fiction Foundation's Graduate Student Essay Prize in 2001 for 'Science Fiction as Pharmacy: Plato, Derrida, Ryman' (published in *Foundation* 86, 2002).

JOAN SLONCZEWSKI teaches molecular biology at Kenyon College, Ohio, and studies *Escherichia coli* survival in extreme acid. Her science fiction explores future medicine, nanotechnology and alien sexualities. *Brain Plague* (2000), nominated for the Nebula Award, shows intelligent alien microbes that enhance human brainpower – at a price. Her Campbell-award winner *A Door into Ocean* (1986) creates a world covered entirely by ocean, inhabited by an all-female race of humans who use genetic engineering to defend their unique ecosystem. In *Daughter of Elysium* (1993) biologists engineer humans to live for thousands of years, then face a revolt by the machines that made it possible. She is currently authoring a major textbook, *Microbiology: A Genomic Perspective* which will include science fiction themes.

BRIAN STABLEFORD'S most recent science fiction project is a six-volume 'Future History' series published by Tor, starting with *Inherit the Earth* (1998). Other recent publications include the apocalyptic comedy *Year Zero* (2000) and a new translation of *Lumen* by Camille Flammarion (2002). He has a BA in Biology and a DPhil in Sociology from the University of York, and has taught at the Universities of Reading and the West of England, and at King Alfred's Winchester. He has been active as a professional writer since 1965, publishing more than fifty novels and 200 short stories as well as several non-fiction books; he is a prolific writer of articles for reference books, mainly in the area of literary history.

GARY WESTFAHL, who teaches at the University of California, Riverside, writes a bi-monthly column for the British science fiction magazine *Interzone* and contributes occasional film reviews and commentaries to the Locus Online website. He is also the author, editor or co-editor of fourteen books about science fiction and fantasy; his authored books include *Cosmic Engineers: A Study of Hard Science Fiction* (1996); *Islands in the Sky: The Space Station Theme in Science Fiction Literature* (1996); and *The Mechanics of Wonder: The Creation of the Idea of Science Fiction* (1998).

GARY K. WOLFE, Professor of Humanities and English and former Dean of University College at Roosevelt University in Chicago, is the author of six books and hundreds of essays and reviews; his most recent book is *Harlan Ellison: The Edge of Forever* (with Ellen Weil) (2002). Currently he is a contributing editor and reviewer for *Locus* magazine. Wolfe has received the Distinguished Scholarship Award from the International Association for the Fantastic in the Arts (1998); the Pilgrim Award for criticism and scholarship from the Science Fiction Research Association (1987); and the Eaton Award for critical work on science fiction (1981). A native of Missouri, Wolfe received his doctorate in English from the University of Chicago.

# FOREWORD

We met in a bedroom of the Royal York Hotel in Toronto in 1971, at the first meeting of the Science Fiction Research Association. There had been an earlier, organizing meeting in New York; it is remembered, in part, for the blackboard exhortation by Dena Brown (then married to Charles Brown, who not long before had started publishing *Locus*, still the main news and reviews magazine of the science fiction field): 'Let's take science fiction out of the classroom and put it back in the gutter where it belongs.' In those days, some fans considered the embrace of academia next to the kiss of death.

That was where we were, in Toronto, caught between our pulp traditions, our love for Edgar Rice Burroughs and A. Merritt and E. E. 'Doc' Smith, and the realization that science fiction was capable of greater sophistication and that it was worthy of study, of scholarship, even of being taught to students. We had already seen evidence that it could be literature in the pages of *The Magazine of Fantasy and Science Fiction*, of *Galaxy*, even of *Astounding*; Kurt Vonnegut Jr was showing that science fiction could break out of the backwaters of general expectations into the eddies of the mainstream, even into best-seller lists, and earn critical acclaim as well, even if it meant taking the label off the books.

The writer and editor Judith Merril was there in Toronto; and the critic Leslie Fiedler, a symbol of the new academic acceptance of science fiction; and Gerald Jonas, who was working on an article for *New Yorker*, had published a science-fiction story himself and later would become the science-fiction book-review editor of the *New York Times*. Robert Scholes showed up at a later meeting, I think. He was another academic convert who would present a series of insightful lectures three years later at Notre Dame (and get them published under the title of *Structural Fabulation*, just as Kingsley Amis had broken the critical ice in a series of lectures at Princeton a decade earlier, published as *New Maps of Hell*).

I do not remember who else was in the hotel room in Toronto, but Phil Klass was there. He had been one of those authors, writing as William Tenn, who had revealed science fiction's potential; he had given up writing to teach English at Penn State University. I remember Phil's presentation in Toronto when he compared his encounter with science fiction with his first glimpse of the model of the solar system at the Hayden Planetarium, the same experience of knee-trembling epiphany of scope. But most of all I remember standing with Phil in front of a window looking out upon the Royal York Hotel grounds and Phil saying, 'We should come up with a canon before someone else does.'

That was where science fiction was back in 1971, filled with hope and anticipation but lacking almost all the tools of scholarship, the reference works, the indexes, the histories, the encyclopedias, the studies and the canon. The present volume, with its list of distinguished international scholars and published by a university press whose parent institution goes back to the Middle Ages, is a symbol of how far science-fiction scholarship has come in thirty years.

Where did it come from?

It all started in the pulp magazines invented in 1896 by Frank A. Munsey. Mostly filled with adventure stories in a variety of locales and periods, they became more specialized beginning in 1915 with the introduction of *Detective Story Monthly* and then *Western Story Magazine* in 1919 and *Love Stories* in 1921. Hugo Gernsback, an immigrant from Luxembourg, had been publishing popular-science magazines with science fiction stories in them. In 1926 he mustered his resources (and his courage) and founded *Amazing Stories*. Soon competitors began to appear, fans and new writers were attracted and a genre was born.

Science-fiction stories and science-fiction writers had been around before, but what they wrote was not quite science fiction and it was not even called science fiction (Gernsback gave it, in 1929, the name that would stick): Verne's adventure novels were called 'voyages extraordinaires' and Wells's stories and novels were 'scientific romances'. Although some critics have claimed that the direction in which Gernsback moved the new category was a blind alley and that it would have been better existing as a kind of mainstream variant, it is difficult to imagine how science fiction would otherwise have developed its sense of identity, a body of informed readers, shared assumptions that sometimes rigidified into conventions and a dialogue among writers, editors and readers that carried science fiction onward and upward.

Of course that is what the critics have attacked: the sense of identity that led to inwardness, insularity, ghetto-ism, fandom, conventions, self-congratulatory awards and all the other paraphernalia. Better, they say, the freedom, the lack of cohesion, the individual artistry of the mainstream.

Rightly or wrongly, the Gernsback tradition, modified by a succession of influential magazine editors beginning with John W. Campbell at *Astounding/Analog* and passing through Tony Boucher and J. Francis McComas of *Fantasy and Science Fiction*, Horace Gold and later Frederik Pohl of *Galaxy* and Michael Moorcock of *New Worlds*, shaped the way science fiction developed. That is what we deal with today, even when the mainstream seems to have broadened to accept the fanciful, and writers who have emerged from the Gernsback tradition seem to be free to venture where they will.

What may be significant, but has been largely overlooked, is that virtually all of the pulp magazines have disappeared except the science-fiction magazines. My conclusion from this (influenced, no doubt, by my early recognition that the science-fiction magazines were different from the other pulps) is that science fiction only seemed to be a part of the pulp-magazine tradition. Rather than emerging from the adventure pulps, science fiction was an outgrowth of the popular-science movement. Even today, *Analog* carries the designation: 'Science Fiction and Fact'. While the other category pulp magazines were supplanted by television, science fiction continues (diminished in circulation but surviving), even in the face of burgeoning science-fiction programming in film and on television.

The teaching of science fiction was started by fans. Sam Moskowitz taught evening classes at the City College of New York in 1953 and 1954. Mark Hillegas taught the first regularly scheduled course at Colgate University (New York State), in 1962, followed by Jack Williamson at Eastern New Mexico University and Tom Clareson at the College of Wooster (Ohio). From there courses proliferated, not only in English departments but in physics, chemistry, sociology, anthropology, history and others. Such courses are both less adventurous and better organized today.

Scholarship was another extraordinary journey. A single academic study, by Philip Babcock Gove, was published in 1941, followed in the postwar period by J. O. Bailey's *Pilgrims Through Space and Time* and Marjorie Hope Nicolson's *Voyages to the Moon*. But most of the tools of scholarship, like the postwar publication of science fiction in books, was provided by amateurs, by dedicated fans, some of them ascending to scholarly objectivity, such as Donald H. Tuck, Donald B. Day, the New England Science Fiction Association, Everett F. Bleiler and Sam Moskowitz.

Academic journals were created, first by fans in academic positions, then by more traditional scholars; Tom Clareson created *Extrapolation* in 1959, and *Foundation* began in Britain in 1972 and *Science-Fiction Studies* in 1973. All have moved around and changed editors from time to time, but they manage to persist and serve slightly different communities. Academic conferences on science fiction, that began with a section at MLA in the late 1950s, grew into the Science Fiction Research Association's annual meeting, the Eaton Conference at the University of California, Riverside and the International Conference on the Fantastic in the Arts, now in Fort Lauderdale; more specialized conferences now are held frequently throughout the year, and in recent years there have been important conferences in Britain, France, Greece and elsewhere.

Just as the mainstream publishers took over the task of publishing from the fans, academic scholars began to assume their traditional roles in the field, bringing to the study greater rigour, better focus and more resources. But even the scholarly field, inside and outside the academy, remains motivated more by a love for the field itself than occurs in other disciplines. Some science-fiction academic publishing houses have come and gone, including Advent (a fan publishing enterprise), Starmont House and Borgo Press. Greenwood Press and McFarland are still active in the field, and a number of university presses have been receptive to science-fiction texts, including Oxford University Press, one of the pioneers, beginning in the 1960s with Bruce Franklin's *Future Perfect*, I. F. Clarke's *Voices Prophesying War* and Mark Hillegas's *The Future as Nightmare*, a series of single-author studies in the 1980s, and continuing with Edward James's *Science Fiction in the Twentieth Century* in 1994. Today both Wesleyan and Liverpool University Presses maintain specialist science-fiction series, and Cambridge University Press has commissioned this book.

Now we enter a new period marked by general acceptance of science fiction as a respectable area of scholarship, widespread popularity of science fiction in film (the top ten best-grossing films of all time are mostly science fiction or fantasy) and the approximately two thousand books of science fiction and fantasy published each year (many of them, to be sure, and often the most popular, media tie-ins). But we now have most of the basic critical tools we need. John Clute and Peter Nicholls have produced substantial encyclopedias; Hal Hall, indexes to reviews; William Contento, indexes to collections and anthologies; and substantial contributions also from Marshall Tymn, and Mike Ashley in Great Britain. And the scholars are gathering.

James Gunn

# ACKNOWLEDGEMENTS

The editors would like to thank Brian Ameringen, Austin Benson, Paul Barnett, Jim Burns, David A. Hardy, David Langford, Michelle Le Blanc, Caroline Mullan, Colin Odell, Claude Pehrson, Roger Robinson and Jim Thrall for their help, and all the contributors (particularly John Clute and Ken MacLeod) for their cooperation and assistance. We should like to dedicate the book to George Hay (1922–1997), founder of the Science Fiction Foundation, who worked tirelessly for the academic recognition of science fiction in Britain.

# CHRONOLOGY

1905 Rudyard Kipling, 'With the Night Mail'
1907 Jack London, *The Iron Heel*
1909 E. M. Forster, 'The Machine Stops'
1911 Hugo Gernsback, *Ralph 124C 41+*
1912 J. D. Beresford, *The Hampdenshire Wonder*
  Garrett P. Serviss, *The Second Deluge*
  Edgar Rice Burroughs, 'Under the Moons of Mars'
1914 George Allan England, *Darkness and Dawn*
1915 Charlotte Perkins Gilman, *Herland*
  Jack London, *The Scarlet Plague*
1918 Abraham Merritt, 'The Moon Pool'
1920 Karel Čapek, *R. U. R.: A Fantastic Melodrama*
  W. E. B. Du Bois, 'The Comet'
  David Lindsay, *A Voyage to Arcturus*
1923 E. V. Odle, *The Clockwork Man*
1924 Yevgeny Zamiatin, *We*
1926 Hugo Gernsback starts *Amazing Stories*
  *Metropolis* (dir. Fritz Lang)
1928 E. E. Smith, *The Skylark of Space*
1930 Olaf Stapledon, *Last and First Men*
  John Taine, *The Iron Star*
  *Astounding Science-Fiction* launched
1932 Aldous Huxley, *Brave New World*
1934 Murray Leinster, 'Sidewise in Time'
  Stanley G. Weinbaum, 'A Martian Odyssey'
1935 Olaf Stapledon, *Odd John*
1936 *Things to Come* (dir. William Cameron Menzies)
1938 John W. Campbell, Jr. (as Don A. Stuart), 'Who Goes There?'
    Lester del Rey, 'Helen O'Loy'
1939 Stanley G. Weinbaum, *The New Adam*
1940 Robert A. Heinlein, 'The Roads Must Roll'
  Robert A. Heinlein, '"If This Goes On –"'
  A. E. Van Vogt, *Slan* (book 1946)
1941 Isaac Asimov, 'Nightfall'
  L. Sprague De Camp, *Lest Darkness Fall*
  Robert A. Heinlein, 'Universe'
  Theodore Sturgeon, 'Microcosmic God'
1942 Isaac Asimov, 'Foundation' (book 1951)
  Robert A. Heinlein, *Beyond This Horizon* (book 1948)
1944 C. L. Moore, 'No Woman Born'

Robert A. Heinlein, *The Moon is a Harsh Mistress*
Damon Knight, ed., *Orbit 1* (annual original anthology)
Keith Roberts, 'The Signaller'
*Star Trek* first broadcast in the USA
1967 Samuel R. Delany, *The Einstein Intersection*
Harlan Ellison, ed., *Dangerous Visions* (anthology)
Roger Zelazny, *Lord of Light*
1968 John Brunner, *Stand on Zanzibar*
Philip K. Dick, *Do Androids Dream of Electric Sheep?*
Thomas M. Disch, *Camp Concentration*
Stanislaw Lem, *Solaris*
Anne McCaffrey, *Dragonflight*
Judith Merril, ed., *England Swings SF* (anthology)
Alexei Panshin, *Rite of Passage*
Keith Roberts, *Pavane*
Robert Silverberg, *Hawksbill Station*
*2001: A Space Odyssey* (dir. Stanley Kubrick)
1969 Michael Crichton, *The Andromeda Strain*
Ursula K. Le Guin, *The Left Hand of Darkness*
1970 Larry Niven, *Ringworld*
1971 Terry Carr, ed., *Universe 1* (annual original anthology)
Robert Silverberg, *The World Inside*
1972 Isaac Asimov, *The Gods Themselves*
Harlan Ellison, ed., *Again, Dangerous Visions* (anthology)
Barry Malzberg, *Beyond Apollo*
Joanna Russ, 'When It Changed'
Arkadi and Boris Strugatsky, *Roadside Picnic*
Gene Wolfe, *The Fifth Head of Cerberus*
Science Fiction Foundation begins the journal *Foundation*
1973 Arthur C. Clarke, *Rendezvous with Rama*
Thomas Pynchon, *Gravity's Rainbow*
Mack Reynolds, *Looking Backward, from the Year 2000*
James Tiptree, Jr, *Ten Thousand Light Years from Home*
(collection)
Ian Watson, *The Embedding*
*Science-Fiction Studies* begins publication
1974 Suzy McKee Charnas, *Walk to the End of the World*
Joe Haldeman, *The Forever War*
Ursula K. Le Guin, *The Dispossessed*
1975 Samuel R. Delany, *Dhalgren*
Joanna Russ, *The Female Man*

FARAH MENDLESOHN

# Introduction: reading science fiction

*The Cambridge Companion to Science Fiction* is intended to provide readers with an introduction to the genre and to its study. To this end, we have divided this book into three parts: an historical overview of the field which discusses the major authors and editors, the people and market forces which have shaped the literary structures of the field; a section on critical approaches to science fiction (sf); and finally a collection of essays exploring some of the issues and concerns which have been considered by both critics and writers to be intrinsic to the genre. The first language of all of the contributors is English, and the book concentrates almost entirely on the English-language sf that has, for the last century, dominated the field.

The structure we have adopted makes a number of assumptions: it assumes that you, the reader, know what sf is, and that everyone who has contributed to this book shares the same criteria. This second statement is the more contentious. Science fiction is less a genre – a body of writing from which one can expect certain plot elements and specific tropes – than an ongoing discussion. Its texts are mutually referential, may be written by those active in criticism (something we have tried to reflect) and have often been generated from the same fan base which supports the market. The reader's expectations of sf are governed less by what happens than how that happening is described, and by the critical tools with which the reader is expected to approach the text. Yet the critical tools are themselves contentious: sf is a battleground between different groups of fans, and different groups of critics. When this book is reviewed, some will object to the number of thematic essays we have included, and others will object to the assertion, contained in a number of essays, that sf emerges in the twentieth century, preferring to include within the definition texts written in the nineteenth or earlier centuries. These objections emerge from the very nature of the beast that is sf: a mode of writing which has seemed to exist at variance from the standards and demands of both the literary establishment and the mass market (because, whatever else it is, sf literature is not *popular*, even while 'sci-fi' movies pack the cinemas).

Alongside these issues is the absence of any specific textual analysis in this book. Because sf is a discussion, a collection of essays on 'representative' texts would in many ways have been unrepresentative: too much sf is written as an argument with the universe to allow some of the best works to be filleted from their context, and this is evidenced by the extent to which certain names crop up repeatedly in the essays. Only where a specific canon of texts has emerged around a particular theme or mode have our contributors been able to offer sustained textual analysis.

But the case can be made that the best way to understand what sf *is*, is to map our theories on to an exemplar text, a text that demonstrates the theories from which many of the critics contributing to this book proceed. Rather than make sweeping statements about the nature of sf based primarily on the classics – ideas which might be challenged by the most recent contributions to the field, and which would rapidly reveal that most sf texts only perform perhaps two-thirds of the theoretical demands which we impose on sf – we shall begin this *Companion* by examining those ideas which structure sf as demonstrated in a very specific text by one of the best contemporary authors: Greg Egan's *Schild's Ladder* (2002).[1] This hard sf space opera is curiously susceptible to such mapping. It contains within it the very history of the genre, the ideas which underpin the critical discourse. Let us start with the one idea that most often baffles colleagues in genre criticism: that sf is a discussion or a mode, and not a genre.

If sf were a genre, we would know the rough outline of every book that we picked up. If it were a mystery, we would know that there was 'something to be found out'; if a romance, that two people would meet, make conflict and fall in love; if horror, that there would be an intrusion of the unnatural into the world that would eventually be tamed or destroyed. But Egan's *Schild's Ladder* offers all three of these outlines. Cass, a scientist, wants to find out whether the mathematical equations named after Sarumpaet hold true; Tchicaya, many years later, is driven to find out what is on the other side of the disruptive border that Cass's disastrous experiment has created. If this is not enough to match the book with the mystery genre, it becomes imperative two-thirds of the way in to discover who has sabotaged *Rindler*, the investigative space station, and the novel is instantly recognizable as a 'thriller'. The border itself offers horror: will our protagonists succeed in holding back the new universe before it devours Earth? This is an sf novel, not a film, so there is not necessarily the happy resolution demanded by Hollywood: authors such as Stephen Baxter and John Barnes have become notorious for killing off the human race. And finally there is the romance between Tchicaya and Mariama: childhood sweethearts, separated for almost seven hundred years, their romance would be at the heart of many novels. But this is sf, and as I shall show later, romance means something very different in sf.

Having demonstrated that sf is quite happy to extract its plot structures from any available genre, and thus each individual book could potentially be identified with one of these genres rather than with sf, we need to consider whether sf does 'own' a narrative. It is rarely considered in these terms, but if sf does have an immediately recognizable narrative it is centred on what has been termed the 'sense of wonder'.

The sense of wonder is the emotional heart of sf. David Nye has described this reaction as the appreciation of the sublime whether natural, such as the rings of Saturn, or technological: a space station or rocket ship (see Gwyneth Jones, chapter 11 in this volume).[2] For the first fifteen years of the development of genre sf (from the mid-1920s), it *was* the basic narrative of most fiction in the US magazines, as the titles – *Amazing*, *Astounding*, *Thrilling Wonder* – suggest. The earliest sf relied on the creation of a new invention, or an arrival in a new place. For the readers of this material this was enough; one could stand and stare at the flying city, or gasp at the audacity of the super-weapon. The tone was primarily descriptive, the protagonist unfamiliar with his/her surroundings describing to the reader, or auditing a lecture on our behalf. Almost all stories ended either in universal peace or with the destruction of invention and inventor because the writers either lacked the skill to go beyond the idea and employed the explosion as the sf equivalent of 'I woke up and it was all a dream', perhaps in order to avoid any sense of *consequence*; John Clute has argued that the secret is that

'Doc' Smith and his peers – and A. E. Van Vogt, who walked alone – may have loved the task of conceiving futures, but, at the same time, each of these sf writers manifestly displayed a very deep distrust and fear of anything that hinted at any of the unfolding 'real' futures that have refilled the water holes of our infancy with mutagens. The Lensmen series is escapist, as much good fiction is; and we love it for that, but it does not escape 1930, it escapes the future.[3]

The result was a sense of wonder combined with presentism. But this core sense of wonder continues to power sf. The first thirty-five pages of *Schild's Ladder* are self-contained: a classic short story, emulating the achievements of early sf, and exemplifying the fundamental role of the sense of wonder in the construction of what we mean by sf. For the sake of a theorem Cass has her mind sent 370 light years from Earth and embodied in a form 2mm high. The plot is deceptively simple: Cass seeks the help of aliens to test a proof of Sarumpaet's mathematical theory in the safety of deep space. Older and wiser than we, they counsel caution and break the experiment down into fifteen smaller experiments. When they finally permit the entire experiment to be enacted, it still goes wrong and the resulting 'explosion' begins to swallow the universe. And the 'short-story' ends. In the tradition of that early genre sf we have the sense of wonder (the possibilities of maths); the wise aliens (although in this case they are post-humans); the show of hubris; and the cold equations of the universe, the traditional sf substitute for divine punishment, halting human ingenuity in its tracks. Small points of wonder – the size to which Cass is reduced, the body which can live on light, the space station itself – punctuate the text, ensuring that we cannot become blasé.

But there are reasons I have suggested that *Schild's Ladder* is an exemplar text. Science fiction has not remained static. As Nye argues, the sense of wonder is itself a fragile thing, made more difficult to achieve by familiarity, and although for a while bigger, better and more complicated inventions and icons may supply this, the visceral response is vulnerable to ennui. *Schild's Ladder* is fascinating because it precisely maps the development from the sense of wonder to other literary structures that, building on the sense of wonder, become the mode of sf. The first of these is what Istvan Csicsery-Ronay has described as 'the grotesque'[4] but which we can think of as 'consequences'. The sense of wonder allowed one to admire the aesthetics of the mushroom cloud; the sense of the grotesque led the writer and reader to consider the fall-out. Science fiction began to shift to the consideration of consequences in the late 1930s thanks in part to the editors F. Orlin Tremaine and John W. Campbell (see chapters 2 and 6 in this volume), and this shift is marked in *Schild's Ladder* in the opening sections of the second part. The thought experiment, the 'what if?' (which Darko Suvin calls the novum),[5] is crucial to all sf, and has led to the most popular alternative interpretation of 'sf': speculative fiction. It is here that sf most departs from contemporary literature, because in sf 'the idea' is the hero.

*Schild's Ladder* begins with a thought experiment made literal, the testing of Sarumpaet's theory; the main driver appears to be the consequences of that experiment. But throughout the novel we also have the thought experiment made metaphor: physics becomes the crowbar with which we break open the universe, the code to preserve intellect and character, in themselves a matter of sublime beauty. One character, himself 'mere' digitisation made flesh, describes how '"When I was ten years old, all I gave my sweetheart was a pair of projections that turned the group of rotations in four dimensions into principal bundles over the three-sphere"' (p. 97). (She loved them.) All of these descend from an apparently secondary 'what if', about the nature of personality – what are the consequences of freeing ourselves from corporeality? This is actually much more challenging than the initial experiment which threatened to destroy the universe. This kind of structure is the classic double bluff of sf: setting up one thought experiment within another, to force the reader to look out of the corner of his/her eye at the context of the adventure, mystery or romance. Although the driver of many an sf novel depends on a specific scientific problem, the structure and forms of the genre/mode are much more embedded in this contextual issue, because while that first thought experiment may provide the sense of the sublime, it is the combination of the hidden 'what ifs' and the initial thought experiment that create what Darko Suvin has called cognitive estrangement; 'the cognitive nucleus of the plot codetermines the fictional estrangement itself'.[6]

Cognitive estrangement is tied inextricably to the encoded nature of sf: to style, lexical invention and embedding. Cognitive estrangement is the sense that something in the fictive world is dissonant with the reader's experienced world. On a superficial level this difference may be achieved by shifts of time, place and technological scenery. But if that is all that is done, the resultant fiction is didactic and overly descriptive. The technique common in early sf is known contemptuously as the 'info-dump': a character lectures a captive audience about something they could be expected to know but which we do not. It is a very difficult thing to avoid, and at the moment of conceptual breakthrough[7] when the critical insight is won, and the world is revealed as bigger or different than one thought, it can be the only tool a writer has to convey information. Even Egan cannot resist this in *Schild's Ladder*. When the Sarumpaet theory is finally overturned, Egan is forced to allow one character a two-page public lecture (pp. 88–9), mitigated by allowing the point-of-view protagonist to be slightly less familiar with the material than others in the audience, by couching this didacticism as a plea for 'forbearance' on behalf of the new theory, and by allowing the point of view to assume that others in the audience are irritated. It is a cheat, but a clever one.

To be really effective, sf has to be subtle. Over the past seventy years the community of sf writers has developed a tool kit, the absence or recreation of which is usually the hallmark of outsider sf (fiction written by professional writers which either claims to have invented a new genre, or which vigorously denies its categorization of science fiction). The most obvious, and the one which newcomers to the genre notice immediately, is the use of language in science fiction. As Gwyneth Jones argues (chapter 11), 'the reading of a science fiction story is always an active process of translation'.

Language is not trustworthy in sf: metaphor becomes literal. 'He gave her his hand' or 'he turned on his side' raise numerous possibilities in the mind of the sf reader, involving, perhaps, detachable body-parts or implanted electronics. In addition, the sf writer may set up estrangement by the deliberate construction of new, technological metaphors such as 'The sky above the port was the color of television, tuned to a dead channel.'[8] But there is still the expectation that one will read literally whatever is on the page, whether 'he caught sight of an undigested stretch of calf, still bearing traces of the last inhabitant's body hair and musculature' (Egan, *Schild's Ladder*, p. 35) or invented words such as 'Qusp'. Their effectiveness in creating dissonance relies on the expectation that the reader will either understand what is written or will fill in the gap, creating meaning where none is provided. These two techniques are crucial to the sf project and they are cumulative. Science fiction has come to rely on the evolution of a vocabulary, of a structure and a set of shared ideas which are deeply embedded in the genre's psyche. It is no longer necessary, for example, for authors to describe the means by which their interstellar ships are propelled across vast distances, a simple reference to 'FTL' ('faster-than-light') will collapse several pages of description. Such hand-waving is one of the hallmarks of hard sf (see Kathryn Cramer, chapter 13). Yet sf produces its own metaphor. Le Guin's *The Dispossessed* begins: 'There was a wall, it did not look important . . . even a child could climb it . . . an idea of a boundary. But the idea was real . . . What was inside it and what was outside it depended upon which side of it you were on.'[9] Because we are sf readers we know that this wall is going to be both a portal into the adventure and a metaphor for narrative. In those first five lines, Le Guin generates both estrangement and story.

Egan uses the archaeology of science fiction to seed his text with meaning. It allows him to leak information into his created world. Yann, an acorporeal – a concept underpinned by what we might call the 'legacy texts'[10] of William Gibson and Vernor Vinge – can refer to 'anachronauts [expected] to arrive at the *Rindler* any day now – preceded by a few megatons of fusion by-products – and announce that they've come to save the universe' (*Schild's Ladder*, p. 52) and while we might not get the meaning, we know we *should*. We are linked to the fusion torch-ships of Heinlein and others, can make assumptions about cryonics and are referred directly to the Terran supremacy fiction fostered by John W. Campbell in the pages of *Astounding Science Fiction*. The sf history of the universe is recapitulated in one sentence, but the anachronauts are not fully explained for another fifty pages. We must work to find steady ground.

But we are also being made fun of. The anachronauts are themselves an sf legacy, what John Clute describes in chapter 4 as 'exudations of style, not signals of substantive shaping advocacy'. Obsessed by sex and the idea of gender conflict they have gone from planet to planet looking for the 'central story of the future' (chapter 4), a narrative impervious to evidence. Egan's anachronauts recapitulate James Tiptree Jr's assertion that those who claim to protect us frequently model the phantom aggressor on themselves (see Veronica Hollinger, chapter 8). Until they meet Tchicaya's father, an adolescent too confused and in love to lie, they have been made fun of by the descendants of humans who have told them the kind of stories used to fool anthropologists since the days of Margaret Mead. And the anachronauts also function as a sly dig at those critics of sf who condemn a book because it does not conform to their particular political position, a figure not confined to the political left.

In addition to using legacy texts to layer his world, Egan also creates his own embedding. Our understanding of who and what the anachronauts are is built up from small clues until the moment of breakthrough where, in the tradition of villains everywhere, they spit their motivation into the narrative. But equally, Egan estranges us from our assumptions about the primary actors in the novel, building up the sense that these people are not us. Cass, the initial protagonist, is recreated 2 mm high and 'hermetically sealed against the vacuum . . . Being hermetically sealed against the vacuum and feeding on nothing but light took some getting used to' (*Schild's Ladder*, p. 5); but the notion of body transfer is unquestioned, because in modern sf the protagonists are not strangers in their land; they are competent within their universe and have no need either to explain to us, or demand explanation for themselves.[11] These people have a different sense of what 'self' is; boundaries have to be continually negotiated. 'When the means existed to transform yourself instantly and effortlessly, into anything at all, the only way to maintain an identity was to draw your own boundaries. But once you lost the urge to keep on drawing them in the right place, you might as well have been born *Homo Sapiens*, with no real choices at all'(p. 6): this is a line that effortlessly drops in the most vital information, that these people are not humans. But as our cultural understanding of the body is not monolithic, neither is theirs, and there are some post-humans who prefer to hang on to their birth body, some who maintain active backups, others whose backups are there solely in the event of death and many who prefer to live mostly digitized, opting for bodies only to achieve specific interactions. Death has as many different meanings in this culture as there are modes of existence.

Neither are they gendered like humans. Building on the legacies of feminist writers, Egan has preserved gender but divorces it from the body, playing a very neat trick by blithely using names with vowel endings for both sexes, in contradiction to Western expectations. Our first hint of dissonance is at the end of the flashback sequence:

> between his legs, the skin was newly red and swollen . . . Touching it was like tickling himself . . . And he could still change his mind, change his feelings. Everything was voluntary, his father had explained. Unless you loved someone

deeply, and unless they felt the same towards you, neither of you could grow what you both needed to make love together . . . Every couple grew something different, just as every couple would have a different child.     (pp. 77–8)

At this stage this sounds like nothing more than the myths parents tell their children to protect them. The final moment of revelation must wait until Tchicaya is taken to bed by Rasmah.

> 'Oh, look what we made! I knew it would be beautiful. And I think I have something that would fit here, almost perfectly. And here. And maybe even . . . *here*!'
>
> Tchicaya gritted his teeth, but he didn't stop her moving her fingers over him, inside him. There was no more vulnerable feeling than being touched in a place that had not existed before, a place you'd never seen or touched yourself . . .
>
> Nature had never had much imagination, but people had always found new ways to connect.     (pp. 161–2)

But who they choose to connect with and why is also unstable. In the first section of the novel, Cass is destabilized because her corporeality leads her to assume that sex is the most intimate of acts, whereas Rainzi simply does not think that way. He is offering to share the universe with her. Our attention is forced to consider what we mean by 'the opposite sex' or as Wendy Pearson points out in chapter 10, 'queer'. If both 'sexes' come with the same equipment and the same potential to penetrate and be penetrated, and gender has become more about corporealty and acorporeality than male and female, it is perfectly possible to argue that the whole discourse of humanity has been queered in *Schild's Ladder*.

These are very different creatures from ourselves, yet this is never explicitly spelled out. As James Gunn points out (Foreword), it is the layering, embedding and shorthand endemic to sf that rescues the genre from didacticism. But this is not a mere negative: this essential technique (not unique to sf, but very much more conscious in the genre than elsewhere) shifts the real narrative of sf in directions unfamiliar to readers of the contemporary novel. In avoidance of didacticism Egan moves his fictional world to centre stage. No novelist in mainstream fiction would expect description to stand in for characterization, but sf, in making cognitive estrangement storyable,[12] insists that the world be treated as character (see chapters 10 and 11 in this volume). And here we turn to another characteristic of sf. Much of early sf mistook weirdness for landscape, but some authors have successfully elevated place to the level of character. This can be done in a straightforward manner: in both Murray Leinster's 'The Lonely Planet'[13] and Judith Moffett's *Pennterra* (1987) the planets turn out to be alive. But more fundamental is the way in which a planet becomes intrinsically interesting, its story vital to the way in which the occupants live their lives: Le Guin's *The Left Hand of Darkness* (1969) and *The Dispossessed* (1974) link political systems to landscape as does Kim Stanley Robinson's Mars trilogy (see chapter 16 in this volume). Brian Aldiss's Helliconia trilogy is the masterpiece in this trend: the individuals who live through the seasons on Helliconia merely occupy the ecological niches of story, and the protagonist is the planet. In *Schild's Ladder* we must wait a long time for this element of sf. The space station, fascinating though it is, does not capture the imagination. It is the other side, the Bright, the alter-vacuum with its drifting vendeks and airflowers, which engages the senses of both readers and protagonists, and from its discovery, the nature of the book shifts dramatically and again in ways which underscore the difference between sf and the mainstream.

The Bright is discovered by Tchicaya and Mariama when they are trapped in a space capsule together, and Mariama's Qusp (her recorded personality) is embedded in Tchicaya's kidney. Science fiction likes its romance visceral. It is not possible to get closer to someone than to ride inside their body, but sf also likes the ambiguous and the ethereal – without bodies there cannot be sex and sf remains one of the few genres in which intimate relations are marginal. *Schild's Ladder* is no exception. Sex is used to indicate the differences between the forms of human which now exist. Yann cannot take sex seriously; its neural rewards are too unsubtle. Sex does function as a signifier of friendship and community, but it is not where the romance lies. Tchicaya and Mariama are attracted not to each other but to the glories of the cosmos, to the real romance at the heart of any sf, the romance of the universe. For sf is perhaps the last real bastion of Romantic fiction: sf protagonists fall in love with the macrocosm. Where mainstream fiction writes of the intricacies of inter-human relationships, the discourse of sf is about our relationship to the world and the universe. The great events (wars, moon landings, famines) or the great ideas (evolution, alien contact, immortality) are foregrounded. In *Schild's Ladder*, Tchicaya and Mariama are not conducting their affair against the shaping force of a great discovery: they are conducting their discovery of the universe against the unwelcome distraction of unresolved emotions. It is this reversal of romance, the insistence that romance is *out there* rather than internal, that frequently results in non-sf critics judging sf deficient in characterization and emotion. At the very point of the novel where one might expect our protagonists to fall into each other's arms, they decide not to bother. 'Nothing could have lived up to four thousand years of waiting. Except perhaps an original theorem' (p. 246) or 'The seed for a universe, lying in the gutter' (p. 248).

Yet entwined with the wonder is a note of alienation. This is a cold romanticism in which we are forever excluded from our object of love, and alienation is as much a part of sf as is the joy of discovery. The alienation at the heart of sf is most evident in the sense of the uncaring universe exemplified in hard sf by the concept of the 'cold equations' (to use the title of Tom Godwin's sf story), those fixed rules that decide whether we live or die, irrespective of whether we love – the universe is a harsh mistress. *Schild's Ladder* depends on the chill that emanates from the scientific superstructure of the text: Tchicaya and Mariama may fall in love with the Bright, but it is not sentient and like any ecology, will kill them if they do not adapt.

But sf also values alienation as the central element of character. Sf of the 1940s through the 1960s overused the idea of the alienated, isolated individual as genius – there is little question that it reflected the angst of generations of bookish adolescents – and although the conceit is much diminished in sf, the trope retains its power: isolation and alienation are as much a factor in *Schild's Ladder* as they are in that classic of sf angst, Van Vogt's *Slan* (1940). Tchicaya and Mariama have both succumbed to the idea that 'different' is the same as superior. In their own adolescence, their self-absorption, their conviction that their own lives were at the centre of the universal narratives, led them to hide the discovery of alien life. As adults they meet unreconstructed *homo sapiens* who, having extended that distorted self-narrative into an ideology, themselves demonstrate willingness to destroy that which is other. One legacy of Marxism, feminism and postmodernism (see chapters 7, 8, 9) has been the ability to tell new stories, to inscribe the other into the picture of the world. Part of Egan's achievement in *Schild's Ladder* is to make the new world's voice powerful. The universe, its equations still chilly, corrects the anachronauts rather forcibly. We learn again that it is the idea that is plot and character here, and it can survive the death of any of the protagonists.

Science fiction is part of a polysemic discourse. Texts are vulnerable to a multiplicity of interpretations, each of which produces a different landscape of sf, as reflected in the numerous academic and 'fan' canons which have emerged over the past eight decades. As critics are increasingly drawn from communities of fans, even the once hard divisions between the 'fan' canon (Heinlein, Asimov, Clarke) and the 'academic' canon (Dick, Le Guin, Ballard) blur. Each of our contributors would draw Egan's book differently. It can be read as a space opera, as hard sf, through and with an eye to biological speculation. Helen Merrick and Wendy Pearson might pick up on the attempts Egan has made to go beyond the heterosexual imperative, while maintaining a binary structure for social relations. The radical shift in perception results in a configuration of sexuality not susceptible to our categorization and naming devices. Queer theory, according to Pearson, emphasizes fluidity and liminality, not fixed binaries or alternatives. Alongside this, Hollinger would simply note that it is now almost impossible to write a plausible sf novel that does not acknowledge feminism. In contrast, I suspect that this novel would not appeal to either Marxist or postmodernist critics, for neither the means of production, nor any sense of politics shapes this novel. The book is colour-blind, in that there is no colour, which can be read as either post-race, or allowing us to write our own prejudices on to the text (see Elisabeth Anne Leonard, chapter 19). *Schild's Ladder* is an appropriate text for both Edward James and Ken MacLeod (chapters 16, 17), for its technotopia demonstrates both the limits of the forms and the occasionally artificial plotting required to introduce contention. The novel might even be read as alternative history (see chapter 15), in the sense that this is not *our* future which Egan narrates: his fusion ships cannot descend from an Earth that has turned its back on manned space exploration. Most important is the influence that the historical chapters, written by Brian Stableford, Brian Attebery, Damien Broderick and John Clute have on our reading of this and other novels. Sf is a built genre. It is its history; without these chapters one could only skate the present.

## NOTES

1. For further discussion see: Russell Letson, *Locus*, May 2002, pp. 37, 61; Paul Di Filippo, at http://www.SciFi.Com; and Adam Roberts, at http://www.thealienonline.net.
2. David Nye, *The American Technological Sublime* (Cambridge, MA: MIT Press, 1984), pp. 14–15.
3. John Clute, introduction to *Galactic Patrol, Gray Lensman, Second Stage Lensman, Children of the Lens*, by E. E. Smith (Baltimore, MD: Old Earth Books, 1998), pp. xii–xiii.
4. Istvan Csicsery-Ronay, Jr, 'On the Grotesque in Science Fiction', *Science-Fiction Studies* 29 (2002), pp. 71–99.
5. Darko Suvin, *Metamorphoses of Science Fiction: On the Poetics and History of a Literary Genre* (New Haven, CT: Yale University Press, 1979), p. 63.
6. *Ibid.*, p. 15.
7. Peter Nicholls argues for the centrality of 'conceptual breakthrough' in Nicholls, ed., *The Encyclopedia of Science Fiction* (London: Granada, 1979), pp. 134–6.
8. William Gibson, *Neuromancer* (1984) (London: Grafton, 1986), p. 9.
9. Ursula K. Le Guin, *The Dispossessed* (London: Gollancz, 1974), p. 5.
10. A phrase inspired by the 'legacy code' in Ken MacLeod's *Cosmonaut Keep* (2000), p. 27: it is an IT term for code from the past, retained because it works and is difficult to modify without unintended consequences.
11. The protagonists' experience of recreation and multiplication of lives is a direct descendant of Camille Flammarion's *Lumen* (1887) (see Brian Stableford, chapter 1), as sf has sought a technical means to fulfil the fantasy of reincarnation.

Body-swapping functions as an sf concept because it is built on the ruins of many different facilitating devices.

12. John Clute, in his chapter on Howard Waldrop, in Richard Bleiler, ed., *Supernatural Fiction Writers: Contemporary Fantasy and Horror* (New York: Charles Scribner's Sons, 2003), p. 952.

13. 'The Lonely Planet' (1949), in J.J. Pierce, ed., *The Best of Murray Leinster* (New York: Del Rey, 1978), pp. 274–307.

# I
# THE HISTORY

# 1

BRIAN STABLEFORD

# Science fiction before the genre

## The origins of science fiction

The word 'science' acquired its modern meaning when it took aboard the realization that reliable knowledge is rooted in the evidence of the senses, carefully sifted by deductive reasoning and the experimental testing of generalizations. In the seventeenth century writers began producing speculative fictions about new discoveries and technologies that the application of scientific method might bring about, the earliest examples being accommodated – rather uncomfortably – within existing genres and narrative frameworks.

One genre hospitable to sf speculation was that of utopian fantasy, whose usual narrative form was the imaginary voyage. The rich tradition of sf travellers' tales was launched by one of the first and foremost champions of the scientific method, Francis Bacon, in *New Atlantis* (written *c.*1617; published 1627), although the importance of technological progress to social reform had earlier been recognised by Johann Valentin Andreae's account of *Christianopolis* (1619) and Tommaso Campanella's description of *La Città del Sole* (*The City of the Sun*, written 1602; published 1623). Most subsequent utopian fantasies took scientific and technological advancement into account, but relegated it to a minor role while matters of social, religious and political reform remained centre stage. Nor were those writers who took account of scientific progress always enthusiastic about it; Baconian optimism prompted a backlash of hostility from those who perceived a threat to religious values in the secularizing tendencies of religion and the materialistic encouragements of technology.

The imaginary voyage was also the usual narrative form of scathing satirical fantasies, and scientists became satirical targets in Margaret Cavendish's *The Blazing World* (1666) and the third book of Jonathan Swift's *Gulliver's Travels* (1726). Such works founded a tradition of 'anti-science fiction', whose reliance on similar motifs and narrative strategies has always resulted in its subsumption within the genre whose ambitions it opposes. Given the importance of scepticism and theoretical dissent to the advancement of science and the near-oxymoronic quality of the 'science fiction' label, this confusion is not entirely inappropriate.

The more extreme versions of the fantastic voyage overlapped with the standard format of religious fantasy, the dream story. Whenever seventeenth- and eighteenth-century imaginary voyages found it convenient to cross interplanetary space their devices became phantasmagorical, and dreaming remained the only plausible means of gaining access to the future until the late nineteenth century. Another pioneer of the scientific revolution, Johannes Kepler, was the first to couch an earnest scientific argument – a representation of the Copernican theory of the solar system – as a visionary fantasy. His *Somnium* (*A Dream*, 1634) also includes an ingenious attempt to imagine how life on the moon might have adapted to the long cycle of day and night.

Although most early accounts of lunar voyages are calculatedly ludicrous, the proposition that the moon and the planets were other worlds was a central contention of the heliocentric theory of the solar system. That theory became an important champion of the cause of science in its contest against religious faith because the Christian Church had adopted the geocentric cosmology favoured by Aristotle into its faith-supported world-view. Francis Godwin's farcical account of *The Man in the Moone* (1638) may, therefore, be placed among the ancestors of sf as confidently as John Wilkins's earnest essay celebrating the *Discovery of a World in the Moon* (1638) – to which a supplement was added in 1640, proposing that men would one day journey to the moon.

Such discussions were less risky in Protestant England than in Catholic France, but Pierre Borel's *Discours nouveau prouvant le pluralité des mondes* (*A New Discourse Proving the Plurality of Worlds*, 1657) and Cyrano de Bergerac's flamboyant *L'Autre Monde – The Other World*, two fragments of which were published in 1657 and 1662 – prepared the way for Bernard de Fontenelle's enormously popular *Entretiens sur la pluralité des mondes* (*Discussion of the Plurality of Worlds*, 1686). Fontenelle's adaptation of the classical dialogue into a casual and flippant 'conversation' was calculated to defuse criticism, but it helped pave the way for the development of more naturalistic speculative fictions. Throughout the eighteenth century, however, such fictions were handicapped by the lack of any plausible narrative devices capable of opening up the imaginative frontiers of space and time.

Although most satirists were satisfied with the moon as an extraterrestrial venue, a tradition of more wide-ranging cosmic voyages was founded by Athanasius Kircher's *Itinerarium Exstaticum* (*Ecstatic Journey*, 1656). Cosmic tours taking in all the known worlds of the solar system became a hybrid sub-genre, fusing religious and scientific fantasies, usually incorporating utopian and eschatological imagery within the same framework. Attempts to describe a universe in which the sun was merely one star had little alternative but to adopt the form of visionary fantasy, however, even when the vision took the form of a voyage through space. Such works as Gabriel Daniel's *Voyage au monde de Descartes* (*Voyage to the World of Descartes*, 1692) and Christian Huygens's *Cosmotheoros* (1698) struggled to find an appropriate narrative form.

The most ambitious cosmic visions of the eighteenth century were those allegedly experienced in 1743–5 and reported in *Arcana Coelestia* (1749–56) by the Swedish mystical theologian Emmanuel Swedenborg, strongly influenced by Swedenborg's early work in physics, geology and mathematics. In France, the tradition of cosmic voyages was encouraged by a new imaginative licence – often involving the casual deployment of magical devices borrowed from Antoine Galland's translation of the *Arabian Nights* – associated with the fashionability of fantastic fiction. *Voyages de Mylord Céton dans les sept planètes* (*Journeys of Lord Seton in the Seven Planets*, 1765) by Marie-Anne de Roumier-Robert was the most extravagant, employing a narrative template established by the Chevalier de Béthune's *Relation du monde de Mercure* (*The World of Mercury*, 1750).

The gradual removal of terra incognita from maps of the Earth's surface helped to force utopian and satirical images out into space, although the remoter regions of the southern hemisphere remained useful to such writers as Gabriel de Foigny in *La Terre australe connu* (1676) and Restif de la Bretonne in *La Découverte australe par un homme volant* (*The Discovery of the South by a Flying Man*, 1781). Ludvig Holberg's *Nils Klim* (1741) pointed out another way to go, but the interior of the Earth was always a minority choice, although the adventurous *Le Passage de pôle arctique au pôle antarctique* (*The Passage from the North to the South Poles*, 1780) might have attracted more attention had it not remained unattributable. A more significant variation on the cosmic voyage theme was, however, employed in the *conte philosophique* by Voltaire, *Micromégas* (1752), which brought visitors to Earth from Sirius and Saturn.

Many French works, along with several translations from English, were reprinted in a thirty-six-volume series of *Voyages imaginaires* produced by Charles Garnier in 1787–9. This attempt to define and exemplify a genre might have been even more influential had it not been interrupted by the Revolution; even so, it provided a vital landmark for Camille Flammarion – who included many of its constituent works in his pioneering history of cosmological speculative fiction constructed in *Les Mondes imaginaires et les mondes réels* (*Imaginary Worlds and Real Worlds*, 1864) – and Jules Verne, who described his own works, collectively, as *Voyages extraordinaires*.

The adaptation of traditional narrative frameworks to the work of serious speculation laboured under several handicaps. Travellers' tales, even in their most earnest utopian mode, were infected by a chronic frivolity that increased as the travels extended into regions inaccessible to ships and pedestrians. Literary dreams, even at their most gravely allegorical, were by definition mere phantoms of the imagination, demolished by reawakening. The transformation of moral fables into Voltairean *contes philosophiques* was hampered by the calculated artificiality of their traditional milieux and exemplary characters. These problems became more acute as the philosophy of progress made the future an imaginative realm ripe for exploration. Utopian speculation entered a 'euchronian' mode once Louis-Sebastien Mercier had led the way in *L'An deux mille quatre cent quarante* (*The Year* 2440, 1771) – which soon prompted the production of more cynical accounts of futurity, such as Cousin de Grainville's *Le Dernier Homme* (*The Last Man*, 1805) – but the only obvious alternative to dreaming as a means of gaining access to the future was sleeping for a long time. This was no help to a contemporary narrator if the intelligence gained could not be returned to the present. The problem of designing and developing appropriate narrative frames for scientific *contes philosophiques* inevitably became acute during the nineteenth century, and was not easily solved.

## Experiments in science-fictional method

The first writer to grapple with this problem in a wide-ranging experimental fashion was Edgar Allan Poe. The earliest poem by Poe to see eventual publication was 'Sonnet – to Science', written in the early 1820s, and his career culminated in *Eureka* (1848), an extraordinary poetic essay on the nature of the universe newly revealed by astronomical telescopes. The imaginative thread connecting these two works ran through Poe's entire career. As his appreciation of the aesthetics of scientific discovery grew, his attempts to find literary means of communicating and celebrating the wonders of science became more varied and more inventive.

Although the prefatory essay on the necessity of verisimilitude attached to reprints of Poe's lunar voyage story 'Hans Phaal' (1835; revised 1840 as 'The Unparalleled Adventure of One Hans Pfaall') was not intended to be taken seriously, it highlighted the problem implicit in extending travellers' tales beyond the Earth's surface. Although balloons had enabled a few intrepid aeronauts to get off the ground, they were not a convincing means of extraterrestrial exploration, and Hans Pfaall's attempt to outdo the hero of Willem Bilderdijk's pioneering *Kort verhaal van eene aanmerklijke luctreis en nieuwe planeetokdekking* (1813) never seemed convincing even to its author. Despite its self-taunting sarcasm, however, Poe's preface became the first tentative manifesto for modern sf.

Poe experimented with new frameworks for futuristic speculation in 'The Conversation of Eiros and Charmion' (1839), a dialogue of the dead whose protagonists recall the near-future destruction of Earth by a comet, and 'The Colloquy of Monos and Una' (1841) before producing 'Mesmeric Revelation' (1844), which recognizes and emphasizes the necessity of establishing a more authoritative species of visionary fantasy for science-fictional use. He also used mesmerism as a device in 'A Tale of the Ragged Mountains' (1844) and 'The Facts in the Case of M. Valdemar' (1845); the latter added the further device of mimicking a 'scientific paper' – a prose form then in its infancy – thus paving the way for *Eureka*.

A few British writers contemporary with Poe grappled with the problem of finding appropriate narrative frameworks for bold scientific speculation, without any conspicuous success. Sir Humphry Davy's posthumously published *Consolations in Travel* (1830) was formulated as a series of dialogues extrapolating responses to a cosmological vision. In the same year that Poe published *Eureka*, Robert Hunt – a significant pioneer of the popularization of science – published *The Poetry of Science*, but the metaphysical visions in Hunt's novel *Panthea* (1849) owe more to the 'Rosicrucian romances' popularized by Edward Bulwer-Lytton (building on foundation-stones provided by J. V. Andreae) than to the scientific method for which Hunt gave up his own Romantic aspirations. Hunt's *Poetry of Science* inspired William Wilson to coin the term 'science-fiction' in *A Little Earnest Book Upon a Great Old Subject* (1851), but the only instance of the new genre Wilson could find was R. H. Horne's *The Poor Artist* (1850), a fable in which an artist discovers the wonders of the world as beheld by the eyesights of different creatures.

Modern historians of sf often locate the origins of British scientific romance in the works of Mary Shelley, although the Gothic trappings of *Frankenstein* (1818) place it firmly within the tradition of anti-science fiction, and *The Last Man* (1826), a fatalistic disaster story, is equally antithetical to the philosophy of progress. Neither work made its influence felt immediately, but both became formative templates heading powerful traditions of imaginative fiction. The Frankenstein formula of an unruly and unfortunate artefact bringing about the downfall of its creator became established in the last decade of the nineteenth century as the principal narrative form of anti-science fiction, and still retains that status, while *The Last Man* became grandparent to an entire genre of elegiac British disaster stories, more directly fathered by Richard Jefferies's *After London* (1885). One early work derivative of *Frankenstein* that did offer some tentative championship of progress was *The Mummy! A Tale of the Twenty-Second Century* (1827) by Jane Webb

Loudon, but explorations of the future remained few and tentative for many years. Notable exceptions include *The Air Battle* (1859) by 'Herrmann Lang', which anticipates what was soon to become an important British genre of future war fiction, and *The History of a Voyage to the Moon* (1864), where Poe's demand for more 'verisimilitude' in interplanetary fiction was taken up by the pseudonymous 'Chrysostom Trueman', who employed an early 'antigravity' technology to transport his protagonists to a lunar utopia.

Poe's American contemporary Nathaniel Hawthorne described imaginary scientific experiments in several of his moral tales, but his deep suspicion of the scientific world-view placed him in the antagonistic tradition; 'The Birthmark' (1843) and 'Rappaccini's Daughter' (1844) are early exemplars of a sceptical attitude deploring the excesses and perversions of what would nowadays be called 'scientism'. Other nineteenth-century American writers following in Poe's footsteps were mostly inclined to a similar caution. Fitz-James O'Brien's 'The Diamond Lens' (1858) and Ambrose Bierce's 'Moxon's Master' (collected 1909) are usually read as conservative moral tales, although the latter item is flirtatiously ambiguous. Edward Everett Hale's space flight satire 'The Brick Moon' (1869) is unconvincing, but he set an important precedent by producing the first significant fictionalization of an essay in alternative history, 'Hands Off!' (1881). Frank R. Stockton took advantage of the increasing familiarity of science-fictional devices by employing them as launch-pads for playful flights of fancy in such tales as 'The Water-Devil' (1874) and 'A Tale of Negative Gravity' (1884).

Thanks to Charles Baudelaire, their French translator, Poe's works became far more influential in France than in his native land, and it was there that the cause of finding more appropriate narrative frameworks for sf was taken up most urgently and most adventurously. Jules Verne toyed briefly with Poesque short forms before deciding that the imaginary voyage offered far more scope for interstitial scientific discourse. The essence of Verne's method was the carefully constrained extrapolation of contemporary technology, and he became famous for the application of hypothetical locomotive technologies to laborious exploration and leisurely tourism. Verne made the most convincing nineteenth-century attempt to import a measure of verisimilitude into an extraterrestrial voyage in *De la terre à la lune* (*From the Earth to the Moon*, 1865), but his conscience forbade him to land his moonshot – because he had no plausible way to return it to Earth – and his quarrelsome travellers ended up merely making a trip *Autour de la lune* (*Round the Moon*, 1870).

Verne's earliest *voyages extraordinaires* included several boldly imaginative works, the most extravagant of all being *Voyage au centre de la terre* (*Journey to the Centre of the Earth*, 1863) and *Vingt mille lieues sous les* mers (*Twenty Thousand Leagues under the Seas*, 1870), but he became convinced that the key to success was the moderation of his imagination. His publisher Hetzel apparently refused to publish an adventurous vision of twentieth-century Paris in the future which Verne penned in the early 1860s (it was not published until 1994). Verne's imaginative discipline became so stern that several of the more adventurous works credited to him in his later years required imaginative injections from his enthusiastic disciple Paschal Grousset – who signed himself André Laurie – or his son Michel Verne. Jules Verne was, however, solely responsible for the extraterrestrial fantasy *Hector Servadac* (1877) and the flying machine story *Robur le conquérant* (*Robur the Conqueror*, also translated as *The Clipper of the Clouds*, 1886). The most important of the works in which Grousset had a hand was *Les Cinq cents millions de la bégum* (*The 500 Millions of the Begum*, also translated as *The Begum's Fortune*, 1879), which contrasts utopian and dystopian images of technological development, while Michel's most impressive 'posthumous collaboration' with his father was the fantasy of historical recurrence 'L'Eternel Adam' (1910). Unfortunately, Verne's belated sequel to Poe's *The Narrative of A. Gordon Pym* (1837), *Le Sphinx des glaces* (*The Sphinx of the Ices*, translated as *An Antarctic Mystery*, 1897), meticulously squeezed all the imaginative virility out of its predecessor, contriving a bathetic quasi-naturalistic reduction of all its ominous wonders.

Poe's influence is also manifest in the works of Camille Flammarion, another pioneer of the popularization of science. Flammarion, who also took considerable inspiration from Humphry Davy, was more imaginatively ambitious than Verne, although he struggled in vain to find narrative frameworks appropriate to his ambition. The most daring item in *Récits de l'infini* (*Stories of Infinity*, 1872), expanded for separate publication as *Lumen* (1887), is a dialogue between a human questioner and a disembodied soul whose ability to travel faster than light has allowed him to view and remember former incarnations on a large number of alien worlds, each of which has life-forms adapted to its particular physical circumstances. No other nineteenth-century work is so thoroughly imbued with a sense of wonder at the universe revealed by astronomy and the Earth sciences. Flammarion incorporated a synoptic account of *Lumen*'s schema into a painstakingly didactic account of a reincarnation on Mars in the patchwork *Uranie* (1889), and his account of *La Fin du monde* (translated as *Omega. The Last Days of the World*, 1893) is also a patchwork, concluding with a rhapsodic prose poem.

Hetzel's restraint of Jules Verne's imagination was encouraged by his desire to serialize Verne's novels in an educational magazine for young readers, and this tactic inhibited Verne's influence both at home and abroad. Although

Verne's works were read by adults as well as children, the works of other 'Vernian' writers – who sprang up in some profusion in France, Britain and Germany – were usually marketed as juveniles. The most prolific of Verne's French disciples were Pierre d'Ivoi and Gustave le Rouge; the most inventive writers featured in British boys' papers were Francis Henry Atkins – who wrote as 'Frank Aubrey' and 'Fenton Ash' – and George C. Wallis; the leading German Vernians were Robert Kraft and F. W. Mader.

The introduction of Vernian fiction into America initially followed the same path, but was always distinctive by virtue of its cultural context. Stories about young inventors comprised one of a number of marketing categories formulated by the publishers of 'dime novels', alongside westerns and detective stories. Edward S. Ellis's pioneering account of *The Steam Man of the Prairies* (1868) was, in fact, a western, as were many of the items in story series featuring inventors such as Frank Reade and Tom Edison Jr. The hybridization of inventor fiction and westerns emphasized the importance of the myth of the frontier to American attitudes to technological development. The two genres retained a crucial spiritual affinity which persisted for a hundred years.

So powerful was the myth of the West as a place where the future was to be found and made, however, that American Vernian fiction soon began to outstrip the ambitions of European Vernians. Writers like Frank R. Stockton, in *The Great War Syndicate* (1889) and *The Great Stone of Sardis* (1898), and Garrett P. Serviss, in *The Moon Metal* (1900) and *A Columbus of Space* (1909), helped pave the way for the development of popular sf of a distinctively American kind.

## The evolution of scientific romance

British speculative fiction received a vital boost in 1871 when *Blackwood's Magazine* published George T. Chesney's account of 'The Battle of Dorking'. This account of British defeat following a German invasion provoked numerous replies in kind, founding a genre of future war stories that remained prolific until the outbreak of the actual Great War in 1914. Its early practitioners favoured mock-nonfictional formats, often following Chesney's example – which was subtitled 'Reminiscences of a Volunteer' – in presenting their accounts as 'memoirs', but as time went by the accounts of future conflict became increasingly novelistic. Another important precedent set in 1871 was the initially anonymous publication of the most science-fictional of Bulwer-Lytton's occult romances, *The Coming Race*, featuring a technologically advanced subterranean utopia. Samuel Butler's flamboyant utopian satire *Erewhon* (1872), including a parody of Darwinistic evolution applied to machinery, provided a further stimulus, as did the first translation of Verne's *Journey to the Centre of the Earth*.

Britain might have been more hospitable to scientific speculation had it not been for the fact that the standard format of Victorian fiction was the three-volume novel beloved of the circulating libraries. Building descriptions of significantly different other worlds, whether futuristic or alien, requires a great deal of narrative labour, but the task is better suited to sketchy outlining than to detailed elaboration. Such three-decker futuristic fantasies as Edward Maitland's *By and By* (1873) and Andrew Blair's *Annals of the Twenty-Ninth Century* (1874) founder under their own ponderous weight, in stark contrast to the deftest of the Poesque tales produced in America, which occupied the opposite limit of the broadening spectrum of speculative fiction.

The future war story popularized by Chesney offered a solution to the awkward problem of how to make technological advancement dramatic. From the point of view of progressively minded writers the device involved the unfortunate cost of concentrating heavily on military technology, but that was not initially a deterrent. The crucial point in the evolution of future war stories arrived when they made the leap from propagandistic pamphlets to serialization in a host of new popular periodicals, which entered into a fierce circulation war in the 1890s. A relatively pedestrian account of 'The Great War of 1892' compiled by military experts, including Rear-Admiral Colomb, which was serialized in 1891–2, was immediately upstaged by George Griffith's lurid account of the exploits of heroic 'Terrorists' armed with airships, submarines and high explosives in *The Angel of the Revolution*, whose anti-imperialistic sentiments immediately called forth a right-wing backlash in E. Douglas Fawcett's account of the exploits of *Hartmann the Anarchist*. All three of these works were reprinted in book form in 1893, after which the steady trickle of future war stories became a flood.

Griffith's casual deployment of as-yet-non-existent arms and armour was rapidly standardized, and the escalation was such that when Griffith began his last future war story in 1906, *The Lord of Labour* (published posthumously in 1911), his weapons of choice were nuclear missiles and disintegrator rays. Other journalists persuaded by their editors to write future war serials included Louis Tracy, author of *The Final War* (1896), and William Le Queux, author of *The Invasion of 1910* (1906), both of whom went on to write scientific romances of other kinds. One of the most adventurous early contributors to the new genre, M. P. Shiel, also made his entry by this route with 'The Empress of the Earth' – reprinted as *The Yellow Danger* (1898) – although he was the chief British disciple of Edgar Allan Poe.

Although the expansion of the future war genre into a much broader speculative genre of 'scientific romance' was tentatively begun by others it was not until H. G. Wells got involved that anyone replicated Poe's determination to explore the utility of a whole range of narrative frameworks. The sudden surge of new periodicals provided the perfect arena for Wells to conduct his experiments in speculation. The earliest were cast as brief journalistic essays, of which the most adventurous was 'The Man of the Year Million' (1893), but as soon as he began to adapt the ideas in these essays into fictional form he discovered the limitations of such travellers' tales as 'Aepyornis Island' (1894) and such visionary fantasies as 'The Remarkable Case of Davidson's Eyes' (1894).

By the time Wells made his third attempt to fit an appropriate fictional frame around a speculative account of the future evolution of life on Earth – initially published as 'The Chronic Argonauts' (1888) – he was very conscious indeed of the necessity of replacing dreams as a means of exploring possible futures. The idea of mesmerically induced 'true visions' no longer commanded the least shred of plausibility, so he took advantage of articles by C. H. Hinton collected in *Scientific Romances* (1886), which had popularized the idea of time as a 'fourth dimension', to provide an apologetic jargon for a new facilitating device: *The Time Machine* (1895). This imaginative exercise had little in common with Jules Verne's modest extrapolations of locomotive technology, as Verne was quick to recognize and complain, but Wells had not taken the trouble to make his time machine seem plausible to sympathetic readers because he expected them to take the notion seriously as an actual possibility; he knew how necessary some such device had become as a means of opening the future to serious speculative scrutiny.

Wells's time machine became the first of a series of facilitating devices that opened up the farther reaches of time and space to a kind of rational enquiry that had previously been severely handicapped by its reliance on obsolete narrative frameworks. The crucial invention of *The Time Machine* was the establishment of a paradigm example of a whole new class of narrative devices. The antigravity technology of Cavorite, employed by Wells in *The First Men in the Moon* (1901), was the most obvious equivalent of the time machine and its most necessary supplement. The publication dates of these two works defined the brief interval in which Wells produced all his important scientific romances; not only did he never use the time machine or Cavorite again but he never invented or used any significant facilitating device after 1901.

As soon as the twentieth century had begun, moved by the earnest passion of his strong socialist convictions, Wells gave up wide-ranging exploration of the infinite range of future possibility in favour of a much less interesting quest to discover and comment upon the particular form that the future actually would take. The first philosophical novel subjecting the possibilities of futuristic fiction to scrupulous analysis, Anatole France's *Sur la pierre blanche* (*The White Stone*, 1903), hailed Wells as the only writer prepared to venture into the future as an open-minded explorer rather than a vulgar prophet intent on painting his own hopes or anxieties on its blank canvas, but by the time that judgement appeared in print it was no longer true. Even so, Wells single-handedly laid the groundwork for the distinctive methods of modern sf, employing the narrative technique he had developed in *The Time Machine*, gaudily seasoned with melodrama, to reinvigorate the narrative framework of the moral *conte philosophique* far more effectively than anyone had previously contrived.

*The Island of Dr Moreau* (1896), *The Invisible Man* (1897) and *The War of the Worlds* (1898) are all painstaking moral fables, albeit of an unprecedentedly zestful and unusually realistic kind, cleverly assisted by the narrative labour that made their central devices plausible. Wells's other moral fables in melodramatic guise include 'The Star' (1897) and 'The Empire of the Ants' (1904), but he always remained willing to develop such fables in more traditional forms, as he did in *The Wonderful Visit* (1895), 'The Man Who Could Work Miracles' (1898) and 'The Country of the Blind' (1904). He also remained content, as and when the mood moved him, to employ perfectly straightforward visionary fantasies, as in 'Under the Knife' (1896) – although 'The Crystal Egg' (1897) does make use of a facilitating device of sorts.

Precedents had been set for Wellsian speculative fiction by such cautionary tales as Grant Allen's 'Pausodyne' (1881) and 'A Child of the Phalanstery' (1884), and by such extended *contes philosophiques* as W. H. Hudson's *A Crystal Age* (1887) and Walter Besant's *The Inner House* (1888), but Wells imported such powerful narrative energy and sturdy conviction into his works that he transformed the methodology of speculative fiction, with almost instantaneous effect. Indeed, he revealed far more potential than he sought to exploit even in his brief fervent phase. Although his demonstration that moral fables could be couched as gripping and violent thrillers was welcome news to at least a few would-be moralists, *The Island of Dr Moreau*, *The Invisible Man* and *The War of the Worlds* spawned far more imitations whose writers were only interested in the melodramatic potential of monstermakers, alien incursions and scientifically assisted criminals.

Wells's work was, therefore, an invitation to writers of action-adventure fiction enthusiastic to work on wider stages in a more spectacular manner than naturalistic fiction would ever permit, as well as to speculative fabulists. There was, inevitably, a certain parting of the ways between writers whose primary interest was in futuristic and other-worldly costume drama and writers who were seriously concerned to explore future possibilities associated with the advancement of science and technology, but the overlap between the two remained considerable, and the artful combination of the two kinds of ambition has always been able to exploit a powerful synergy.

It is perhaps regrettable that Wells never followed up his most useful discoveries. With one exception – the awkward but enterprising mock-naturalistic novella 'A Story of the Days to Come' (1897) – his post-*Time Machine* ventures into the future all fell back on more traditional modes of presentation, including suspended animation in *When the Sleeper Wakes* (1899) and visionary fantasy in *The Dream* (1924). Nor did he make any further use of his new means of space travel, tending to fall back on Vernian space-guns in other interplanetary tales (he could never bring himself to accept the potential of rockets). When Wells did use pseudoscientific facilitating devices after 1901, he did so in a tokenistic fashion whose casualness was almost insulting, as in *In the Days of the Comet* (1906).

Although his work grew out of the same milieu as the future war sub-genre, Wells was a latecomer to that branch of speculative fiction, and he was virtually alone among its writers in deploring the destruction that such a war might bring. His anticipation of tank warfare in 'The Land Ironclads' (1903) was followed up by an account of *The War in the Air* (1908) as witnessed by its potential victims. These two stories now seem far more prophetic than the jingoistic flood of novels which took it for granted that 'the war to end war' would be won by the British – and thus provided the slogan under which the actual Great War could recruit its cannon fodder – but in this respect too, Wells relented; his atomic war story *The World Set Free* (1914) was the first of several works in which he welcomed the prospect of a destruction of civilization, on the grounds that nothing less would clear the way for socialist reconstruction. There was, however, no shortage of twentieth-century writers ambitious to write the 'Wellsian' works that Wells himself would not.

## Proliferation and diversification

Wells's influence at home and abroad was mediated by local circumstance. In Britain the extension of scientific romance beyond the margins of future war fiction was exploited by future war chroniclers such as Fred T. Jane and M. P. Shiel, in the apocalyptic fantasies *The Violet Flame* (1899) and *The Purple Cloud* (1901). George Griffith, a relentless borrower of other writers' ideas, soon progressed to interplanetary romance in *A Honeymoon in Space* (1901), although he also became a prolific writer of 'karmic romances' in a vein popularized by Edwin Lester Arnold and Henry Rider Haggard.

The broader horizons of scientific romance attracted a host of assiduous new recruits. Robert Cromie – who felt that Wells had stolen the thunder of his interplanetary romance *A Plunge into Space* (1890), which had employed an antigravity device similar to Chrysostom Trueman's – offered his own take on the implications of Darwin's theory of evolution in *The Crack of Doom* (1895). William Hope Hodgson embedded a cosmic vision in *The House on the Borderland* (1908) before publishing the far-futuristic phantasmagoria *The Night Land* (1912), which outdid *The Time Machine* in supplying an account of the death of the Earth as anticipated by the theory of Lord Kelvin (which held that the sun's heat was generated by gravitational collapse, and could not last more than a few million years). J. D. Beresford followed the fine evolutionary fantasy *The Hampdenshire Wonder* (1912), tracing the career of a superhuman born out of his time, with the elegiac disaster story *Goslings* (1913) and a series of visionary *contes philosophiques* collected in *Signs and Wonders* (1921).

Many members of the new generation of professional writers created by the new periodicals dabbled in scientific romance as they dabbled in detective fiction and adventure stories. The most notable were Arthur Conan Doyle, whose tentative pre-Wellsian *The Doings of Raffles Haw* (1891) was far surpassed by his series chronicling the adventures of Professor Challenger begun with *The Lost World* (1912) and *The Poison Belt* (1913), and Rudyard Kipling, whose 'With the Night Mail' (1905) and 'As Easy as A.B.C.' (1912) imagine the dramatic transformation of future society by air transport and air power. Minor writers who helped formularize genre templates included C. J. Cutcliffe Hyne, who employed the Frankenstein formula in numerous stories published under the pseudonym Weatherby Chesney, and the disaster-story writer Fred M. White.

This activity was curbed as the popular periodicals moved beyond their experimental phase, having discovered that other genres were more popular with larger audiences; the long-anticipated Great War delivered an abrupt *coup de grâce*. The bitter legacy of disenchantment left by the war lasted far longer than the fighting, very obviously reflected in such dire anticipations of the destruction of civilization by war as *The People of the Ruins* (1920) by Edward Shanks and *Theodore Savage* (1922) by Cicely Hamilton. Although those writers of imaginatively ambitious scientific romance who survived the war tried to continue their work in that vein they found it very difficult to do so, and the most adventurous scientific romances of the early postwar years – E. V. Odle's *The Clockwork Man* (1923), Edward Heron-Allen's *The Cheetah Girl* (1923) and S. Fowler Wright's *The Amphibians* (1925) – were released into a hostile environment whose inhospitability was not to relent until the 1930s.

In France the continuing influence of Poe, Verne and Flammarion was quickly combined with Wellsian elements by such writers as J.-H. Rosny *aîné*, the pioneer of the novel of prehistory. Rosny had already adapted that sub-genre to more adventurous speculation in the alien visitation story 'Les Xipéhus' ('The Xipehus', 1887), as well as dabbling in Flammarionesque visionary fantasy in 'La Légende sceptique' (1889), but the influences of Flammarion and Wells are fruitfully combined in 'La Mort de la terre' ('The Death of the Earth', 1910) and *Les Navigateurs de l'infini* (*Navigators of Infinity*, 1925). Albert Robida, who had built a career as a writer and illustrator by cleverly satirizing Jules Verne and future war fiction, also became more adventurous towards the end of his career, in such novels as the time-reversal fantasy *L'Horloge des siècles* (*The Clock of the Ages*, 1902). Flammarionesque notions of serial extraterrestrial reincarnation remained important in French speculative fiction, providing a logic for the striking visionary fantasy *Force ennemie* (*Enemy Force*, 1903) by John-Antoine Nau – which won the first Prix Goncourt – but they were melodramatically combined with Wellsian influences in such novels as Octave Joncquel and Théo Varlet's 'Martian epic', *Les Titans du ciel* (*The Titans of Heaven*, 1921) and *L'Agonie de la terre* (*Agony of the Earth*, 1922). In France as in England, however, the Great War was a drastic interruption inhibiting the genre's development and lending encouragement to its sceptical and pessimistic elements.

Elsewhere in Europe, where no traditions of scientific romance had taken root before the importation of Verne and Wells, the Great War had even more dramatic effects. Although the German Wellsian, Kurd Lasswitz, produced three speculative novels, including the monumental *Auf Zwei Planeten* (*On Two Planets*, 1897), his influence – and that of the highly imaginative Paul Scheerbart, whose *Astrale Novelletten* were collected in 1912 – was effaced by the war and its aftermath. The Russian revolutions of 1917 interrupted a burgeoning tradition including such innovative works as Valery Brussof's futuristic fable 'Respublika yuzhnavo kresta' (1905) and rocket pioneer Konstantin Tsiolkovsky's ground-breaking account of extraterrestrial colonization *Vne zemli* (*Out of the Earth*, 1916). The futuristic socialist rhetoric of Alexei Tolstoi's *Aelita* (1922) founded a very different tradition, although Mikhail Bulgakov managed to produce the fine Wellsian satire 'Rokovy'e yaitsa' ('The Fatal Eggs', 1922) before being silenced.

Because the USA came late into World War I and was remote from its battlefields, the interruption of the domestic tradition of American speculative fiction was much less pronounced. Even more important, the effect of the war on American attitudes to technological progress was much less caustic. As in Europe, the development of late nineteenth-century American speculative fiction had been handicapped by the lack of convincing narrative frames. Tentatively adventurous works by Edward Bellamy, including *Dr Heidenhoff's Process* (1880) and 'The Blindman's World' (1886), and Edgar Fawcett, including *Solarion* (1889) and *The Ghost of Guy Thyrle* (1895), were hamstrung by their formulation as visionary fantasies. Bellamy overcame the barrier in his best-selling utopian romance *Looking Backward, 2000–1887* (1888), whose last chapter defiantly cast aside the conventional apology that it was all a dream, but Fawcett never could, even though he took the trouble to preface *The Ghost of Guy Thyrle* with a defiant manifesto for a new genre of 'realistic romances'.

As in the UK, it was an explosion of new periodicals in the 1890s that opened up market space for experimental exploitation by such writers as Jack London, whose Wellsian short stories such as 'A Thousand Deaths' (1899) and 'The Shadow and the Flesh' (1903) paved the way for the prehistoric fantasy *Before Adam* (1906) and the apocalyptic fantasy *The Scarlet Plague* (1912). Like Wells, London was a committed socialist, and his political fantasy *The Iron Heel* (1907) carried forward a sceptical tradition founded by Ignatius Donnelly's spectacular dystopia *Caesar's Column* (1890), the most extreme of many reactions to Bellamy's account of a peaceful evolutionary transition from capitalism to socialism.

The ready availability in the USA of cheap paper made from woodpulp encouraged the rapid growth of 'pulp magazines' specializing in garish melodramas, which inherited the commercial genres identified by the dime novels. One of the many new sub-genres developed in this medium consisted of uninhibited extraterrestrial adventure stories, pioneered by Edgar Rice Burroughs's extraordinarily influential 'Under the Moons of Mars' (1912; reprinted as *A Princess of Mars*). This was an unashamed dream story which did not trouble to establish a plausible mechanism for its hero's abrupt transplantation to the planet Mars. Although the image of Mars presented in the story owed something to speculative descriptions offered by the astronomer Percival Lowell in such books as *Mars as the Abode of Life* (1908), Burroughs used the ideas he borrowed as a backdrop for a fantasy of extraordinary derring-do.

Almost all of the colourful fantasies written in imitation of *A Princess of Mars* were essentially dream stories, although relatively few of them were as scornful of facilitating devices – even Burroughs, when he began to write a similar series set on Venus, condescended to employ a spaceship. Many of the writers, having read H. G. Wells, were enthusiastic to deploy pseudoscientific jargon in support of their facilitating devices, and some went so far as to use it to attain and define new imaginative spaces. J. U. Giesy employed a variant of Flammarionesque reincarnation to transport the hero of *Palos of the Dog*

*Star Pack* (1918) across interstellar distances. Ray Cummings pioneered the microcosmic romance in the hybrid Wells/Burroughs pastiche 'The Girl in the Golden Atom' (1919). Ralph Milne Farley extended the idea of radio broadcasting to include matter transmission in *The Radio Man* (1924). Once their preliminary journeys were complete, however, pulp fantasies of this kind became straightforward costume dramas in which stereotyped heroes fought sneering villains and grotesque monsters in order to win the hands of lovely heroines.

Burroughs's chief rival as a pulp fantasist was Abraham Merritt, an unashamed master of purple prose who was even less concerned to cloak his facilitating devices in scientific jargon. Even so, his ground-breaking story 'The Moon Pool' (1918) gave a new gloss of plausibility to the folkloristic notion that our world is juxtaposed with far more fantastic 'parallel worlds' which can be reached via magical portals. This device was immediately borrowed by other pulp fantasists, most notably 'Francis Stevens' (Gertrude Barrows Bennett), who elaborated it considerably in the futuristic *The Heads of Cerberus* (1919).

Pulp-dependent writers who were ambitious to produce morally challenging works, including Jack London and Upton Sinclair, usually had to issue their political fantasies in other formats, although Victor Rousseau Emanuel – who used his forenames as a pseudonym in the USA – was able to serialize *The Messiah of the Cylinder* (1917), a ringing ideological reply to Wells's *When the Sleeper Wakes*, and George Allan England serialized the political fable *The Golden Blight* (1912) before becoming the third major pulp fantasist with a trilogy of post-holocaust romances begun with *Darkness and Dawn* (1912–13; collected in book form 1914). England was, however, unable to serialize his angry condemnation of predatory capitalism *The Air Trust* (1915).

It was the gaudy exotica of pulp fiction rather than these more earnest speculative fictions that provided the backcloth for Hugo Gernsback's invention of the new genre of 'scientifiction', although the popular science magazines in which it was first featured, including *The Electrical Experimenter* and *Science and Invention*, were not themselves pulps. Scientifiction was a didactic enterprise intended to spread enthusiasm for the various technological devices (including radio sets) that Gernsback imported and sold. Although it was extremely crude in literary terms, and had no more interest in moral fabulation than any other kind of pulp fiction, it had perforce to develop new methods of story-telling in order to fulfil its didactic purpose.

The format that early writers of scientifiction found most useful was a variant of the conversation piece: anecdotal tall tales spiced with technically inclined questions. Series of this type, in which zany scientists and inventors would explain their new ventures to curious innocents, included Gernsback's own accounts of 'Baron Munchausen's New Scientific Adventures' (1915–17) and Clement Fézandie's Doctor Hackenshaw series (1921–5); they established a method of using a mock-comedic mask for the exposition of extravagant ideas that was carried forward into genre sf when Gernsback founded the first scientifiction magazine, *Amazing Stories*, in 1926. Gernsback was, however, almost as great an admirer of Burroughs and Merritt as he was of Jules Verne and H. G. Wells; he encouraged both American writers to produce more speculatively inclined works so that he could publish them, and when their responses were lukewarm he encouraged other writers to take over that particular crusade.

While it was still gestating in its pulp womb, therefore, American sf had already brought about a zygotic fusion of European scientific romance and American other-worldly exotica, lightly leavened with casually extravagant tall tales of scientific miracle-making. It was from this point that the collaborative work of horizon-expansion, social extrapolation and moral re-sophistication which has been the labour and triumph of modern science fiction began anew.

# 2

BRIAN ATTEBERY

# The magazine era: 1926–1960

The period of sf history from 1926 to 1960 can justly be called the magazine era. Even though many well-known works appeared in other venues during this period – books, comics, movies, and even radio plays – sf magazines such as *Astounding Science Fiction* were chiefly responsible for creating a sense of sf as a distinctive genre.

Science fiction is not only a mode of story-telling but also a niche for writers, a marketing category for publishers, a collection of visual images and styles and a community of like-minded individuals. All of these aspects of the genre took on their most familiar guises within the magazines that dominated the field for half a century. The magazines exerted considerable influence on sf's form and subject matter; the nature of magazine publishing and distribution, and, in particular, boom-and-bust cycles within the industry, have likewise played a part in shaping what is written and read. In addition, the location of most of the magazines' publishers in the USA has strengthened the association between sf and American culture, both in the United States and abroad.

## Origins of the science fiction magazine

The first English-language magazine entirely devoted to sf was Hugo Gernsback's *Amazing Stories*, founded in 1926. Nineteenth-century literary magazines, such as *Blackwood's* and *The Strand* in the UK and *Putnam's* and *Atlantic Monthly* in the USA, had occasionally published works of fantasy and what might be called proto-science fiction alongside more realistic fare. Early in the twentieth century, a number of inexpensive periodicals, called pulp magazines because of the poor-quality woodpulp paper on which they were printed, included sf stories by writers such as Jack London and Edgar Rice Burroughs as one of several categories of exotic adventure. Burroughs's first novel, *A Princess of Mars*, was first published in one of these pulps, *All-Story Magazine*, in 1912. A fair number of stories that can be considered sf appeared alongside the more usual supernatural fare offered in the magazines *The Thrill Book* (1919) and *Weird Tales* (1923–54, with fitful revivals). Elsewhere in the world, a few magazines combined sf with other kinds of fiction or with scientific articles: a very early example of the latter combination was the Swedish *Hugin* (1916–20).

Gernsback's *Amazing*, however, was the first not only to limit its fictional contents to stories of scientific extrapolation and outer-space adventure but also to attempt to define the genre which the editor initially called 'scientifiction', but began to refer to as 'science fiction' by 1929. An editorial in the first issue called for more examples of 'the Jules Verne, H. G. Wells and Edgar Allan Poe type of story – a charming romance intermingled with scientific fact and prophetic vision'. By singling out and reprinting some of these writers, Gernsback made them sf writers after the fact, inventing a tradition to support his ambitions. He hoped that such stories would 'supply knowledge that we might not otherwise obtain – and . . . supply it in a very palatable form'.[1] In other words, sf, as he envisioned it, was primarily a teaching tool, but one that did not make its teaching obvious.

The best way to sneak in scientific content was to offer readers the traditional pleasures of popular fiction. John Cawelti, in his study of popular story-telling formulas, groups those pleasures under the headings of adventure, mystery and romance.[2] Adventure could come in the form of conflict between humans and aliens or struggle against the unforgiving environment of outer space. Romance was usually supplied in perfunctory form – a fainting heroine hidden away by villains through most of the action and restored to the hero's arms at the last possible moment. It was  mystery, in early magazine sf, that took the most distinctive form. Many stories in the pulp magazines revolved around solving a problem through scientific means: scientific information was doled out throughout the tale, usually by characters explaining to one another. This technique can be viewed as an aesthetic flaw; it certainly slows the action down and hardly demands realistic characterization. However, if one thinks of the sf story as a scientific mystery, in which the reader is invited to accompany the characters on a voyage of discovery, then these blocks of explanation – known in sf circles as 'infodumps' or, more kindly, as 'expository lumps' – function like the gathering of clues by a detective. Each additional fact about a planetary orbit or an atomic engine leads us closer to the 'conceptual breakthrough' that Peter Nicholls, in *The Encyclopedia of Science Fiction*, identified as the central action and emotional payoff in much sf.[3]

In the four decades dominated by the sf magazines, the level of sophistication and stylistic distinction evolved from E. E. 'Doc' Smith's ray-guns-and-rockets adventure stories in the 1920s to Cordwainer Smith's intricate and evocative future histories in the 1950s. Yet the extremes represented by these two (unrelated) Smiths both fit Gernsback's basic description: the one is clearly an outgrowth of the other.

In the invention of the sf magazine, three separate publishing traditions came together. First, there was the literary mode to which Gernsback refers, a mode often called 'scientific romance'. In his prospectus, the mode was exemplified by Poe, Verne and Wells but other examples could include Shelley, Hawthorne, Melville, Bulwer-Lytton, Twain and Kipling. Second was the collection of popular story-telling formulas that developed in dime novels and pulp magazines. Third was scientific journalism.

This last form is one whose history has always been closely linked with sf. H. G. Wells began as a journalist popularizing scientific ideas, and a number of scientists from J. B. S. Haldane to Carl Sagan have tried their hands at both magazine articles and sf stories in attempts to convey ideas to a larger public. Science fiction magazines have regularly included columns devoted to science fact. Hugo Gernsback's own publishing career began in 1908 with a periodical called *Modern Electrics*, an attempt to interest readers in and educate them about new developments relating to electronic communications. Radio was the hot new technology in 1908, preceding rocketry as a hobby for would-be inventors and junior engineers. Even twenty years later, sf magazines were filled with radio-related terms such as 'triodes' and 'heterodyning', which must have conveyed the same sense of with-it novelty that 'virtual reality' and 'cyborg' suggested in the 1990s.

Gernsback intended his first magazine not only to educate but also to convert his readers to the habit of thinking about the future. He assembled some of his own predictions about future technology into a loose narrative and published the resulting novel in serial form in 1911–12 under the title *Ralph 124C 41+*. Upon selling his interest in *Modern Electrics* in 1913, he started a similar publication called *Electrical Experimenter*, renamed *Science and Invention* in 1920. One issue of that magazine, August 1923, was a special 'scientific fiction' issue. Under all three mastheads he continued to run the same mix of science fact, how-to articles and futuristic fiction. *Amazing Stories* kept the same mixture – and probably the same core of readers – but altered the proportions.

## Fictional formulas in the pulp magazines

The kind of fiction published in the magazine revealed its popular science and formula fiction parentage more obviously than its literary sources. Characterization was perfunctory and plots were often thinly disguised westerns, mysteries or lost-world romances. Several writers helped to translate these older formulas into what is now generally called 'space opera'. The best remembered of these is 'Doc' Smith, whose Skylark and Lensmen series rarely go out of print. A typical Smith adventure might involve one of his interchangeable heroes coming across a spaceship in distress, single-handedly defeating a band of space pirates, making friends with a bizarre but good-natured alien and rescuing a beautiful woman. The quality that made Smith's space opera stand out from that of most of his contemporaries was his ability to build one episode upon another to create a sense of ever-broadening vistas opening up for the reader. The Lensmen series, for instance, begins with a local conflict on Earth and ends up depicting a universe torn between godlike forces of good and evil (an effect partly lost when the first volume, *Triplanetary*, was republished in book form and Smith added an introduction to explain upfront the conflict between the evil Eddorians and the good Arisians). At each stage, the heroes acquire more powerful technology and more superhuman powers of their own to face ever more shadowy villains. Many of the plot devices developed by Smith still appear in movies and television shows.

Although Hugo Gernsback was interested in the genre's educational function, he accepted stories like Smith's in which the science was shaky but the tone properly reverential towards experimentation and technology. The definition of sf could be stretched to fit even a writer of Poesque horror, if he was as popular with readers as H. P. Lovecraft turned out to be. Many contributors to the early sf magazines were experienced pulp writers, not specialists in scientific speculation but adaptable professionals willing to supply the new market with variations on what they had been writing for detective, western or general adventure magazines.

The emphasis on – or sometimes the pretence of – scientific teaching in early magazines meant that other elements slipped through without much acknowledgement by either editor or fans. Results were mixed. On one hand, most of the fiction was stylistically weak, awkwardly constructed and marked by a naive 'gee whiz' attitude toward its gadgets and settings. On the other hand, a few writers such as Stanley Weinbaum and C. L. Moore (Catherine Moore) found freedom within the pages of the pulp magazines to explore truly 'amazing' situations and unconventional scenarios. Weinbaum became famous for creating some of the first sympathetic aliens in stories such as 'A Martian Odyssey' (1934), while Moore explored exotic scenes and complex emotions in stories such as 'The Bright Illusion' (1934). Though sometimes overwritten, their work is less formulaic, not only than that of their fellow pulp writers, but also than most of the writing for the 'slick' magazines of the day. Within the pulp sf magazines, so long as a story invoked images of futuristic machines or mist-shrouded towers, the writer was free to violate most conventions regarding character and plot.

That is not to say that such conventions did not exist. Less talented or less daring writers wrote endless variations on the tale of the young scientist who saves the world and wins his mentor's approval with a daring new invention. Marriage to the elder scientist's daughter often reinforced the fairy-tale nature of these stories. Using this basic plot structure, the writer could introduce variations regarding the nature of the threat (aliens, rival scientists, natural disasters) and the invention (a time machine, a device to accelerate evolution, a death ray). The tone could be sombre, rapturous or comic. The ending, though, was nearly always happy, a vindication of the young hero's character and the reader's beliefs. If many of the incredible invention stories concluded with astounding explosions, the author thereby allowed the hero to escape from the long-term consequences of his ingenuity.

Illustrations in the magazines of the 1930s generally matched the fiction in combining lovingly conveyed machines and unearthly vistas with blandly indistinguishable human beings. Though *Amazing*'s first cover artist, Frank R. Paul, was not very good at portraying people, he was able to produce seemingly endless modifications of the basic rocket ship and, despite the poor printing quality of the pulps, to create convincingly alien spaces and beings. He and his successors translated writers' words into images – spaceships, domed cities, goggle-eyed creatures – that are still being used to represent the future in advertisements, movies and television shows.

In a sense, the artwork, the scientific articles, the almost interchangeable stories and even the advertising in the pulp magazines represented a single continuous flow of information about the technological future. Reading one of these magazines from cover to cover is like watching an evening of television on one of the more focused cable networks. Nothing stands out; nothing is supposed to. Characters from one story reappear in another like guest stars in a situation comedy. Sometimes they have new names: Professor Brown instead of Professor Stone. Other times, they have the same name, for writers were encouraged to repeat popular scenarios as series, such as the ongoing adventures of Professor Aloysius O'Flannigan in stories by Amelia R. Long. If there were no A. R. Long stories in a particular issue, however, a fan of the series could find the same ingredients in stories by Eando Binder or R. R. Winterbotham.

The *Amazing Stories* formula found an immediate and eager audience. According to Mike Ashley, the most reliable historian of the magazines, *Amazing* reached a circulation of over 100,000 within just a few months.[4] This success stimulated other publishers to create their own sf magazines. The magazine's first direct competitor was started up, oddly enough, by Hugo Gernsback, who had overextended himself financially and lost control of his own creation in a bankruptcy proceeding in 1929. *Amazing Stories* went on under the editorship of Arthur Lynch and then T. O'Conor Sloane, while Gernsback started up, in quick succession, *Science Wonder Stories*, *Air Wonder Stories* and *Science Wonder Quarterly*, all in 1929. These were later merged into *Wonder Stories*. Other magazines began to appear, their titles indicating their indebtedness to the *Amazing Stories* formula: *Astounding Stories* (1930), *Astonishing Stories* (1931), *Marvel Science Stories* (1938), *Startling Stories* (1939). Most were owned by companies such as Munsey or Clayton, which issued whole families of pulp magazines.

## Thought variants in the Campbell era

One of these newer magazines, *Astounding Stories*, introduced a term that sums up much pulp magazine sf. Its editor, F. Orlin Tremaine, used the term 'thought-variant story' to describe a particular blend of philosophical speculation and fiction, but in a sense all the stories published in the magazines of the 1920s and 1930s were thought variants: jazz-like improvisations on familiar themes. Though any one story differs little from the next, the cumulative variations added up to a real evolutionary shift in the genre by 1937, when John W. Campbell, Jr replaced Tremaine as editor of the magazine that Campbell renamed *Astounding Science-Fiction*.

Campbell and his magazine *Astounding* stand for the second era of the sf magazines as Gernsback stands for the first. The period that begins with his editorship is often called the Golden Age of sf, and many of the best-known writers in the field first appeared in his magazine. However, part of Campbell's success was a matter of building on Gernsback's inventions, which included not only the fictional content but also the standard format: the chatty editorials, the advertising (for radio kits, scientific publications, correspondence courses, razors and body-building regimens) and, perhaps most significantly, the letters from fans. Some of the fans who wrote in demonstrated considerable understanding of the genre's history and possibilities. Their discussions represent the first attempts to create a critical theory devoted specifically to sf. In 1926, one letter-writer, G. Peyton Wertenbaker, reminded the editor that the effectiveness of 'scientifiction' lay not in its imparting of technical information but in its ability to rouse emotion by portraying 'things vast, things cataclysmic, and things unfathomably strange'.[5]

Another correspondent, Miles J. Breuer, complained in 1928 that poor literary craftsmanship did more harm to the genre than scientific accuracy could compensate for.[6] Both Wertenbaker and Breuer became important contributors of stories as well as opinions, and the letter columns of *Amazing* and the other pulps turned out to be the first public venue for many fans-turned-writers, such as John Beynon Harris (better known as John Wyndham) and

Isaac Asimov. Tremaine tried to turn the letters column in *Astounding Stories* into a venue for purely technical 'Science Discussions', but his successor, Campbell, quickly brought back the old free-ranging conversation under its former name of 'Brass Tacks'.

By encouraging such feedback, the magazines fostered a sense that readers could help shape the genre. This impression was enhanced by Gernsback's decision as early as 1914 (in *The Electrical Experimenter*) to sponsor story contests for new writers. These competitions helped break down the barrier between professional and fan, writer and reader. They also chipped away at gender barriers – one of the contest winners at *Amazing* was Clare Winger Harris, who became the first regular female contributor to the sf pulps.

After coming together on the pages of the magazines, readers and writers of sf also began to correspond directly with one another and to meet in person. These informal associations evolved into local fan clubs, a number of which came together in 1934 to form the Science Fiction League in 1934. The League soon broke up, but its offshoots carried on the fan tradition of meeting, arguing, publishing non-professional magazines for one another and generally behaving more like equal partners than passive consumers. One group, the Futurians, included many of the most important writers in the next generation: Frederik Pohl, Damon Knight, Judith Merril, Cyril Kornbluth, Isaac Asimov and James Blish. Three of those, Blish, Knight and Merril, also became important critics, pointing out logical flaws in sf stories and praising those writers who embodied scientific ideas in compelling narratives. Their efforts, and the willingness of fans to explore new fictional directions, helped transform the genre into something more sophisticated than its pulp beginnings.

John Campbell was himself a fan turned writer and editor. His agenda for *Astounding* – the avoidance of mysticism ('the boys don't like mysticism'),[7] the awareness of his audience as 'technically trained, mature men',[8] and his belief that his primary audience constituted an almost wizardly caste, an elite in-group who could get things done by knowing the universe's rules – dominated the field in the 1940s and remained influential for decades beyond that. Though he stopped writing fiction soon after he became an editor, Campbell found a number of writers who could express his vision of the orderly, knowable universe and the place of the scientifically minded man within it. Robert A. Heinlein set the pattern for the *Astounding* hero: the tough, taciturn engineer who uses reason and practical know-how to solve seemingly insurmountable problems. Those solutions could be harsh ones. In Heinlein's early story 'The Roads Must Roll' (1940), the engineer hero Gaines is in charge of keeping an elaborate system of automated highways working. He faces what seems to be a mechanical failure but is really an act of sabotage by disaffected workers. Heinlein deftly suggests that it is the application of Gaines's engineering knowledge to a human situation that restores order. As John Huntington has pointed out in *Rationalizing Genius* (1989), 'The technocratic hero is rewarding precisely because he or she seems to be able to make decisions purely "rationally".'[9] So long as the solution is neat and efficient, the human cost (never borne by the engineer himself) seems worthwhile. The story glorifies Gaines and his core of managers and disparages the striking workers, whose concerns are merely personal and emotional.

Another famous *Astounding* story, written by Tom Godwin but significantly shaped by Campbell, involves a shuttle pilot on a mercy mission who discovers a young woman stowaway on board his vessel. The laws of physics, which the title of the 1954 story terms 'The Cold Equations', determine that the stowaway cannot be saved, but the mission can if he is willing to sacrifice her life. Throughout the story, the pilot searches for an alternative that would leave her alive, but the editor insisted that the pilot and the author play by the rules. As the stowaway learns the facts, she too comes to accept the inevitability of the cold equations, and chooses to step out of the airlock of her own accord. It is a shocking ending, but in a curious way a happy one, for it reaffirms the core values held by the technological elite that Campbell called 'the boys'. The pilot completes his mission; his knowledge saves the day if not the girl.[10]

A major innovation in magazine fiction from the 1940s on was the imagined application of experimental method and technological innovation not to physical problems but to fundamental questions about society and the mind. One such application of scientific principles to society can be found in Isaac Asimov's stories about Hari Seldon, later assembled into the novel *Foundation* and its sequels (1951–86). These stories, beginning with 'Foundation' in 1942, depicted Seldon as the creator of a scholarly society that was established to prevent a future Dark Age. Seldon's statistically based discipline of 'psychohistory' allowed him both to predict the fall of a galactic empire and to alleviate the effects of that fall. People in large groups, according to the theory, behave as predictably as molecules in a fluid. No one molecule's course can be anticipated, but the flow of the mass can be charted reliably. This faith in predictive social science led not only Asimov but a number of other writers as well to begin considering social dynamics more seriously, writing stories that emphasized politics, religion and other collective activities. The result was a richer form of fiction than the super-science adventures of earlier decades.

The attempt to apply scientific principles to the workings of the human mind had an odder result. Amid sober stories about natural law and complex

investigations of social trends, the magazines of the 1940s and 1950s published a great many stories about telepathy and other forms of extrasensory
perception, or so-called 'psi powers'. Campbell considered these to be as
valid scientifically as any speculation about alien environments or rocket
ship engineering. One of his favourite writers of psionic fiction was A. E. Van
Vogt, who was otherwise the antithesis of Campbell-era sf. Rather than writing the rigorously logical stories that Campbell encouraged from Asimov or
Heinlein, Van Vogt produced dreamlike narratives about psychic supermen
in hiding, such as Jommy Cross in the enormously popular *Slan* (serialized
in 1940). Van Vogt's fiction is energetic and vivid, but often barely coherent.
His protagonists resemble fairy-tale heroes more than Heinlein's competent
engineers. They are guided along the way by characters who might as well
be wizards; their psychic gifts are thinly disguised wishing-rings and cloaks
of invisibility.

Another writer whose sf tended to shade off into fantasy was L. Ron
Hubbard. A popular writer for *Astounding* and also for Campbell's fantasy
magazine *Unknown*, Hubbard is nowadays better known for starting up first
a psychological theory called dianetics and then a religion called Scientology.
Both are characterized by the belief that the mind's untapped powers could
transform ordinary humans into psychic supermen, a theme that also dom-
inates Hubbard's fiction. Van Vogt became a follower of Hubbard's ideas,
and so, up to a point, did Campbell. Campbell wrote editorials extolling dianetics but a habit of religious scepticism kept him from accepting Scientology
wholeheartedly.

Though Campbell's own ideas about science sometimes seem to confuse
'the magic that works' with magic pure and simple, when it came to the
depiction of credible futures in fiction he had a good eye and a sure editorial
hand. He insisted on prose that was at least coherent and efficient, and he
demanded characters as believable as those in slick magazines such as *The
Saturday Evening Post*. He asked his writers to write about the future as
if they were writing for audience living in that future – in other words, to
stop explaining everything and simply let the wonder grow out of the story-
telling itself. Heinlein proved to be a master at this technique, dropping one-
word hints that opened up whole worlds of strangeness. In 'The Menace
from Earth' (1957), for instance, he suggests what it might be like to live
in a moon colony simply by having his narrator mention travelling on a
'slidebelt', and referring to people from Earth as 'groundhogs'. Unlike most
earlier writers, Heinlein felt no need to describe the technology that must
lie behind the former term or the social attitudes summed up in the latter.
His readers could fill in the blanks because of their familiarity with the
genre.

Many novels that are now considered sf classics either appeared in their entirety in *Astounding* or grew out of short stories published there. Besides Asimov's Foundation stories, these include Henry Kuttner's *Mutant* (1953), all the later installments of E. E. 'Doc' Smith's Lensmen series (1948–54), Hal Clement's *Mission of Gravity* (1954) and Frank Herbert's *Dune* (1965). Some of these writers, such as Kuttner and Smith, had written for Gernsback, but they essentially remade themselves to meet Campbell's expectations.

Another indication that *Astounding* was the most influential magazine of the 1940s is that thirty-two of the thirty-five stories reprinted in the first major sf anthology, Raymond Healy and J. Francis McComas's *Adventures in Time and Space* (1946), had first appeared on its pages. The other magazines that survived the wartime paper crunch generally got Campbell's leftovers. They survived by reprinting older material, by carrying on the older tradition of interplanetary adventure and by bringing out work by writers whose taste and politics collided with Campbell's opinions.

### Science fiction for grown-ups: the 1950s

Even as *Astounding* was reaching its peak, however, a different sort of sf was beginning to find its way into the lesser magazines. A few writers in the 1940s began to experiment with style and narrative technique – sure ways not to get published in *Astounding*. The early work of Ray Bradbury, Alfred Bester and Cordwainer Smith was published in other periodicals. Other writers who had already appeared in *Astounding* began to explore more personal voices and visions, for which they had to seek out more congenial markets. Those markets suddenly boomed around 1950, when a new set of magazines came into existence to challenge the ascendancy of *Astounding* and when a few book publishers began to seek out sf novels (mostly reprints from the magazines at first).

It is difficult to pick one of the magazines to represent the new era. One possibility is *The Magazine of Fantasy and Science Fiction*, founded in 1949 and edited by Anthony Boucher and J. Francis McComas. Another is *If*, in which the first part of James Blish's masterpiece of speculative theology, *A Case of Conscience* (1958), appeared in 1953. A third is creaky old *Amazing*, transformed by new assistant – and later managing – editor Cele Goldsmith in 1956. All of these magazines published major works of sf that Campbell would probably not have touched. All the editors encouraged new writers and new directions for established writers. Boucher and Goldsmith, in particular, looked for sophisticated themes and stylistic distinction.

A listing of stories published in these magazines seems, at first glance, to represent all the best output of the 1950s. Walter Miller's *A Canticle for Leibowitz* appeared in *Fantasy and Science Fiction* from 1955 to 1957. Miller brought not only a distinctive style and emotional depth but also a strong sense of historical precedent to this story of rebuilding civilization after nuclear holocaust. The same magazine also published Zenna Henderson's wistful tales of the exiled aliens she called the People, Daniel Keyes's most famous story 'Flowers for Algernon' (1959) and stories by non-sf regulars such as Kingsley Amis and C. S. Lewis, whose presence helped offset the American dominance of the field.

The magazine that did the most to strengthen the British presence within sf, however, was the London-based *New Worlds*, which began as a fanzine called *Nova Terrae* but metamorphosed into a professional magazine in the American mode in 1949. Its existence helped revive the tradition of British speculative fiction, which had flagged since the days of H. G. Wells. In his novel *Childhood's End* (1953), whose first part was published in *New Worlds* as 'Guardian Angel' (1950), Arthur C. Clarke managed to combine the efficient story-telling of American sf with Wells's social awareness and Olaf Stapledon's visionary grandeur. Part utopia, part comic variation of the alien-invasion story, *Childhood's End* finishes with a haunting image of the mutated children of Earth destroying their world as they leave material existence behind. Other writers who contributed to the *New Worlds* British renaissance included Brian Aldiss, John Brunner and J. G. Ballard. Yet interestingly the most popular sf author in Britain in the 1950s was John Wyndham, who had published in the American pulps before the war, but who made his name in the 1950s through the paperback publication of novels such as *The Day of the Triffids* (1951). Science fiction writers would soon be publishing straight into paperback, rather than emerging from the magazines.

The most representative – and perhaps most important – sf magazine of the 1950s was *Galaxy Science Fiction*, founded in 1950 by Horace L. Gold. The ambience of a typical *Galaxy* story is smart, edgy, urban and faintly paranoid. Central characters are often variations on a type: the chain-smoking, rumpled-suit-wearing, martini-drinking adman who claims he would rather be editing a weekly newspaper in the country. Women characters are not usually very satisfactory: some are aliens in disguise, and nearly all are inexplicable in their motivations and perceptions – though Gold did try to include 'at least one story that appealed to women' in every issue.[11] Few *Galaxy* stories take place in space. The opening scene, until things get weird, might almost be a *New Yorker* sketch of the same period.

The best of those stories are told with the assurance and finesse of one of these *New Yorker* pieces by regulars such as James Thurber or E. B. White.

Such story-telling requires a combination of circumstances including a gifted editor paying the best rates in the business, a close circle of mutually critical writers and an audience ready for greater sophistication in style and theme. That audience included longtime readers, who had worked their way through Gernsback's primary and Campbell's secondary courses in sf and were ready to go on to higher education. It also included readers new to the field. According to A. J. Budrys, Gold always intended to reach

> a great untapped market of mundane readers – the people to whom he insisted that he was the editor of *Galaxy* magazine, *not* of *Galaxy* science fiction. At his card table every Friday night were not just Frederik Pohl, Bob Scheckley [*sic*], and the fellow whom Jerry Bixby nicknamed 'Ayjay' Budrys, but also such persons as the modern composers Louis and Bebe Barron and John Cage, radio and TV executives, and people on the editorial staffs of major slick magazines.[12]

One of those guests was Alfred Bester, a scriptwriter who was eventually to edit a slick magazine himself (*Holiday*). He had done some sf writing in the 1940s, and Gold tried to talk him into contributing to *Galaxy*. According to Bester, after he reluctantly offered a few ideas for possible stories,

> At this point his professionalism took command and, still via the telephone machine, he discussed the ideas, took them apart, put them together again, and combined and recombined them with me in a wonderful series of editor–author sessions. The crux of those conferences was that we respected each other and could accept or reject each other's suggestions without loss of face or temper. It was an ideal collaboration, and out of it came the novel.[13]

The novel in question was *The Demolished Man* (1953), a tour de force of satire, lyricism, stylistic playfulness and classic sf invention. His even more impressive follow-up, *The Stars My Destination* (1956), draws on such familiar plot devices as space piracy and psychic supermen, but combines them with literary experimentation in the tradition of William Blake and Arthur Rimbaud. Bester's hero Gully Foyle has his senses cross-wired in a manner suggesting Rimbaud's poetry and develops into a heaven-challenging anti-hero straight out of one of Blake's epics. The epigraph of the book is drawn from Blake's 'The Tyger'.

In addition to Bester's two classic novels, Gold published such satirical works as Pohl and Kornbluth's exploration of advertising and consumerism, *The Space Merchants* (1953); other major works from *Galaxy* include Theodore Sturgeon's 'Baby Is Three', the core novella of his novel of evolution and ethics, *More Than Human* (1953) and Ray Bradbury's

'The Fireman', which became *Fahrenheit 451* (1953). The magazine published major stories by Philip K. Dick, William Tenn, Margaret St. Clair, Avram Davidson, Fritz Leiber, Damon Knight and Katharine MacLean. It fostered the careers of newer writers such as Edgar Pangborn, Mark Clifton, Kurt Vonnegut and, perhaps most importantly, Cordwainer Smith (Paul Linebarger).

Smith's association with *Galaxy* began with 'The Game of Rat and Dragon' in 1955 and continued through the next decade and a half. The rats of that story are also its dragons: deadly predators lurking in the other-dimensional space through which interstellar ships must pass. Only telepaths can sense the approach of dragons, but human telepaths alone are not fast enough to shoot off the light-bombs that destroy them. They must have partners. Midway through the story, the reader realizes that the elegant, diminutive, ferocious Partners with which the human 'pinlighters' must work are ordinary cats. Typical Smith touches in this story are its unexpected juxtapositions, such as rat-hunting cats teamed with space-going warriors; its evocative names – we meet cats named Murr, Lady May and Captain Wow; the unconventionality of its heroes, who include an old priest and a little girl; the personal cost to those heroes of their victories; and the odd, lilting language used to evoke strange visions.

The work of writers such as Bester and Smith is more than workmanlike. It is challenging, disturbing, elegant, witty and surprisingly fresh even decades later. It has hardly a trace of the old pulp formularization. The writers' voices are distinctive, rather than blending into a continuous flow of sf discourse. Any paragraph of a Cordwainer Smith story is recognizable as no one else's work. By the end of the 1950s, the best magazine sf was comparable to fiction published in more traditional literary venues, and readers were already getting a taste of the experiments that were to characterize the next decade's New Wave.

At the beginning of the magazine era, popular sf often defined itself by contrast with literary fiction. When Aldous Huxley's *Brave New World* was published in 1932, a reviewer in *Amazing Stories* saw it primarily in terms of its failure to meet the expectations of magazine readers. 'From the point of view of the scientific fiction fan', the reviewer (credited only as C.A.B.) said in an essay titled 'Highbrow Science Fiction', 'this book is a decided flop.' One of the reviewer's objections had to do with the raciness of Huxley's dystopian novel, for overt sexuality was strictly excluded from the sf magazines at the time. The bigger objection, however, was that 'Mr Huxley either dislikes science, particular its possible future development, or that he does not believe in science.'[14] It was not enough for Huxley to predict cloning, artificial wombs, recreational drugs and the social changes following on those innovations. Nor did his inventive style and daring characterization count for much. He was supposed to say something uplifting about science and to provide the emotional payoffs that come with adventure, mystery and romance. Otherwise, his novel might be literature, but it was not really sf.

By the 1950s, however, reviewers such as Damon Knight and James Blish welcomed highbrow fiction into the field. Blish (writing under his critical pen name of William Atheling, Jr) discusses Huxley among several other '"outside" authors', including George Orwell, Bernard Wolfe and Kurt Vonnegut, who brought something fresh to sf tropes. Publishing outside the sf community, they did not need to worry about finding new angles on old plot devices. Rather, they could concern themselves with '*thinking about something*' through their fiction.[15] Knight was a little more hesitant to welcome literary dabblers into the category of sf, but he did list as classic works within the genre Karel Čapek's novel *War with the Newts* (1937), and Eugene Zamiatin's (or Evgeny Zamyatin's) brilliant dystopia *We* (1924).[16]

Just as the early issues of *Amazing Stories* helped to create a tradition for sf by pulling in nineteenth-century writers of scientific romance, these reviews helped expand and deepen the field by incorporating twentieth-century traditions of surrealism, satire and utopian speculation. They also recognized that sf could be produced in countries other than the United States: Huxley's England, Zamiatin's Russia, Čapek's Czechoslovakia. Even works that bore only the slightest resemblance to the standard scientific adventure were recommended to the sf readership: Olaf Stapledon's visionary trip through the cosmos called *Star Maker* (1937), J. R. R. Tolkien's fantasy epic *The Lord of the Rings* (1954–5) and Mervyn Peake's eerie *Titus Groan* (1946) were all seen by reviewers as relevant to the genre's expanding horizons and growing ambitions.

This is not to say that sf had become indistinguishable from the literary mainstream. Critics outside the genre rarely paid attention to its achievements, and works such as *Brave New World* were rarely acknowledged to be sf except by fans. One such critic, Arthur Koestler, stated outright that 'Swift's *Gulliver*, Huxley's *Brave New World*, Orwell's *Nineteen Eighty-Four* are great works of literature because in them the oddities of alien worlds serve merely as a background or pretext for a social message. In other words, they are literature precisely to the extent to which they are not science fiction.'[17] Though sf had achieved considerable maturity as a genre by the end of the 1950s, it was still seen by outsiders in terms of pulp formulas and movie monsters. A greater measure of acceptance came partly as a result of the movement of the field away from its origins.

## Emerging from the magazines

By the 1960s, the era of magazine sf was coming to an end; that is, the field could no longer be characterized primarily in terms of its periodicals. This change could be seen first in the format of the magazines themselves. Whereas the early pulps looked almost like comic books, the later magazines more nearly resembled paperback novels. The folio-sized pages and garish covers of *Amazing* gradually gave way to digest-size and a more subtle presentation. The first magazine to switch sizes was *Astounding*, under the paper restrictions of the Second World War. At the time, the switch was seen as a loss of visibility on the newsstands, but it had the unexpected benefit of making the magazine seem more grown-up and more literary. All the major magazines of the 1950s were published in digest form, *Amazing Stories* being the last pulp-sized survivor. *Galaxy*, which was partly underwritten by a prosperous Italian publishing firm, was given an especially sleek look. It was, in essence, a monthly series of original anthologies, and it demonstrated to the publishing world the viability of such anthologies, and of science fiction as a category for book publication.

This new possibility coincided with a major disruption of the magazine market. At the end of the 1950s the primary distributor, the American News Service, was declared a monopoly and had to divest itself of its local holdings. As a direct result, twenty magazines (of various sorts) folded immediately and the others took severe hits in their circulation.[18] The more prosperous magazines were able to keep going, but sf ceased to be identified primarily as a magazine form. Shorter forms, from short-short stories to novellas, gave way to novels and even multi-volume series. In marketing terms, the brand names under which sf could be sold ceased to be *Astounding* or *Galaxy* and would become specialized categories such as military sf and science fantasy or individual authors such as Heinlein and Asimov. It is significant that the major magazine of the 1980s and 1990s was called *Isaac Asimov's Science Fiction Magazine*.

The transformation from magazine to book format involved some sacrifices. Despite editorial whims and market downturns, the magazines had allowed the development of surprising new themes, forms and techniques – nearly anything could be accommodated as part of a reliable mix. The relatively small scale of the magazine market also fostered artistic independence. A magazine was like the small independent film as opposed to the Hollywood blockbuster, which has to meet the expectations of the broadest possible audience. Magazines have subscribers and more-or-less guaranteed space on newsstands. Books must be promoted. Even now, well after the heyday of the magazines, most innovation within the field takes place in the remaining magazines or in their contemporary equivalents. The latter include small press volumes, semi-professional publications and on-line publishers.

It remains to be seen whether these outlets will be enough to foster the wild talents and random mutations of an earlier era. Though much of the fiction from the pulp era is quaint and forgettable, some is not. And without those earlier efforts, the genre would not be what it has become.

## NOTES

1. Mike Ashley, *The Time Machines: The Story of the Science-Fiction Pulp Magazines from the Beginning to 1950* (Liverpool: Liverpool University Press, 2000), pp. 49–50.
2. See John G. Cawelti, *Adventure, Mystery, and Romance* (Chicago: Chicago University Press, 1976).
3. Peter Nicholls, ed., *The Encyclopedia of Science Fiction* (London: Granada, 1979), pp. 134–6.
4. Ashley, *Time Machines*, p. 51.
5. *Ibid.*, p. 57.
6. *Ibid.*, pp. 57–58.
7. 'To Mr. R. M. Williams', 23 March 1953, in *The Complete Collection of the John W. Campbell Letters*, compiled by Perry A. Chapdelaine, Sr. (Microfilm. Franklin TN: A. C. Projects, 1987), Reel 4.
8. 'To Dr Welland A. Hause', 7 January 1952, in ibid., Reel 3.
9. John Huntington, *Rationalizing Genius* (New Brunswick, NJ: Rutgers University Press, 1989), p. 74.
10. Tom Godwin's 'The Cold Equations' was first published in *Astounding Science-Fiction*, August 1954, and reprinted many times, as in Robert Silverberg, ed., *The Science Fiction Hall of Fame Vol. 1* (New York: Avon, 1970), pp. 543–69.
11. Horace Gold, 'Gold on Galaxy', in Frederik Pohl, Martin H. Greenberg and Joseph F. Olander, eds., *Galaxy: Thirty Years of Innovative Science Fiction* (Chicago: Playboy Press, 1980), p. 6.
12. Algis Budrys, 'Memoir: Spilled Milk', in *ibid.*, p. 169.
13. Alfred Bester, 'Horace, Galaxyca', in *ibid.*, p. 424.
14. 'Highbrow Science Fiction', *Amazing Stories* (April 1932), p. 86.
15. William Atheling, Jr [James Blish], *The Issue at Hand* (Chicago: Advent, 1973), p. 142.
16. Damon Knight, *In Search of Wonder* (Chicago: Advent, 1967), pp. 11, 17.
17. Quoted by Knight, *ibid.*, p. 2.
18. Barry Malzberg, 'Introduction: The Fifties', in Barry N. Malzberg and Bill Pronzini, eds., *The End of Summer: Science Fiction of the Fifties* (New York: Ace, 1979), p. 2.

# 3

DAMIEN BRODERICK

# New Wave and backwash: 1960–1980

The 1960s – like the turn of the twentieth century, and the apocalyptic, futuristic millennial years 2000 and 2001 – carried a special freight of nervous expectation. While atomic weapons still had limited capabilities, public perception was of a world facing imminent destruction, and people daily suppressed their anticipation of radioactive doom from the skies. That terror had been manifest, in disguised form, in earlier sf tales and movies of monsters, horrific transformation and alien invasion. By late 1962, the world actually faced just such a science-fictional threat – the Cuban missile crisis, when nuclear war seemed about to erupt – and saw it narrowly averted. Two images epitomize this turbulent, paradoxical era: the brief, grainy film frames of President Kennedy's assassination in November 1963, and the equally indistinct television coverage, live from the moon, of Neil Armstrong's first step into the lunar dust in July 1969. These were beamed about the planet via a medium, television, that just forty years earlier had been, in the contemptuous phrase journalists love, '*mere* science fiction'.

After the generally straitlaced, vapid fifties, and despite repressed dread, the sixties would be a metaphor and icon for psychic unbuttoning, diverting potential political rage into self-indulgence. Obsessed with style, teens and twenties reached first for simple raunchy pleasure in popular music and other entertainment media – to the distress of an older generation – and then for complexity and engagement. The growing moral crisis of the Vietnam War was not resolved until American defeat and withdrawal from south-east Asia in the early 1970s; partisans in the conflict would find literary expression, in part, through upheavals in the way sf was written, published and read. In this chapter, the emphasis will be almost entirely on sf from the West – Britain, the USA, Australia and other Anglophone outposts. Significant work was being done in the USSR and its satellites – by Stanislaw Lem in Poland, especially, and by Russians such as the Strugatsky brothers – but despite efforts to translate and publish the best work, it had little effect on sf's main trajectory until more recent decades.

While it is not absurd to view history as a succession of ten-year tableaux, alternative perspectives are equally valid. A human generation is roughly twenty-five years long, birth to parenthood. Certain punctuations leave their generational mark on a whole culture, especially disruptive warfare or atrocious natural catastrophe. In the West, the two global wars created just such markers. By 1918 and 1945, many young men in their prime were dead; millions more had been separated from home for years. The routine cycle of marriage and childbirth was disrupted. Both wars were followed by a baby boom, particularly the second, which coincided with a period of feverish technical growth and new abundance. One might expect the children of those epochs to make their cultural mark *en bloc*, in their late teens or early twenties. So it proved with the emerging field of sf in the 1940s, although military service disturbed the expected pattern somewhat, delaying the full flowering of Golden Age sf for several years. A raft of the most brilliant Western sf writers of that period had been born around 1920, and roughly a generation later, in the mid 1940s, we find another loose cluster.

Those growing up after the Second World War had great expectations, and chafed under them. Education, especially to university level, increased manyfold, with a post-Sputnik scare boost for the sciences and engineering, but also with greatly increased places throughout the West for humanities students. Paperback books filled every back pocket; beatniks declaimed rough, angry and sensual poetry. So if politically it seemed in some ways the dreariest of times, it was also hopeful, striving, experimental. A high point of kinetic sf modernism in the 1950s, the vibrantly knowing sf prose of Alfred Bester (and other savvy, literary writers such as Theodore Sturgeon and Cordwainer Smith) was one goal for emulation by the smart kids who went through college in the late fifties and early sixties, wolfing down John Webster, Arthur Rimbaud, James Joyce and Jack Kerouac alongside engineering or physics classes. Ambitious in ways unknown to most meat-and-potatoes sf readers, they thrilled the innocent with vivid language, bold imagery and a profoundly sceptical analysis of the world even as they unsettled an old guard who found these modernist experiments a betrayal of everything in the established rules of sf.

### The New Wave

The emergent movement, a reaction against genre exhaustion but never quite formalized and often repudiated by its major exemplars, came to be known as the New Wave, adapting French cinema's *nouvelle vague*. Auteurs such as Jean-Luc Godard and François Truffaut broke with narrative tradition at the start of the sixties, dazzling or puzzling viewers with tapestries of jump cuts, meanderings, all-but-plotless immersion in image. Christopher Priest appropriated the term for an sf almost equally disruptive, existentially fraught and formally daring, that evolved around the British sf magazine *New Worlds* in the mid to late 1960s.

Alfred Bester had provided a kind of advance imprimatur. In February 1961, as fiction reviewer for the most literary of sf venues, *The Magazine of Fantasy and Science Fiction*, he boiled over in a scornful denunciation of his peers. 'The average quality of writing in the field today is extraordinarily low.' He meant not stylistic competence – 'it's astonishing how well amateurs and professionals alike can handle words' – but thought, theme and drama. 'Many practicing science fiction authors reveal themselves in their works as . . . silly, childish people who have taken refuge in science fiction where they can establish their own arbitrary rules about reality to suit their own inadequacy.'[1]

By the early sixties much sf had become complacent, recycling with minor modification a small number of tropes and ideas. The previous decade's sf had suffered in microcosm just the sort of preposterous, trashy pseudo-ideas that would blossom as the 'Age of Aquarius' and form the basis of an ever-expanding retreat from Enlightenment science and values – the New Age movement – eerily, a feature of the end of the twentieth century predicted and deplored in Robert Heinlein's Future History as 'the Crazy Years'.

Most of these loony tunes – the allegedly psionic Hieronymus Machine that worked even better if you took out the resistors and left only the circuit diagram, the Dean Drive, a sort of antigravity machine, even a sophistical advocacy of slave-holding – were warbled by John W. Campbell, Jr, usually regarded as Golden Age sf's founding father and fearless proponent of science and gung-ho technology in an era of renewed superstition. During 1960, his famous and influential magazine, *Astounding*, changed its name to the less ludicrous *Analog*, in a bid for respectability and lucrative advertising, but his irascible editorials pressed on with the promotion of strange ideas, deliberately against the liberal grain. His magazine slowly lost popularity among the young even as its bizarre quirks foreshadowed the flight from reason that would go hand in hand, among hippies and housewives alike, with chemical self-medication in the quest for existential meaning and transcendence in a cruel world where, as even *Time* magazine noted in a famous cover story of 1965, God was dead.

Alexei and Cory Panshin have argued that the driving impulse of Golden Age sf was a 'quest for transcendence'.[2] That quest did not falter in the sixties; if anything, it intensified. By the seventies, its febrile flush was fading, and a kind of rapprochement emerged between the New Wave's radical stylistics, and those arduously won techniques of the 'lived-in future' that Heinlein and others had devised, if not yet quite perfected. Perhaps surprisingly, the earliest index of this continuing hunger for transcendence was Heinlein's own award-winning *Stranger in a Strange Land* (1961), which by the sixties' end was a best-selling cult novel on campus and beyond, as was J. R. R. Tolkien's trilogy *Lord of the Rings* (1954–5; in one volume, 1968) – the canonical twentieth-century fantasy, yet one developed with the rigour of an alien-populated sf landscape. In mid decade, Frank Herbert's *Analog* serials *Dune World* and *The Prophet of Dune* (1963–5) appeared in revised book form as *Dune* (1965), perhaps the most famous modern sf novel. It manipulated superbly the longing that Bester had mocked so ferociously: an adolescent craving for imaginary worlds in which heroes triumph by a preternatural blend of bravery, genius and psi, helped along in this case by a secret psychedelic drug, *melange*. The deep irony of *Dune*'s popular triumph, and that of its many sequels, is Herbert's own declared intention to undermine exactly that besotted identification with the van Vogtian superman-hero. It is in this crux, as much as in the stylistic advances and excesses of the New Wave, that the sixties made its mark on sf, and sf made its even greater mark on the world.

Critic John Clute, in an essay with the deliciously absurd New Wave title 'Scholia, Seasoned with Crabs, Blish Is' (1973), diagnosed James Blish's central sf texts as 'Menippean satires', a borrowing from Northrop Frye's *Anatomy of Criticism* (1957).[3] Third-century BC philosopher Menippus prefigured a kind of seriocomic idea-centred fiction quite unlike the character-focused novel perfected in the nineteenth century and taken by literary scholars of the mid-twentieth century (and by many even today) as almost the only allowable version. Heinlein's *Stranger* is a clear candidate. Its characters are stylized, mouthpieces for systems of ideas paraded and rather jerkily dramatized. In this case, the ideas advanced included 'free love' – still rather shocking in the early sixties – a sort of relativist 'Thou-art-God' religiosity and scornful hostility to such established doctrines as democracy. Young Valentine Michael Smith had been raised in isolation by aliens and hence with altered access to reality (in accordance with the linguistic theory of Benjamin Lee Whorf) due to unique Martian semantics, and was now a redemptive gift to humanity. The novel's cast were at once collective (sharing a 'Nest', bonded near-telepathically and given miraculous powers by the inscrutable Martian language), authoritarian (happily serving under their whimsical 'Boss', Jubal Harshaw, one of the great figures of sf and surely a skewed portrait of Heinlein), yet libertarian. It was an unstable compound, and efforts by stoned hippies who had read the book to put its ideals into practice came predictably unstuck – as the novel's paradigms, primitive Christianity and Mormonism, had done. Unfortunately, none of them could think in Martian. Still, the wistful fantasy filled a void left by the death of God, if only for a giddy semester.

Presumably Heinlein did not really believe that changing linguistic habits could give you miraculous powers, although more than one of his stories used this trope. By contrast, it seems clear that Frank Herbert did intend his ornate, baffling sequence about the Atreides supermen and women of the year 10,000 to induct readers into a sort of advanced consciousness. Like a Sufi or Zen master, Herbert wished to prod his readers toward enlightenment, a moment of *satori* or insight that would free them from mechanical adherence to routine, habit and the dull complacency of the previous decade. Regrettably, his technique served better as a hypnotic. Hundreds of thousands of readers, probably millions, revelled in the adventures of Paul Muad'Dib, embattled heir to the desert planet Arrakis or Dune. The books overflowed: female Jesuits (the Bene Gesserit, with their centuries-long eugenics breeding program), the mysterious Arab-like Fremen, blue-eyed from the drug *melange* and driven by visions and artful myth, the great savage worms like sand whales, Mentat supermen with enhanced minds able to think as fast as the forbidden computers, galactic intrigue and warfare . . . It remains a heady blend, if rather clunkily wrought, and carried the main vector of Golden Age sf toward a kind of apotheosis.

Except that Herbert had hidden a hand-grenade in his wish-fulfilment – so artfully that it blew up in his editor's face. Declining the sequel, *Dune Messiah*, Campbell complained with forthright coarseness: 'The reactions of science-fictioneers . . . over the last few decades has [*sic*] persistently and explicitly been that they want *heroes* – not anti-heroes. They want stories of strong men who exert themselves, inspire others, and make a monkey's uncle out of malign fates!'[4] Slyly, Herbert had meant exactly to subvert that facile template, and his secret instinct resonated with the writers of the emerging New Wave if not with older sf fans. 'What better way to destroy a civilization, society or a race than to set people into the wild oscillations which follow their turning over their judgment and decision-making faculties to a superhero?'[5] That was nearly a full generation, of course, after several self-declared supermen and their viciously subhuman regimes were toppled in Europe at the cost of millions of lives. It was a lesson that sf never quite learned until New Wave writers began to peel open the ideological myth of supreme scientific competence and galactic manifest destiny.

## Inner space

The first begetter of this heretical tradition, or at least most prominent, is often held to be James Ballard, whose account of an uprooted childhood in wartime Singapore, brought to a close by the distant science-fictional flash of a nuclear weapon bursting over Japan, would be filmed by Steven Spielberg in 1987 as the movie *Empire of the Sun*.

J. G. Ballard was launched in an unlikely venue: the venerable, dull pages of John Carnell's British magazines *New Worlds* and *Science Fantasy*, which against the odds were also responsible for Brian W. Aldiss, John Brunner and several other brilliant autodidact harbingers of the revolution. Strictly, these few slick British innovators were fifties writers, but each came into his – or very, very rarely her – own during the ferment of the sixties' New Wave. With his achingly dry surrealist wit, clarified prose and devotion to recurrent 'properties' (empty swimming pools, damaged astronauts, catastrophic and numinous landscapes), Ballard was from the outset a goad to traditionalists. By that very token, he was a gift to the quirky US anthologist Judith Merril, whose *Year's Best SF* series featured his work, together with an increasingly agitated propaganda for new ways of writing something she dubbed 'speculative fiction' – new ways that were generally, in the larger literary world, rather old. Alongside unnerving tales by Aldiss, Ballard and Cordwainer Smith, Merril paraded pieces by Borges, Romain Gary, Dos Passos, Lawrence Durrell, plus the usual literate-to-brilliant sf suspects: Asimov, Bradbury, Clarke, Zenna Henderson, Algis Budrys. In 1960, impeccably, she selected Daniel Keyes's superb 'Flowers for Algernon', a gentle emergent superman story with a bittersweet twist; today, it seems scarcely sf at all, more like Norman Mailer's account of the Apollo Moon landing. By 1965 Merril had Thomas M. Disch's bleak, absurdist 'Descending', the louche poetry of Roger Zelazny's 'A Rose for Ecclesiastes' and Ballard's paradigmatic 'The Terminal Beach': 'In the field office he came across a series of large charts of mutated chromosomes. He rolled them up and took them back to his bunker. The abstract patterns were meaningless, but during his recovery he amused himself by devising suitable titles for them . . . Thus embroidered, the charts took on many layers of cryptic association.'[6] As, indeed, did Ballard's ever stranger body of work. When Carnell's *New Worlds* expired of terminal blandness in 1964, a youthful Michael Moorcock tore to its rescue, changing the magazine utterly as its backlog cleared. Now, with Ballard as house patron saint, and under the sign of William Burroughs, the New Wave began to roll relentlessly toward sf's crusted shores. Donald Wollheim found Norman Spinrad's gonzo novel *Bug Jack Barron*, serialized in *New Worlds*, a 'depraved, cynical, utterly repulsive and thoroughly degenerate parody of what was once a real SF theme'.[7] Still, the undeniable detritus carried along with the New Wave was not necessarily welcome even to devoted surfers.[8] Half the names on *New World*'s contents pages are now forgotten – Langdon Jones, Michael Butterworth, Roger Jones – and some were pseudonymous:

'Joyce Churchill' hid M. John Harrison, a fine artist who grew disenchanted with sf's mode (although he released a new sf novel, *Light*, in 2002). What is striking in retrospect is how enduring, even so, the impact of the major New Wave writers has been, and the longevity of its biggest names: Ballard (although he has largely abandoned sf), Aldiss, Moorcock himself and so-journing Americans during the swinging sixties: brilliant funny, caustic John Sladek (d. 2000), Pamela Zoline, Samuel R. Delany, Thomas Disch, Norman Spinrad. The work of Robert Silverberg, formerly a prodigious writing ma-chine, deepened markedly in a New Wave direction after 1967, winning him a special Campbell Memorial award in 1973 'for excellence in writing'. Still, James Blish, another important writer-critic, was disenchanted by the hype and declared the Wave washed-up by the decade's close.[9]

Its brief moment is displayed in raucous glory in several anthologies: Merril's proselytizing *England Swings SF* (1968; in Britain, *The Space-Time Journal*), Harlan Ellison's immensely ambitious fusion of New Wave and American can-do, *Dangerous Visions* (1967), Spinrad's *The New Tomorrows* (1971) and Damon Knight's important long-running not-quite-New Wave series of original anthologies, *Orbit* (1966 and later), showcasing such off-beat and consequential talents as R. A. Lafferty, Gene Wolfe, Joanna Russ, Kate Wilhelm and Gardner Dozois. The mood of bewildered antagonism from the old guard is caught perfectly in Isaac Asimov's bitter remark, cited by Ace Book's editor Donald Wollheim on the jacket of Merril's showcase: 'I hope that when the New Wave has deposited its froth, the vast and solid shore of *science fiction* will appear once more.' Wollheim had already taken care to distance himself, to comic effect. On the back jacket, in bold red capitals, he shouted:

THIS MAY BE THE MOST IMPORTANT SF BOOK OF THE YEAR

and underneath, in black and a smaller font:

(or it may be the least. You must judge for yourself!)

By 1968, however, Wollheim had proved himself an editor of some courage, if little discrimination, publishing amid a constant drizzle of mediocre consumer product several exceptional novels at the margins of the New Wave: Delany's romantic, flushed *The Jewels of Aptor* (1962), *Babel-17* and *Empire Star* (1966) and *The Einstein Intersection* (1967). Ursula K. Le Guin's first Hainish novels (*Rocannon's World*, 1964; *Planet of Exile*, 1966; *City of Illusion*, 1967) appeared under the dubious Ace imprint. Le Guin's triumph at the cusp of the seventies as the thoughtful, elegant anthropologist of sf and fantasy, begun with *A Wizard of Earthsea* (1968), was established with *The Left Hand of Darkness* (1969) under a revitalizing Ace Special imprint by New Wave-sympathetic editor Terry Carr and confirmed by *The Dispossessed: An Ambiguous Utopia* (1974).

An error easily made when considering these several trajectories is to suppose that one literary movement follows another in a parable of progress, dinosaurs giving way to eager young mammals – or, in an allegory of regression, gains arduously accumulated are lost to the onrush of barbarians. Neither image is valid. Writers, publishers and readers are always somewhat out of step. By the time a 'fashion' is visible, built from the latest work available to readers, a year or more has passed since those texts were created and sold. Unless a movement is geographically concentrated – as the London *New Wave* scene largely was – mutual influence straggles.

Moreover, in a marginal mode like sf, read most enthusiastically by the penniless young, genre history is piled up indiscriminately in libraries and second-hand book stores. Near the start of the 1960s, fresh inductees to the sf mythos could read the latest coolly ironic Ballard slap at bourgeois prejudice or Zelazny MA-trained gutter poetry – 'where the sun is a tarnished penny, the wind is a whip, where two moons play at hot-rod games, and a hell of sand gives you the incendiary itches'[10] – then turn at once to a paperback of 'Doc' Smith's tone-deaf Lensmen series from the Golden Age and earlier, meanwhile soaking up scads of Asimov, Heinlein, annual 'Year's Best' gatherings and comic book adventures. We must apply Stephen Jay Gould's evolutionary insight: in every era most species are simple life-forms, fitted almost from the outset to a range of environments and tremendously persistent. So the classics of sf, at least until fairly recently, have always remained alive in the humus. Certainly that was so in the 1960s and 1970s, when the backlists of many publishers formed a reliable backstop to their annual income.

Nor is the distinction between New Wave and Old as simple as pessimism versus triumphalism. Several sets of coordinates overlap, to some extent by accident. It is true that much of the 'experimental' sf of the 1960s took a gloomy cast, while the continuing mainstream of commercial sf was distinctly upbeat, constructing a universe in which technological salvation arrives through virtuous human efforts. Was that distinction *necessarily* echoed in the contrast between a disruptive textuality seeking to enact its ideas in richly modernist symbol and vocabulary, versus traditional sf's adherence to a 'clear windowpane' theory of writing? It is more likely that stylistic differences derived from the filiations (and education) of its writers.

Even if the science of classic sf was often laughable or wholly invented, it did borrow something structurally important from the lab: scientific papers, after all, are meant to rid themselves of any taint of the subjective, uttering their reports in a disembodied, timeless Voice of Reason (even as those

findings are acknowledged to be fallible, provisional, awaiting challenge).
New Wave writers – and those signing up as established middle-aged veterans, such as Philip José Farmer – took, as their model, narratives drenched
in artful subjectivity, even when, as in Ballard's remote constructs, personality seemed wilfully denied. From the outset, it was impossible to mistake
Ballard's dry voice and curious obsessions: 'Later Powers often thought of
Whitby, and the strange grooves the biologist had cut, apparently at random,
all over the floor of the empty swimming pool.'[11] Or in his pungent, non-
linear 'condensed novels': '**Narcissistic**. Many things preoccupied him during
this time in the sun: the plasticity of forms, the image maze, the catatonic
plateau, the need to re-score the C.N.S., pre-uterine claims, the absurd –
i.e., the phenomenology of the universe . . .'[12]

The brilliantly iconoclastic Philip K. Dick was forging a powerful new
vision from sf's generic trash, which he dubbed 'kipple'. Dick was driven
by routine commercial urgencies, but something wonderful happened when
his hilariously demented tales ran out of control inside the awful covers
of pulp paperbacks. Australian critic Bruce Gillespie has posed the central
quandary, not just of Dick's œuvre but for sf as a maturing yet weirdly
shocking paraliterature: 'how can a writer of pulpy, even careless, prose and
melodramatic situations write books that also retain the power to move the
reader, no matter how many times the works are re-read?' Part of his answer
is that Dick repeatedly takes us on an 'abrupt journey from a false reality to
a real reality' or, in the extreme case, 'a roller coaster ride down and down,
leaving behind ordinary reality and falling into a totally paranoid alternate
reality. By the book's end, there is nothing trustworthy left in the world.'[13]

## Entropy machines

Just that existential vertigo is arguably the key to New Wave textuality, sometimes masked as an obsession with *entropy*, the tendency of all organized
matter and energy to degrade towards meaningless noise and inanition. Certainly that is how many traditionalists viewed their rivals, and who could
blame them when faced with an exultantly transgressive cut-up collage from
Thomas M. Disch's *Camp Concentration*, serialized in *New Worlds* in 1967:

> **The Parable of the Sun and the Moon**
> The king arrives unaccompanied and enters the parenchyma . . . The dew Pia
> watering it, dissolving layers of trodden gold. He gives it to the toadstools.
> Everything comes in. He divests himself of his skin. It is written: *I am the Lord
> Saturn*. The epithesis of sin. Saturn takes it and careens (Hoa). All things are
> Hoa. He, when once it has been given Him, illapses into prepared matter. O
> how fall'n. (Squab, upon a rock.)[14]

This delirious passage runs on for pages at a pivotal point in Disch's superbly crafted evocation of a sanctimonious genius growing much smarter, and bleakly insightful, under the baleful influence of a genetically engineered syphilis virus. It left conventional sf readers cold or outraged, even as Samuel R. Delany found it 'far and away *the* exemplar of Disch's work, and by extension of the gathering New Wave project'.[15] Disch was entirely ignored by voters for the Hugo Award (hundreds of self-selected fans at the annual world sf convention) and even the Nebula (chosen by fellow sf writers). He would achieve no recognition until 1980; by then, his interests had moved elsewhere, to the genre's loss.

Still, such awards did recognize works of talent as well as less interesting candidates: Nebulas (started in 1965) went in the sixties to Herbert's Hugo-winning *Dune*, Keyes's *Flowers for Algernon*, Delany's *Babel-17* and *The Einstein Intersection*, only to offer the 1968 prize to Alexei Panshin's competent but not extraordinary *Rite of Passage* rather than Delany's bravura *Nova* or Keith Roberts' *Pavane*, now credited as the finest of all 'alternate histories'. Hugos were won by Walter M. Miller, Jr's *A Canticle for Leibowitz* (1960, but parts published in the 1950s), a mordant cycle tracking the recovery, after nuclear war, of technical knowledge guarded by monastic 'bookleggers', by Heinlein's *Stranger in a Strange Land* and by Roger Zelazny's New Wave-influenced *Lord of Light* (1967) (a mythopoeic reworking of Hindu and Buddhist imagery), as well as by Clifford Simak's sentimental, pedestrian *Way Station* (1963) rather than another nominee, Kurt Vonnegut, Jr's exquisite and funny *Cat's Cradle*. In a different medium, though, both old and new combined dazzlingly in Stanley Kubrick's 1968 movie from an Arthur C. Clarke script, *2001: A Space Odyssey* and Kubrick's 1971 *A Clockwork Orange*, both Hugo winners. It seemed for a moment as if sf might be about to come in from the cold.

Everyone agrees that it is inappropriate to judge a book by its cover, although for most of sf's commercial existence it has been shudderingly difficult to do anything else. Might we more reliably judge a book by its title? The shift from the lurid action-adventure 1950s to the more polished, sensitive sf of the 1960s might be gauged by considering some gauche short story and book titles from the earlier decade: 'Lord of a Thousand Suns' (1951), 'Sargasso of Lost Starships' (1952), 'Captive of the Centaurianess' (1952), *War of the Wing-Men* (1958), *The Enemy Stars* (1959).

Contrast those with several measured titles by Poul Anderson, who in 1997 would be selected a Grand Master of the Science Fiction Writers of America: 'Deus Ex Machina', 'World of No Stars', 'The Road to Jupiter', *The Man Who Counts* and a graceful, elegiac borrowing from Rudyard Kipling, *We Have Fed Our Sea*. These titles are more typical of a later generation, one senses, shaped by the revolution of the mid-1960s. The odd reality, though, is that the second set of titles is just Anderson's original choice for these sombre, haunting tales, which were brutally retitled by editors who figured they knew how to titillate 1950s' patrons. Surely those editors were wrong, since customers for 'Captive of the Centaurianess' were not dissatisfied by Anderson's lyrical if sometimes thumping prose. One apparent transition from the fifties to the sixties and seventies, then, is more illusory than real, a tactic of crass marketing adjusted to a somewhat less barbarous newsstand ambience.

In the 1960s, popular taste – as registered in the Hugo awards for shorter fiction – favoured a kind of excessive or hysterical posturing, mostly marked in several Harlan Ellison titles (matched by the overwrought contents): '"Repent, Harlequin!" Said the Ticktockman' (1965) through to 'Adrift Just Off the Islets of Langerhans: Latitude 30° 54′ N, Longitude 77° 00′ 13″ W' (1975). Such titles reveal the market's mood as plainly as 'Sargasso of Lost Starships'. In a fit of verbal thrift, Ellison won a 1978 Hugo with 'Jeffty is Five'. Things were calming down.

After the flash and filigree of the sixties, the next decade can seem rather docile, even disappointing. It is widely regarded as an interval of integration and bruised armistice. David Hartwell, scholar and important sf editor (who bought both Herbert's *Dune* and, fifteen years on, Gene Wolfe's incomparable Book of the New Sun and its successors), declared: 'There was much less that was new and colorful in science fiction in the 1970s and early 1980s, given the enormous amount published, than in any previous decade . . . [It was] a time of consolidation and wide public acceptance.'[16] Campbell died in 1971, and Ben Bova revived *Analog* by encouraging such literate writers as Joe Haldeman. At the end of the seventies, in the first edition of his magisterial *Encyclopedia of Science Fiction*, Peter Nicholls ran the two preceding decades together, noting an ongoing and complex generic cross-fertilization. 'The apparently limitless diversity opening up is an excellent sign of a genre reaching such health and maturity that paradoxically it is ceasing to be one.'[17]

This bursting open of a previously secluded or mockingly marginalized narrative mode happened on the largest possible scale in 1977. Two prodigiously successful movies were released: *Star Wars* and *Close Encounters of the Third Kind*, vigorous and even numinous (if equally set at child's-eye level), unabashedly revived and exploited the sense of wonder known until then mostly to the few hundred thousand devotees of print sf – and the many who watched bad monster movies and clumsy early episodes of *Star Trek*, which premiered in 1966. In part this success was enabled by technical advances that finally came close to matching the immense spectacle of space travel, physical transformation and sheer luminosity of metaphor that had always worked at a dreamlike level in classic sf. That impulse has not yet faltered, carrying sf/fantasy (of a rather reduced, simplified kind) to the point where it accounts for most of the highest-grossing films of the last two and a half decades.

### Blending of new and old

Meanwhile, though, the generic hybrids of Old Wave and New, enriched by techniques drawn from modernist general fiction, myth, art and movies, rose to broad popularity among sf readers. As with most scientific experiments, it was granted that many had failed (one might say that their hypotheses had been falsified), yet they led towards genuine improvement. Ursula K. Le Guin's stately, beautifully rendered and felt fiction had little in common with the crude adventure tales that characterized early commercial sf, but neither did many polished routine tales. As in the greater world, political issues continued to bubble and deepen: feminism, renewed in the mid-1960s, found utopian and critical expression in sf, from sex-role reversals and other simple adaptations of standard patriarchal commonplaces through to the authentically subversive novels and stories of Joanna Russ (especially her technically dazzling *The Female Man*, 1975). It is arguable that Anne McCaffrey's endless Pern sequence, begun with 1968 Hugo winner 'Weyr Search', remade fairy tales into ecological planetary romances. Popular women writers such as McCaffrey, Joan Vinge and Marion Zimmer Bradley, Brian Attebery has commented, become more interesting if you ask of their work 'what is a female hero?'[18]

At the same time, gay writers such as Samuel R. Delany, who was also black and hence doubly alienated from the established order, used sf to confound prejudice and illuminate otherness – something sf had prided itself on doing since the 1950s, yet had rarely managed to achieve. Delany's most ambitious novel of the period, *Dhalgren* (1975), became a million-selling success, but not, by and large, among sf readers. His *Triton* (1976) was even less congenial, featuring a bitterly misogynistic man whose lack of insight into his woes within a diversified utopia is only worsened after a sex change.

Adjustments to fresh possibilities are found on many of the Hugo, Nebula and Campbell Memorial Award ballots of the 1970s. Few remained untouched by a drenching from the New Wave, by then ebbed. Brunner's *Stand on Zanzibar* (1968), technically adventurous in borrowing formal devices from Dos Passos, was a kind of New Wave hybrid, and had been sampled in *New Worlds*. Le Guin's *The Left Hand of Darkness* (1969) searchingly testing the nature of gender, won both Hugo and Nebula, but the following year so did Larry Niven's far less subtle *Ringworld* (1970), in some ways a direct descendent of Heinlein and Pohl in the 1950s yet marked, arguably, by Hemingway's minimalism. Hemingway's influence could be seen later in Joe Haldeman's *The Forever War* (1974), also a dual winner, which interrogated Heinlein's contentious *Starship Troopers* (1959) from the basis of Haldeman's own brutal experience of the Vietnam War. Old-timers were not absent: Arthur C. Clarke won Hugos for both *Rendezvous with Rama* (1973) and *The Fountains of Paradise* (1979), exemplars of what his old friend Asimov had hoped to find after the foam settled. So too, in its way, was Asimov's own *The Gods Themselves* (1972), Hugo and Nebula winner; his satirical naturalism – portraying the practice of real science – blended uneasily with a truly alien (and even sexy) adjacent universe.

The drift towards convergence can be seen in several awarded novels at the end of the seventies: Kate Wilhelm's *Where Late the Sweet Birds Sang* (1976; Hugo), a cautionary tale of global pollution and human clones when those ideas were still new; Frederik Pohl's *Gateway* (1977; Hugo, Nebula, Campbell), told with sidebars and divagation; Vonda McIntyre's feminist *Dreamsnake* (1979; Hugo and Nebula); and Gregory Benford's masterful *Timescape* (1980; Campbell), probably the best sf novel combining plausible science and politics, wrapped around a fascinating idea: causality disruption via signal to the past.

None of these prize-winners was as radical in form as their New Wave antecedents, although the superb, cryptic fiction of Gene Wolfe, trialed during the 1970s in Damon Knight's anthology series *Orbit*, blossomed into full maturity at the cusp of the 1980s with the opening volume of his Book of the New Sun. Inevitably, even insiderly popular taste missed some of the most profound or innovatory works of the period: Disch's *On Wings of Song* (1979) caught a Campbell Memorial Award, as had Barry N. Malzberg's dyspeptic *Beyond Apollo* (1972), scandalously, but was otherwise scanted. Lucid, enamelled and very enjoyable essays in world-building, now apparently forgotten, include M. A. Foster's *The Warriors of Dawn* (1975), which introduced the mutant Ler, and the saga of their coming, *The Gameplayers of Zan* (1977). In 1974 John Varley introduced an increasingly detailed and delicious transhuman solar system – Heinlein as wrought by a post-New Wave hand. Jack Vance's 'Demon Princes' sequence (1964–81) was quirky, ironic space opera sprinkled with mock-authoritative footnotes. Ian Watson's impressive debut, *The Embedding* (1973), was runner-up for a Campbell; the mandarin density of its Chomskian linguistics, radical politics and alien invasion made it one of the finest novels of the decade. Another runner-up was John Crowley's *Engine Summer* (1979); disregarded by fans, Crowley was fated, with Wolfe, to be one of the enduring talents in the new, enlarged hybrid form that was now sf.

## The academy discovers sf

Theorized criticism of sf, previously almost unknown, opened the sixties with spectacular ructions over British novelist-academic Kingsley Amis's laid-back Princeton University lectures on sf, *New Maps of Hell* (1960), and closed the seventies with Professor Darko Suvin's formidably formalist and Marxist *Metamorphoses of Science Fiction* (1979), and a batch of other studies variously intelligible or obscure. None, of course, reached the paradoxical contortions and laborious *faux*-Francophone discourse familiar in subsequent decades, except perhaps Suvin's own, Fredric Jameson's (whose Marxist-structuralist essays provided dense, darkly illuminating insight into Dick, Le Guin and others) and Delany's critical collection *The Jewel-Hinged Jaw* (1977), and his intensively close reading, influenced by Roland Barthes's proto-deconstruction, of a Disch story, *The American Shore* (1978). Positioned midway was Robert Scholes (coining a term dead at birth, 'structural fabulation'), a structuralist sliding relentlessly toward semiotics and deconstruction. With Eric Rabkin, he combined essays and exemplary stories in *Science Fiction: History, Science, Vision* (1977).

At the furthest extreme from these academics were several sadly lame works of advocacy from the Old Wave, especially editors Lester del Rey (*The World of Science Fiction*, 1979) and Donald Wollheim (*The Universe Makers*, 1971). M. John Harrison's wickedly accurate dissection tells how vile and misjudged Wollheim's efforts seemed at the start of the seventies: 'Its awful prose style, rising like thick fog from the depths of its author's private grammar, permits only brief, tantalising glimpses of subject matter and intent.'[19] Wollheim stood firmly against the dismal entropic embrace of the New Wave, with its artsy nay-saying and repudiation of mankind's glorious galactic destiny. It was hard to reconcile with his early support for Delany, Le Guin, Zelazny and even Merril.

Academic journals began to appear – *Foundation* in the UK (1972–) and the US *Science-Fiction Studies* (1973–); argument over the New Wave flourished in the major ephemeral US fanzines, especially Dick Geis's *Science Fiction Review* and Frank Lunney's *Beabohema*. Perhaps as importantly, shrewd essays in fanzines from the rest of the world began to puncture sf's complacency: essays by Australians John Foyster and Bruce Gillespie on Aldiss, Ballard, Blish, Dick, Cordwainer Smith; by German Franz Rottensteiner on Heinlein and Stanislaw Lem (until then unknown beyond Poland); and by Lem on Dick, much of this translated initially for Australian fanzines such as *Science Fiction Commentary*.

One way to understand the long, slow eddies of those two decades, and the two generations they represented – one fading (but due for a startling resurgence in the 1980s, as Asimov, Clarke, Heinlein, Herbert, and Pohl reached toward belated best-sellerdom), the other growing into comfortable dominance – is to adapt Professor Scholes's simplified analysis of literary theory (via Roland Barthes) in his *Textual Power* (1985).[20] He detects three primary ingredients in every encounter with texts: reading, interpretation and criticism. Emphasizing each in turn, these can serve as useful windows into major forms of fictive endeavour: naturalist realism, modernist symbolism and postmodernist deconstruction. (A somewhat similar model is Joanna Russ's 'naive', 'realist' and 'parodic' or post-realistic.)[21] Deconstructive fiction is not as user-unfriendly as it sounds – it is embodied radiantly in all those reeling reality-disruptions of Philip K. Dick's novels and stories that form the core of several highly popular movies (including some, like *Pleasantville* (1998), that fail to acknowledge his influence, now pervasive).

On this three-phase analysis, it is arguable that sf before the 1960s was predominantly *empirical* or *readerly:* however gaudy or galactic its venue, you accepted what was on the page as if seeing it through clear glass. With the New Wave, sf convulsed belatedly into the crisis of modernism that half a century earlier had shaken mainstream high art, opening its texts to a radically *epistemological* or *writerly* invitation to endless reinterpretation. Beyond the end of the seventies, the prescient spirit of Dick invited a new generation of sf innovators towards a postmodern gesture: deep *ontological* doubt, a profound questioning of every reality claim.

This no longer applies to most sf of the eighties, nineties and later. The seductive rise of mass-media 'sci-fi' tore sf away from its elaborated specialist roots, carelessly discarded its long history. Science fiction consumers now start again from scratch, again and again. For the best sf, though, accepted or consensus versions of reality have become the landscape, the postulate, to explore or explode with corrosive and hilarious doubt. Without the frenzy and exhilaration of the New Wave experimenters, this aperture might not have opened, and without the diligent consolidation of the subsequent decade it might have remained where Dick's penny-a-word genius found it: eating dog food at the foot of the rich man's table.

## NOTES

1. Alfred Bester, 'A Diatribe Against Science Fiction', *Magazine of Fantasy and Science Fiction*, May 1961, reprinted in *Redemolished*, compiled by Richard Raucci (New York: ibooks, 2000), pp. 400, 403.
2. Alexei and Cory Panshin, *The World Beyond the Hill* (Los Angeles: Jeremy P. Tarcher, 1989).
3. John Clute, 'Scholia, Seasoned with Crabs, Blish Is', *New Worlds Quarterly 6* (London: Sphere, 1973), pp. 118–29.

4. Cited by Timothy O'Reilly, *Frank Herbert* (New York: Frederick Ungar, 1981), p. 188.
5. *Ibid.*, p. 5.
6. Ballard, reprinted in Judith Merril, ed. *10th Annual SF* (New York: Dell, 1966), p. 259.
7. Cited in M. John Harrison, 'A Literature of Comfort', in *New Worlds Quarterly* 1 (London: Sphere Books, 1971), p. 170.
8. Colin Greenland's usefully analytical and admirably waspish study, *The Entropy Exhibition* (London: Routledge & Kegan Paul, 1983), emphasizes Moorcock's role.
9. Blish (writing as 'William Atheling, Jr'), 'Making Waves', in Atheling, *More Issues at Hand* (Chicago: Advent, 1970), p. 146.
10. 'A Rose for Ecclesiastes' [1963], in Merril, ed., *10th Annual SF*, pp. 211–48.
11. 'The Voices of Time', 1960, in Ballard, *The Four-Dimensional Nightmare* (1963) (Harmondsworth: Penguin, 1965), p. 11.
12. 'You and Me and the Continuum', 1966, reprinted in Ballard, *The Atrocity Exhibition* (1969) (London: Panther, 1972), p. 106.
13. Bruce Gillespie, 2001, interviewed by Frank Bertrand, 'My Life and Philip K. Dick': http://www.philipkdick.com.
14. Thomas M. Disch, *Camp Concentration* (London: Panther, 1969), p. 102.
15. Samuel R. Delany, *The Jewel-Hinged Jaw* (New York: Berkely Windhover, 1978), p. 181.
16. David G. Hartwell, *Age of Wonders* (New York: McGraw-Hill, 1984), p. 182.
17. Peter Nicholls, ed., *The Encyclopedia of Science Fiction* (London: Granada, 1979), p. 287.
18. Personal e-mail communication.
19. M. John Harrison, 'To the Stars and Beyond on the Fabulous Anti-Syntax Drive', in *New Worlds Quarterly* 5 (London: Sphere Books, 1973), p. 236.
20. Robert Scholes, *Textual Power: Literary Theory and the Teaching of English* (New Haven: Yale University Press, 1985), p. 22.
21. Joanna Russ, 'The Wearing Out of Genre Materials', *College English*, 33:1 (October 1971); reprinted in *Vector* 62 (November-December 1972), pp. 16–24.

# 4

JOHN CLUTE

# Science fiction from 1980 to the present

It is, to begin with, a problem in perception. The nature of sf during the last two decades of the twentieth century can be seen as a classic figure-ground puzzle.[1] One angle of perspective on the era gives us a vision of the triumph of sf as a genre and as a series of outstanding texts which figured to our gaze the significant futures that, during those years, began to come to pass. But under a second angle of perspective, the high profile of sf as a shaping vision becomes indecipherable from the world during these years: in this perspective, sf gradually burned through the categories that gave it the defining potency of genre, and became fatally indistinguishable from the world it attempted to adumbrate, to signify: which is a way of saying, to *differ* from. Both perspectives, after the nature of figure-ground puzzles, co-exist.

This chapter can be understood to adhere to both perspectives.

Much happened in the two decades between 1980 and 2000. The sf readership broadened and diffused; no longer could it be claimed (a claim only made in any case with any plausibility about some forms of American sf before 1980) that sf was primarily read, or could be profitably written for, adolescent males. Written sf was increasingly presented in the form of books, while magazines declined. Written sf itself lost its unquestioned status as the default form of the genre; indeed, many consumers of sf ideas and iconography now accessed that material solely through film, television and computer gaming, without in fact actually reading sf at all. And an increasingly high proportion of that sf which continued to appear in written form turned out – on examination – to consist of versions of sf works which had first appeared in other media; the copyright in spin-offs from enterprises like *Star Trek* or *Star Wars*, which proliferated through the 1980s and 1990s, was in almost all cases owned by the enterprises in question, for whom written sf constituted a kind of infomercial for a fixed product.

These spin-offs, which represented the industrialization of the old cottage firm of sf, were fundamentally distinct from sf as a form of literature which claimed to be about how the world might change, for the focus of the spin-off is not on the future as a ground for thought experiments, or on the joy of text, but on the product it advertises: which is a way of saying, the past. If any form of sf may be said to have become fatally indistinguishable from the media- and consumption-ridden world we live in, and incapable of *differing* from that world in any useful sense, then the spin-off is that form. Therefore, though much of eighties and nineties sf is in fact owned by corporations, written sf based on enterprises whose homebase is not written sf, and whose function is essentially promotional, will not be referred to again in this chapter.

More important than this to the central body of sf readers – by this we mean readers of autonomous sf texts – was a transformation of the genre due to ageing. What might be called the biological model of sf – a model by which the sf genre could be understood as an entity that was born and came to maturity within the span of a human life – finally became, somewhere in the past two decades, too tortured to work in the imaginations of sf writers, editors, publishers, readers, fans, critics. By 1990 or so it was no longer possible for that sf affinity subculture group to conceive of sf itself as a kind of 'organism' whose origins could be accessed through human memory, and whose phases were the phases of a human life. American sf – which began as a genre around 1925, enjoyed an adolescence and a Golden Age before 1940 or so and matured steadily through the Eisenhower years – no longer had a human lifespan. The men and women who had manned sf from the beginning, and whose faces were the faces of sf in the minds of those who read sf, were almost all dead. (The only founding sf figure who remained active into the twenty-first century was the extraordinary Jack Williamson, whose publishing career as a professional writer had lasted seventy-four years by 2002.) Science fiction, which had seemed young or young-at-heart for almost the whole of the twentieth century, no longer confirmed the biological metaphor implicit in such images. Its past was dead documents, dead magazines, dead authors, dead memories; living words. The past of sf was now unmistakably heavier in the mind's eye than its present. As the new century began, sf had clearly become something no longer 'biological' in any sense; it had become something far more complexly integrated into the world than it had been.

Since 1980, the relationship between sf and the world, a relationship which could be described as a kind of mutual harnessing, had altered, therefore, almost out of all recognition. The genre which differed from the world in order to advocate a better one – or the genre which spanielled at heel the sensationalist virtual reality world we will now arguably inhabit till the planet dies – had become by 2000, in triumph or defeat or both, an *institution* for the telling of story. This institution continued to figure the future in ways useful and pleasurable to its readers; or it dissolved into a world so complex and future-irradiated that sf was just another voice in a Babel of mission statements; or both. We can perhaps gain some conceptual grasp of this complex double portrait of sf in 2000 by tracing two patterns of change.

The first dynamic of change has been noticed frequently: that there is a decreasing resemblance between the world we inhabit today and the future worlds advocated, with some consistency of voice and vision, in the American sf of the previous half-century. It may caricature classic sf to claim that, in 1980, the genre as a whole still told one story about how the world might – in fact, should – develop. But though we must hedge that caricature with qualifications – granting that dozens, perhaps hundreds, of sf stories of significance failed to argue that central story of the future – the old sf story, as it struggled to prevail through the last decades of the century, did remain easy to recognize. It was a First World vision, a set of stories about the future written by inhabitants of, and for the benefit of readers who were inhabitants of, the industrialized Western world, which dominated the twentieth century; simplistically, it was a set of stories about the American Dream.

In this Dream, progress was achieved through an invasive understanding of nature that led to the control of nature, through miracles of applied opportunity-grabbing science; through the penetration of frontiers; through the taming of alien peoples on other worlds; through an establishment of hierarchical centralized governances throughout the galaxy. Even as late as the twenty-first century, much routine sf assumed without argument that this form of progress remained storyable, that its fascination as a big story about visible triumphs overrode its implausibility as prophecy. Many of the significant writers of the past twenty years, such as Greg Bear or David Brin or C. J. Cherryh or Dan Simmons or Sheri Tepper in the USA, and Brian Aldiss (whose long sf career climaxed in the revisionist Helliconia space operas of the 1980s) or Iain Banks or Stephen Baxter or Gwyneth Jones or Paul J. McAuley or Ken MacLeod in the UK, subjected the dream of twentieth-century sf to scrutinies of varying intensity.

Whatever the case today, classic sf was deeply tied to a vision of the future whose fabric – the tools, the weapons, the technologies, the means, the armies, the emperors, the flows of capital, the waves of culture – could be seen in the mind's eye. Multi-causal structures of explanation were almost never engaged upon in an sf story for which the world needed to be visible. But that visible world was deeply loved, even after it had become a kind of historical fiction, a form of defensive nostalgia in the minds of many, for a world sufficiently seeable to shape. Much of the history of sf in the 1980s and 1990s can be seen as a reluctant farewell (as in the work of Bear and his cohort) to that world of transformations which were seen to be believed, that vision of the future which, almost deliberately, ignored the transistor, described computers in terms of bulk rather than invisible intricacies, failed to anticipate the nanoware-driven world we may now be entering. But it was this high visiblity of its subject matter, this figural intensity, that may have at the same time shielded us from the fact that sf's high-profile icons no longer meant now what they once meant: that in 2000 those icons are exudations of style, not signals of substantive shaping advocacy.

But the shield is porous. A recessional mood about the subject matter and techniques of the genre, a lack of security about the interestingness of sf as a tool for cognition and imaging, has permeated the field for years now, and has had arguably one significant effect. The 'dinosaurs' of sf – men (mostly) such as Jack Williamson, Robert A. Heinlein, Isaac Asimov or Frederik Pohl, those who had begun to gain fame by 1950 or so – stayed remarkably active. But many of the writers who had come into their own in the 1970s, and who might have been expected to enter their years of true pomp in the 1980s, did not in fact follow that course. Writers such as Octavia E. Butler, Samuel R. Delany, Thomas M. Disch, Ursula K. Le Guin, Joanna Russ and John Varley either wrote less than was expected of them, or shifted their main attention from sf altogether. Their own attempts to renew the genre, which can be crudely understood as attempts at restyling an engine which had nearly run out of fuel, became history.

After 1980, there was some sense that sf was running on inertia, that too many of its creative thinkers had decamped. Until the information explosion began dramatically to impact upon our lives in the 1980s, sf as a genre may have been wrong in many of its advocacies of the future, but it had never been *outmoded*. By around 1990, however, when the Internet began radically to shape our sense of the nature of the real world, sf as a set of arguments and conventions was in some disarray. It had been blindsided by the future. The only form of sf to grapple imaginatively with at least some aspects of the dizzying new order was Cyberpunk, a term coined by sf writer Bruce Bethke in 1983 to describe novels and stories about the information explosion of the 1980s (hence 'Cyber', from cybernetics), most of them picturing a dense, urban, confusing new world in which most of us will find that we have been disenfranchised from any real power (hence 'punk'). But Cyberpunk, beginning with William Gibson's *Neuromancer* (1984), had as it were o'erleaped the sheer vast mundanity of the information explosion, in order to create a *noir* megalopolis of inner space, imaginatively dense but clearly not directed towards explicating or illuminating the revolutions in the routines of individual and corporate life that were transforming the daylight hours first of the industrialized world, and soon afterwards the world entire. Cyberpunk did not domesticate the future; it treated the future as a god. It was, in any case, deeply resented by many older writers, who thought of Cyberpunk as an abandonment of the sf story – which of course it was. So the crisis was in fact deep.

This leads us to the second dynamic of change. A genre such as sf had rapidly to adjust its sights in order to apprehend the new, or its heart would die, just as the peripheries of sf – the water margins occupied by spin-offs (see above) and commercial series whose function was not to apprehend the new but to rent space in it – were dying. And the job was taken on. If the world of information was not something sf anticipated – Vernor Vinge's 'True Names' (1981) being almost the sole attempt to anticipate the technologies involved in something like the Internet – and if, therefore, sf writers had a great deal of catching up to do in order to describe a world which (shamingly) already existed, then it must be said that they succeeded in short order. It is a marker of the sharp intelligence of the sf writers who came to maturity since 1980 that they have indeed materially caught up with the world, that they have transformed a genre which was not designed for the twenty-first century, that they have exposed the genre of sf to the corrosive invisibilities of information.

So there has been a slow transformation of sf into a genre capable of understanding the world in terms of information, a genre whose individual tales are capable of figuring the world as though it were information that, once 'read', could be manipulated. As the new century advances, we come closer and closer to realizing that the new sf descriptions of the world-as-information may be genuine descriptions of the case; and that the storylike utterances we make may have become instruction kits for manipulating the new world. Information is power. Information is *words* of power. The world is a case we can alter. It is almost as though the words of sf had become flesh: as though the advocacies of the old sf had become sea-changed into intimate, literal engines of change.

It is, however, a thin partition between the uttering of a storyable idea about the future, and acting as a spokesperson for the venture capitalist who wants to obtain copyright on the future. After 2000, triumph (understanding the worlds we can speak) and failure (uttering projections for owners) have become very nearly the same thing. Can sf, as a set of cognitions which differ from the world, exist in a world which takes on the colouring of our thought? What now is figure, what now is ground? What now is difference, what now is mission statement?

This broad-brush portrait of the changing nature of sf over the past two decades has slighted, as we have made clear, the great mass of routine sf whose main function is to provide reliable entertainment, usually in series formats, and it has deliberately ignored the equally great mass of product written-to-hire (a common sf term for this is 'sharecropped', a term once used to describe tenant farmers) for owners of sf products. Nor does it fairly acknowledge the fact that much of the greatest sf of the period deliberately avoids any near-future setting – the sort of setting into which these issues inevitably protrude; that much of the greatest sf between 1980 and 2000 is, in fact, space opera. This portrait has also ignored one other category of sf: the great writer.

In any one world, in any one century, relatively few creative figures may be called great, though many more may be deemed important. In the genre of sf, it could be argued that H.G. Wells came close to being a great writer, while being at the same time a writer of great importance to the genre. Robert A. Heinlein and Isaac Asimov, neither of them writers of great stature, were of undoubted importance to the evolution of sf. Philip K. Dick hovered at the edge of a greatness only perceivable through an understanding of the sf motifs he transformed and on which he laid his imprint; his importance to the field, though initially indirect, has only grown since his death in 1982.

Between 1980 and 2000 there is only one writer whose creative grasp and imprint and prolificacy – and what might be called parental density, that density of creative being which generates the anxiety of influence in literary children, who may only be able to wrestle and come to terms with the parent after many years – are so unmistakably manifest that one may plausibly use the word 'great' in describing his work. That writer is Gene Wolfe. He may be, as a creator of autonomous works of art, the greatest writer of sf in a century which saw many hundreds of writers do their work with high ambition and remarkable craft; he is, however, far from the most important sf writer of the century, and is by no means a writer of great significance in determining the nature of flow of his chosen genre during the years of his prime, which extend throughout the period under discussion.

A synoptic view of a collective enterprise such as the genre of sf must nec-essarily deal with those writers whose influence – whether or not we have a high opinion of their œuvres as autonomous works of art – is centrally colle-gial; and whose own works reflect in turn the influence of others in the long conversation of genre. But synopsis can become travesty when confronted with the essential *strangeness* of the great writer; and any survey of a field or an era – such as this volume – fails at the moment it attempts to domesticate that strangeness.

Though Gene Wolfe is not therefore an exemplary figure of the past two decades of sf, he remains an author whose works are so deeply imbricated in the genre that it is absolutely impossible to think of them as transcending genre (any critic who argues works, in order to be good, must 'transcend' genre, has almost certainly displaced a dis-ease with genre itself into a rhetoric of escape that is both traitorous to the text and condescendingly escapist about the nature of art and story); rather than transcending genre, they are genre wrought to the uttermost.

His central work comprises three multi-volume novels which join, arguably, into one meta-novel. The first is The Book of the New Sun, the 'confessions' of an Apollo-Christ figure named Severian, which comprise *The Shadow of the Torturer* (1980), *The Claw of the Conciliator* (1981), *The Sword of the Lictor* (1982) and *The Citadel of the Autarch* (1983), plus a recounting of his later life in *The Urth of the New Sun* (1987). Narrated with indirections and traps whose crystalline fundament recalls Jorge Luis Borges or Vladimir Nabokov, and permeated with a dark Catholic sensibility resembling that, one might guess, of a fully grown G.K. Chesterton, this far-future tale, which quotes many of the century's sf tropes, does not in the end resemble any other work but – as though we viewed it through one of the many mirrors in the text – itself. The second novel, The Book of the Long Sun, presents the biography of a priest-saviour named Silk who tries (unlike Severian) to tell the truth and to illuminate the pocket universe he is born into; it comprises *Nightside the Long Sun* (1993), *Lake of the Long Sun* (1994), *Calde of the Long Sun* (1994) and *Exodus from the Long Sun* (1996). The tale depicts several human communities' last days aboard a generation starship which had left Earth (Urth) centuries earlier, and which arrives at its destination at about the time Severian, back home, begins his quest for the world-transcending god within him. Immediately following upon this is The Book of the Short Sun, comprising *On Blue's Waters* (1999), *In Green's Jungles* (2000) and *Return to the Whorl* (2001), and in which the memoirist of the previous novel becomes a central character of this, as he searches for Silk on two devastating planets. Modernist dazzlements confound us throughout this final tale, as the narrator becomes the narrated, the book he writes becomes the Book that writes his fate, and Silk – one of the very few genuinely good characters in a century of dark creations – reaches his apotheosis, and goes fishing for men among the further stars. We learn nothing of the past two decades here, nothing of the intricate harnessing of sf and world that has increasingly marked them; we learn, though, how words can mean, how works of art may dream a scholar soul, how souls may shine through the revels of making.

We return to the 'merely' significant, and attempt to point out some figures of merit in the roil of change. Several fine full-length novels were published as the 1980s began, but the tale which began the task of refocusing the genre – after the half-century of relatively unexamined fit between generic goals and our understanding of the nature of the times – was Vernor Vinge's 'True Names' (1981). It is a cusp tale. Its narrative tone, the simply outlined protagonists who carry the story, its inherent *Analog*-style cheerfulness about the technologies outlined, look backward to the great days. But its prefiguration of an Internet world, complete with code-protected covens of technogeeks ambitious to exercise godling sway over the mundane world, looks straight forward towards the end of the real century, and prefigures many of the concerns of sf writers today, faced as they are with a world in which iterations of data and the unfoldings of story threaten to become immiscible, a perplexity treated as a problem to solve by the Australian Greg Egan, whose career began with the unremarkable *An Unusual Angle* (1983), but whose work of the 1990s and later, beginning with *Quarantine* (1992), can be understood as nearly pure models of universes decipherable into codes.

After this work of insight into the immediate, Vinge shifted his concerns from the near future, and in *A Fire Upon the Deep* (1992) and *A Deepness in the Sky* (1999) wrote two highly complex space operas whose arenas of action – the galaxy itself, intricately configured into storyable form – made possible the telling of tales about worlds that differed radically from near-future Earth. It is arguable that sf writers of this period, who were the first to take the space opera/planetary romance configuration seriously, created by doing so the period's most interesting platform for the analysis, and the acting out in the creative imagination, of human possibilities. Even Gene Wolfe's unrelentingly complex meta-novel can be, at least in part, understood as an exploration of space opera and planetary romance. About Vinge's two big novels, there is no doubt. But Vinge, though he wrought space opera to a high pitch, did not of course invent the form; with 'True Names', on the other hand, he can be seen as the godfather of Cyberpunk.

If one adds to 'True Names' the visual and iconographic influence of Ridley Scott's *noir*-hued *Blade Runner* (1982) – a film adaptation of Philip K. Dick's *Do Androids Dream of Electric Sheep?* (1968) – then one can perceive some of the mulch of influences from which William Gibson created the profound metaphor of cyberspace in *Neuromancer* (1984). Gibson was notoriously ignorant of computer technology, and certainly did not work on one when he wrote the novel; his sorting of a storyable version of the inside of the world of information was essentially a *literary* coup: cyberspace is a literary metaphor of very considerable brilliance, and if the world in 2003 in some ways resembles the world he created – and if its writers' obsessional use of counterfactual images of downloading seems to have translated that metaphor into an article of faith – then it is because the world, and the writers who articulate the world, have *imitated* Gibson. It is surely not the other way round: Gibson, by his own testimony, was too incompetent to imitate the world.

The interior, download world depicted in *Neuromancer* is a multi-dimensional dream arena in which actions – which may here be defined as outcomes of highly improbable data densities – and actors – who may be defined in precisely the same terms – aspire dizzyingly to the power of gods. What Gibson's empowered protagonists find, however, is that the gods are already in residence, that the interior world of cyberspace is not a free arena but a godgame – a term derived from John Fowles's *The Magus* (1966), in which a magus figure rules the game of the world from behind the scenes. This double intuition of *Neuromancer* about the nature of the world to come – that we are hugely empowered, that we are essentially powerless – may be the most profound metaphor constructed by an sf writer for the experience of living in the 1980s and 1990s, as a constructed century sank downwards towards a constructed millennium.

That double intuition lies at the heart of the whole Cyberpunk movement – a 'movement', like most literary movements, more gesticulated at than lived by its ostensible participants; Gibson himself denies being a member – whose practitioners and texts deeply offended the old guard of the sf that had begun to seem addled whenever it attempted to deal with the near future of the world. Cyberpunk writers, loosely defined, included Gibson's colleague and collaborator, Bruce Sterling, whose *Mirrorshades: The Cyberpunk Anthology* (1986) articulated as aggressively as possible the argument that Cyberpunk stories constituted a kind of modular for surfing the new world; and Pat Cadigan, whose *Mindplayers* (1987), *Synners* (1991) and *Fools* (1992) presented a far more destabilized, invasively fragmenting world, hotly dangerous to any traditional sense that human beings were autonomous entities. Much cosmetic Cyberpunk was written in the 1980s, and before the end of the century its landscapes had become advertising clichés. Writers such as Gibson, Sterling or Cadigan had long since migrated elsewhere.

In only one way, perhaps, does *Neuromancer* look back to the earlier days of sf, when the genre (as we have noted) seemed to occupy a kind of organic shape in time and space; Gibson's novel was published by Ace Books, in the second of a series of 'Ace Specials' edited by Terry Carr (the first series was issued in the 1960s). These Ace Special series, both of them restricted to paperback originals, and the second restricted as well to first novels, served as a conduit – or an artery – for the best new writers in the field to publish their works within a familiar, collegial context. It would perhaps be the last time that young emerging writers might seem to be members of a family, and be so welcomed.

William Gibson was not the only author to gain in this fashion a family launch and imprimatur. Kim Stanley Robinson's first novel, *The Wild Shore* (1984), also appeared in the series, beginning the book career of the most conspicuously *non*-Cyberpunk writer to come out of the period. (In the mid-1980s, a factitious war was promulgated, by Bruce Sterling in the main, between the Cyberpunk writers and 'Humanists' such as Robinson; little was demonstrated, or learned, by this attempt at creating an internecine conflict within a genre whose walls were, if not dissolving, in a state of terminal fracture.) Robinson sedulously applied the cognitive tools of traditional sf – worlds clearly described in terms paraphrasable into argument; protagonists consciously geared into the world-historical processes which unpack history; technological innovations as substantive engines of visible change – to a sober, highly intelligent, sometimes unrelenting set of visions both utopian and dystopian. *The Wild Shore* and its two thematic sequels, *The Gold Coast* (1988) and *Pacific Edge* (1990), constitute a trilogy of speculative outcomes for American communities of the near future: as enclaves dominated by other states; as a congested, polluted, treeless Orange County America; as a conscious ecology-aware small-scale set of utopian communities. The Mars trilogy – *Red Mars* (1992), *Green Mars* (1993) and *Blue Mars* (1996) – makes an immensely detailed case for humanity's inhabiting of Mars, and suggests procedures for making our potentially planet-disrupting move there something to celebrate rather than mourn.

This is, of course, sf as advocacy, and reminiscent in that sense of the sf of 'big story' writers such as Heinlein and Asimov. But by making no bones about his advocacies, by *exposing* them as advocacy through the explicit patterning of his series, Robinson clearly distinguishes himself from his honoured predecessors. It is vital, he demonstrates, precisely to expose the arguments sf texts promote, to make them more powerful, but also more honest, more chaste. The stakes, as we argued above, are high. They are for Robinson as well. By the twenty-first century, he thinks, 'rapid technological development on all fronts [has combined] to turn our entire social reality into one giant science fiction novel, which we are all writing together in the great collaboration called history'.[2]

The publication of Howard Waldrop's first novel, *Them Bones* (1984), in the Ace Specials series was an early marker of the popularity, in the last years of the second millennium, of time travel/alternate history tales, stories which turn back from the terrors of the near future and which take the past as a legitimate field for thought experiments. The danger in doing this is that of turning the past into a vast vaudeville, and its significant actors into mummers capable of donning any role. Waldrop makes a melancholy glory of this danger; Kim Newman, slightly later, in books such as *Anno Dracula* (1992), transforms the vaudeville into *grand guignol*; Connie Willis, in *Lincoln's Dreams* (1987) and *Doomsday Book* (1992), used time travel not as a fulcrum with which to dislodge history, but as a portal into domestic minds, private tragedies, a route out of the savaged turmoil of the near future into worlds where fate, though it might be terrible, was sufficiently compact that it could be grasped; and the industrious Harry Turtledove, author of numerous alternate histories, fixes the past into templates, upon which entertainments may be mounted.

Lucius Shepard, the most explicitly literary writer of modern American sf after Avram Davidson, also published his first novel in the Ace Specials; in a technique increasingly to be found as the decades passed, *Green Eyes* (1984) mixes sf and fantasy and horror, almost as though by this means gaining some focus on the increasingly intertextual fabric of reality of a closing, self-referential, nostalgic era. It is a commonplace that self-referentiality marks the creative output of any *fin de siècle* – periods when history seems as distressed as an old painting, times when we seem to have reached the end of our tether – but Shepard adds a peculiar moral intensity to the mix, extracting from his wealth of sources – *Kallimantan* (1990) is for instance elaborately drawn from Joseph Conrad's 'Heart of Darkness' (1899), which is also a century-ender – a language rich in judgemental nuance. Though he does not directly father later writers such as Jonathan Lethem, his example prepares a place for novels such as Lethem's *Girl in Landscape* (1998), a deadpan planetary-romance morality elaborately drawn from John Ford's great western film, *The Searchers* (1956), also a late-genre deadpan morality whose effect is subcutaneous.

Michael Swanwick's Ace Specials novel, *In the Drift* (1985), was a tentative essay in the epic-by-episode (also known as the fix-up), a series of peephole views of a strife-ridden post-catastrophe America; but his later novels focused intensely on their exemplary targets. In the course of a quest plot, *Vacuum Flowers* (1987) transacts our solar system where it has become extraordinarily difficult – through bio-engineering and other carefully calibrated engines of change – to pin down what a human is, where a human lives and how human societies work; it is perhaps the first novel successfully to import into traditional sf structures the conceptual loosening afforded writers by both Cyberpunk and genetic engineering. *Stations of the Tide* (1991) also provides a model for sf, also attempts to render the onrush of the new into storyable form. Its description of cyberspace in terms of the Renaissance Theatre of Memory does much to capture the intricate interplay we are now experiencing between the world and the words which embody the world.

If Iain Banks had been American rather than Scottish, he may too have found a home, with Terry Carr, for one of the sf novels he had drafted before actually publishing his first novel, *The Wasp Factory* (1984), in England; it is not sf though it is surely a tale of the fantastic, and launched his double career. The sf novels published as by Iain M. Banks – though they were manifestly composed by an author very familiar with the American forms of sf, which deeply affected British sf through the twentieth century; and though they manifestly benefit from the plot-oriented, kinetic intensity of American models of space opera – offer a radical commentary on some of the inherent assumptions about the plot-friendly entrepreneurial freedoms enjoyed by space-opera protagonists in galaxies governed by rigid oligarchies. The best of them – from *Consider Phlebas* (1986) to *Look to Windward* (2000) – play seriously in a galaxy-wide arena governed by comities which lay few obligations upon their citizens, and which may be defined as post-scarcity. It has become a cliché in the analysis of Earth-bound systems of economic activity that they are based on one party's gaining from the possession of scarce commodities, and that scarcity, when it does not occur naturally, will be enforced; Banks, and those he has inspired, make the iconoclastic suggestion that, somewhere, somewhen, energy will be sufficient to needs, and scarcity will not exist. It seems obvious that this sort of argument, which differs from current political and cultural sanctities, lies at the heart of a healthy sf.

Banks was the first new British writer of space opera in some time. He was soon followed by two figures, whose difference from him and from each other gives some sense of the range of recent British sf responses to end-of-century interplays between genre and reality. Paul J. McAuley's 1980s space-opera venues, sometimes ironized to the point of aridity, seemed increasingly richer as the 1990s progressed. *Eternal Light* (1991) was joyfully baroque in its play with cosmogonic matters; and the Confluence trilogy – *Child of the River* (1997), *Ancients of Days* (1998) and *Shrine of Stars* (1999) – may be the only sf text successfully to show the deep influence of Gene Wolfe, and at the same time to parlay that anxiety of influence into a novel (the three books are one story) that both honours Wolfe and assesses dramatically some of the fractures that mark his œuvre. Like The Book of the New Sun, and with a plotline similarly ouroboral, Confluence unfolds a view of evolved humanity so complexly divergent that the reader's initial response is of intoxication; only slowly do we understand that, within the tropical jungle of life thousands of generations distant, iron laws apply: biology; ecology; entropy. In the end, that which flourishes in one cycle is mulch for that which is born to seem to rule the next. It is obvious enough that McAuley's vision of a cyclical future differs radically from our orthodox hope, here on Earth in 2003, that we may still hitch our wagon to the arrow of time.

The second successor to Banks, Stephen Baxter, differs in his own way from orthodoxies we may continue to adhere to, here on Earth, for as long as we remain alone in the universe. In his Xeelee series – from *Raft* (1991) to *Vacuum Diagrams* (1997) – Baxter creates a hard sf world in which, even more devastatingly than is the case in Vernor Vinge's contemporaneous space operas – humanity is an exiguous, relatively primitive species clutching to the sidelines of galactic history, destined never to take stage-front. In an abstract fashion – which still has a hot-ice intensity – Baxter places humanity in an essentially Third World relationship to the action of advanced species. But the most radical Third World sf was written by two Americans and one British: Paul Park, whose *Coelestis* (1993) is planetary romance perceived through the eyes of the dispossessed; Maureen F. McHugh, whose novels from *China Mountain Xhang* (1992) to *Nekropolis* (2001), being set on Earth itself, strictly challenge our assumption that sf, having become a literature about manipulating the terms that define the world, can in truth speak for that world entire; and Jon Courtenay Grimwood, whose novels challenged the politics of dispossession, first in a post-Napoleonic alternative future (*redRobe*, 1999) and then in an alternative Middle East (*Pashazade*, 2001 and *Effendi*, 2002).

In the meantime, two American careers which had begun in the late 1970s reached their peak in the mid 1980s, just as the Ace Specials cohort began to dominate; a subsequent decline in their influence did not necessarily mark a decline in quality of work.

Orson Scott Card reached the apogee of his productive career with *Ender's Game* (1985), in which an incredibly smart young boy with something like an absolute sense of topology rises to the top of the tree in an Army school, where he and his mates train in simulated environments for their eventual transfer to the front in the expected continuation of war between humanity and repulsive Buggers. After he wins the final wargame for humanity, Ender Wiggins discovers (typical of 1980s sf, the distinction between reality and VR is here put to question) that he has been in fact conducting, through simulations, a real war, and has extirpated the enemy. He then discovers that the Buggers were innocent of aggressive intent. Nothing in the novel's numerous sequels, which extend through the 1990s, comes close to equalling the effect of this concluding discovery.

Greg Bear also reached a peak in 1985, with the publication of *Blood Music* and *Eon*. The first is a kind of apotheosis of the hive-mind tale; in this case, humanity as a whole is transfigured into an immense organism, with only a rote modicum of regret for the meat-puppet past. *Eon* in turn apotheosizes the sf tale of the sense-of-wonder artefact; the vast asteroid which is initially discovered proves, despite its huge intricacy, to be little more than the stopcock at the end of a multi-dimensional tunnel which extends, it may be, to infinity. In both tales, a kind of genial impersonality of narrative irradiates Bear's cognitive powers, giving an impression that he is writing to us from somewhere far distant, in space or time; that the world into which he is depositing these tales of transcendence is only a particular, and perhaps rather minor example or case of the worlds that may be, up the line. In this, Bear differs productively from the prevailing doctrine about the history of our times: that our case is terminal.

Both Card and Bear write tales which use space opera and planetary romance formats, though not as fulsomely as David Brin, whose Uplift series humanizes Bear's chilly afflatus; or as complicatedly as C. J. Cherryh, whose many space operas have been incorporated into a vast mega-series whose very scale connotes an earned seriousness of intent; or as devotedly as Sheri S. Tepper, whose novels – such as *The Gate to Women's Country* (1988) or *Grass* (1989) or *Six Moon Dance* (1998) – treat their planetary settings, intimately, as liveable; or as enterprisingly accessible as Lois McMaster Bujold; or as omnivorously as Dan Simmons. Simmons's Hyperion Cantos – *Hyperion* (1989), *The Fall of Hyperion* (1990), *Endymion* (1996) and *The Rise of Endymion* (1997) – could be described as cosmogony operas, for they undertake to shape *everything* into one baroque entelechy. The series as a whole may be seen as the culmination of everything here suggested about space opera as a theatre illuminating humanity's wares, stagecraft, mortal savvy, mortal stupidity, godly reach.

Most of the writers of the greatest significance in the 1990s, as we have noted, began their careers in the 1980s. Authors such as Ted Chiang or China Miéville, whose careers began in the 1990s, will certainly begin to define the fields of the fantastic during the first decade of the twenty-first century. Almost certainly, these two writers, and their colleagues, will continue to explore the fissiparous hot zones that still divide one genre of the fantastic from another. This is an exploration begun in the 1990s, with novels such as Michael Swanwick's *The Iron Dragon's Daughter* (1993), but it is only with the new century that what one might call genre-morphing has become a central defining enterprise within fantastic literature.

Two final novels of the 1990s can serve to return us to our initial swivel of perspective on the genre during the decades of our remit, and suggest that sf, as developed and mutated over the past decades, can still visibly figure the world to come.

Bruce Sterling's *Distraction* (1998) seems radically to disavow a central tenet of classic sf: that truth will out; that between the beginning and the end of the storyline of an sf tale the veils of illusion and ignorance, which conceal us from the conceptual breakthrough that opens our eyes to the truth, will be dissolved; that the intersubjectivities and allures of the veil are *less real* than the single truth which outs. In the world of *Distraction*, set a few decades into the twenty-first century, that central tenet of pre-1980 sf is mocked to destruction. The protagonist of the tale is a spin-doctor who understands that a world comprised of codes is a world infinitely malleable; that what you see – the veil – is an exfoliation of world-choices; that, quite profoundly, what you see (that is, what you code for) is what you get. This understanding of the codes of the world we are at the verge of inhabiting could only have been articulated through a knowing use of the organon of the genre of sf.

Because it is set in a non-alternate history past, Neal Stephenson's *Crypto-nomicon* (1999) has been treated by some critics as a 'mundane' novel. But *Cryptonomicon* is a novel about the world, a radical recasting of history since the Second World War as a conspiracy of data; and it could be argued that any novel which is about the world shares a structural identity with the most overt tale of sf. Sf is that set of stories, more precisely, which *argues* the world; which argues the *case* of the world. It is important and likely, but not necessary, that that argument promulgates outcomes that have not yet become the case in reality. That *Cryptonomicon* is set in the past of the world is inessential in any argument that understands it, correctly, as an sf text about understanding the world as a set of instructions the world must adhere to.

These novels are pure sf. By articulating the world, they differ from the world. They demonstrate the continued usefulness of the trusted and tested toolkits of sf. They are adherent to the underlying, shaping urgency of the genre. They speak to the future of the genre. To save the genre from the ground of instant habituation, as they seem so clearly to demonstrate, the answer may be as simple as this: that the right way to figure sf is to write it.

## NOTES

1. 'Figure-ground' or 'figure and ground' refers to ambiguous drawings in which the same part can be seen as either figure or ground, as invented by Gestalt psychologists; see also Necker cube.
2. Kim Stanley Robinson, 'Introduction', *Nebula Awards Showcase 2000* (New York: Roc, 2002), pp. 1–2.

# 5

MARK BOULD

# Film and television

## Science fiction film: the first fifty years

In the first book of film theory, written in 1915, Vachel Lindsay imagined a modern America transformed into a permanent World's Fair. Central to his poetic vision of the coming technocracy was the cinema, whose 'prophet-wizards will set before the world a new group of pictures of the future' surpassing even Jules Verne, Edward Bellamy and H. G. Wells.[1] Lindsay's peculiar rhetoric has obvious resonances with the interplay of entertainment, education and prophecy in Gernsback's model of scientifiction, but as the manifesto for a new kind of cinema it found few, if any, adherents – not least because sf cinema had been developing in a different direction since the Lumière brothers' *Charcuterie méchanique* (*The Mechanical Butcher*, 1895). A one-minute, single-scene short, it showed a pig being fed into a machine from which various cuts of pork soon emerge. Audiences might well have also seen the film projected in reverse, and one of its imitators, *Dog Factory* (Porter, 1904),[2] utilized this basic technique to depict a machine that reconstituted strings of sausages into whatever breed of dog the customer required.

The first twenty years of sf cinema were dominated by similar one-reel trick movies which exploited the basic special effects made possible by undercranking or overcranking the camera, split screens, dissolves, stop-motion and reversed footage. Such narratives as these films possessed hinged on X-rays, elixirs, giant insects, flying bicycles, hair-restoring tonics, supercars, dirigibles, invisibility and the mysterious powers of electricity, magnetism and monkey glands. Notable practitioners of the form include J. Stuart Blackton, Walter R. Booth, Segundo de Chomon, Ferdinand Zecca and Georges Méliès, the stage magician with whom it is most commonly associated. His earliest sf shorts, the automaton comedy *Gugusse et l'automaton* (*The Clown and the Automaton*, 1897) and the transplant comedy *Chirurgien americain* (*A Twentieth Century Surgeon*, 1897), have not survived. His most famous film, *Le Voyage dans la lune* (*A Trip to the Moon*, 1902) is, like many literary voyages to the moon, a mild satire on terrestrial social relations and organization; but, more importantly for an understanding of the nature and development of sf film, it is primarily a compendium of special effects whose 'story merely frames a display of cinema's magical possibilities'.[3]

For many years early cinema was considered to be structured around a conflict between two competing aesthetics: realism, as represented by the Lumières' *actualités*, and fantasy, as represented by Méliès's *féerie* films. More recently, Gunning has noted a key continuity between these supposed opposites. Until the emergence of a properly narrative cinema around 1908–14, filmmaking was primarily concerned with the presentation of spectacle, whether the presentation of landscapes and events favoured by the Lumières or the trickery pioneered by Méliès. Gunning calls this non-narrative cinema the cinema of attractions, arguing that such 'apparently different approaches . . . unite in using cinema to present a series of views to audiences, views fascinating because of their illusory power'.[4] The most extreme version of this use of actuality film was to be found in Hale's Tours, a chain of cinemas which until 1906 exhibited non-narrative travel pieces, usually shot from trains, in cinemas designed to simulate carriages, complete with conductors and sound effects. However, as early as 1895, Robert Paul and H. G. Wells had applied for a patent to construct a more complex projection device *cum* exhibition space to simulate a fantastic journey through time similar to those described in Wells's *The Time Machine* (1895). Although their plans came to nothing, the experience they envisaged producing is merely more elaborate than, not different from, that of the actuality-based Hale's Tours. Much later innovations (widescreen ratios, 3-D, IMAX, studio tours) would replicate these efforts to transform the exhibition space into one of overwhelming spectacle. Films such as *Brainstorm* (Trumbull, 1983), *Dark City* (Proyas, 1998) and *The Matrix* (Wachowski brothers, 1999) would draw on cutting-edge cinema technology to narrativize and investigate the possibilities inherent in the cinema of attractions. As song-and-dance numbers, chase sequences and special-effects extravaganzas demonstrate, the hegemony of narrative cinema remains incomplete. It has never succeeded in banishing non-narrative attractions or completely narrativizing the spectacle.

The special position afforded to spectacle within narrative sf cinema is evident in the feature-length sf movies which began to appear around 1915. Proclaimed by its title card to be 'The First Submarine Photoplay To Be Filmed', *Twenty Thousand Leagues under the Sea* (Paton, 1916) then informs the audience that 'The submarine scenes in this production were made possible by the use of the Williamson inventions, and were directed under the personal supervision of the Williamson brothers, who alone have solved the secret of under-the-ocean photography.' The first actual footage in the film is of the inventors Ernest and George Williamson removing their hats and bowing to the camera, and narrative progression regularly gives way to lengthy views of the seabed and aquatic life, including real sharks and a fake giant octopus. *Paris qui dort* (*The Crazy Ray*, Clair, 1923), in which a scientist develops a ray which stops motion and sends the world to sleep, draws on less complex technologies to provide its moments of spectacle. In addition to magnificent shots of Paris and the Eiffel Tower, animated graphics depict the broadcast of the ray and freeze-frames represent the sleeping world. Although the special effects are few, they nonetheless demonstrate the typical unwillingness of the sf movie to subjugate effects and spectacle to narrative logic. When the ray is switched off, there is a montage of Paris waking up, but although the effect of the ray is nearly simultaneous across the city, each shot of a frozen Paris waking up cuts to a shot of another part of frozen Paris, which then wakes up. The montage of Paris being frozen is similarly staggered. Thus the duration of these sequences is artificially extended, contravening temporal logic in order that the audience can savour the spectacle. (The effect of the climactic electromagnetic pulse in *Small Soldiers* (Dante, 1998) is likewise prolonged by a sequence of set-pieces.) The lengthy and elaborate special effects sequences of *The Lost World* (Hoyt, 1925) are situated within a narrative structure which suggests that the reason for adapting Doyle's novel was to reach a juncture where the movie had to devote screen time to exploiting advances in stop-motion animation, a pattern repeated in *King Kong* (Cooper, Schoedsack, 1933). Although the effects technologies have changed, the logic and structure of films such as *Jurassic Park* (Spielberg, 1993) and *Pitch Black* (Twohy, 2000) remain much the same.

Throughout the silent period, sf cinema demonstrated little in the way of self-awareness about its generic identity, although several distinct sub-genres did emerge. The appearance of Halley's comet in 1910 inspired the first sf disaster movie, *The Comet* (director unknown, 1910). A cycle of future war movies was initiated by Leo Stormont's 1909 multi-media performance *England Invaded*. Movie serials such as *The Exploits of Elaine* (Gasnier and Seitz, 1914) and *Lady Baffles and Detective Duck* (Curtis, 1915) recounted the adventures of scientific detectives. The pacifistic *Himmelskibet* (*The Airship*, Madsen, 1917) and the satirical *Aelita* (Protazanov, 1924) introduced the interplanetary adventure. *One Hundred Years After* (director unknown, 1911) and *The Last Man on Earth* (Blystone, 1924) misogynistically satirized gender equality. The 1920s saw an increasing number of movies and serials featuring mad scientists (*A Blind Bargain*, Worsley, 1922; *Alraune* (*Unholy Love*) Galeen, 1928) or master criminals (*Luch Smerti* (*Death Ray*), Kuleshov, 1925; *Blake of Scotland Yard*, Hill, 1927) as well as a cycle of movies about rejuvenation (*The Young Diana*, Capellani and Vignola, 1922; *Sinners in Silk*, Henley, 1924).

In addition to numerous adaptations of sf by authors such as Marie Corelli, Guy du Maurier, Hans Heinz Ewers, Camille Flammarion, William Le Queux, Maurice Renard, Mary Shelley, Robert Louis Stevenson, Alexei Tolstoy, Verne and Wells, the silent period also saw sf movies by a number of major directors, including Michael Curtiz, D. W. Griffiths, Fritz Lang, Jean Renoir, Maurice Tourneur, Paul Wegener and Robert Wiene. Among these, Lang was the most significant for the development of sf cinema. *Der Goldene See* (1919) and *Das Brilliantenschiff* (1920), the first two parts of the uncompleted four-part *Die Spinnen* (*The Spiders*), follow the globetrotting efforts of their sportsman-explorer hero to thwart the designs of a global criminal organisation. *Spione* (1928), an equally breakneck adventure, pits its hero against an international spy ring. The exotic settings, suspenseful narratives and sf trappings of these early technothrillers anticipate the adventures, respectively, of Doc Savage and James Bond. Lang also directed two of the most significant cinematic dystopias. *Doktor Mabuse, der Spieler* (*Dr Mabuse, the Gambler*, 1922) depicts an estranged vision of Weimar Germany, so decadent as to be as susceptible to Mabuse's financial manipulations as various characters are to his powerful hypnotic suggestions. This nightmarish breakdown of society is extended in *Das Testament des Dr Mabuse* (*The Testament of Dr Mabuse*, 1933), an ambiguously anti-Nazi film, in which society is terrorized by Mabuse's criminal organization even after his descent into madness and sudden death. (Lang's final film, *Die tausend Augen des Dr Mabuse* (*The Thousand Eyes of Dr Mabuse*, 1960), offers a panoptical dystopia, in which police surveillance systems are as extensive and intrusive as those of the inexplicably revived criminal genius.) *Metropolis* (1926) is a spectacular evocation of the modern city, built upon class exploitation and brought to the brink of apocalypse. The towering skyscrapers and abstract machinery suggest the triumph of reason, but the sufferings of the narcotized workers, messianic religiosity and hysteria about female sexuality indicate not only a residue of irrational premodern forms but the terrible toll of modernity. The much-criticized denouement, in which the boss's son marries a worker (thus joining head and hand through the mediation of the heart), is perhaps more symptomatic of an irresolvable dilemma than a failure of imagination. *Die Frau im Mond* (*The Girl in the Moon*, 1929) again places stunning special effects at the service of an inadequate narrative, this time about the first trip to the moon. Its greatest significance lies in its painstaking attention to procedural detail, particularly during the launch scenes, and its fetishization of scientific accuracy (Lang employed Willy Ley and Hermann Oberth as scientific advisers). This pedantic approach to the spectacular would recur in later sf movies, such as *Destination Moon* (Pichel, 1950) and *2001: A Space Odyssey* (Kubrick, 1968), and become strangely eroticized in the technophilic model-work of various Gerry Anderson productions (for example, the opening sequence of *Thunderbirds Are Go*, Lane, 1966).

A more immediate Langian influence can be found in the monumentalist sf of the late 1920s and early 1930s, typically concerned with gigantic architectural feats. Modern metropolises can be found in *High Treason* (Elvey, 1929), *Just Imagine* (Butler, 1930), *Kosmitchesky Reis* (*The Space Ship*, Zhuravlev, 1935) and *Things to Come* (Menzies, 1936). *F.P.1. Antwortet Nicht* (Hartl, 1932; also shot in French and English versions, the latter as *F.P.1 Doesn't Answer*) is about the construction and sabotage of a mid-Atlantic platform designed to enable transatlantic flights to land and refuel. *Der Tunnel* (Bernhardt, 1933), also shot in a French version and remade as *The Tunnel* (Elvey, 1935), focuses on the construction of a transatlantic tunnel, and *Gold* (Hartl, 1934; also shot in a French version) features an atomic reactor designed to convert lead into gold. However, the celebration of the modern machine-age one might expect to find in such movies is blunted by an anxiety about the alienation from nature and people that seems to inevitably accompany such technological expansion – a tension embodied in the humanoid robots of *Metropolis* and *Gibel Sensaty* (*Loss of Feeling*, Andreievsky, 1935). Probably the only sf films of the period to be unequivocally modern are avant-garde shorts such as *The Birth of the Robot* (Lye, 1935) and *Equation: x + x = 0* (Fairthorne and Salt, 1936). It is unsurprising then to find massive catastrophes striking the Earth in *La Fin du monde* (*The End of the World*, Gance, 1930) and *Deluge* (Feist, 1933).

In the first decade of talking pictures, sf was crossed with the quintessentially modern American film genre, the musical, in such bizarre ventures as *Just Imagine, It's Great to Be Alive* (Werker, 1933), *The Big Broadcast of 1936* (Taurog, 1935) and *The Big Broadcast of 1938* (Leisen, 1938). Equally unusual collisions with the premodern occurred in *A Connecticut Yankee* (Butler, 1931), in which Will Rogers wisecracks about the New Deal while tanks overrun Camelot, and *The Phantom Empire* (Brower and Eason, 1935), in which singing cowboy Gene Autry discovers an underground city of super-science. However, the primary site of this dynamic interaction, and the dominant form sf cinema took during the 1930s, was the mad-scientist movie. Throughout this cycle the modern and the premodern meet in the *mise-en-scène*. Fabulous electrical laboratory equipment hums and sparks and sputters in run-down gothic turrets in *Frankenstein* (Whale, 1931) and *Bride of Frankenstein* (Whale, 1935). *The Invisible Man* (Whale, 1933) sees cutting-edge scientific research conducted in the drawing rooms of country houses and rustic pub lodgings, and considers the social transformations being wrought by mass communication media. In *Island of Lost Souls* (Kenton, 1933), Dr Moreau's experiments in vivisection take place in a carceral compound encircled by a perpetually dark jungle in which irrational half-men lurk. The psychosexual currents of an especially sadistic colonialism run deep beneath this outpost of rational civilization. Central to the cycle, if barely sf, is *The Black Cat* (Ulmer, 1934), a tale of perverse sexuality, psychological obsession, satanic worship and retribution. Set in a house with remarkable modern architecture and decor, but built on the site of a wartime massacre in the Hungarian mountains, it – more than any other sf or horror movie of the period – articulates something of the trauma of the first properly industrialized war. The archaism of the cycle's typically gothic setting and mode are often interrogated at key moments by an impressively mobile camera which self-consciously intrudes its quintessentially modern perspective, most strikingly in *Doctor Jekyll and Mr Hyde* (Mamoulian, 1932), which opens with a three-and-a-half minute sequence shot exclusively from Jekyll's point of view. Along with movie serials, the tail-end of this cycle was the mainstay of sf cinema during the 1940s.

There were about ninety sf or marginally sf movie serials between 1914 and 1955. Simply plotted, episodic adventure narratives with usually twelve or fifteen instalments, movie serials were aimed primarily at juvenile audiences; they suffered shrinking budgets and a long slow decline throughout the 1940s and into the mid-1950s. Pre-eminent among the sf movie serials of the sound period is *Flash Gordon* (Stephani, 1936), adapted from Alex Raymond's comic strip. With an unprecedented $350,000 budget (three times the average cost of a movie serial), and sets, props, models, footage and music borrowed from other films, it was a massive box-office success. Nostalgic remembrance has tended to mute its sexually charged narrative and fetishization of scantily clad hero and asphyxiation-prone heroine. Several other serials attempted to replicate its space operatics, notably *Undersea Kingdom* (Eason and Kane, 1936) and *Buck Rogers* (Beebe and Goodkind, 1939). More typically, though, sf elements were unleashed in a contemporary (thus cheaper) setting, as in *The Fighting Devil Dogs* (Witney and English, 1938), *The Mysterious Dr Satan* (Witney and English, 1940) and *King of the Rocket Men* (Brannon, 1949). For all their intermittent verve, the movie serials' financial restrictions – manifested in their cardboard characters, melodramatic situations, repetitive structures and straight-faced presentation of loopy plots – have largely banished them from histories and critical discussions of both sf and cinema. Nowadays, their appeal is largely camp.

The 1930s also saw adaptations of Karel Čapek, H. Rider Haggard, James Hilton, Renard, Sax Rohmer, Shelley, Curt Siodmak, Stevenson, Wells and Philip Wylie, but there was little noteworthy sf cinema during the 1940s.

## The 1950s boom and after

The 1950s witnessed an sf movie boom centred in the USA, although a significant number of movies were also made in Europe, Asia and Latin America. Hollywood's major, minor and poverty-row studios all dabbled in the genre, but it remained largely the province of independent producers. The boom commenced with the first of several sf movies produced by George Pal, *Destination Moon* (Pichel, 1950). Co-written by Robert Heinlein, adapting his 1947 novel *Rocketship Galileo*, and shot in a near-documentary style, it is a resolutely sober and undramatic account of the first moon mission. Taken alongside its departure from the gothic expressionism of many earlier sf movies, its final caption – 'THIS IS THE END OF THE BEGINNING' – could be seen to announce the start of a genuinely sf cinema; but, with the exception of its flat visual style, later films found little in it to imitate. A better origin point for the boom might, in fact, be *Rocketship X-M* (Neumann, 1950): rushed into production to cash in on *Destination Moon*, and released first, it was opportunistic, exploitative, melodramatic and sometimes amateurish, and featured a dire warning about nuclear war.

Although the following year saw a number of sf movies, including *The Day the Earth Stood Still* (Wise, 1951), *The Thing (from Another World)* (Nyby, 1951) and Pal's *When Worlds Collide* (Maté, 1951), the only major sf movie of 1952 was the marginal *Monkey Business* (Hawks, 1952), and the boom might have quickly played out. Warren has argued that the heavily promoted and extremely successful 1952 re-release of *King Kong* played an important role in revitalizing the apparently moribund genre, prompting the production of monster movies such as *The Beast From 20,000 Fathoms* (Lourié, 1953) and *Them!* (Douglas, 1954).[5] Their scenes of terror and urban destruction were matched in Pal's *War of the Worlds* (Haskin, 1953), a loose adaptation of Wells's novel which replaces the Martian tripods with craft more akin to flying saucers; other movies to exploit the decade's flying-saucer craze included *Invaders from Mars* (Menzies, 1953), *This Island Earth* (Newman, 1955), *Forbidden Planet* (Wilcox, 1956) and *Plan 9 from Outer Space* (Wood, Jr, 1956).

Accounts of 1950s US sf movies typically stress the themes of anti-communism and nuclear anxiety. The latter is evident in a number of recurring tropes: scenes of mass destruction; radioactively generated monsters, mutants and giant insects; the repeated validation of military-scientific collaboration; aliens concerned about the proliferation of nuclear weapons into space; alien civilizations destroyed by nuclear conflicts; and consolatory religious subtexts. However, although the decade did throw up hysterically anti-communist movies such as *Invasion USA* (Green, 1952), *Red Planet*

*Mars* (Horner, 1952) and *The 27th Day* (Asher, 1957), the suggestion that the paranoia suffusing many 1950s sf movies is about communism is as banal as it is difficult to sustain.

An instructive example is *The Whip Hand* (Menzies, 1951), in which the hero, stranded in an isolated village, discovers communists plotting biological warfare. The movie was actually completed a year earlier (as *The Man He Found*), and in that unreleased version the hero found Nazi fifth-columnists. This opportunistic shift from Nazis to communists, both typically depicted as producing terrorized and mindlessly conformist hierarchical societies, suggests that the propaganda and ideology of the period generated and played upon deep-seated anxieties about regimentation and dehumanization, the sources of which can as easily be found in Eisenhower's placid decade. In this respect, the most important American sf movie of the time is *Invasion of the Body Snatchers* (Siegel, 1956), in which unemotional alien facsimiles covertly replace the human population. Often considered an allegory of communist infiltration, the movie offers little to support such a reading. Rather, automated technologies and gynaecological imagery indicate a concern with production and reproduction. The narrative centres on a sexually active unmarried couple and a well-off, smugly hedonistic, childless couple. These 'deviants' are pursued and persecuted by 'pod-people' who precisely replicate small-town conformism. Furthermore, the movie's imagery of contagion and dehumanization, often associated with communism, was also central to contemporary discourses about everything from mass culture, marijuana, motherhood and McCarthyism to homosexuality, civil rights, juvenile delinquency and rock'n'roll.

The most important 1950s American sf director was Jack Arnold, whose *It Came from Outer Space* (1953), *Creature from the Black Lagoon* (1954), *Tarantula* (1955), *The Incredible Shrinking Man* (1957) and *The Space Children* (1958) sympathized with their monsters. Arnold's evocations of the possibilities inherent in a landscape without figures brought lyricism to a frequently bland-looking genre. More typical of the turn the genre took in the late 1950s is Roger Corman, with his ultra-low budget output and targeting of a teenage audience. Following the success of Hammer's *The Curse of Frankenstein* (Fisher, 1957) and *Dracula* (Fisher, 1958) and TV screenings of the 1930s Universal horror movies, he played a major role in rechannelling the genre towards horror. With few exceptions (*X – The Man with X-Ray Eyes*, Corman, 1963; *Robinson Crusoe on Mars*, Haskin, 1964; *Sins of the Fleshapoids*, Kuchar, 1965), the USA produced little further sf of note until the late 1960s, largely restricting itself to comedies (*The Absent-Minded Professor*, Stevenson, 1961; *The Nutty Professor*, Lewis, 1963), nuclear warnings (*On the Beach*, Kramer, 1959; *Fail Safe*, Lumet, 1964), and

James Bond parodies (*Our Man Flint*, Mann, 1965; *The Silencers*, Karlson, 1966).

In the UK, the mad-scientist movie took comic form in *The Perfect Woman* (Knowles, 1949), a farce involving a robot, mistaken identities and a fetishistic interest in women's underwear, and *The Man in the White Suit* (Mackendrick, 1951), which strikingly captures conservative terror of innovation. The 1950s and 1960s were dominated by bleak narratives of alien invasion, nuclear threat and out-of-control science, such as *The Quatermass Xperiment* (Guest, 1955), *X the Unknown* (Norman, 1956), *Village of the Damned* (Rilla, 1960), *The Damned* (Losey, 1961), *The Day the Earth Caught Fire* (Guest, 1961), *The Mind Benders* (Dearden, 1963) and *No Blade of Grass* (Wilde, 1970). In contrast to these often dour movies, British sf cinema also offered the frequently startling colour of Hammer's Frankenstein movies and the exotic locations of the James Bond series.

Throughout this period Japan produced three basic kinds of sf movie: the *kaiju eiga* or monster movie, inaugurated by *Gojira* (Honda, 1954), anglicized as *Godzilla*; space opera, beginning with *Chikyu Boeigun* (*The Mysterians*, Honda, 1957); and anti-nuclear warnings such as *Dai sanji Sekai Taisen – Yonju-Ichi no Kyofu* (*The Final War*, Hidaka, 1960). In France, several of the filmmaker-critics associated with *Cahiers du cinéma* and the *nouvelle vague* made sf movies, including *Un amour de poche* (*A Girl in his Pocket*, Kast, 1957), *Les Yeux sans visage* (*Eyes Without a Face*, Franju, 1959), *La Jetée* (Marker, 1962), *Alphaville* (Godard, 1965), *Fahrenheit 451* (Truffaut, 1966) and *Je t'aime, je t'aime* (Resnais, 1967). Mexico, West Germany and Spain all produced major examples of surgical sf, including *El Ladrón de Cadáveres* (*The Robber of Corpses*, Méndez, 1956), *Die Nackte und der Satan* (*The Head*, Trivas, 1959) and *Gritos en la Noche* (*The Awful Dr Orloff*, Franco, 1962). From the USSR came interplanetary adventures such as *Planeta Burg* (Klushantsev, 1962), and from Czechoslovakia, Karel Zeman's dazzling adaptations of Verne, the best of which is *Vynález Zkázy* (1958). From Italy came the pop-camp classics *Barbarella* (Vadim, 1967) and *Diabolik* (Bava, 1967), a sub-genre to which producer Dino De Laurentiis would later contribute *King Kong* (Guillermin, 1976), *Flash Gordon* (Hodges, 1980) and *Dune* (Lynch, 1984).

## Origins of TV sf

Stableford has argued that the history of sf as a popular genre can be divided into three stages: between 1930 and 1960 it emerged and developed in the pulp magazines; from 1960 to 1990, it was located in book publishing; since 1990, the primary site of popular sf has been TV (a category under which he subsumes film).⁶ Although there are problems with this schema, it does identify an undeniable trend: the massive growth of sf across a wide range of media, largely as a consequence of the practices and processes of globalization, conglomerization and fragmentation pursued by the multinational corporations which now dominate the media industries. One of their central strategies is to develop concepts/packages to sell world-wide, through their own subsidiaries or franchise deals, in as many different media and product forms as possible. The prime example of such synergy, regardless of genre, is the sprawling *Star Trek* franchise, which has to date spawned five live-action series, an animated series, nine movies, hundreds of novels and other books and mountains of tie-in merchandising. One of the keys to its success has been its fan-following, particularly its vociferous and often genuinely creative organized fandom. Although no other sf series approaches *Star Trek* in these respects, similar industries and followings have grown up around shows such as *Doctor Who* (1963–89), *Babylon 5* (1993–8) and *The X-Files* (1993–2002). Nothing about TV sf's origins indicated that it would achieve such significance in the global media.

TV sf began in the late 1940s and early 1950s, when much of the medium's output was still broadcast live. If the production values of these shows now look extraordinarily amateurish, it is indicative of the extent to which the very fact of TV no longer seems miraculous. In the USA, TV sf began with rudimentary space operas such as *Captain Video and His Video Rangers* (1949–55) and *Tom Corbett, Space Cadet* (1950–5), in which self-righteous, square-jawed heroes championed conformist values while fighting evil. (Such hero types remain common in TV sf; for example, no matter how cynical or sceptical the protagonists of *The X-Files* or *Seven Days* (1998–2001) become about America, they continue to uphold its values and institutions.) Among these space operas, *Tom Corbett* stands out, both for its higher production values and, courtesy of scientific advisor Willy Ley, its obsession with scientific accuracy. Most, however, followed *Captain Video*'s example, preferring exciting plots to scientific plausibility.

By the mid 1950s, TV sf began to receive more serious treatment. Walt Disney collaborated with Ley, Heinz Haber and Werner von Braun to produce three influential programmes ('Man in Space', 1955; 'Man and the Moon', 1955; and 'Mars and Beyond', 1957) on the realities of space exploration. *Science Fiction Theatre* (1955–7) produced topical single dramas, while *The Man and the Challenge* (1959–60) and *Men into Space* (1959–60) offered relatively realistic dramas about preparing for and venturing into space. Sf also began to appear with some regularity in prestigious drama anthology series such as *Westinghouse Studio One*, *TV Playhouse*, *Desilu Playhouse* and *Goodyear Television Playhouse*. This range of shows and the kind of stories they told, which tended to subjugate science to a blend of adventure, soap opera, topicality (sometimes even seriousness) and moralizing, largely established the parameters of American TV sf. This can be observed in shows as varied as *The Twilight Zone* (1959–64), *The Outer Limits* (1963–5), *Voyage to the Bottom of the Sea* (1964–8), *Lost in Space* (1965–8) and *Star Trek* (1966–9), through to *Quantum Leap* (1989–93) and *Sliders* (1995–2000). Notable exceptions to this pattern can be found among the 1960s fantastic family sitcoms. *The Jetsons* (1962–3) exploited the comedy inherent in depicting unchanged humans in a vastly changed world, while *My Favorite Martian* (1963–6) based its comedy on the potentially subversive misunderstandings inherent to a clash of cultures. Between them, they provided the two basic templates for TV sf comedy. Examples of the former type include *The Hitchhiker's Guide to the Galaxy* (1981), *Red Dwarf* (since 1988) and *Futurama* (since 1999); among the latter are *Mork and Mindy* (1978–82), *ALF* (1986–90), *Goodnight Sweetheart* (1993–9) and *Third Rock from the Sun* (1996–2001).

In the UK, the birth of TV sf was intertwined with the birth of TV drama. Well into the 1950s, aesthetic debates at the BBC focused on the cosy address of the TV to the family audience gathered around a nine- or fifteen-inch screen in their own home with the lights down low, and on the intimacy that TV allowed. Unlike film, actors crafted a continuous live performance; unlike the stage, the camera enabled the audience to get up close. This resulted in a tendency to privilege close-ups of the actor and a more muted style of (nonetheless continuous) film-like performance. Writer Nigel Kneale and director/producer Rudolph Cartier sought ways to move away from the dominance of the intimate, to reduce the close-up to one stylistic choice among many. Their preference for fast-moving narratives in which people did things and things happened on a larger scale led them to sf. One of the contradictory impulses at the heart of the genre is the desire for stories to happen on a grand scale (planets in peril, invasions from other worlds) but also a need to follow individual actions, to humanize the events. This tension structures Kneale and Cartier's collaborations on three tremendously successful six-part *Quatermass* adventures – *The Quatermass Experiment* (1953), *Quatermass II* (1955) and *Quatermass and the Pit* (1958–9) – and their controversial adaptation of *Nineteen Eighty-Four* (1954). The imaginative and technical dilemmas posed by this dynamic tension is, arguably, the defining characteristic of British TV sf, not least of all because budgetary constraints often foreground it. For example, one of the most memorable moments in *Doctor Who* comes in 'Genesis of the Daleks' (1975), in which the Doctor, called upon to destroy his evil arch-enemies at the moment of their creation, is torn by the grandest of ethical dilemmas: should he commit genocide in order to prevent future wars and genocides? However, the sets, costumes, repetitive plot and clichéd moralizing all undermine the potential seriousness of this moment.

## From the counter-culture to *Star Wars*

Although other nations have continued to produce sf movies, from the late 1960s onwards the USA reasserted its dominance in the field. *Night of the Living Dead* (Romero, 1968), *Planet of the Apes* (Schaffner, 1968), *Wild in the Streets* (Shear, 1968), *THX 1138* (Lucas, 1970), *Glen and Randa* (McBride, 1971) and *The Crazies* (Romero, 1973) resonated strongly with counter-cultural concerns about nuclear weapons, the American invasion and occupation of Vietnam, the anti-democratic relationship between business and government, civil rights and youth politics. This provided the genre with a new sense of relevance, which can also be observed in various episodes of *Star Trek*. Indeed, critical discussions of *Star Trek* tend to focus on its ability to address such concerns. For example, those who would champion its liberal vision of an egalitarian future often note the presence on the bridge of Lieutenant Uhura (Nichelle Nicholls), an African-American woman; those who would censure its failure to adequately imagine such a utopia, point to her role as an exotic, mini-skirted switchboard operator, persistently positioned on the margin or in the background. Similarly, some argue that the Borg are the Federation's dark opposite; others explore the striking similarities in their conformism and their drive to assimilate other cultures. A more pointed criticism of the franchise might concern itself with the ways in which it reveals the limitations of liberal discourse.

This sense of contemporary relevance was continued in a cycle of ecologically themed movies, such as *The Andromeda Strain* (Wise, 1970), *Silent Running* (Trumbull, 1971) and *It's Alive* (Cohen, 1973), but it rapidly gave way to a revenge-of-nature cycle (*Frogs*, McCowan, 1972; *Phase IV*, Bass, 1973) and a spate of disaster movies. Completely out of step with counter-cultural concerns, but tremendously popular nonetheless, were the various 'SuperMarionation' TV series produced in the UK by Gerry and Sylvia Anderson. *Supercar* (1961–2), *Fireball XL5* (1962–3), *Stingray* (1964–5), *Thunderbirds* (1965–6) and *Joe 90* (1968–9) tended to celebrate the 'white heat of technology' and patriarchal command structures. Only the darkest of them, *Captain Scarlet and the Mysterons* (1967–8), ever seemed in tune with a decade of civil disobedience and anti-imperialist guerrilla wars, although the series inevitably sided with a global military and Euro-cool consumerism.

Major 1960s sf directors included John Frankenheimer (*The Manchurian Candidate*, 1962; *Seven Days in May*, 1964; *Seconds*, 1966) and Peter

Watkins (*The War Game*, 1966; *Privilege*, 1967; *Gladiatorerna* (*The Peace Game*), 1969; *Punishment Park*, 1971), but neither of them could match Stanley Kubrick's success in rendering the genre so utterly cinematic. *Doctor Strangelove* (1964), *A Clockwork Orange* (1971) and, especially, *2001: A Space Odyssey* (1968) demonstrate a darkly comic vision and a suspicion of technology counterpointed by a determination to explore the formal limits of filmmaking and its apparatuses. Although directors such as Ridley Scott, Terry Gilliam, Luc Besson and Jean-Pierre Jeunet would bring as distinctive visual styles to sf moviemaking, only Andrei Tarkovsky, in *Solaris* (1972), *Stalker* (1979) and *Offret* (*The Sacrifice*, 1986), has treated the genre with comparable wit and rigour.

1970s sf witnessed continued occasionally successful attempts at movies of contemporary relevance: *Westworld* (Crichton, 1973), *The Stepford Wives* (Forbes, 1974), *The Terminal Man* (Hodges, 1974), *The Man Who Fell to Earth* (Roeg, 1976). However, much livelier material could be found in sex-ploitation (*Flesh Gordon*, Benveniste and Ziehm, 1974; *Spermula*, Matton, 1976), blaxploitation (*Dr Black, Mr Hyde*, Crain, 1976) and such Children's Film Foundation movies as *Egghead's Robot* (Lewis, 1970) and *Kadoyng* (Shand, 1972). The decade also saw sf become increasingly self-aware, a trend most evident in comedies such as *Schlock* (Landis, 1973), *Sleeper* (Allen, 1973), *Dark Star* (Carpenter, 1974), *Death Race 2000* (Bartel, 1975) and the camp excess of *Dr Phibes Rises Again* (Fuest, 1972) and *The Rocky Horror Picture Show* (Sharman, 1975). Unsurprisingly, the latter are British movies. If *Doctor Who*'s fantastic intertext, with its idiosyncratic disregard for the boundaries of genre and consistency of mood and tone, was indicative of the vibrancy of the fantastic in British popular culture in the 1960s and after, then several other shows of the period with occasional sf elements, in-cluding *The Avengers* (1961–9), *The Saint* (1962–8), *Adam Adamant Lives!* (1966–7) and *Jason King* (1971–2), added a swinging London flavour to pop-camp sf. Foremost among such series was *The Prisoner* (1967–8), whose self-conscious deployment of whimsy, sf and spy story clichés and the image of the modern, along with its steadfast refusal to make consistent or coher-ent sense and its final metaleptic evasion of closure, exposed the absurdity of the processes of modernity. In the 1970s, British TV sf typically took on a darker tone, as in Terry Nation's post-holocaust *The Survivors* (1975–7) and the grim space opera *Blake's 7* (1978–81).

## When it changed: *Star Wars* and after

*Star Wars* (Lucas, 1977) and *Close Encounters of the Third Kind* (Spiel-berg, 1977) represent a turning point in American cinema, simultaneously confirming the potential profitability of the new style of effects-driven, cross-marketed, heavily merchandised, saturation-booked blockbuster pioneered by *Jaws* (Spielberg, 1975), and the ability of such fundamentally juvenile narratives to appeal to a global audience. Central to their success was the sensuous elaboration of production design and special effects, and (as the box-office failure of *Flash Gordon* (Hodges, 1980) suggests) their doggedly straight-faced presentation. Immediate attempts to recapture the audience and replicate the success of these movies included *Superman* (Donner, 1978), *The Black Hole* (Nelson, 1979), *Star Trek – The Motion Picture* (Wise, 1979), *Battle Beyond the Stars* (Murakami, 1980) and the TV series *Battlestar Galactica* (1978–80) and *Buck Rogers in the 25th Century* (1979–81). *Alien* (Scott, 1979) and *Blade Runner* (Scott, 1982) targeted an older market segment, with similarly mixed success, although they were eventually recognized as exemplifying debates about postmodernity, embodiment and identity which have since dominated many areas of cultural study.

After the success of the *Star Wars* sequels and *E.T. – The Extraterrestrial* (Spielberg, 1982), the 1980s witnessed a further juvenilization and sentimentalization of sf, often accompanied by a turn to comedy, in *Back to the Future* (Zemeckis, 1985), *Cocoon* (Howard, 1985), *Explorers* (Dante, 1985) and *Weird Science* (Hughes, 1985). Such movies demonstrate not only the extent to which sf ideas and imagery had become integrated into the popular imagination, but also the shift in 1980s sf cinema away from the social towards the magical resolution of personal problems. This is perhaps an inevitable result of the changing economics and production context of the New Hollywood, as much as it is an articulation and ideological mystification of the right-wing political retrenchment that took root in the West in the late-1970s.

Although sf movie-making has become increasingly linked to the production of expensive visual effects, there has nonetheless been a constant flow of lower-budget movies, many of which betray the kinds of intellectual ambition, political sophistication or narrative inventiveness absent from bigger-budget productions. Comedies such as *Der Grosse Verhau* (*The Big Mess*, Kluge, 1970) and *Iron Bread* (Pei, 1970) mock the pretensions of the 'serious' sf movie; while movies such as *Otel 'U Pogibshchego Alpinista* (*The Dead Mountaineer Hotel*, Kromanov, 1979), *Chronopolis* (Kamler, 1982), *Born in Flames* (Borden, 1983), *The Brother from Another Planet* (Sayles, 1984), *O-Bi, O-Ba – Koniec Cywilizacji* (*O-Bi, O-Ba – The End of Civilization*, Szulkin, 1985), *Friendship's Death* (Wollen, 1987) and *Incident at Raven's Gate* (de Heer, 1988) demonstrated that sf movies could achieve the more typically literary goals of defamiliarization, astonishment, coherent speculation, political commentary and closely textured world-creation.

Lower-budget filmmaking has also provided many of the more inventive action-adventure sf movies since the late 1970s: *Piranha* (Dante, 1978), *Alligator* (Teague, 1980), *Mad Max 2* (Miller, 1981), *Repo Man* (Cox, 1984), *The Terminator* (Cameron, 1984), *Trancers* (Band, 1984), *The Stuff* (Cohen, 1985), *Zone Troopers* (Bilson, 1985), *Tremors* (Underwood, 1989), *Darkman* (Raimi, 1990) and *Megaville* (Lehner, 1990).

The most important director to emerge in this context is David Cronenberg, whose many sf-horror cross-overs, including *Shivers* (1974), *Rabid* (1976), *The Brood* (1979), *Scanners* (1980), *The Fly* (1986) and *Dead Ringers* (1988), manipulate the imagery of medicine, trauma, sexual desire, the surgical and the organic, to conduct an ongoing interrogation of human embodiment and identity. His major achievement is *Videodrome* (1982), which inflects his usual concerns through a series of disturbing images and a destabilizing narrative incoherence, opening up a troubled space in which the politics of fantasy, desire, ubiquitous media, cyborging technology, ideology and propaganda interweave and implode.

Since the mid 1980s, cinematic sf has often seemed to be dominated by a handful of directors: Steven Spielberg (*Jurassic Park*, 1993, and its 1997 and 2001 sequels; *A.I. – Artificial Intelligence*, 2001); James Cameron (*Aliens*, 1986; *The Abyss*, 1989; *Terminator 2: Judgment Day*, 1991); Paul Verhoeven (*RoboCop*, 1987; *Total Recall*, 1990; *Starship Troopers*, 1997; *The Hollow Man*, 2000); Roland Emmerich (*Universal Soldier*, 1992; *Stargate*, 1994; *Independence Day*, 1996; *Godzilla*, 1998); and John Carpenter, slowly declining from the vigour of *Escape from New York* (1981) and *The Thing* (1982). Alongside the work of these big-name directors and the expensive flops (*Waterworld*, Reynolds, 1995; *The Postman*, Costner, 1997), the period has also seen a number of lucrative movie series, including *Alien, Back to the Future, Batman, The Matrix, Men in Black, Mission: Impossible, Teenage Mutant Ninja Turtles* and *The X-Men*, and failed attempts to launch series (*Judge Dredd, The Avengers*). There have also been a number of movie cycles, of which the most populous featured *Alien* imitators, cyborgs or post-holocaust road warriors. Such trends are to be expected in a global cinema dominated by the particular production, distribution and exhibition practices of the New Hollywood, with its drive to produce event movies to be resold in various forms in multiple markets. Pre-sold titles, exploitable contents and images, and hybrid narratives with an ability to appeal to multiple audience segments have become the goal.

Two other recent trends in sf film and TV can also be traced to the new organization of the culture industries. First, there is the growing interrelationship between between film and TV, which has seen films adapted from TV shows: *Jetsons – The Movie* (Hanna and Barbera, 1990), *Lost in Space*

(Hopkins, 1998), *My Favorite Martian* (Petrie, 1999); remakes of movies: *The Nutty Professor* (Shadyac, 1996), *The Planet of the Apes* (Burton, 2001); TV shows developed from movies: *Timecop* (1997), *Stargate SG-1* (since 1997), various animated and live-action *RoboCop* spin-offs; and TV shows developed/produced by movie 'auteurs': Oliver Stone's *Wild Palms* (1993), James Cameron's *Dark Angel* (since 2000). This is complemented by a further series of interrelations with the computer-game industry. Second, there is the trend towards producing non-sf movies which draw on the genre's full range of special effects while appealing to a much larger audience: *Apollo 13* (Howard, 1995), *Titanic* (Cameron, 1997), *Saving Private Ryan* (Spielberg, 1998). This has in turn produced a series of sf movies which are simultaneously overwrought family melodramas: *Deep Impact* (Leder, 1998), *Armageddon* (Bay, 1998) and *Mission to Mars* (De Palma, 2000).

However, this extensive control of the media industries by multinational corporations has not succeeded in squeezing out more marginal productions. Stuart Gordon continued to make unpretentious action-adventure sf with *Fortress* (1992) and *Space Truckers* (1997). Japanese *anime* such as *Akira* (Otomo, 1988), *Oneamisu No Tsubasa* (*Wings of Honneamise*, Yamaga, 1987/1994) and *Kokaku kidotai* (*Ghost in the Shell*, Oshii, 1995), and strange live-action movies such as *Ganheddo* (*Gunhed*, Harada, 1989), *Tetsuo* (*The Iron Man*, Tsukamoto, 1989) and *Tetsuo II: Body Hammer* (Tsukamoto, 1991) found international success. The New Queer Cinema produced *Poison* (Haynes, 1991), and from Hong Kong came such near-future action fantasies as *Dongfang San Xia* (*The Heroic Trio*, Qifeng, 1992), *Gauyat Sandiu Haplui* (*Saviour of the Soul*, Kwai, 1992) and *Yaoshu dushi* (*The Wicked City*, Kit, 1992). Other quirkily imaginative movies of the period include *Miracle Mile* (DeJarnatt, 1990), *Wax, or The Discovery of Television Among the Bees* (Blair, 1991) and its hypermedia remix *Waxweb* (1999), *Acción Mutante* (de la Iglesia, 1993), *Cube* (Natali, 1998), *Pi* (Aronofksy, 1998), *Avalon* (Oshii, 2000) and *Daehakno-yeseo maechoonhadaka tomaksalhae danghan yeogosaeng ajik Daehakno-ye Issda* (*Teenage Hooker Became Killing Machine in Daehakno*, Nam, 2000). The significance of these movies lies in the way that they prove the ongoing vitality of a genre which has become increasingly common property.

Nowadays, TV sf relies on types of character interaction common to soap opera, while the limited varieties of closure available to series TV has rendered it conventional and conservative. Blockbuster cinema, in which sf has played a large part since the 1970s, is often criticized for the way in which it permits the production of spectacle to override more traditional concerns with character development, narrative coherence and thematic elaboration, and thus produces extremely conservative texts. Similarly, computer games also seem to restrict innovation to the realm of technical considerations. This is not to suggest that lower-budget filmmaking is never conservative in the stories it wishes to tell and the ways in which it wishes to tell them, but to point to the greater opportunities (and necessity) for inventiveness which come with financial restrictions. While none of the movies listed in the above paragraph could be considered models of coherent character, narrative or theme, they nonetheless succeed in negotiating the relationship between narrative and spectacle in ways that are consistently interesting. They provide hope for a diverse, challenging and distinctive audio-visual sf.

## NOTES

1. Vachel Lindsay, *The Art of the Moving Picture* (1915; New York: Modern Library, 2000), p. 183.
2. In what follows, the name which follows the title of a film is that of the director or directors.
3. Tom Gunning, *D. W. Griffiths and the Origins of American Narrative Film: The Early Years* (Urbana: University of Illinois Press, 1994), p. 41.
4. *Ibid.*, p. 41.
5. Bill Warren, *Keep Watching the Skies!* (Jefferson, MO: McFarland, 1997), p. xiv.
6. Brian Stableford, 'The Third Generation of Genre Science Fiction', *Science-Fiction Studies* 23 (1996), pp. 321–30.

# 6

GARY K. WOLFE

# Science fiction and its editors

More than in any other popular genre, and for that matter more than in most publishing in general, sf's editors and publishers have from the beginning played a highly visible and sometimes controversial role in the evolution and ideology of the field and its readership. While relatively few readers of other genres such as mystery and romance are even aware of the names of the magazine and book editors who select and sometimes shape the texts that collectively define those fields, sf editors have from the beginning played a more visible and sometimes even celebrated role; it is perhaps indicative of this that the leading American mystery award is named the Edgar, after Edgar Allan Poe, while the most publicized sf award, the Hugo, is named after an editor and publisher, Hugo Gernsback. By the same token, the Hugos (voted on by fans and awarded at the annual World Science Fiction Convention) have since 1973 included a category for 'Best Professional Editor,' while the Edgar Award includes no such category (although its Ellery Queen Award, originally intended for collaborations, has sometimes gone to editors and publishers instead). Science fiction editors are frequent guests at fan conventions, and a substantial number of readers can trace their first allegiance to the field by citing the work of anthologists from Judith Merril to Gardner Dozois, or (in an older generation) to the magazines of Gernsback, John W. Campbell, Jr, or Horace Gold. Equally important, the ongoing dialogue of ideas, and increasingly of styles and forms, that has defined the field's sometimes insular identity, is in large measure the result of quite deliberate editorial intervention, often accompanied by editorial position papers and even manifestoes. This is not to suggest that sf is or has been a 'managed literature', but it is a literature that has often and sometimes loudly proclaimed a sense of mission, and this mission has in large measure been articulated and promoted by the field's editors.

As early as 1864, Jules Verne's publisher Pierre Hetzel began shaping an audience for sf with his *Magasin d'éducation et de recréation*, which serialized several of the novels (including *Vingt mille lieues sous les mers*) that over the next few decades would establish Verne's reputation as 'the father of science fiction', and the end of the century saw early versions of the famous pulp magazines from such publishers as Frank Tousey (*The Frank Reade Library*) and Frank Munsey (*Munsey's Magazine, The All-Story*, the latter featuring early works by Edgar Rice Burroughs, A. Merritt, and others). During this period it is evident that editors as much as authors were feeling their way towards what many of them perceived as a new form of fiction, providing sinecures for writers whose fantastic tales might otherwise have gone unpublished and generating models and markets for later writers entering the field. Eventually, through selective reprints of older works, the editors of sf magazines played a crucial role in helping to shape what became a kind of consensus canon of classic stories – a canon further refined by a subsequent generation of anthologists. Still later, as sf moved increasingly towards the novel as a dominant form and gained a stronger foothold in commercial book publishing, editors working for publishing houses continued to shape the direction of the field.

## The magazines

By the time *Amazing Stories*, the magazine most commonly cited as the first sf magazine, appeared in 1926, its editor and publisher Hugo Gernsback had already begun to cultivate an audience through earlier magazines such as *Science and Invention*, and throughout his career as an editor he consistently treated sf as a personal duchy, creating fan organizations, soliciting letters to the editor and in general contributing so visibly to the rise of 'fandom' that the reader-voted awards of the annual World Science Fiction Convention are named Hugos in his honour. Given such legendary status within the sf community, it is sobering to remember that Gernsback's tenure as an editor of any significant influence lasted only a decade, and his editorship of *Amazing Stories* for only thirty-seven issues. Following a bankruptcy in 1929, he lost control of the magazine and quickly began a similar one called *Science Wonder Stories* (later *Wonder Stories*). But *Amazing Stories* had already cemented the notion of sf as a viable market category, helping readers develop a common sense of the field's lineage (the first two issues, consisting entirely of reprints, each included work by Verne, Poe and Wells), and promoting what arguably was the first operational notion of what the genre ought to be – essentially science lessons clothed in simplistic adventures. Ironically, the most successful work published in *Amazing Stories* during Gernsback's tenure, E. E. Smith's *The Skylark of Space*, barely qualified as a science lesson at all, but instead established the template for the 'space opera', which would become one of sf's most cherished sub-genres among fans, and damning evidence of the genre's chronic sub-literariness among outsiders.

The success of *Amazing Stories* quickly led to other sf magazines – the so-called 'pulp era' – and to competing market strategies which, at least indirectly, reflected competing notions of what this new field ought to be about. Gernsback's hold over the field began to evaporate in the face of these new markets, which proved attractive to writers not least because of Gernsback's famously miserly pay rates, which alienated popular writers such as Edgar Rice Burroughs and H. P. Lovecraft; even *The Skylark of Space* had been bought at the scandalous rate of less than a seventh of a cent per word. Following Gernsback's departure, *Amazing* began to decline under the uninspired editorship of T. O'Conor Sloane, Gernsback's former managing editor, then nearly eighty years old. But in January 1930 another magazine debuted which would eventually prove the most influential of all: *Astounding Stories of Super-Science*, later changed to *Astounding Stories*, then to *Astounding Science-Fiction* and, decades later, to *Analog*.

Under the initial editorship of former adventure-magazine editor Harry Bates and influential assistant editor Desmond Hall, *Astounding* helped re-define sf in terms of fast-paced adventure tales in exotic settings; Bates and Hall, writing as Anthony Gilmore, even collaborated on the popular 'Hawk Carse' series, as though providing a model for the kind of fiction they sought. The notion of sf as merely a subset of adventure fiction was at odds with Gernsback's more didactic aesthetic, but it would gain even further purchase in 1938, when former fan Raymond Palmer assumed the editorship of *Amazing*, now under the control of the Ziff-Davis magazine chain. The following year Palmer began another magazine, *Fantastic Adventures*, which together with the new *Amazing* did much to establish the lurid, juvenile stereotype of the sf pulp. (In later years, in both *Amazing* and other magazines, Palmer strained the credibility of the field even further by linking sf with pseudo-scientific cults involving lost continents and UFOs.)

But at the same time yet a third aesthetic was entering the field: in 1933, the editorship of *Astounding* passed from Bates to veteran pulp editor F. Orlin Tremaine, who announced that each issue would include at least one 'thought-variant' story, based on either an entirely new idea or a radical re-visioning of a familiar one. Though relatively few of these 'thought-variants' are widely read today (one famous example was Murray Leinster's 'Sidewise in Time' (1934), an early treatment of the parallel-universe theme), the policy was among the first examples of an sf editor recognizing that the potential of the field may lie largely in its speculative content rather than as a platform for action tales or science lessons. This idea would move to the centre of the field when one of the magazine's most popular contributors, John W. Campbell, Jr, replaced Desmond Hall as assistant editor and, in 1937, replaced Tremaine as editor.

Campbell's thirty-four year reign as editor of *Astounding* – detailed more fully in Brian Attebery's chapter in this volume – is not only the longest in sf magazine history, but easily the most influential. From the Gernsback tradition, he demanded a degree of scientific plausibility, but also insisted on competent stories with credible characters and detailed, 'lived-in' settings – the model for which eventually became Robert A. Heinlein's 'future history' series. Campbell virtually moulded the young Isaac Asimov into the model of what he believed an sf author should be, but also published space opera by E. E. Smith, hyperkinetic adventures by A. E. Van Vogt and L. Ron Hubbard and rustic humour by Henry Kuttner. Despite the blunt and often right-wing technocratic opinions that paraded through his endless editorials, he provided a home for humanist and even sentimental writers such as Theodore Sturgeon and Clifford D. Simak. In fact, among some readers the term 'Campbellian science fiction' is virtually synonymous with 'Golden Age', so manifestly more rigorous were the authors Campbell developed than the majority of pulp writers who preceded them. But this 'Golden Age', like the Gernsback era before it, actually lasted little more than a decade; by the early1950s Campbell's own odd enthusiasms for such schemes as L. Ron Hubbard's Dianetics (first introduced in *Astounding* in 1950), together with the rise of Anthony Boucher and J. Francis McComas at *The Magazine of Fantasy and Science Fiction* (founded 1949 as *The Magazine of Fantasy*) and H. L. Gold at *Galaxy Science Fiction* (founded 1950), had begun to erode the leadership role of *Astounding*.

During the 1940s, other sf magazines continued to flourish with more limited agendas. The space opera was kept alive by such magazines as *Planet Stories*, edited by Malcolm Reiss from 1939 through 1955, both *Amazing Stories* and *Wonder Stories* survived in various incarnations (the latter with a successful companion magazine, *Startling Stories*), and Campbell himself helped promote popular fantasy with *Unknown* (later *Unknown Worlds*) from 1939 to 1943. *Unknown* may have had a nascent effect on the development of sf as well; since it published many of the same authors as *Astounding* (Jack Williamson, Theodore Sturgeon, Fritz Leiber), it may have helped lead to the blurring of genre boundaries that became evident in later decades. In all, more than three dozen sf magazines were introduced between 1939 and 1950, many with clearly defined niches. One such niche worth noting was the reprint magazine: in 1939, the Munsey Company launched *Famous Fantastic Mysteries* under the editorship of Mary Gnaedinger, initially to reprint stories from older Munsey magazines. With its companion *Fantastic Novels*, the magazine not only brought older narrative traditions into the pulp marketplace, but helped introduce this newer generation of readers to 'classics' by A. Merritt, Ray Cummings and others. Classic reprints also made up the bulk of the *Avon Fantasy Reader* (1947–52) essentially a series of anthologies rather than a magazine, edited by Donald A. Wollheim and featuring Wells, Dunsany, Merritt, William Hope Hodgson and others (a companion *Avon Science Fiction Reader* lasted only three issues). Such reprint venues provided readers with a sense of the field's historical depth and its alliance with other fantastic genres, thus helping to shape the emerging canon of historically important authors.

In the 1950s, a newer generation of sf editors began to promulgate a view of sf that was both more socially liberal and broadly literary than anything Gernsback or Campbell had imagined. Social and economic satire became associated with Gold's aggressively hands-on editorship of *Galaxy* – which in its first few years published Alfred Bester's *The Demolished Man* (viewed by some historians as virtually a collaboration with Gold, so heavy was Gold's involvement), Robert A. Heinlein's *The Puppet Masters* and the stories which would become Frederik Pohl and C. M. Kornbluth's *The Space Merchants* and Ray Bradbury's *Fahrenheit 451*. Stylistic elegance became the hallmark of Anthony Boucher and J. Francis McComas at *The Magazine of Fantasy and Science Fiction*, which featured classic reprints as well as new fiction, and mixed literary fantasy with its sf. While the 1950s saw a boom in sf magazines that outstripped any previous era, with more than sixty new titles introduced during the decade, it was largely the directions established by *Galaxy* and *Fantasy and Science Fiction* that defined the tenor of the decade. Gold may not have single-handedly introduced irony into sf, but his interest in satire led to the publication in *Galaxy* of many of the acerbic tales of Robert Sheckley, as well as the darker satire of C. M. Kornbluth's 'The Marching Morons' and such absurdist economic fables as Frederik Pohl's 'The Midas Plague'. It is not surprising that Kurt Vonnegut, Jr's first appearances in an sf magazine were in *Galaxy*. Gold's willingness to entertain new voices led to the publication of early stories by Richard Matheson and, perhaps most dramatically, of 'Cordwainer Smith' (Paul Linebarger), whose radically defamiliarized and linguistically sophisticated fiction remains influential today. When Frederik Pohl assumed the editorship of *Galaxy* in 1961 – along with that of its lower-budget but more popular companion magazine *If* – this sense of impending revolution became even more pronounced, not only with additional Cordwainer Smith stories, but with unorthodox new fiction from Harlan Ellison, Robert Silverberg, R. A. Lafferty, Philip K. Dick and Roger Zelazny.

Some of these authors had been publishing sf for years, but for Ellison and Silverberg in particular, the *Galaxy* stories represented a new freedom of voice. *If*, meanwhile, combined traditional 'classic' sf (Heinlein, Van Vogt, even E. E. Smith) with authors who came to be associated with the 'New Wave' (Ballard, Delany, Ellison, including the latter's famous 'I Have No Mouth and I Must Scream'), despite Pohl's editorially stated objections to the movement.

The 'New Wave' itself, at least as a definable movement, was as much a creation of editors as of authors. Although it is often conveniently dated from Michael Moorcock's assumption of the editorship of the British magazine *New Worlds* in 1964, the magazine itself had existed in various incarnations since 1939 and had been published continuously since 1946 with John Carnell as editor. During the next two years, a colloquy of writers and fans met regularly at a London tavern (later memorialized in Arthur C. Clarke's collection *Tales from the White Hart*), eventually forming a company to assume publication of the magazine, which thus became one of the first successful sf magazines to escape the limitations of chain publishers. Brian Aldiss, John Brunner and Kenneth Bulmer became contributors, later joined by Ballard, Colin Kapp and James White. When declining circulation led to plans to fold the magazine in 1963, it was rescued by publisher David Warburton, who, at Carnell's suggestion, named Moorcock editor. Moorcock, in editorials, immediately began to proclaim a 'renaissance', and he featured an essay by Ballard touting the American novelist William Burroughs as a kind of model for the new sf. But at the beginning, Moorcock included much traditional sf together with the more adventurous work of himself, Ballard, Aldiss and such American writers as Thomas M. Disch and Roger Zelazny – dramatically establishing a contrast, which quickly became a controversy, between the old and new schools.

Without the accompanying proclamation of revolution, a similar contrast was also apparent in certain American magazines of this period. In addition to Pohl, the editor who may have done most to promote it was Cele Goldsmith, who had assumed the editorship of *Amazing* and *Fantastic* in 1958, and who featured the work not only of Disch, Zelazny, Aldiss and Ballard, but of Ursula K. Le Guin, Philip K. Dick and David R. Bunch. In retrospect, it may have been the eclecticism rather than the revolutionary impulses of these editors that provided the model for Gardner Dozois of *Isaac Asimov's Science Fiction Magazine*, whose long tenure (since 1986) is the most significant among sf magazine editors in the last several decades, and whose mix of literary stories (sometimes only minimally sf) with genre material has incorporated 'New Wave' and traditional sensibilities with far less controversy. Like *Interzone* in England (founded in 1982 by an editorial collective, but latterly edited by David Pringle alone), *Isaac Asimov's Science Fiction Magazine* features stories that incorporate elements of nearly all eras of recent science fiction history, indicating, perhaps, that the genre's various historical movements and styles have not been abandoned so much as subsumed.

## The anthologists

While the history of modern sf can, and often has been, written as the history of magazine editors, anthologists have also shaped the canon of the field for the better part of six decades, preserving stories that might otherwise have been ephemeral and helping establish a taxonomy of key themes and styles. Since so much of sf in its first several decades was confined to magazine publication (which could only support novels in the form of occasional serials or linked stories), the anthology became a crucial mechanism for introducing the genre into bookstores, circulating libraries and eventually classrooms. The first sf anthology clearly identified as such, Donald A. Wollheim's *The Pocket Book of Science Fiction* (1943), also established what would become an important link between the field and the then-nascent paperback industry. Later, a series of large hardbound anthologies edited by Groff Conklin, Raymond Healy and J. Francis McComas, John W. Campbell, August Derleth and others in the 1940s and early 1950s not only made their way into bookstores and libraries, but also gained the support of mainstream publishers such as Crown, Random House and Simon and Schuster, who at the time would hardly have considered mounting a line of novels from this still questionable genre. Editor Anthony Boucher once estimated that between 1949 and 1952, some 42 per cent of sf titles published were anthologies or story collections, compared to about 5 per cent in the novel-dominated mystery field.

Equally important, the anthologies afforded subsequent generations of readers, too young to have followed the pulps of the 1930s and 1940s, an opportunity to develop an historical sense of the field, its ongoing dialogue of ideas and techniques and its emerging canon of influential writers and stories. *Astounding*'s historical pre-eminence, for example, was no doubt enhanced by the editors of the 'big books' of sf that appeared between 1946 and 1952: no fewer than thirty-one of the thirty-five stories in Raymond Healy and J. Francis McComas's *Adventures in Time and Space* (1946, later, as *Famous Science Fiction Stories*, long kept in print as part of Random House's Modern Library) came from this magazine; adding to this the four Crown anthologies produced by Groff Conklin (*Best of Science Fiction*, 1946; *Treasury of*

*Science Fiction*, 1948; *Big Book of Science Fiction*, 1950; *Omnibus of Science Fiction*, 1952) and John W. Campbell, Jr's *Astounding Science Fiction Anthology* (1952), we find that nearly 140 stories from this single magazine were reprinted in these hardcovers in a six-year period. Still drawing heavily on *Astounding*, Conklin went on to pioneer the 'theme' anthology, illustrating how writers had developed dialogues on certain recurring tropes, with such titles as *Invaders of Earth* (1952), *Science Fiction Adventures in Dimension* (1953), *Science Fiction Thinking Machines* (1954) and *Science Fiction Adventures in Mutation* (1955).

Of the prolific anthologists of this era, only August Derleth argued for a more eclectic view of the field, including in his several anthologies selections from such magazines as *Weird Tales* and seeking deep historical roots in *Beyond Time and Space* (1950), which featured Plato, Lucian, Kepler and Francis Godwin alongside Wells, Stapledon, Sturgeon, Heinlein and Bradbury. To a great extent, the first short-fiction canon of sf was forged through the anthology movement of the 1950s. Of the twenty-six stories in Robert Silverberg's 1970 anthology *The Science Fiction Hall of Fame* – a collection of the best all-time sf stories as voted by the membership of the Science Fiction Writers of America – no fewer than fourteen had been collected in at least three anthologies or author collections prior to 1960, one (Arthur C. Clarke's 'The Nine Billion Names of God') as many as five times. And *The Science Fiction Hall of Fame* itself quickly demonstrated its own influence on the canon, at least in the academic sense: a 1996 survey conducted by the journal *Science-Fiction Studies* revealed it to be easily the most frequently assigned anthology as a text in sf literature courses offered in the United States and Canada, despite the availability of a number of anthologies specifically designed as college texts.

Anthologists helped shape the field in other crucial ways as well. In 1949, Everett F. Bleiler and T. E. Dikty published *The Best Science Fiction Stories, 1949*, inaugurating a tradition of annual 'year's best' anthologies that has continued in various incarnations and under various editors ever since. The Bleiler/Dikty series lasted until 1956, the same year that Judith Merril began what may have been the most influential of all such series, which lasted until 1968. Merril's ambitious agenda to expand the range of what might be considered sf – she included stories by John Steinbeck and Eugene Ionesco, and at one point even a *Pogo* comic strip by Walt Kelly – helped establish the notion that a 'year's best' might be used not merely as a recognition of excellence, but as a brief in support of a particular view of the field and its possibilities. By the mid 1970s, there were as many as four such anthologies appearing in a given year, each arguing for a somewhat different view of what the field was, or ought to be. Beginning in 1977, Gardner Dozois became the longest-running editor of such anthologies, editing one series from 1977 to 1981 and another from 1984 on, and for much of the 1990s enjoyed an unchallenged hegemony in the field. But in 1996 David Hartwell, arguing against what he perceived as a blurring of sf's identity in the Dozois annuals, began his own series.

Yet another manner in which anthologists altered the nature of the marketplace – and by extension the kinds of sf that could get published – began in 1951 when Raymond J. Healy, who together with J. Francis McComas had edited *Adventures in Time and Space,* published *New Tales of Space and Time*, pioneering the 'original anthology' of previously unpublished stories (although an earlier example, Donald A. Wollheim's *The Girl With Hungry Eyes*, had appeared from Avon in 1949), a trend which continued throughout the 1950s with Frederik Pohl's influential *Star Science Fiction* series (1953–9). Pohl's series, from Ballantine Books, also demonstrated the potential of the original anthology as a series, providing authors with instant access to book publication and an alternative to the relatively low-paying magazine markets. In the 1960s and 1970s, the original anthology series emerged as a major, and more risk-taking, competitor to the magazines, notably with John Carnell's *New Writings in SF* (1964–78, with Kenneth Bulmer editing after 1973), Damon Knight's *Orbit* (1965–80), Terry Carr's *Universe* (1971–87) and Robert Silverberg's *New Dimensions* (1971–81).

Anthologies have also helped provide a focus for what passes for literary movements in the sf field. If the New Wave in England was largely the construct of magazine editor Michael Moorcock, in the US it gained much of its identity and visibility from three key anthologies: Judith Merril's appallingly titled *England Swings SF* (1968), apparently conceived as a vanguard of a 'British invasion' comparable to that of rock music earlier in the decade, and Harlan Ellison's *Dangerous Visions* (1967) and *Again, Dangerous Visions* (1972), in which the introductions and afterwords by Ellison and his contributors proclaimed revolution at least as much as the stories themselves. Although, like Pohl, Ellison disdained the notion of a 'New Wave', he actually used the French equivalent of the term in describing *Dangerous Visions* as a demonstration of the '"nouvelle vague"', if you will, of speculative writing.'[1] Decades later, a similarly manifesto-like introduction, in Bruce Sterling's *Mirrorshades: The Cyberpunk Anthology* (1986), helped define the cyberpunk movement of the 1980s. And the 'renaissance' in Australian sf during the 1990s gained wide attention thanks to original anthologies such as Jack Dann and Janeen Webb's *Dreaming Down-Under* (1998) – a deliberate attempt to echo Ellison's *Dangerous Visions*, an Australian 'year's best' series begun by Jonathan Strahan and Jeremy Byrne in 1997, and David G.

Hartwell and Damien Broderick's *Centaurus: The Best Australian Science Fiction* (1999).

## The book editors

As the sf novel market emerged in the 1950s, a third kind of editor gained prominence in addition to the magazine editors and anthologists. While several specialty publishing houses, such as Arkham House, Shasta and Fantasy Press, had been formed in the 1940s to promote sf and fantasy in book form, most were the work of enthusiasts and fans still somewhat in awe of their authors, and professional editorial direction, by most evidence, was fairly minimal. This began to change in 1949 when two commercial publishers, Frederick Fell and Doubleday, decided to inaugurate programmes of sf. Fell concentrated on anthologies (Bleiler and Dikty's *Best Science Fiction Stories*, Donald A. Wollheim's *Every Boy's Book of Science-Fiction* and others), but Doubleday, with Walter Bradbury as its new sf editor, undertook serious efforts to develop new properties from promising writers. In that first year alone, Bradbury helped Isaac Asimov develop the novel that eventually became *Pebble in the Sky* (after failing to persuade Doubleday's board to take an interest in the Foundation series) and suggested to Ray Bradbury (no relation) that his various Martian stories published in the pulps could be collected as a linked sequence under the title *The Martian Chronicles*. According to Ray Bradbury, *The Illustrated Man* was also sold to Walter Bradbury on the same day. Under Walter Bradbury's guidance, Doubleday quickly emerged as the premier commercial publisher of hardbound sf in the 1950s, its eminence in the field rivaled only by the mostly paperback Ballantine Books.

Ballantine, founded in 1952 by Ian and Betty Ballantine (and initially headquartered in their New York apartment), is perhaps more important than any other publisher in establishing the long-standing linkage between sf and the paperback. As a student at the London School of Economics, Ian Ballantine had written an academic thesis on paperback publishing, and in 1939 he spearheaded the American distribution of England's Penguin line of paperbacks, which had begun in 1935 – four years before the vaunted American 'paperback revolution' began with Robert de Graff's Pocket Books in 1939. When the war interrupted Ballantine's supply of British paperbacks, he undertook a publishing programme of his own, adding cover illustrations to the print-only covers of the original Penguins. Allen Lane, Penguin's original publisher, was distressed by this, and it contributed to the differences in philosophy that led Ballantine to separate from Penguin in 1945. By August of that year, Ballantine and a hastily assembled group of editors and directors had founded Bantam Books, which would quickly prove to be the leading competitor to De Graff's Pocket Books. But by the early 1950s, over-production and unfavourable publicity in the paperback industry (which, along with comic books, became a focus of the notorious Select Committee on Current Pornographic Materials of the US House of Representatives, popularly known as the Gathings Committee) led to a series of crises, and Ballantine departed from Bantam in June 1952 to begin his own line. Although its original plan featured simultaneous hardcover and paperback editions, Ballantine soon became known principally as a paperback house, inaugurating its sf line in 1953 with Frederik Pohl and C. M. Kornbluth's *The Space Merchants*, followed by major works from Arthur C. Clarke, Theodore Sturgeon, Ray Bradbury and others. Ballantine's choice of Richard Powers's semi-abstract and surrealist artwork for the majority of the sf covers is also sometimes credited with having helped free the genre both from its pulp associations and from the lurid earlier history of American paperbacks.

At the same time that Ballantine was promoting the image of a more speculative and literary model of sf, Donald A. Wollheim at Ace Books was doing much to preserve the colourful adventure tradition of the pulps. Ace, founded by A. A. Wyn in 1953, featured more garish cover art (often by Ed Valigurski) and introduced the concept of the 'Ace Double' – two short books bound back-to-back, in what amounted to a two-for-one pricing gimmick. Wollheim, the sf editor at Avon from 1947 to 1952, had already demonstrated a talent for disguising relatively sophisticated work in pulpish packages – his paperback series at Avon introduced C. S. Lewis's *Out of the Silent Planet* trilogy to a mass-market audience – but at Ace he promoted an astute mix of theme anthologies (edited by himself), pulp space operas and newer authors: Harlan Ellison, Samuel R. Delany and Ursula K. Le Guin saw their first sf paperback publications as Ace Doubles. Terry Carr joined Wollheim at Ace in 1964, and proved to be an equally astute and even more innovative editor, introducing a series of 'Ace Specials' which included the first publications of such now-classic works as Le Guin's *The Left Hand of Darkness* and, when the series was revived after a hiatus of several years, William Gibson's *Neuromancer*. Carr and Wollheim also collaborated on a series of 'year's best' anthologies (although they later separated to produced competing annuals), and Carr initiated the important *Universe* series of original anthologies.

Wollheim left Ace in 1972 to form his own sf publishing enterprise, DAW Books (the name taken from his initials), where he continued to promote swashbuckling sf adventure tales, mixed with a good deal of fantasy and a series of retrospective author collections; among the most significant of the new sf writers he published was C. J. Cherryh. DAW Books was one of the first examples of an editor becoming a brand-name imprint in sf, and the distinctive yellow spines, cover art and typography reinforced this brand identity. Five years later, in 1977, Del Rey Books became another example, as an imprint of Ballantine Books. Judy-Lynn del Rey had been an unusually successful editor at Ballantine since 1973 – the year before Ian and Betty Ballantine left the company – and her most notable achievements included not only attracting new and veteran talent, but developing methods of pro-moting genre literature to best-seller status with such titles as Stephen R. Donaldson's fantasy trilogy *The Chronicles of Thomas Covenant the Un-believer*. (Although she was married to sf author and editor Lester del Rey, the imprint was named for her.) Although, like Wollheim and Carr, del Rey emerged more from the sf community than from the ranks of professional book editors, the marketing savvy that she developed helped promote the notion of the professional sf book editor, one whose background and ex-pertise lay specifically within the field, in contrast to earlier editors such as Walter Bradbury, who had been assigned to 'handle' sf as part of a broader range of editorial duties.

In England, a formal programme of sf publishing was not inaugurated until 1961, by Victor Gollancz (under the editorship of his nephew Hilary Rubinstein), although Gollancz had demonstrated interest in fantastic liter-ature since the firm's founding in 1928, and would eventually hire Malcolm Edwards, one of the most important British editors of the 1970s and later. In the early 1950s, however, support for sf was evident only through indi-vidual editors at a handful of publishing houses, one example being Charles Monteith at Faber and Faber, who reportedly rescued William Golding's *Lord of the Flies* (1954) from the 'slushpile' and who later not only com-missioned Brian Aldiss's first book, the non-sf *The Brightfount Diaries* (1955), but also published Aldiss's first sf novel, *Non-Stop*, in 1958. Other publishers, such as Weidenfeld and Nicolson and Grayson and Grayson also established sf lists, although not labelling them as such, and Michael Joseph (who had published John Wyndham's *The Day of the Triffids* in 1951) inaugurated a series of 'Novels of the Future', edited by the then sixty-seven-year-old novelist Clemence Dane, in 1955; John Christopher was among the authors featured. In the paperback field, sf publishing was unfortunately characterized in England in the 1950s by the undistin-guished (and sometimes appalling) production-line novels of firms such as Curtis Warren and Badger Books, which characteristically featured works written to specification by a stable of in-house writers, often using house pseudonyms.

By the 1980s, the discovery that certain genre works could be shrewdly marketed into best-sellers, together with the huge built-in sales of fiction linked to movies and TV (such as *Star Trek* or *Star Wars*) and added pressure on publishers from the increasingly dominant chain bookstores, exacerbated what had already been a long-standing tension in publishing between literary merit and market viability. Historically, with its comparatively narrow but dependable market, sf may have been less affected by this than mainstream fiction, but now that informal exemption had all but evaporated. The book editors who emerged in the 1970s and 1980s thus faced a new kind of challenge – a genre that was steadily growing more literary and complex and a market that rewarded the most familiar kinds of formula fiction. Among the best-known examples of this dilemma was the fate of Timescape Books, an imprint of Simon and Schuster and Pocket Books edited by David Hartwell from 1981 to 1984. Since the early 1970s Hartwell had established himself at several publishing houses as a strong advocate of literary sf, and his short tenure at Timescape produced some of the major works of the period – most notably Gene Wolfe's *Book of the New Sun* tetralogy, but also important titles by Gregory Benford, Michael Bishop and Philip K. Dick. Widely honoured within the field, the Timescape titles seldom attained the best-seller status that was now regarded as at least a potential for sf, and this, coupled with the general economic contraction of the early 1980s, led to the premature demise of what was among the most intelligently edited series of modern sf titles. Hartwell continued to be an influential and innovative editor, mostly at Tor Books (which has also employed such other important contemporary editors as Beth Meacham and Terri Windling, and which eventually became the leading American publisher of sf), and later editors were still able to develop specialized and sometimes semi-independent sf lines (Bantam Spectra, founded under Lou Aronica at Bantam in 1985; Baen Books, founded by Jim Baen in 1984; while in Britain Malcolm Edwards developed the sf line at Gollancz; John Jarrold developed Earthlight for Simon and Schuster; and Tim Holman Orbit, for Little, Brown). But the new economics of publishing and book distribution, which continued to accelerate throughout the 1990s, redefined the role of editors in crucial ways, often casting them in the role of advocates for the field's expanding literary possibilities while market pressures seemed to demand an increased reliance on proven formulas. By the beginning of the present century, authors of major blockbuster titles or franchise tie-ins seemed barely to be edited at all, while some of the most innovative writers came to depend on the determination and integrity of the field's most unsung champions. Although an argument might reasonably be made that much of sf's persistently marginal status in the literary arena is the result of editorial exigency or stubbornness during the field's formative years, it is almost certain that the field could not have evolved to its modern level of complexity and variety without the energetic and persistent advocacy of its best editors.

## NOTE

1. Harlan Ellison, in Ellison, ed. *Dangerous Visions* (Garden City, NY: Doubleday, 1967), p. xx.

# 2

# CRITICAL APPROACHES

# 7

ISTVAN CSICSERY-RONAY, JR

# Marxist theory and science fiction

## Marxism, science fiction and utopia

Marxist theory has played an important role in sf criticism, especially in the last third of the past century. Since the 1960s, many of the most sophisticated studies of sf have been either explicitly Marxist in orientation or influenced by Marxist concepts adopted by feminism, race-criticism, queer theory and cultural studies. Although relatively few critics and writers in the genre have been avowed adherents of Marxism, sf and the closely related genre of utopian fiction have deep affinities with Marxist thought in particular, and socialist thought in general. In its simplest terms, sf and utopian fiction have been concerned with imagining progressive alternatives to the status quo, often implying critiques of contemporary conditions or possible future outcomes of current social trends. Science fiction, in particular, imagines change in terms of the whole human species,[1] and these changes are often the results of scientific discoveries and inventions that are applied by human beings to their own social evolution. These are also the concerns of the Marxist utopian and social imagination.

Marx's system combined a sophisticated critique of the capitalist economic system, a conception of history as the dialectical process of human self-construction, and a vision of a universally just and democratic way of life in the future as the goal of human history. Although Marxism's role as a political practice and prophetic mode has weakened with the collapse of the Soviet bloc and the ascendancy of multinational capitalism, many of its key concepts have been adopted by other critical social movements and branches of scholarship. Race-critical and feminist thought has borrowed the Marxist historical model, substituting people of colour and women for the working class as emphasized historical agents. It frequently models racism and sexism on bourgeois ideology, as racial hegemony and patriarchy are modelled on the capitalist mode of production. Thus marginalized humanity acts like the proletariat in a model of progressive coming-to-consciousness and revelation of the contradictions between ideology and its practice. Cultural studies have employed fundamental Marxian concepts to trace the dialectical relations of social groups to entrenched power and to each other through the medium of culture.[2]

From its earliest forms, utopian fiction has depicted imaginary just and rational societies established in opposition to exploitative worldly ones. Marx was famously reluctant to describe the utopian society that would succeed the successful proletarian revolution, describing it only in the vaguest terms in the conclusion of the *Communist Manifesto*. Nonetheless he affirmed its importance as an historical goal. Marx also valued technology as a vital tool of human liberation. He believed that in a just world technological innovations were the guarantors of human freedom from toil, just as they were also the means of mass enslavement in an exploitative order. These ideas were forged in Marxist thought into a story of social and technological liberation that had clear affinities with the basic stories of sf.

Utopian socialist thinking was one of the strongest formative influences on sf of the late nineteenth century, especially in the English-speaking world and Russia. The most important figures in the development of Anglophone sf in the thirty years between the mid 1880s and the beginning of the First World War – Edward Bellamy, William Morris, H. G. Wells and Jack London – were all socialists. Although of these only London was avowedly Marxist, all shared the notion that scientific and utopian romance were allied with the social reform of amoral laissez-faire capitalism. In the West, Wells's influence was greater than Marx's in this context. His utopian writings – in works such as *A Modern Utopia* (1905), *The World Set Free* (1914) and *Men Like Gods* (1923) – enjoyed great international popularity, and his favoured model of a technocratic world-state run by enlightened scientists and engineers dominated much of social thought on the Left before the 1930s.

One would expect Marxism to have influenced conceptions of sf in the Soviet Union, as Marxism-Leninism was the official state philosophy. Utopian sf was an important genre of political fantasy among radicals before 1917, and among the populace at large in the first years of the Revolution. Beginning in the early 1920s, however, Soviet writers were discouraged from writing utopian fantasy that might raise popular expectations and imply criticism of present conditions. The discouragement became active suppression with Stalin's 'doctrine of near limits'. Writers were to concentrate on heroicizing the tasks of the present. Science fiction and utopian fiction, it was claimed, no longer had a role in a socialist society. As a consequence, no serious sf, let alone criticism and theory, was published in the USSR until after the death of Stalin in 1953.[3]

In the late 1950s, grand-scale socialist-utopian sf began to be written again, inspired by Ivan Yefremov's ground-breaking *Andromeda* (1959). A boom of inventive sf followed in the so-called 'thaw' period of the late 1950s and early 1960s, best represented by the work of the Strugatsky brothers. Both Yefremov and the Strugatskys were criticized for deviating from the Party's prescriptions – Yefremov for abandoning the image of 'Socialist Man' and depicting his heroes as quasi-divine, the Strugatskys for depicting characters insufficiently heroic to represent Socialist Man.[4] As reaction intensified during the 1970s and 1980s, Soviet sf writers became increasingly critical, and were often forced to publish in samizdat (privately duplicated underground publications). There was no taste for defending critical sf in Marxist language. Under these conditions, no serious theory of sf was framed in Marxist terms.

In the USA, where sf developed through the pulps into a powerful form of popular literature, socialist ideas had little influence after the First World War. Wells remained the most powerful model in the genre, but American sf writers took from him primarily the justification for a technocratic elite. The model protagonist of US sf was not the socialist scientist working for the scientific reorganization of humanity, but the polymathic engineer-adventurer-entrepreneur embodied in the figure of the individual genius-inventor, Edison.[5] After the Russian Revolution, the community of sf writers became increasingly not only anti-communist, but anti-socialist as well. With the Second World War and its aftermath, anti-communism so pervaded American life that Marxist thought became anathema. A few writers persevered by writing anti-capitalist satires, such as Frederik Pohl and Cyril Kornbluth and the socialist Mack Reynolds, but most sf writers (many of whom, like the Futurians, had Leftist sympathies in the 1930s) had become anti-socialists, and their sf depicted laissez-faire capitalism and individualism as the natural order of the future. Science fiction films gained a new form of popularity by allegorizing McCarthyite hysteria. The word 'utopian' became associated in the popular mind with Soviet communism, and sf of the immediate postwar period was dominated by anti-utopian themes.

This anti-radical and anti-utopian climate changed dramatically in the 1960s. Inspired by the civil-rights struggle and the sudden independence of many of the European colonies, and supported by unprecedented affluence and technological development in the capitalist democracies, an international contestatory culture set itself in opposition to the institutions and policies of the bourgeois state. The movement had an enormous diversity of goals, but they shared two characteristics relevant in this context: a respect for Marxist ideas and what Italo Calvino called 'a utopian charge',[6] a powerful, unformed desire to rid the world of poverty, racism, sexual repression and

economic exploitation – sins that Marxist thought had convincingly theorized as endemic and necessary aspects of bourgeois state-capitalism. This
conjunction had a inspirational effect on the genre of sf, as well. Intellec-
tuals and students initiated a mass-project of imagining alternatives to the
bipolar, irrationally militarized world order of the Cold War. A multitude of
alternative intentional communities were attempted, and cultural life was increasingly marked by criticisms of the status quo from imaginary standpoints
where the problems of the present were resolved, even if uncertainly. Science
fiction became one of the privileged instruments of this current of thought.
Works such as Frank Herbert's *Dune* (1965), Robert Heinlein's *Stranger in
a Strange Land* (1961), Kurt Vonnegut's *Cat's Cradle* (1963) and *Sirens of
Titan* (1959) enjoyed immense popularity unprecedented for works of sf.

The utopian charge was released in many forms: philosophical anarchism,
Left Nietzscheanism, a proto-Green movement, psychedelic libertarianism
and perhaps most influential of all, the conflation of the Marxist critique of
oppression with the Freudian analysis of repression, the so-called Freudo-
Marxism most visibly promulgated by Herbert Marcuse. This constellation
had two, uneasily allied aspects. On the one hand, there was the New Left's
emphasis on utopian critique and liberation from commodification; on the
other, an anti-colonial, revolutionary, quasi-Leninist politics of national,
ethnic and class resistance. The former emphasized critical consciousness of
culture, the latter class-consciousness as a prerequisite for violent resistance
and revolution. The two overlapped primarily in their critique of capitalism.

With time, the popular desire to imagine alternatives and to formulate
imaginative critiques became narrowly limited to cultural theory. The hopeful student uprisings throughout the world in 1968 did not seriously affect the
structure of the capitalist state – nor indeed, in the case of the Prague Spring,
the communist state. In Europe and the US, extremist movements acted out a
violent politics of despair in the name of Leninist revolution, turning people
increasingly towards the protections of increasingly repressive governments.
In Britain, where Marxist thought had remained grounded in trade-union
activism, Marxist cultural theory developed within the context of the practical sociology of class cultures, with little recourse to utopian theory.
Consequently, no body of Marxist sf theory emerged there (despite the
occasional interest in sf shown by Raymond Williams, one of the guiding
theorists of materialist cultural studies).[7]

## New Marxist criticism in the USA

In the USA, by contrast, there was an explosion of interest in sf, not only
by Left academics and students, but in mass culture as well. A new style of

artistically ambitious and politically sophisticated sf took shape, exemplified by the work of Philip K. Dick, Joanna Russ, Ursula K. Le Guin and Samuel R. Delany. The preconditions for the crystallization of a radical sf theory were in place.

In the mid 1970s Marxist theorists of sf found themselves in a dilemma. On the one hand, sf was generally held by educated readers (including most Marxist theorists) to be artistically negligible; moreover, because the vast bulk of sf was written for mass entertainment, it manifestly eschewed social criticism and supported the dominant ideology of bourgeois individualism. This was especially true in the USA, where most sf was produced and consumed. For some Marxist critics, sf was a particularly egregious example of ideological complicity with established capitalist interests. The work of H. Bruce Franklin in the USA, in particular, focused on this aspect of the genre. Franklin's biography of Robert A. Heinlein (1980) identified the notoriously individualistic author with US imperialism in the ongoing Vietnam War. In later essays and the book *War Stars* (1988), Franklin argued more persuasively, if not more subtly, that sf had been a major inspiration, indeed an imaginative engine, for the development of super-weapons of mass destruction, and thus bore a tremendous weight of historical guilt. In these and similar works on sf and the Vietnam War, Franklin set out to illuminate the insidious ideological force of an apparently harmless form of entertainment with the urgency and anger of a insurrectionist critic.[8]

The main developments of sf theory, however, went along a different path. In 1973, Darko Suvin and R. D. Mullen founded *Science-Fiction Studies*, which was to become the primary venue for neo-Marxist criticism of sf. The journal did not profess a single direction and published important sf scholarship by many non-Marxist writers (Mullen himself was not a Marxist), yet it became the home for a group of Marxist theorist-critics who agreed on certain premises and extended each other's ideas. In addition to Suvin, they included Fredric Jameson, Peter Fitting, Tom Moylan, Marc Angenot and Carl Freedman. Although it would be misleading to speak of a *Science-Fiction Studies* 'school', most of these writers relied on, and elaborated, the concept of the 'critical utopia' (as it was to be eventually named by Moylan) as the central core of the sf imagination.

The 'critical utopia' derives from certain ideas important in the tradition of Hegelian Marxism, represented in the works of T. W. Adorno, Walter Benjamin, Ernst Bloch, Antonio Gramsci and Raymond Williams, and certain works of Georg Lukács that analysed culture as an aspect of class-domination in order to construct a disciplined resisting consciousness. This direction had, in a sense, abandoned one of the cherished premises of Marxism: the belief in an imminent emancipatory revolution by the working class. After the success of the Nazis, Soviet communism and state capitalism in manipulating the masses, these thinkers reconceived utopia to signify an emancipatory mode of thought that keeps alive the hope for social justice and equality. Articulated most fully by Bloch, this utopia is simultaneously a wish-dream of a happy and enlightened social life, and a tool with which to identify and attack the ideological obstacles to achieving utopia.

In his book *Metamorphoses of Science Fiction* (1979), Suvin introduced a number of ideas that remain central in sf criticism: cognitive estrangement, the novum and sf's genetic link with utopia. In the notion of cognitive estrangement, Suvin conflated two distinct, but related, ideas of estrangement from earlier literary theory: *ostranenie* (de-familiarization) from the Russian Formalists, and Berthold Brecht's *Verfremdungseffekt* (alienation effect). The Formalists had claimed that art always makes the receiver aware of reality in an intensely fresh way, by subverting and 'roughening' the habitual responses one develops in the routines of everyday existence. Brecht had adapted the Formalists' idea to theatre, proposing that estrangement should be an explicitly political act, which draws the audience's attention to the fact that the spectacle they are witnessing is an illusion, stimulating the crowd to become aware of their situation as passive receivers, an awareness they might then extend to reflection about their similar situation in the manipulated illusion-world of bourgeois domination.

Suvin argued that an sf text presents aspects of a reader's empirical reality 'made strange' through a new perspective 'implying a new set of norms'.[9] This recasting of the familiar has a 'cognitive' purpose, that is, the recognition of reality it evokes from the reader is a gain in rational understanding of the social conditions of existence. Science-fictional estrangement works like scientific modelling: the familiar (that is, naturalized) situation is either rationally extrapolated to reveal its hidden norms and premises (as for example, the fantastic evolutionary projection of the Victorian class system into Morlocks and Eloi in *The Time Machine*, 1895), or it is analogically displaced on to something unfamiliar in which the invisible (because too-familiar) elements are seen freshly as alien phenomena (as in *The War of the Worlds*, 1898, in which British imperialism is displaced on to invading Martians). The specific difference between sf and other estranging genres, such as fantasy, is that sf's displacements must be logically consistent and methodical; in fact, they must be scientific to the extent that they imitate, reinforce and illuminate the process of scientific cognition.

Even more influential in sf theory than cognitive estrangement is Suvin's concept of the novum. The novum is the historical innovation or novelty in an sf text from which the most important distinctions between the world of the tale from the world of the reader stem. It is, by definition, rational, as opposed to the supernatural intrusions of marvellous tales, ghost stories, high fantasy and other genres of the fantastic. In practice, the novum appears as an invention or a discovery around which the characters and setting organize themselves in a cogent, historically plausible way. The novum is a product of material processes; it produces effects that can be logically derived from the novum's causes, in the material and social worlds; and it is plausible in terms of historical logic, whether it be in the history of technoscience or other social institutions.

Suvin adopts the concept of the novum from the work of Ernst Bloch, for whom the term refers to those concrete innovations in lived history that awaken human collective consciousness out of a static present to awareness that history can be changed. The novum thus inspires hope for positive historical transformations. The value of such a philosophy of future orientation for an understanding of sf should be obvious, for sf as a genre depends on its readers' unquenchable desire to imagine more or less plausible transformations of the quotidian, whether those transformations lead to greater freedom, to technological despotism, a linguistically unimaginable transcendence or even merely a different everyday world.

The novum and cognitive estrangement together characterize a mode of thinking that is not only science fictional, but also utopian, as the term is used by Bloch. Together they critique empirical reality and imagine an alternative to it. For this reason Suvin argues that true sf is genetically linked to the genre of literary utopia. Bloch argued that all manifestations of culture, even artistically worthless escapist formulas, include some utopian aspect, if only because they deny conditions as they are and activate wishes to make life manageable and pleasurable. This combination of critical denial and wish-fulfilment is particularly active in sf, since it is concerned with the wishing into being of imaginary worlds constructed on ostensibly rational principles.

Carl Freedman, in *Critical Theory and Science Fiction* (2000), a work very much in the Suvinian mold, has pointed out that Suvin's strictures would lead to the exclusion from the ranks of sf of most works generally viewed as sf but with little 'cognitive' value (such as *Star Wars* (1977) and *E.T.* (1982), for example). 'Science fiction' is consequently both a descriptive and an evaluative term for Suvin: bad sf is not sf. Suvin's criteria for judging the aesthetic worth of sf similarly have less to do with the terms of art than with terms of knowledge of social truth. Freedman suggests that Suvin's category can be made valid by thinking of sf not in terms of real cognition, but as a 'cognition effect' – a rhetorical construction that evokes the sense of true cognition. Freedman notes that the knowledge one gains in a work of sf is often entirely imaginary, although it may be based on solid scientific principles. In other respects, Freedman's conception of sf recapitulates that of Suvin: sf implies critical utopias even when it does not construct them explicitly in the narrative. Freedman goes even further in suggesting that this critical utopian function characterizes all of critical theory after Kant, but most particularly Marxist theory. Science fiction in this sense is the genre whose essence is critical utopian imagining, and thus even nonfictional critical theory might be considered a form of sf, thereby extending the conception of sf and science-fictionality beyond the boundaries of literary genre to encompass philosophical theory.

Most of the critical work of the Marxist scholars associated with *Science-Fiction Studies*, and later also *Utopian Studies*, was devoted to two practical purposes. The first was to identify recent works of sf that could model the dual function of critical utopias, that is, to criticize the status quo and to offer hopeful alternatives, thereby alerting readers to potentially subversive works, and cultivating radical inspiration. Certain works and writers clearly fit the requirements well, since they had helped inspire the idea of a critical utopia in sf in the first place. Foremost among these were Le Guin's *The Dispossessed* (1974), Russ's *The Female Man* (1975), Delany's *Triton* (1976) and Marge Piercy's *Woman on the Edge of Time* (1976). These novels estranged not only the empirical reality, but the concept of utopia itself, in Moylan's words 'rejecting it as blueprint while preserving it as dream'.[10] The second goal was to identify and elaborate the critical-utopian content in those complex sf texts that reveal the irremovable contradictions of bourgeois ideology while they strive to contain and resolve them. The model here was Philip K. Dick, who was the subject of more Marxist analyses than any other sf writer and inspired some of the finest textual criticism by Marxist critics. In Dick they saw a writer who, although averse to all forms of political theory, reflected the paranoia, insecurity and mundane chaos that were the true social conditions of his society. Arguably, these works constitute a canon of the superior texts and writers of the age against which others should be measured. In his book *Demand the Impossible* (1986), Moylan bestows this status on the four works listed above. In a later book, *Scraps of the Untainted Sky* (2000), he expanded the canon to include 'critical dystopias', works whose dark image of society stems from a thwarted utopian desire. It is too soon to know whether these works – Kim Stanley Robinson's Orange Country trilogy (*The Wild Shore*, 1984, *The Gold Coast*, 1986 and *Pacific Edge*, 1990), Octavia Butler's Parable books (*Parable of the Sower*, 1993, *Parable of the Talents*, 1998), and Marge Piercy's *He, She and It* (1991;

UK, *Body of Glass*) – will be accepted as a canon similar to that of critical utopias.

## Jameson: unimaginable futures

A different path was taken by Fredric Jameson, perhaps the most sophisticated and influential Marxist cultural theorist in the Anglophone world. He approached sf in terms of the problematics of 'generic discontinuities', world-reduction and spatialization that would later be transformed into themes in his writings on postmodernism. For Jameson, sf was interesting less as a source of critical utopias, than as a space to analyse the aesthetic problems of form, genre, character and setting through which contemporary science fiction worked out ideologically fundamental problems of the late-modern world view. As is characteristic of the oblique approach of all of Jameson's work, he singled out eccentric and emphatically non-canonical texts – works that cannot be identified with utopian, let alone Marxist thought: Brian Aldiss's *Non-Stop* (USA: *Starship*) (1958), Le Guin's *The Left Hand of Darkness* (1969) (rather than the 'canonical' *The Dispossessed*), Dick's *Dr Bloodmoney* (1965) (rather than *Ubik*) and Vonda McIntyre's *The Exile Waiting* (1975).

Jameson's work in the 1980s departed from the mainline of utopian Marxist sf criticism. The latter strove to assert the positive, enlightening and hope-giving potential of sf as the bearer of historical consciousness in the dark age of totalitarian capitalism. Jameson, by contrast, concentrated on the concept of negative totality, which, in his usage, came to stand as the dialectical opposite of utopia. In this sense, totality is the concept of the total system of capitalist relations to which the world is subject. In his most influential essay in sf theory, 'Progress versus Utopia' (1982),[11] Jameson argued that science fictions are fantastic displacements of the present's ideological contradictions into the future; at best, major reflective works of sf can make us aware that we are unable to imagine any utopian transformations. 'Progress versus Utopia' presages Jameson's well-known concept, articulated in *Postmodernism, The Cultural Logic of Late Capitalism* (1991), of the need for, and the extreme difficulty of, 'cognitive mapping' of the totality of hegemonic supranational capitalism.[12]

Jameson's interest in using sf to help make such a cognitive map has continued, in his use of Dick and J. G. Ballard to represent the breakdown of modernist space–time in *Postmodernism*, and in more hopeful recent essays on the Mars trilogy of Kim Stanley Robinson, one of the few sf writers who treats Marxist and utopian ideas as having vitality in the future.

## Postmodernism and cyborg socialism

The critical utopian current of Marxist sf theory has been criticized for being narrow, if deep.[13] Restrictive in its normative conception of the genre, it has tended to look for ideal types and exemplars, which acquire canonical status. Because most sf is ideologically and aesthetically compromised, the utopian Marxist theorists have avoided dealing with the virtues of many of the works that have had the greatest mass appeal. Their construction of the genre has been, de facto, from the top down. They have, arguably, abdicated saying much about sf as a cultural institution, or about the hybrids and mutants that might arise out of the actually existing genre. Contemporary Marxist sf theory from the European tradition can be accused of paying insufficient attention to the ways technoscientific innovations have transformed social life globally – to their potential to transform the means of production, and with them world models, cultural values and human bodies. Jameson has taken on the challenge, after a fashion, in his work on postmodernism and Third World cinema, but his interest in this area is primarily in the effect of technology on art, drawing conclusions about world-currents through elite artefacts. Quick to view technosocial changes in terms of negative totality, Jameson rarely treats the phenomena that occupy the attention of sf readers, sf writers and the multitudes of people who think science-fictionally – that is, of being rapidly and chaotically immersed in new technologies that lead to new kinds of knowledge and new possibilities of social evolution.

The distance of this line of theory from feminism is striking. Although their critical canon includes a few feminist works (mainly by Piercy and Russ), critical utopian theorists have shown relatively little interest in feminist theory, which has actually become a science fiction-like enterprise in some of its manifestations. Feminist thought, in turn, has increasingly turned away from the Marxist analytic to which it once owed its progressive historical model. An important exception is Donna Haraway, whose profoundly influential reconceptualization of the cyborg fuses the sf imagination, historical materialism and feminism. For Haraway, contemporary technoscience has decisively promoted the breakdown of categories previously thought to be natural and inviolable – such as those between the genders, between animals and humans and between humans and machines. As identities are broken down and dispersed, the network of connections, created originally as a tool for the extension of capitalist domination, has ironically created a new form of social being, the cyborg. The cyborg in Haraway's usage is obliquely modelled on the proletariat and on women under patriarchy; it is an exploited class of beings that is capable of a form of class-consciousness, and hence subversive of and eventually capable of wresting control over the technoscientific network.

Haraway's world-picture is explicitly derived from sf, from which she wrested the notion of the cyborg and transformed it into the positive agent of historical transformation. In her audacious vision 'the boundary between science fiction and social reality is an optical illusion'.[14] She has used her model for powerful readings of the works of Octavia Butler, Joanna Russ and other feminist sf writers.[15] Haraway's work is in many ways more intimately connected than that of the critical utopians with the technoscientific languages that pervade postmodern culture, and that have become the currency for sf writers. Moreover, as a theory of political networks, cyborg theory also implies forms of activism – and this activism often envisions itself in terms of the 'ironic myths' of sf. At the same time it must be said that Haraway, too, has shown little interest in sf as a cultural practice, restricting herself to texts that speak to cyborg feminism.

It is telling that neither of the two most important directions of Marxist sf theory refers to the other's work. Marxist sf theory may thus be at a point when it can no longer claim to be adequate for a radically fluid postmodern reality, or at the threshold of a synthetic view that will be useful for 'mapping' the social metamorphoses of cyborg science and the efflorescence of sf that attends it.

## NOTES

1. James Gunn, Introduction, in Gunn, ed., *The Road to Science Fiction. Volume 6: Around the World* (Clarkston, GA: Borealis, 1998), p. 17.
2. Cf. Cary Nelson, *et al.*, 'Cultural Studies: An Introduction', in Lawrence Grossberg *et al.*, eds. *Cultural Studies* (New York: Routledge, 1992), pp. 5ff.
3. See Leonid Heller, *De la science-fiction soviétique* (Geneva: L'Age d'homme, 1979), pp. 52ff.
4. *Ibid.*, pp. 66–9, 78.
5. On the Edisonade, see Brooks Landon, *Science Fiction after 1900* (New York: Twayne, 1997), pp. 42–9.
6. Italo Calvino, *The Uses of Literature* (New York: Harcourt, 1982), p. 247.
7. Williams's previously unreprinted essay of 1956, 'Science Fiction', appears online at http://www.depauw.edu/sfs/documents/williams.htmessays. His 'Utopia and Science Fiction' appeared in *Science-Fiction Studies* 5:3 (November 1978), pp. 203–14.
8. H. Bruce Franklin, 'Star Trek in the Vietnam Era', *Science-Fiction Studies* 21:1 (March 1994) and 'The Vietnam War as American SF and Fantasy', *Science-Fiction Studies* 17:3 (November 1990).
9. Darko Suvin, *Metamorphoses of Science Fiction* (New Haven, CT: Yale University Press, 1979), p. 6.
10. Tom Moylan, *Demand the Impossible* (London: Methuen, 1986), p. 61.

11. *Science-Fiction Studies* 9:2 (July 1982), pp. 147–58.
12. My discussion of Jameson's cognitive mapping owes much to Tom Moylan's *Scraps of the Untainted Sky* (Boulder, CO: Westview, 2000), pp. 56–62.
13. Cf. Patrick Parrinder, 'Revisiting Suvin's Poetics of Science Fiction', in Parrinder, ed., *Learning from Other Worlds* (Liverpool: Liverpool University Press, 2000), pp. 36–50.
14. Donna Haraway, *Simians, Cyborgs, and Women* (New York: Routledge, 1991), p. 148.
15. Haraway discusses the sf basis of her cyborg in 'A Cyborg Manifesto' reprinted in *ibid.*, pp. 176–81.

# 8

VERONICA HOLLINGER

# Feminist theory and science fiction

Boy meets girl. Boy loses girl. Boy builds girl.
> (Anonymous, 'The Shortest Science Fiction Story Ever Written')

[I]t lifted her heart to think of the stories being written now, new stories, stories of the Free. That was why writing was so important.
> (Suzy McKee Charnas)[1]

## Feminist reading

Like most theoretical projects, feminist thought has generated a variety of conceptual models that, in turn, suggest particular reading strategies encompassing diverse and sometimes conflicting perspectives.[2] Many feminist scholars undertake humanist-oriented literary analysis, while the materialist critiques of Marxist and socialist feminists and the philosophical deconstructions of French feminists have posed challenges to such relatively straightforward reading practices. Some of the most powerful recent critiques of subject and gender construction have been undertaken by queer-feminists such as Teresa de Lauretis and Judith Butler (see Wendy Pearson and Helen Merrick in this volume). Other critical models, of particular interest in the context of sf, have been suggested by cyber-theorists such as Donna Haraway and N. Katherine Hayles, who are concerned with how developments in contemporary science and technology – for instance, advances in reproductive and communications technologies – are shaping and will continue to shape the lives of women. Whatever their founding assumptions, however, all feminist theories resist the ideological self-representations of the masculinist cultural text that traditionally offers itself as the universal expression of a homogeneous 'human nature'. As history since the Enlightenment has demonstrated, more often than not the subject of that universal 'human nature' has been white, male and middle-class. In the narratives of this subject, women have tended to play supporting roles as the 'others' of men – emoting bodies to their reasoning minds and nature to their culture. Only rarely have women been represented as subjects in their own right.

Unlike some theoretical positions – for example, deconstruction or phenomenology – feminist theory has developed as part of a consciously political project. Quite simply, feminism works to achieve social justice for women. It aims to render obsolete the patriarchal order whose hegemony has meant inequality and oppression for women as the 'others' of men. In other words, feminism desires nothing less than to change the world. Feminist reading, then, is not just reading *about* women; it is reading *for* women. In some instances, feminist reading remains more or less consonant with a text's own overt interests and emphases. In other cases, however, the feminist reader is what Judith Fetterley has termed a 'resisting reader',[3] one who activates elements in a text which may be neither dominant nor deliberate. In this instance, feminist reading will often amount to a critique of a particular text's narrative project.

One very obvious example of early sf's masculinist orientation is Lester del Rey's story, 'Helen O'Loy' (1938). The title character – whose name deliberately recalls the beautiful Helen of Troy – is a robot programmed to be the perfect woman; del Rey's narrator describes her as 'one part beauty, one part dream, one part science'.[4] It does not take a very sophisticated reading to appreciate how this story, a rather conventional power fantasy about the creation of artificial life, participates in Western culture's long-standing marginalization of women. As in many stories of this kind, the result is a 'woman' built to the specifications of men, a 'woman' with virtually no individuality or agency, a technological triumph that displaces women.[5] While the scientific project in this story is not unlike that of Mary Shelley's early nineteenth-century Faustian over-reacher, Victor Frankenstein, Shelley's character pays heavily for what he accomplishes in his 'workshop of filthy creation',[6] losing everyone dear to him before himself suffering a miserable death. In glaring contrast, del Rey's scientist, product of a national and historical moment at once more naive and more optimistic about the potential of burgeoning technology, gets to live happily ever after with the perfect 'woman'.

Although sf has often been called 'the literature of change', for the most part it has been slow to recognize the historical contingency and cultural conventionality of many of our ideas about sexual identity and desire, about gendered behaviour and about the 'natural' roles of women and men. 'Helen O'Loy' represents gender as an essential feature of human nature. It assumes that the social roles played by women and men *as women and men* are ahistorical, that they will remain largely unchanged even in the distant future. Feminist reading not only notes the literal absence of women in del Rey's narrative universe, but also undertakes to examine critically the features of the artificial replacement – the simulacrum of perfect lover and perfect wife – whose representation serves to maintain this absence.

It is heartening to juxtapose 'Helen O'Loy' against a story published only a few years later by the very popular Golden Age writer, C. [Catherine] L. Moore.[7] 'No Woman Born' (1944) is the story of Deirdre, a world-famous actor and singer, 'the loveliest creature whose image ever moved along the airways'.[8] After her body is destroyed in a theatre fire, she sets out to rebuild her career using the gleaming metallic body designed for her by the scientist Maltzer. Most of Moore's long story unfolds around the question of whether or not Deirdre is still a woman, indeed whether or not she is still human. These oppositions – 'real' woman against 'imitation' woman, natural body against techno-body – structure the conflict between Deirdre, who plans to resume her performing career in spite of her cyborg status, and the two men who are closest to her, Maltzer, her 'maker', and Harris, her manager. The more Deirdre proves to them that she can still cast her spell over an audience – 'She threw her head back and let her body sway and her shoulders shake, and the laughter, like the music, filled the theater ... And she was a woman now. Humanity had dropped over her like a tangible garment'[9] – the more they worry that she has become a kind of monster. Although Maltzer, in a fit of egocentric guilt, compares himself to Shelley's Frankenstein, however, Deirdre is no Helen O'Loy: 'I'm not a Frankenstein monster made out of dead flesh. I'm myself – alive. I'm not a robot, with compulsions built into me that I have to obey. I'm free-willed and independent, and ... I'm human.'[10]

'Helen O'Loy' demonstrates sf's conventional blindness to potential changes in how women and men are defined and constructed as individuals with differently sexed bodies, differently informed desires, and differently gendered social roles. In contrast, 'No Woman Born' demonstrates the potential of science fiction to disrupt its own constructions of the feminine in particular, and of the sex/gender system in general, while making clever use of some of the same strategies found in male-authored sf – notably, a male point-of-view character and the association of the feminine with the monstrous.[11] Through the figure of its cyborg/subject, Moore's story avoids constructing a simple opposition between the natural body and the technological body. It also raises doubts about 'woman' as an essential definitional category and it questions the distinction between *being* a woman and *performing* femininity.

In spite of the still popular conception of sf as inherently masculinist, it is in the interests of feminist readers to look closely at its potential for imaginative re-presentations of the gendered subject, for re-presentations of difference and diversity. As Teresa de Lauretis has argued, one crucial facet of the feminist project is 'the telling of new stories so as to inscribe into the picture of reality characters and events and resolutions that were previously invisible, untold, unspoken (and so unthinkable, unimaginable, "impossible")'.[12]

## Utopia and defamiliarization

'Helen O'Loy' is a fantasy about the gendered power of science written decades before the Anglo-American and European feminist revolutions of the 1960s and 1970s began to have a significant impact on the sf field. This does not mean, however, that women were not actively involved as readers, writers and fans in the years preceding these upheavals.[13] Many readers locate the 'origin' of sf in Mary Shelley's *Frankenstein* (1818), a text which lends itself to strong feminist interpretations. The work of popular writers such as Leslie F. Stone, Francis Stevens, C. L. Moore, Naomi Mitchison, Leigh Brackett, E. Mayne Hull, Andre Norton and Marion Zimmer Bradley during the 1930s, 1940s and 1950s helped to establish a tradition that in turn provided some of the necessary impetus for the explosion of writing by women in the 1970s, notably including Ursula K. Le Guin's ground-breaking study of gender's grip on human culture in *The Left Hand of Darkness* (1969) and Joanna Russ's formally experimental deconstruction of female subjectivity in *The Female Man* (1975). This is also the period during which feminist authors virtually reinvented the genre of utopian fiction, producing classics such as Marge Piercy's *Woman on the Edge of Time* (1976), James Tiptree, Jr's 'Houston, Houston, Do You Read?' (1976) and the first two novels of Suzy McKee Charnas's Holdfast Chronicles, *Walk to the End of the World* (1974) and *Motherlines* (1978). It is also significant that many challenges to the conventions of male/female relations have focused on a radical critique of these relations as based in the inequities of what Adrienne Rich first identified as 'compulsory heterosexuality'.[14] This is attested to by an influential body of lesbian and queer-feminist sf and utopian fiction, ranging from 'When It Changed' (1972), Russ's elegiac depiction of the all-women planet of Whileaway at the moment when it is visited by men for the first time in six hundred years, to the award-winning stories collected in *Flying Cups and Saucers: Gender Explorations in Science Fiction and Fantasy* (1998).[15]

Analogous to feminist reading, feminist sf is not simply sf about women; it is sf written in the interests of women – however diversely those interests are defined by individual writers. It is a potent tool for feminist imaginative projects that are the necessary first steps in undertaking the cultural and social transformations that are the aims of the feminist political enterprise.

As Joanna Russ observed in a landmark essay on feminist utopias, these 'utopias are not embodiments of universal human values, but are reactive; that is, they supply in fiction what their authors believe society...and/or women, lack in the here-and-now. The positive values stressed in the stories can reveal to us what, in the authors' eyes, is wrong with our own society.'[16] In Tiptree's unnerving 'Houston, Houston, Do You Read?', for example, Lady Blue explains why her all-female future society must 'put down' three male astronauts who have arrived from the past:

> Of course we enjoy your [male] inventions and we do appreciate your [male] evolutionary role. But you must see there's a problem. As I understand it, what you protected people from was largely other males, wasn't it?...But the fighting is long over. It ended when you did, I believe. We...simply have no facilities for people with your emotional problems.[17]

As feminist theoretical models – abstract constructions of the subject, of representation, of sexual difference – become fleshed out in the particularized worlds of the sf imagination, sf articulates and explores those models through its narrative experiments and, in the ongoing dialectical relationship between abstraction and concretization, feminist theory continues to influence the development of the new worlds and new futures of the genre. The resulting stories are not simply programmatic 'mirrors' of particular theoretical arguments, of course, but rather they incorporate those arguments into the lives and actions of imagined human subjects in imaginary worlds, subjecting them to detailed fictional examination. In Le Guin's terms, such stories are 'thought experiments' whose purpose is 'not to predict the future...but to describe reality, the present world'.[18]

Feminist theory contests the hegemonic representations of a patriarchal culture that does not recognize its 'others'. Like other critical discourses, it works to create a critical distance between observer and observed, to defamiliarize certain taken-for-granted aspects of ordinary human reality, 'denaturalizing' situations of historical inequity and/or oppression that otherwise may appear inevitable to us, if indeed we notice them at all. The concept of defamiliarization – of making strange – has also, of course, long been associated with sf.[19] Octavia Butler's award-winning 'Bloodchild' (1984) presents a fictional defamiliarization of human reproduction that is as chilling in its own way as is Mary Shelley's depiction of the creation of artificial life. Gan, Butler's protagonist, is one of a group of humans who have sought escape from slavery on Earth only to find a more complex imprisonment among the long-lived lizard-like aliens known as Tlic. Driven both by his deep affection for the alien T'Gatoi and by his powerlessness as a member of a subject species, Gan agrees to incubate T'Gatoi's young in his own body.

The experience of 'giving birth' is not only physically painful but is also potentially fatal. Like many humans before him, Gan will give his physical body over to the requirements of T'Gatoi's alien system of reproduction at least in part to safeguard his family's limited freedom in the 'Preserve'. In the terms of Butler's brilliant exploration of the conflicted nature of women's reproductive experiences as at once liberatory and enslaving, Gan thinks of himself both as a full participant in 'a kind of birth' and as a 'host animal'.[20] In 'Bloodchild', a 'natural' physical experience that virtually defines what it means to be a 'woman' is defamiliarized, assigned to a male character, embedded in an estranged context that politicizes one of the most 'natural' of human experiences/relationships. Like so many sf stories by women writers, 'Bloodchild' undermines our readerly tendencies to naturalize certain aspects of human nature and human experience as 'essentially feminine' or as 'essentially masculine'; it resists any too-easy conflation of the sexed body with the culturally determined gendered behaviours that are imposed upon that body. 'Bloodchild' suggests, in fictional terms, the theoretical recognition that gender is *not* a body, but a position.

As one of the very few black writers of sf, Butler also presents very complex human–alien interactions that dramatize how our experiences of sex and gender are inextricably intersected by experiences of race (see Elisabeth Anne Leonard in this volume). Very similar to the events in Butler's acclaimed Xenogenesis trilogy, in 'Bloodchild' humans and aliens develop a disturbingly symbiotic relationship – humans require the protection of their alien 'patrons' on 'the Preserve' and the aliens require human host bodies – but, as all too often happens in real-world relations marked by gender and race, the lines of power tend to run all one way. In the narrative arc of Butler's fictions, human characters in oppressive situations must deploy whatever limited control is available to them, compromising as necessary in order to survive.

Another kind of defamiliarization is accomplished in Emma Bull's *Bone Dance* (1991), a feminist revision of 1980s cyberpunk. Subtitled 'A Fantasy for Technophiles', the novel is set in a post-apocalyptic future whose hard-boiled tonalities and textures owe much to the future as constructed in William Gibson's quintessential cyberpunk novel, *Neuromancer* (1984) (see John Clute in this volume). Bull's protagonist, Sparrow, is a small-time trader who makes a living scavenging, repairing and selling the products of pre-apocalyptic technologies, and the novel's narrative voice is as toughly *noir* as anything in earlier cyberpunk novels. In contrast to the extrapolative 'realism' of *Neuromancer*, however, the events in *Bone Dance* unfold against a background of Tarot readings, and voodoo is a consensual belief system which works effectively on events in the material world. The generic indeterminacy of the novel is parallelled by the gender indeterminacy of Bull's protagonist, who is perceived by other characters as sometimes female and sometimes male. As one character complains to Sparrow, 'You do a chameleon thing – that makes you seem female when you're with a woman, and male when you're with a man.'[21]

Sparrow is a genetically engineered *cheval* created to be 'ridden' by the Horsemen, themselves customized products of this future's military technology. As such, s/he is a neutral body, one which can appear either female or male, one which is simultaneously 'natural' and 'technological'. As a *cheval* who has developed independent consciousness, Sparrow is also one of the many monsters – if not literally female, then certainly metaphorically feminized – imagined in sf by women. S/he is a figure who escapes labels, who unsettles expectations, who suggests new ways to conceive of the subject. *Bone Dance*, a novel which interweaves 'hard' science fiction with fantasy, is an anomaly in its play with generic conventions, just as Sparrow is an anomaly in Bull's construction of the multi-gendered subject. Marked by postmodern ideas of the subject as multiple and contradictory, Sparrow is both female and male; her/his 'identity' is dependent more upon the preconceptions of observers – including, of course, readers of the novel – than upon any actual physical make-up. *Bone Dance* is a good example of how the fictional discourses of sf can literalize, unconfined by the generic limitations of realism, some of the complex theoretical metaphors of the subject suggested by contemporary feminist theory, and thus can extend the project of feminist defamiliarization from the abstractions of theoretical discourse into the powerfully involving pleasures of genre fiction.

## Feminist re-presentation

In spite of literary sf's proven capacity for articulating and exploring feminist theoretical models in original and challenging ways, many feminist theorists and critics have tended to overlook it, discounting it as a form of escapist popular fiction with little aesthetic appeal and even less political relevance. This situation has improved steadily over the past two decades, however, and a number of important full-length studies of feminist sf – as well as innumerable essays and articles – have appeared since 1980.[22] Another critical strand of particular interest is the work of contemporary cyber-theorists such as Donna Haraway and N. Katherine Hayles, whose primary focus is on developments in science and technology, and who read sf texts as 'thought experiments' specifically relevant for the ways in which they explore the influence of science and technology on the lives of human individuals. In Haraway's terms, 'Science fiction is generically concerned with the interpenetration of boundaries between problematic selves and unexpected others and with the exploration of possible worlds in a context structured by transnational technoscience.'[23]

As many studies have noted, sf by women writers, and specifically by feminist writers, has made frequent and significant use of two appropriately 'monstrous' figures, the alien and the cyborg, through which to explore the perspectives and experiences of hegemonic culture's traditional 'others'. Eleanor Arnason's *Ring of Swords* (1993) is a wonderfully entertaining example of the complexity with which the figure of the alien can be deployed by a feminist writer to explore issues of difference as they arise in the interactions between 'problematic selves and unexpected others'. *Ring of Swords* is, among other things, a satiric revision of Robert A. Heinlein's classic story of human–alien warfare, *Starship Troopers* (1959). Heinlein's novel is conventionally masculinist in its construction of the 'Bugs', aliens so completely alien/different/unknowable that the only possible response to them is war:

> both races [humans and Bugs] are tough and smart and want the same real estate . . . But does Man have any 'right' to spread through the universe? Man is what he is, a wild animal with the will to survive, and (so far) the ability, against all competition . . . The universe will let us know – later – whether or not Man has any 'right' to expand through it.[24]

Like *Starship Troopers*, *Ring of Swords* introduces a situation which promises war between two equally aggressive species, humans and *hwarhath*. If anything, Arnason's *hwarhath* are even more convinced of their ethical superiority than are the human beings who may soon be fighting them. Where Heinlein's novel is structured according to events in the alien–human war, however, Arnason's novel is structured as a series of diplomatic events, narrating as it does the extensive negotiations undertaken by her decidedly non-heroic central characters in their efforts to avoid an all-out war. Whereas in Heinlein's novel the vast differences between the humans and the 'Bugs' obviate any possibility of detente, in Arnason's novel it is exactly the similarities between humans and aliens that threaten to result in war. In this ironic comedy of errors, one of the human negotiators admits that 'We expected to find aliens who were different from us, really different. We didn't expect to find aliens who are very similar with some striking differences. It has us off balance'.[25]

Among these few striking differences is the radical gender differentiation between male and female *hwarhath*. Not only is it far more extreme than in any real-world human culture, but it is also confusingly mapped along some very unexpected axes of difference: males are fighters, yes, but women are negotiators, exercising complete control of most non-military aspects of *hwarhath* culture and politics. So separate are the lives of males and females in this alien culture that same-sex sexual activity is the norm, but Arnason's text does not simply defamiliarize the unthinking heterosexual assumptions of most real-world human cultures through the construction of a conventionalized alien homosexuality. Through its depiction of the physical relationship between the human Nicholas Sanders and the *hwarhath* First-Defender Ettin Gwarha – same sex, different species – *Ring of Swords* unsettles the homosexual/heterosexual binary that it initially seems to introduce. As a result, Arnason's novel richly rewards not only feminist but also queer-theoretical readings (see Wendy Pearson in this volume), suggesting a parallel between human sexual differences and the differences between humans and aliens in her fictional universe. The more we become familiarized with the conventions of *hwarhath* culture and politics, the more we realize how artificial these conventions are, and the more the text invites us to consider how equally artificial are the conventions of human culture.

In 1985, Haraway published her very influential 'Manifesto for Cyborgs', a powerful socialist-feminist examination of technoculture as an ineluctable influence on contemporary life in the West; since then, the figure of the cyborg has become a privileged theoretical representation in feminist cultural studies of science and technology.[26] For Haraway, feminist sf writers are 'theorists for cyborgs', and sf itself is a particularly valuable imaginative arena within which to consider how science and technology are disrupting and revising many conventional ideas about human subjectivity and human embodiment. In Haraway's terms, 'The cyborgs populating feminist science fiction make very problematic the statuses of man or woman, human, artifact, member of a race, individual identity, or body.'[27]

C. L. Moore's Deirdre is an early example of the many significant cyborg figures in sf stories by women writers. Perhaps the most tragic figure of this kind is the protagonist of Tiptree's 'The Girl Who Was Plugged In' (1973), a proto-cyberpunk story published a decade before Haraway's 'Manifesto' by one of sf's most darkly ironic writers. This story reminds us that even cyborg identity does not guarantee freedom from the constraints of the sex/gender system. Even the cyborg may become enmeshed in and diminished by a too-faithful performance of femininity. Tiptree's protagonist, P. Burke, 'the ugly of the world',[28] is the body that must be hidden away, the abjected female body. In Tiptree's story, she willingly allows her grotesque body to be confined in a hi-tech cabinet while her mind remotely operates the beautiful but soulless cloned body of Delphi, who is described as 'porno for angels' but who, nevertheless, is 'just a vegetable'[29] without someone controlling her from a distance. P. Burke learns how to 'run' her body-at-a-distance as a beautiful woman, while she herself remains out of sight, wired into the system, a controlling brain, loved, finally, not as a human individual but – by Joe, her trainer – as 'the greatest cybersystem he has ever known'.[30] She is willing to sacrifice anything in order to 'be' the beautiful body that is the only body that matters in her image-drenched future society.[31] Within the plot development of this futuristic fairy tale, P. Burke falls in love with a lovely young man, is loved reciprocally as the beautifully feminine Delphi, and dies – both as P. Burke and as Delphi – when she tries to express this love directly, without technological mediation, to the horrified object of her affections.

Feminist science critics such as Haraway read sf for the ways in which it creatively (re)imagines our lives as contemporary cyborgs shaped by the projects of science and technology. They recognize the political urgency of feminist participation in the articulation of possible futures. At this present historical moment, technological anxiety and technological optimism are inextricably interwoven as never before, making the links between models of feminist thought and the narratives of feminist and woman-authored sf more significant than they have ever been. As Linda Janes concludes in her consideration of Haraway's description of sf (given above),

> Science fiction has become perhaps the quintessential genre of postmodernity in its characteristic representations of futuristic 'tomorrowworlds', inhabited by aliens, monsters and cyborgs which draw attention to artificiality, simulation and the constructed 'otherness' of identity. Through its focus on difference and its challenges to fixed categories of identity (which is a characteristic concern of postmodern theory), science fiction also offers potentially fertile ground for feminist analysis and practice.[32]

## NOTES

1. Suzy McKee Charnas, *The Conqueror's Child* (The Holdfast Chronicles, 4) (New York: Tor, 1999), p. 50.
2. This chapter is much indebted to the historical research undertaken by Helen Merrick, as well as to the work of all the feminist writers, fans and scholars who, over the years, have contributed to the development of the feminist sf community.
3. Judith Fetterley, *The Resisting Reader: A Feminist Approach to American Fiction* (Bloomington: Indiana University Press, 1978).
4. Lester del Rey, 'Helen O'Loy' (1938), reprinted in Robert Silverberg, ed., *Science Fiction Hall of Fame* (New York: Avon, 1971), pp. 62–73, at p. 62.
5. This kind of displacement has a long tradition in Western story-telling. For a detailed historical critique of the figure of the 'machine-woman', see Andreas Huyssen's 'The Vamp and the Machine: Fritz Lang's *Metropolis*', in *After the Great Divide: Modernism, Mass Culture, Postmodernism* (Bloomington: Indiana University Press, 1986), pp. 65–81.

6. Mary Shelley, *Frankenstein* (1818) (New York: Bantam, 1981), p. 39.
7. See also Susan Gubar, 'C. L. Moore and the Conventions of Women's SF', *Science-Fiction Studies* 7 (March 1980), pp. 16–27.
8. C. L. Moore, 'No Woman Born' (1944), reprinted in Lester del Rey, ed., *The Best of C. L. Moore* (New York: Ballantine, 1975), pp. 236–88, at p. 236.
9. *Ibid.*, p. 265.
10. *Ibid.*, pp. 278–9.
11. For the (gendered) authorial masquerades performed by women sf writers, see Jane L. Donawerth, *Frankenstein's Daughters* (Syracuse, NY: Syracuse University Press, 1997), especially, pp. 109–76. James Tiptree, Jr famously published award-winning stories for over a decade before it was discovered in the late 1970s that s/he was 'really' Alice Hastings Bradley Sheldon.
12. Teresa de Lauretis, 'Feminist Studies/Critical Studies: Issues, Terms, and Contexts', in de Lauretis, ed., *Feminist Studies/Critical Studies* (Bloomington: Indiana University Press, 1986), pp. 1–19, at p. 11.
13. See Helen Merrick's '"Fantastic Dialogues"', in Andy Sawyer and David Seed, eds., *Speaking Science Fiction* (Liverpool: Liverpool University Press, 2000), pp. 52–68, for a compelling analysis of the complex history of women's participation in the early years of the genre. One of the earliest surveys of women in sf was undertaken by sf writer and editor Pamela Sargent in the introduction to her first edited anthology, *Women of Wonder: Science Fiction Stories by Women about Women* (New York: Vintage, 1975), pp. xiii–lxiv.
14. Adrienne Rich, 'Compulsory Heterosexuality and Lesbian Existence', *Signs: A Journal of Women in Culture and Society* 5:4 (1980), pp. 631–60.
15. *Flying Cups and Saucers: Gender Explorations in Science Fiction and Fantasy* (Cambridge, MA: Edgewood Press, 1998), edited by Debbie Notkin and The Secret Feminist Cabal, is an anthology of winners of the Tiptree Award, presented annually since 1991 for stories that explore, expand and challenge our ideas about gender.
16. Joanna Russ, 'Recent Feminist Utopias', in Marleen S. Barr, ed., *Future Females: A Critical Anthology* (Bowling Green, OH: Bowling Green State University Popular Press, 1981), pp. 71–85, at p. 81.
17. James Tiptree, Jr, 'Houston, Houston, Do You Read?', in Vonda N. McIntyre and Susan Janice Anderson, eds., *Aurora: Beyond Equality* (Greenwich, CT: Fawcett, 1976), pp. 36–98, at pp. 96–7.
18. Ursula K. Le Guin, 'Introduction', *The Left Hand of Darkness* (1969) (New York: Ace, 1976), no pagination.
19. Darko Suvin's definition, in *Metamorphoses of Science Fiction* (New Haven, CT: Yale University Press, 1979), is discussed by Istvan Csicsery-Ronay in this volume.
20. Octavia Butler, 'Bloodchild' (1984), reprinted in Pamela Sargent, ed., *Women of Wonder: The Contemporary Years* (1995), pp. 123–40, at pp. 132 and 134.
21. Emma Bull, *Bone Dance* (New York: Ace, 1991), p. 143.
22. See, for example, the titles by Barr, Donawerth, Larbalestier, Lefanu, Roberts and Wolmark in these notes and in Further Reading.
23. Donna Haraway, 'The Promises of Monsters: A Regenerative Politics for Inappropriate/d Others', in Lawrence Grossberg, Cary Nelson and Paula Treichler, eds., *Cultural Studies* (New York: Routledge, 1992), pp. 295–337, at p. 300.

24. Robert A. Heinlein, *Starship Troopers* (1959) (New York: Ace, 1987), p. 147.
25. Eleanor Arnason, *Ring of Swords* (New York: Tor, 1993), p. 250.
26. Donna Haraway, 'A Manifesto for Cyborgs', reprinted in Elizabeth Weed, ed., *Coming to Terms* (New York: Routledge, 1989), pp. 173–204.
27. *Ibid.*, pp. 197 and 201.
28. James Tiptree, Jr, 'The Girl Who Was Plugged In' (1973), in Tiptree, *Warm Worlds and Otherwise* (New York: Ballantine, 1975), pp. 79–121, at p. 80.
29. *Ibid.*, pp. 85, 86.
30. *Ibid.*, p. 120.
31. See Judith Butler on the construction of subject and gender: *Bodies that Matter: On the Discursive Limits of 'Sex'* (New York: Routledge, 1993).
32. Linda Janes, 'Introduction to Part Two', in Gill Kirkup *et al.*, eds., *The Gendered Cyborg: A Reader* (London: Routledge, 2000), pp. 91–100, at p. 92.

# 9

ANDREW M. BUTLER

# Postmodernism and science fiction

Given that sf is notoriously difficult to define, and that postmodernism is (usually) resistant to any absolute definition, any account of postmodernism and sf risks collapsing under the weight of its own hesitations. This chapter will isolate several theories of postmodernism, examine the interplay of postmodernism and sf and offer a brief critique of postmodernism. It should perhaps be taken for granted that much postmodernism reads like sf.

## Definitions

Postmodernism came into critical focus as an approach thanks to an article by Fredric Jameson,[1] and soon became one of the commonest critical approaches to sf. The term pre-dates Jameson; most significantly in architecture 'postmodernism' had been used to designate a particular style which rejected the brutalism of modernism in favour of eclecticism, quoting from earlier styles and mixing aesthetics.

In the 1960s and 1970s 'postmodern' began to be applied to a series of writers active after 1945 whose works demonstrate knowledge of their own fictionality, either by drawing attention to the creative process of narration, by containing books within books or by breaking down boundaries between author and characters – examples include the works of Beckett, Burroughs and Borges. Kurt Vonnegut is perhaps the author who has most featured himself as a character within his own science fictions – partly in the debate about sf in the novels featuring Kilgore Trout, but most clearly in his interventions into such narratives as *Slaughterhouse-5* (1969), drawing on his experience in Dresden after the Allied bombing raid, or *Breakfast of Champions* (1973), especially at the end when he sets his characters free. It should be emphasized that Vonnegut here is just another character, just as Tom Robbins is when doing battle with his typewriter in *Still Life With Woodpecker* (1980) and Robert Sheckley when he tries to get his narrative to work in *Options* (1975).

In Philip K. Dick's *VALIS* (1981) the narrator Phil Dick tells us about the strange events which have been happening to his friend Horselover Fat – events which Dick claims to have happened to him in real life.[2] Robert Galbreath has argued convincingly that added to Philip the choice of names Kevin and David show a completion of Dick's initials, and Kim Stanley Robinson, paralleling a point made by Steve Brown in a review of *The Divine Invasion* (1981), suggests that 'We could say, then, that *The Divine Invasion* ... [was] written by Horselover Fat, while *The Transmigration of Timothy Archer* ... [was] written by "Phil Dick".'[3] Dick was experimenting with split protagonists prior to writing the novel which became *VALIS*, in giving displaced versions of his autobiography to major characters in *Flow My Tears, the Policeman Said* (1974) and in the mental breakdown of Robert/Fred in *A Scanner Darkly* (1977).

These carefully developed metafictions erase the boundaries between fiction and fact, and perhaps induce a level of anxiety on the part of the reader. Elsewhere, such as in the introduction of sf writers as characters in Robert A. Heinlein's *'The Number of the Beast'* (1980) or, most hilariously, the intervention of a task force of sf writers and scientists to save the day at the climax of Jack McDevitt's *Ancient Shores* (1996), it can seem just like self-indulgence – which does not necessarily stop it from being postmodern. There is a thin line between self-indulgence and playfulness.

This quasi-definition of a (literary) postmodernism as one which involves metafiction places postmodernism as the next stage of an aesthetic history after realism and modernism. It can be argued, with this sense of fiction and its rules, that *all* genre fiction is postmodern, not just sf. In the reader's encounter with generic material, an awareness of the structure of story or theme comes to the foreground, and familiarity with other works within the given genre is part of the reading process. Dan Simmons's *Hyperion* (1989) is structured around two works of fiction, one from high culture, the other from low: *The Canterbury Tales* where pilgrims recall narratives to pass the time, and *The Wizard of Oz* (1900) where four characters travel on a journey to have a wish granted. The climax of the volume even draws out the latter parallel for the reader. Geoff Ryman's *'Was . . .'* (1992) also draws upon *The Wizard of Oz*, mixing together the narrative of an actor wanting to play the scarecrow, the life of Judy Garland and a harrowing account of a 'real' Dorothy Gale, who had no escape into a magical land of Oz.

Postmodernism is here a more extreme version of what modernism was. Modernism had been a movement in literature, music, dance, painting and other aesthetic forms which had flourished between the 1890s and the 1930s, reaching a zenith in the immediate aftermath of the First World War.

Following the emergence of Darwin's theories of evolution, Freud's early work on the impact of the unconscious on the conscious mind and then the cosmological and physical theorizing of Einstein among others, humanity was no longer situated as being between animals and angels. Its sense of place within the universe had been undermined and it was necessary to establish a new subjectivity, one which could take into account the growth of the metropolis, with its new social formations and paradoxical phenomenon of thousands of isolated individuals in crowds. Writers such as T. S. Eliot and James Joyce, in their attempts to find new forms of expression, constantly quoted from both high art and low culture; but in the version of postmodernism which follows this modernism, a sense of the democratic outweighs the élitism associated with modernism.

## Jean-François Lyotard

A different kind of postmodernism had been described by French philosopher Jean-François Lyotard in *The Postmodern Condition* (1979); here the postmodern is after the modern, rather than after modern*ism*. By 'modern' he means the period of the Enlightenment in the eighteenth century, during which a number of constitutions intended to create rational states were written – notably those of the United States of America and France. It was the duty (if not the practice) of the citizen to participate in the state, via the public sphere, and to negotiate the powers that the state could wield. Knowledge was liberation, and would set people free.

Lyotard felt that the Enlightenment project had ground to a halt. The rational state had in fact led to totalitarianism in various forms, and knowledge, in the form of information, had become a commodity. In addition, the state was superfluous, as multinational corporations wielded increasing power, and cut across boundaries. Postmodernity here becomes synonymous with the post-industrial or, rather, the complete industrialization of all aspects of society. The postmodern is characterized by 'an incredulity toward metanarratives',[4] those master narratives which legitimate the way of life of a given society – such as the Judaeo-Christian or Islamic traditions. Science is legitimated by repeatable experimentation, but this empiricism breaks down in the sciences of chaos theory, catastrophe, quantum physics and so on: how can the proof be proven?

On the whole sf does hold to a valorization of scientific truth, even if the accuracy of the science may vary. The process of science as an international 'language' with concepts and applications which cut across national boundaries is perhaps one of the reasons why sf after the Second World War increasingly portrays the obsolescence of the nation state, as in the galaxy-spanning government of *Star Trek*, the Balkanization of the USA in Neal Stephenson's *Snow Crash* (1992) or of the UK in Ken MacLeod's *The Star Fraction* (1995). The state, in sf as in postmodernity, is replaced by the multinational corporation: in Jack Womack's *Terraplane* (1988) it is not America versus the Soviet Union, but Dryco, with tendrils across much of the world, defending its economic interests. In dozens of cyberpunk thrillers information becomes a currency, with bodies simply the form in which it is stored; the film of *Johnny Mnemonic* (1995) offers perhaps the best example of this.

Whilst what Lyotard was discussing in *The Postmodern Condition* is postmodernity, he does elsewhere conceptualize 'postmodern*ism*', although the use of the word 'post' is here problematic. He argues that 'modern aesthetics is an aesthetics of the sublime, though a nostalgic one'.[5] In other words, modernism is characterized by an awareness of the void at the heart of society – in morality, in politics, in individual subjectivity – but with the sense that there was a golden age from which the world has fallen. Texts which foreground the void allow some solace through what Lyotard calls 'good forms' – in other words the traditional narrative of an individual facing the challenges of life. Postmodern aesthetics rejects such forms, and 'searches for new presentations, not in order to enjoy them but in order to impart a stronger sense of the unpresentable'.[6] There was no fall, because there has never been a unity. Curiously, there is the sense that the postmodern somehow precedes the modern: although it is unclear whether this is through new forms of presentation becoming familiar and then good forms or a breakthrough by artists in presenting the unpresentable.

To the extent that there is a void in sf it is in the attempt to present the infinity of the universe, the subjectivity of the alien, the pure arbitrariness that what is the case is indeed the case – that the Reformation has taken place, or that the Allies won the Second World War. The Stargate sequence in *2001: A Space Odyssey* (1968) is the most famous experience of a character not merely confronting the void but heading into it, allowing Stanley Kubrick the director the chance to grapple with the next stage of human consciousness, unpresentable because it has to be beyond our ability to understand it. Equally, at the end of J. G. Ballard's 1960s disaster novels such as *The Drought* (1965), the protagonist embraces the cataclysm rather than attempting to escape it.

Further, sf, in its positioning as a non-literary form outside the canon, certainly rejects the consolations of good form. However, its adherence to thriller narrative shapes, odysseys, or detective-like uncoverings of truths about the world, offers consolations which would perhaps not be considered postmodern by a figure such as Lyotard.

## Fredric Jameson

Fredric Jameson was perhaps the most influential theorist of postmodernism, through his 1984 essay, and the 1991 collection of the same name. Jameson is also a critic of sf, and was on the board of consultants of the journal *Science-Fiction Studies* for many years. On at least one occasion he has tried out theories on sf before proceeding to more canonical texts – for example his semiotic reading of Dick's *Dr Bloodmoney* (1965).[7] In the first note to the book version of *Postmodernism*, Jameson writes that 'This is the place to regret the absence from this book of a chapter on cyberpunk, henceforth, for many of us, the supreme *literary* expression if not of postmodernism, then of late capitalism itself.'[8] This is a huge omission; if postmodernism is the cultural logic of late capitalism, then this places cyberpunk as central to the understanding of the period.

As a Marxist thinker, Jameson traces a parallel trajectory between economics and culture, indeed with society in general. Just as the conditions of capitalism produced realist art, so the third phase of capitalism, late capitalism, leads to postmodern aesthetics. He situates a break between epochs at some point in the late 1950s or early 1960s.

For Jameson a postmodern text is not a critical representation of an authentic reality, but is a simulacrum, a copy without an original. Style and fashion are much more important than content, surface more important than depth. The work is ironically performing, rather than sincerely expressing, emotions or feelings of the artist – not that there is a stable identity which is the artist's self-identity any more, as she or he pastiches the styles of others. What results is schizophrenic *écriture*, where there is a breakdown in the meaningful connections between the words or images; at its most basic this may be an eclectic range of allusions, but it could be a bewildering collection of fragments of different voices. Finally, there is the sense of the sublime in the postmodern text, in part in its exhilarating, hysterical disorientation.

A brief filleting of William Gibson's *Neuromancer* (1984) should begin to explicate these elements. This novel demonstrates great linguistic density, Gibson's concern for style perhaps blinding the reader to any shortcomings of the novel, and at times distancing us from the characters and what Gibson as author may feel about them. There is much pastiche here, style-wise, of Tom Wolfe's New Journalism, William Burroughs, Dashiell Hammett and Raymond Chandler, or rather, given this is pastiche ('parody...without a vocation'),[9] of *noir* stylistics and plotting in general. Case, the hapless protagonist, stumbles between crises, barely knowing what's going on, at risk from a femme fatale and being made offers he cannot resist from mysterious Mr Bigs. The resulting textual collage is an example of schizophrenic *écriture*.

Ridley Scott's *Blade Runner* (1982) is also an iconic postmodern text. Like *Neuromancer* there is a patchwork of influences: heavy-handed allusions to Blake's prophetic poems, film adaptations of *The Maltese Falcon* (1941) and *The Big Sleep* (1946), sets and neon lights borrowed from other films, and multi-cultural extras filling the streets. *Blade Runner: The Director's Cut* (1992) removes Deckard's voice-over which had lent him an air of authority and grants more agency to the replicants – their narratives are no longer subservient to his. The information contained in the voice-over had given us information about Deckard's past which had been a guide to his current character. Now he becomes a blank presence without a history, without emotions, on to whom we project the paranoia that he too is a replicant. After all, Rachael, presented as the niece of Tyrell, chief designer of the replicants, did not realise that she was a replicant. Notions of stable identities collapse, dramatizing the idea of the death of the subject, the self.

Elsewhere in *Postmodernism* Jameson returns to a discussion of the works of Philip K. Dick, firstly with a reference to *Now Wait For Last Year* (1966)[10] and then in a third of a chapter devoted to *Time Out of Joint* (1959). Having discussed the films *Blue Velvet* (1986) and *Something Wild* (1986), where the utopian image of a 1950s-style golden age and a violent underbelly are juxtaposed, he notes the way the 1950s in Dick's novel is constructed as an escape from an imagined 1990s. Jameson questions whether the 1950s was an idyll, or whether the past is being constructed in the image we require. He adds: 'of the great writers of the period, only Dick himself comes to mind as the virtual poet laureate of this material'.[11] Dick's 1950s is a virtual one, a nostalgia for the present.

It is unclear how much Jameson embraces the cultural dominant or merely describes it. Whereas other commentators revel in the postmodern confusion, Jameson fears that 'this latest mutation in space – postmodern hyperspace – has finally succeeded in transcending the capacities of the individual human body to locate itself, to organize its immediate surroundings perceptually, and cognitively to map its position in a mappable external world'.[12] Rather than sailing over the edge of an abyss, Jameson wants to find a way of mapping this brave new world.

## Jean Baudrillard

Jean Baudrillard also situates postmodernism in relation to subjectivity and the notion of the divided individual. Whereas the modernist individual was alienated by the speed of the developing metropolis, the postmodernist individual risks obliteration through a geometric increase of the speed of life, and the saturation of the environment with images, messages and other attempts at communication:

> today we have entered into a new form of schizophrenia – with the emergence of an immanent promiscuity and the perpetual interconnection of all information and communication networks. No more hysteria, or projective paranoia as such, but a state of terror . . . an over-proximity of all things, a foul promiscuity of all things which beleaguer and penetrate him, and no halo, no aura, not even the aura of his own body protects him . . . [the individual is] open to everything.[13]

We no longer experience life from where we are, but from the intersections between us and other 'individuals' who are also under attack. With multi-channel TV, the Internet, dozens of different permutations to choose from at the local coffee bar, the individual is bombarded with the rest of the universe.

This terror can be traced in the writings of Philip K. Dick, for example in Richard Kongrosian's fear that he is being turned inside out in *The Simulacra* (1964), a book which Baudrillard has read. Baudrillard's analysis of post-modern space, partly derived from reading Dick, could be used for a wider understanding of sf:

> the new universe is 'anti-gravitational', or, if it still gravitates, it does so around the *hole* of the real, around the *hole* of the imaginary . . . the reader [of Dick] is, from the outset, in a total simulation without origin, past, or future – in a kind of flux of all coordinates (mental, spatial–temporal, semiotic). It is not a question of parallel universes, or double universes, nor real nor unreal. It is *hyperreal*.[14]

The sheer information density of the opening of William Gibson's *Neuromancer* offers the reader direct experience of overload, as she tries to make sense of the world being described:

> Ratz was tending bar, his prosthetic arm jerking monotonously as he filled a tray of glasses with synthetic Kirin. He saw Case and smiled, his teeth a webwork of East European steel and brown decay. Case found a place at the bar, between the unlikely tan on one of Lonny Zone's whores and the crisp naval uniform of a tall African whose cheekbones were ridged with precise rows of tribal scars.[15]

The prose of Jack Womack is even more dense:

> Aiming Bronxward up Broadway our car carried us home; through smoked windows we eyed tripleshifters deconstructing the walls between Harlem and Washington Heights as the northern, higher parts of Manhattan underwent

their own regooding...I'd lived there as a child. We'd grown together in Washington Heights, me and Judy and poor lost Lola, inloading info, street-smarting, grasping our world's way in a moment's breath if and when essentialled; I regooded myself, once I left.[16]

Baudrillard's theory of the simulacrum is that the history of images means that the copy is becoming more desirable. Images are tied in with notions of exchange – one image is exchanged for an idea – and in, say, the history of economics it has become better to exchange goods for money rather than objects. In the postworld war the image has become everything, especially the copy that has no original; the model has replaced the actual, the opinion poll has become more important that the election. Everyday life has become more and more inauthentic – monetary value has come down to noughts and ones in a computer. For Baudrillard such lack of reality has infected the very landscape of America itself, although this infection has been obscured from its inhabitants. Baudrillard suggests that:

> Disneyland is there to conceal the fact that it is the 'real' country, all of 'real' America, which *is* Disneyland . . . Disneyland is presented as imaginary in order to make us believe that the rest is real, when in fact all of Los Angeles and the America surrounding it are no longer real, but of the order of the hyperreal and of simulation. It is no longer a question of a false representation of reality (ideology), but of concealing the fact that the real is no longer real, and thus of saving the reality principle.[17]

This leaves sf as being prophetic of the postmodern age, or being another cause of the sickness which Baudrillard analyses (and is taken to celebrate).

## Postmodernism and the history of science fiction

Science fiction was emerging as a genre at the same time that literary modernism was passing its high-water mark, perhaps in the same way that the gothic emerged with the growth of the realist novel in the late eighteenth century. It is tempting, then, to try and situate sf as the other of literature, or to assume that it follows a similar but delayed evolution to literature. The heterogeneous group of writers in London in the 1960s known as the (British) New Wave, characterized by stylistic experimentation and a wish to make things new, with Michael Moorcock as a central figure and Ballard as its resident genius, offers an uncanny version of a modernist movement forty years on. Cyberpunk, with its echoes of New Wave sensibilities, offers a postmodern movement in sf.

In the most substantial work on the British New Wave, however, Colin Greenland argues that 'British New Wave sf is one more example, or rather many more examples, of the anarchic and ill-defined movement that critics have tried to label "absurdist", "comic-apocalyptic", "Post-Modernist" or even "Post-Contemporary" fiction, "surfiction", and "fabulation"'.[18] Admittedly, when the original draft of Greenland's book was written (as a DPhil thesis), notions of postmodernism were very different. With the benefit of hindsight Greenland adds:

> In *The Entropy Exhibition* I got off on the wrong foot by blindly assuming, in the face of all the evidence, that this was all some sort of answer to the generic limitations of science fiction. It was nothing of the kind. It wasn't even having the conversation. It was the white-hot slurry of garage postmodernism, surging up into the place only Moorcock (with Ballard, Langdon Jones and Charles Platt) were ambitious enough to provide for it. It was nothing of any kind but its own.[19]

But Greenland is not the only critic to use a movement within sf to tell a narrative of postmodernism. In his *Another Tale to Tell*, the American critic Fred Pfeil offers another model of the history of sf which situates the New Wave as the point where sf 'briefly *becomes modernist*',[20] whereas sf prior to about 1960 is either serious utopian/dystopian mapping or masturbatory thrillers for readers with a mental age of thirteen. As serious literary sf runs out of steam, a New Wave of writers such as Joanna Russ, Ursula Le Guin, Philip K. Dick, Thomas M. Disch and, most importantly, J. G. Ballard, make sf modernist. Without this unparalleled intervention, there could have been no Gibson, Bruce Sterling and Octavia Butler, producers of what Pfeil sees as New Age writing, 'which it is at one and the same time "trashier", "pulpier", and far more sophisticated, even more liberatory, than those earlier writings [of the so-called New Wave]'.[21] Pfeil's argument is open to challenge,[22] but it perhaps demonstrates the slipperiness of the notion of postmodernism that one example he gives of modernist 'New Wave' writing, Disch's *The Businessman* (1984), had previously been reviewed by Pfeil as 'a genuinely postmodern literary object'.[23] But then Lyotard has argued that if a work is to be modern, it must first be postmodern.

Brian McHale has offered two book-length interventions into the debate about postmodernism, initially arguing: 'Science fiction...is to postmodernism what detective fiction was to modernism.'[24] McHale's critique is important for his taking seriously writers such as Philip K. Dick and discussing them alongside acknowledged literary greats such as Nabokov, Spark and Borges. In *Postmodern Fiction*, he situates sf and postmodernist fiction as both parallel and overlapping. McHale's *Constructing Postmodernism* attempts to situate sf as paradigmatic of postmodern literature: 'SF is openly and avowedly ontological, i.e., like "mainstream" postmodernist writing it is self-consciously "world-building" fiction, laying bare the process of fictional world-making itself.'[25]

The zenith of the application of postmodernist aesthetics lies between the publication of McHale's two volumes. This criticism can be found in places such as the special issue of *Mississippi Review* 43/44 (1988) which was to be expanded as *Storming the Reality Studio*; in the volume edited by Slusser and Shippey, drawn from the Fiction 2000 conference at Leeds (June 28–July 1 1989); the sf issue of *Semiotext(e)* (1989), edited by Rucker *et al.*; the 'Science Fiction and Postmodernism' issue of *Science-Fiction Studies* (November 1991); and Scott Bukatman's *Terminal Identity* (1993, but written earlier). In such volumes analyses of Gibson and Sterling rub shoulders with studies of Burroughs and Pynchon, and theories from Lyotard, Baudrillard and Jameson are used to study both sf texts and performance artists such as Stelarc or Orlan. Within sf studies, postmodernism became primarily associated with cyberpunk and vice versa, with the postmodernism present within space-opera pastiches such as Simmons's *Hyperion*, Banks's *Consider Phlebas* (1987) and Greenland's *Harm's Way* (1993) or the metafictive games of Gene Wolfe, Pat Murphy and Geoff Ryman, receiving little critical attention.

There are many ironies here. Postmodernist criticism, with its rejection of hierarchies, has limited itself to a small body of texts – at times just *Blade Runner* and *Neuromancer*. Cyberpunk had been envisaged as something ephemeral, a truly postmodern cutting edge, which was declared dead (sometime around 1986) before most people had even noticed it. Nevertheless, the sub-genre continues as cyberpunk, post-cyberpunk, cyberpunk-seasoned[26] or even (my own contribution to the critical insanity) cyberpunk-flavoured fiction.[27] At the same time as postmodern criticism made it acceptable to talk seriously about writers such as Gibson and Sterling, these writers were leaving the genre ghetto.

In retrospect the tension between postmodernism as being descriptive or prescriptive was its downfall: the critique from the Left of a fragmented world seems to have offered an orthodoxy to the Right. Postmodernism had offered a useful analysis of the decentred subjectivity – which unsettled hierarchies of male/female, white/black, heterosexual/homosexual, ruling class/working class and so on – but this new subjectivity fragmented the sense of shared social identity and consciousness at the very point that Reaganomic and Thatcherite ideologies valorized the individual at the expense of the collective. Notions of hybridity may well be empowering, but if everyone's viewpoint is just relative, then the white, male, heterosexual ruling class hegemony can insist on speaking. Carl Freedman has argued that a similar failure of radicalism can be found in cyberpunk, which 'finally resolves into uncritical conservatism'.[28]

Postmodernism's analysis of 1980s America and the rest of the world was largely correct, but an aesthetics of celebrating the sailing for the abyss was no solution; Jameson may have been looking for a cognitive map but very few others were. The subtle politics of Baudrillard's post-Cold War rhetoric about the Gulf War not taking place[29] was not as important as the injustices of the failure to acknowledge Gulf War Syndrome or the wider picture of Middle East politics. Stelarc's exploration of his own intestines can stand as symbolic of those still stuck in the postmodern paradigm.

Nevertheless, postmodernism's analysis of the surface, hysteria, the sublime, the pastiche, the end of history, the waning of affect and the simulacrum over the original has opened up avenues of exploration which have yet to be entirely excavated, particularly with regard to non-cyberpunk sf. The shift in geopolitics from the North Atlantic to the Pacific Rim which coincided with the 1980s and 1990s still warrants exploration, both with the retreat of some of the so-called Tiger economies and with the largely unquestioned racism in the depiction of the Asian hordes in the work of writers such as Neal Stephenson. The politics of the War Against Terror need questioning, especially where it is prefigured or represented in sf. The critic as Zeitgeist surfer, for whom sf began and ended with *Blade Runner* and *Neuromancer*, has moved on to the next trend, but in the meantime sf has been brought to a wider and more astute audience.

## NOTES

1. *New Left Review* (July/August 1984), pp. 53–94.
2. Cf. Lawrence Sutin, *Divine Invasions: A Life of Philip K. Dick* (New York: Harmony, 1989), pp. 208–33.
3. Robert Galbreath, 'Salvation-Knowledge: Ironic Gnosticism in *VALIS* and *The Flight to Lucifer*', in Gary K. Wolfe (ed.), *Science Fiction Dialogues* (Chicago: Academy, 1982), pp. 115–32, at p. 119; Steve Brown, 'The Two Tractates of Philip K. Dick', *Science Fiction Review* 10:2 (1981), p. 11; Kim Stanley Robinson, *The Novels of Philip K. Dick* (Ann Arbor, MI: UMI Research Press, 1984), p. 111.
4. Jean-François Lyotard, *The Postmodern Condition: A Report on Knowledge* (Manchester: Manchester University Press, 1984), p. xxiv.
5. *Ibid.*, p. 81.
6. *Ibid.*
7. Jameson, 'After Armageddon: Character Systems in *Dr Bloodmoney*', *Science-Fiction Studies* 2 (1975), pp. 31–42.
8. Jameson, *Postmodernism, or The Cultural Logic of Late Capitalism* (Durham, NC: Duke University Press, 1991), p. 419.
9. *Ibid.*, p. 17.

10. *Ibid.*, p. 118.
11. *Ibid.*, p. 280.
12. *Ibid.*, p. 44.
13. Jean Baudrillard, *The Ecstasy of Communication* (New York: Semiotext(e), 1988), pp. 26–7.
14. Baudrillard, 'Simulacra and Science Fiction', *Science-Fiction Studies* 18 (1991), pp. 309–13, at p. 311.
15. William Gibson, *Neuromancer* (London: Grafton, 1986), p. 9.
16. Jack Womack, *Elvissey* (London: HarperCollins, 1993), p. 24.
17. Baudrillard, *Simulations* (New York: Semiotext(e), 1983), p. 25.
18. Colin Greenland, *The Entropy Exhibition* (London: Routledge & Kegan Paul, 1983), p. 203.
19. Greenland, 'Jeremiah Cornelius and the Camelot Baseball Embargo', in *Mexicon* IV *Programme Book* (Harrogate: Mexicon IV, 1991), pp. 9–13, at p. 11.
20. Fred Pfeil, *Another Tale to Tell: Politics and Narrative in Postmodern Culture* (London: Verso, 1990), pp. 85–6.
21. *Ibid.*, p. 84.
22. See Andrew M. Butler, 'Modelling Sf: Fred Pfeil's Embarrassment', *Foundation* 72 (1998), pp. 81–8.
23. Pfeil, [Review of Thomas M. Disch. *The Businessman: A Tale of Terror*], *the minnesota review* 23 (1984), pp. 188–91, at p. 188.
24. Brian McHale, *Postmodernist Fiction* (London: Methuen, 1987), p. 16.
25. McHale, *Constructing Postmodernism* (London: Routledge, 1992), p. 12.
26. Geoff Ryman, [Review of *Vurt*], *Foundation* 61 (1994), pp. 90–2.
27. Andrew M. Butler, *Cyperpunk* (Harpenden: Pocket Essentials, 2000), pp. 17–18.
28. Carl Freedman, *Critical Theory and Science Fiction* (Hanover, NH: Wesleyan University Press, 2000), p. 198.
29. Baudrillard, *The Gulf War Did Not Take Place* (Sydney: Power, 1995).

# 10

## WENDY PEARSON

# Science fiction and queer theory

*Axiom 1: People are different from each other.*
It is astonishing how few respectable conceptual tools we have for dealing with this self-evident fact. A tiny number of inconceivably coarse axes of categorization have been painstakingly inscribed in current critical and political thought: gender, race, class, nationality, sexual orientation are pretty much the available distinctions.

(Eve Kosofsky Sedgwick, *The Epistemology of the Closet*)[1]

'We have to hide,' the other said gently. 'You still kill anything that's ... different'.

(Theodore Sturgeon, 'The Sex Opposite')[2]

## Science fiction and the idea of sexuality

Knowing sf's potential for using the future to explore contemporary reality and its alternatives, one might think the genre ideal for the examination of alternative sexualities. Critics of sf have generally agreed that science fiction is a 'literature of ideas'. Indeed, for many people, it is the ideational content of sf that is its primary characteristic. Sexuality is also an idea. In this sense, one might well expect to find an intrinsic compatibility between sf as a genre and the exploration of human sexuality. For many people, however, sexuality – and particularly heterosexuality – can be envisioned only within the category of the 'natural'. To these people, sexuality is quite specifically *not* an idea; it is the very reverse of the ideational – instinctive, sensate, animalistic. It is at once both 'common sense', as in the apparent logic of procreative sex, and unthinkable, since even apparently procreative sex calls into play emotions, positions, actions and desires whose potential for perversity, even if it is merely the perversity of pleasure, are too frightening to contemplate. And yet, even for these people, sex *is* an idea because it is, after all, an ideology and one which contemporary Western societies have tried very hard indeed both to propagate and to control.

This is one argument about the potential of sf to depict sexualities, whether normative or alternative. It is an argument that stems from the approaches to sexuality studies that have come to be collected under the rubric of 'queer theory'.[3] Before going on to examine what queer theory can tell us about how sexuality is explored in sf, however, it is useful to look also at another, related argument about the depiction of alternative sexuality in sf. In the 1980s, when the topic of sexuality in sf began to receive critical attention, it was not uncommon for critics to decry the absence of positive depictions of alternative sexualities in sf. One of the questions the student of sexualities in sf needs to consider then is whether or not sf is or has been a field in which the full range of human imagination can be brought to bear not merely on the technologies of human existence, but on human sociality in all its complexity. In other words, we might ask whether sf has traditionally been better at imagining machines and their conjunctions than it has been at imagining bodies and their possible relationships.

The answer to this question is probably ambivalent. Although there have always been some sf stories which have touched on issues of sexuality in imaginative ways, often allegorically, these have until recently been vastly outweighed by the number of stories which take for granted the continued prevalence of heteronormative institutional practices – dating, marriage, the nuclear family and so on. It is worth noting that the portrayal of sexuality is not absent in much early sf (despite claims that there was no sex in sf prior to the 1960s),[4] merely an unreflexive reproduction of contemporary norms. Merely to give the hero a fiancée, as E. E. 'Doc' Smith does, for example, is to make suppositions about the naturalness of contemporary Western sexual customs. Thus, looking at issues of sexuality in sf is not simply a matter of looking for positive or negative portrayals of homosexuality, but also of understanding the discourses that inform the depiction of sexual relationships in sf. Indeed, stories which are sympathetic to homosexuality do not necessarily involve any sort of unsettling of a heteronormative regime; at the same time, stories which interrogate alternative possibilities for sexual-social structures are not necessarily sympathetic to alternative sexualities. Robert Heinlein's work provides excellent examples of both types of narrative. In *Friday* (1982), the beautiful female protagonist sleeps with both women and men without disrupting the heteronormative structure of her society in the slightest; in addition, the novel makes pejorative references to 'real' homosexuals, who are identified primarily by their unwillingness to perform their gender roles. *The Moon is a Harsh Mistress* (1964) exemplifies the latter type of narrative, as Lunar society permits a variety of options for marriage beyond the basic one-male-one-female model that is acceptable in most contemporary Western cultures – but only so long as these arrangements, whether between three people or twenty, remain exclusively heterosexual.

If attitudes towards sexuality in sf are ambivalent, critical attention to the issue has been close to non-existent. The one exception is the extent of criticism on the sub-genre of the lesbian feminist utopia, but even there the focus has often not been primarily on sexuality per se. A search on the term 'science fiction' on the MLA database yields 4,019 results, yet there are only thirty-four results for sf plus 'sexuality'. A similar search yields 2,081 results for 'homosexuality', but when combined with sf results in citations for only eight articles, of which only two were published before 1990. The only anthologies on sexuality in sf remain Donald Palumbo's *Erotic Universe* and *Eros in the Mind's Eye* (both 1986). James Riemer's contribution to *Erotic Universe* is also the first serious critical analysis of the treatment of homosexuality in sf, other than the introduction to the first edition of Eric Garber and Lyn Paleo's annotated bibliography of alternative sexualities in sf, fantasy and horror, *Uranian Worlds* (1986). The entry for 'sex' in the *Encyclopedia of Science Fiction* (1993) gives a brief overview of historical attitudes towards the depiction of sexuality in sf; however, the one paragraph that deals with homosexuality mentions only Samuel Delany, Thomas Disch, *Uranian Worlds* and the Gaylactic Network. The most notable omissions here are women writers such as Joanna Russ and Marion Zimmer Bradley.

If sf is indeed the literature of ideas, then it is worth asking why it has taken so long for critics to begin to consider what sf has done with ideas about sexuality, particularly since the history of gender in sf demonstrates quite clearly that sf has been a potent field for thinking about some social, rather than technological, issues. The same could be said for race issues, as sf has had a relatively long history of attempting, no matter how inadequately, to depict a differently racialized future. The same cannot, however, be said for depictions of sexuality. While there are an ever increasing number of gay, lesbian and bisexual authors of sf, it is still relatively uncommon to encounter queer protagonists in the works of sf writers who do not identify themselves as queer. It may be possible to argue that this situation is also starting to change: for instance, Maureen McHugh's *China Mountain Zhang* (1992) has a gay protagonist and Ursula Le Guin's *The Telling* (2000) features a woman who loves women, both in novels that are not predominantly about issues of sexuality. Nevertheless, there is an interesting historical divergence between the treatment of race and gender in sf, and the treatment of sexuality.

There are thus a number of important questions that can be asked, using queer theory as a guide, about representations of sexuality and especially of alternative sexuality in sf. We might ask what sorts of sexualities have been depicted in sf and how have these depictions been constructed – are they allegorical, expository, extrapolative and so on.[5] We might also interrogate whether depictions of heteronormative sexualities are indeed conscious extrapolations of the future or failures to imagine a world with a different social set-up at the basic level of sex. We might investigate the relationships between sexuality, sociality and biology. Additionally, we might consider in which directions contemporary sf is headed in its portrayals of sexuality. Finally we might ask how academic and critical work on sf might potentially address the question of sexuality through queer theory.

## The sexual science(s)

When we speak about the representation of alternative sexualities in sf, we are generally referring to depictions of homosexuality. The very terminology by which we describe sexualities can be problematic. One of the quintessential arguments of queer theory is that homosexuality and heterosexuality are seen as natural oppositions in a binary epistemology of sexuality that is specific to a particular cultural moment. In making this argument, queer theory follows the famous assertion by Michel Foucault that our understanding of homosexuality, indeed our very ability to name certain people as homosexuals, is the result of a specific and radical shift in historical conceptions of human sexuality. Foucault says that,

> [a]s defined by the ancient civil or canonical codes, sodomy was a category of forbidden acts; their perpetrator was nothing more than the juridical subject of them. The nineteenth-century homosexual became a personage, a past, a case history, and a childhood, in addition to being a type of life, a life form, and a morphology, with an indiscreet anatomy and possibly a mysterious physiology.

In saying that 'the sodomite had been a temporary aberration[,] the homosexual was now a species',[6] Foucault has sometimes been understood as arguing that no one in the past had a sense of themselves as different from those around them. In fact, there is an important distinction to be made here between cultural and subcultural epistemologies; when Foucault speaks of the homosexual becoming a species, he is referring not to the self-understanding of a gay minority culture, but to the dominant discourses by which the larger culture as a whole has understood human sexuality. Eve Sedgwick extends Foucault's position here when she highlights the extraordinary particularity of this move towards a new categorization not just of what bodies can do, but of what type of bodies are capable of what sorts of actions. As Sedgwick points out, it is a peculiarity of nineteenth-century history that it was the homo/heterosexual binary that became the way in which we understand 'sexual orientation', despite the range of alternative possibilities for describing how people's sexual practices and desires differ.[7]

The consequences of this new categorization were manifold; as homosexuals were named as a category, both the bodies and psyches of this new species became objects to be studied, regulated, treated and punished. By 1870, homosexuality had already begun to be constituted as a subject for medicine, psychiatry and the criminal law; male homosexuality was criminalized in England in 1885. The categorization of homosexuals as a species of person who were sick, perverted or criminal has had effects which have lasted well into the twenty-first century. Portrayals of homosexuals and bisexuals in sf during this period have unsurprisingly tended to reflect societal attitudes towards sexual dissidence. Garber and Paleo note that 'whether a "soul-sick lesbian", an effeminate caricature, a man-hating amazon, or a bloodthirsty vampire, the image of the homosexual was overwhelmingly stereotypical and one-dimensional'.[8] Attempts to represent homosexuality in a sympathetic or non-stereotypical fashion often met with hostility; in the 1950s when Theodore Sturgeon first attempted to sell 'The World Well Lost', one sf editor 'not only rejected the story, but called up every other magazine editor in the field to tell them not to accept the story either'.[9]

Homosexuality was not decriminalized in England until 1967, while in the USA criminal law affecting homosexuals varies from state to state, with many states still using sodomy statutes to criminalize homosexuals. Both the UK and the USA have legislation aimed at prohibiting the 'promotion' of homosexuality. The American Psychiatric Association classified homosexuality as a mental illness until 1973 and remnants of that categorization remain in the contemporary diagnosis of 'gender identity disorder', particularly when applied to children. While medicine has largely ceased to attempt to cure homosexuality through castration, hormone treatments and other such interventions, the initial association of AIDS with gay men in the early 1980s allowed some medical, religious and public discourses to reinscribe the notion that homosexuals are inherently diseased. Perhaps most pertinently for sf as a genre, medical and scientific research aimed at finding an etiology of homosexuality has focused on hormones, brain structure and the search for a 'gay gene'.

It is precisely this last situation that is explored in Keith Hartman's 'Sex, Guns and Baptists' (1998). An *in utero* test for the gene has been invented, and a world has come into being in which many queer fetuses are aborted, while existing queer children are abandoned to government camps. Catholicism becomes a code for gayness because, as gay Private Investigator Drew Parker explains to his homophobic Baptist client, 'there haven't been a lot of gay Baptists born in the last 23 years . . . Or Methodists. Or Mormons.

Or Presbyterians. You all make a lot of noise about being pro-life, but in the clinch . . . you make "exceptions". Not the Catholics though.'[10] The near future USA that Hartman imagines in this story is an extrapolation from both contemporary science and contemporary sociopolitical discourses: fundamentalist Christians exert considerable influence on the political process, particularly as it affects issues related to sexuality (homosexuality, abortion, prostitution, pornography and the meaning of 'family'). The negative consequences of identifying a genetic component to homosexuality in such a political climate are hardly unforeseen. Some geneticists have themselves argued that a foetal test would be one of the first practical results of such a development. Hartman's story neatly illuminates the fact that were there to be hard scientific evidence of a particular etiology of homosexuality, the consequences of this discovery would not be met with neutrality; on the one hand, a 'gay gene' might be used, as in this story, in an attempt to eliminate gayness, while, on the other hand, it could equally well be mobilized to support claims that gayness is a natural inborn trait, like eye colour or handedness, that should simply be accepted by society and protected under human rights law.

While Hartman's work looks at the confluence of the search for a genetic cause of homosexuality and a right-wing political climate, 'Eat Reecebread' (1998) by Graham Joyce and Peter Hamilton[11] explores the consequences of changing basic human sexual biology. More and more 'hermaphrodite' births are taking place and society becomes increasingly fearful and intolerant of those who are neither male nor female, but both. Anti-hermaphrodite laws are passed, 'Hermie' bashings increase and some police officers are actively conspiring to obstruct police intervention into crimes against hermaphrodites. Like Hartman's story, 'Eat Reecebread' is an extrapolation from contemporary scientific inquiry, based this time on reports of increasing incidences of intersex births amongst fish. The hermaphrodite response in 'Eat Reecebread' is to turn genetic science back on their tormentors, releasing the genes that cause hermaphroditism in plasmid-carrying viruses via Reecebread, the story's equivalent of the Big Mac. Hermaphrodites in 'Eat Reecebread' are treated very much as homosexuals have been – queer bashing and even murder are, for example, still prevalent – so that the story works to examine our cultural assumptions about the binary nature of sexed bodies (almost all cultural discourses naturalize the idea that humans come in only two sexes, despite the known incidence – about 1.7 per cent – of intersex births), and also metonymically to explore the societal difficulties confronting queer people.

This twofold attack on contemporary discourses of bodily sex and sexual orientation also serves to foreground the extent to which historical and cultural understandings of sexuality are often linked to ideas of gender. In many cases, sexual orientation is seen less as a type of desire or sexual practice than as a mismatch between sex and gender. In its more extreme forms, this conflation of sexuality with gender can take the form of seeing queer people as betraying their gender. Eleanor Arnason's *Ring of Swords* (1993), one of the decade's most intelligent explorations of gender and sexuality, depicts an alien society for whom homosexuality is normal. By depicting one of the two human protagonists, Nicky Sanders, as a traitor who has gone over to the *hwarhath* side, the novel also reminds the reader of the long history of conflating homosexuality both with gender treachery and with literal treachery – a conflation that was made, for example, both by the Nazis in Germany and by the House Un-American Activities Committee in the USA. However, unlike the two previous examples, both of which assume a biological foundation for difference, *Ring of Swords* sees sexuality as constructed through society's expectations, even though members of both societies see their own sexualities as innate and natural. In particular, the other humans are hard put to understand how Sanders, given that 'he was a perfectly ordinary heterosexual male twenty years ago',[12] could possibly be enjoying not only a long-term homosexual relationship with a particular *hwarhath*, but also a series of promiscuous encounters with other males. How does a 'normal' heterosexual human come to be queer for furry grey aliens? The depiction of sexuality in *Ring of Swords* thus raises many of the same questions that have gone into the debate between essentialists (who believe that people are born either gay or straight) and constructivists (who think that the meaning and expression of human sexuality is predominantly a result of culture); the novel depicts both human and alien sexualities as complex and difficult to explain, especially from within a given culture. In Sanders's attempt to name his own sexuality as 'hom*eo*sexual' instead of 'hom*o*sexual' – *homeo* means 'like' and *homo* 'same' – Arnason also pays attention to the importance of language in articulating differing conceptions of sexuality at different cultural and historical moments.

## Queering sf

The very word 'homosexual' was only invented in 1868 and first used publicly in 1869, while the first use of the word 'heterosexual' occurred in 1880. However, although the word itself did not exist prior to the 1870s, it is certain that people in the past practised sex with members of their own sex. Queer theory has generally attempted to avoid historical anachronism and to signal that the homo/heterosexual binary is a cultural construct by finding alternative terminologies for historical 'gays' and 'lesbians'. Thus, terms like 'same-sex sex', 'alternative sexualities' and 'sexual dissidence' have been used to attempt to name a broad range of sexual practices that would now be categorized under 'gay' or 'lesbian' or 'queer'. Both the semantic and cultural specificity of ideas of gayness, queerness and so on, suggest that anyone genuinely interested in depicting the ways in which sexuality might be conceived in the future needs to think about epistemologies and terminologies as well as actual practices. The range of possibilities is constrained only by the logic of extrapolation and the limits of the author's imagination. Marge Piercy's *Woman on the Edge of Time* (1976), for example, depicts a future in which all humans are naturally bisexual, and societal and biological distinctions between men and women have become irrelevant, while Samuel Delany's *Trouble on Triton* (1976) offers the reader a world in which it is normal to believe that humans have multiple sexes, genders and sexualities and that children are best raised by at least five adults 'preferably with five different sexes'.[13]

As mentioned above, the relatively few portrayals of alternative sexualities in sf until the 1960s were generally negative. The transition to positive representations of homosexuality, if not of challenges to heteronormativity itself, has traditionally been attributed to Theodore Sturgeon's 'The World Well Lost' (1952). Garber and Paleo speak of Sturgeon as having 'single-handedly opened the science-fiction field to explicit gay images'.[14] Most synopses of this story describe the alien couple, who had initially charmed those on Earth, as being deported when it is discovered that they are the same sex. In fact, however, Earth authorities decide to honour the planet Dirbanu's wish to reclaim its refugees in the hope of facilitating trade with a society that has refused to have anything to do with humans. The loverbirds' secret is only discovered by one of the two human crewmembers, Grunty, when they are already en route back to Dirbanu. Indeed, the story is in many ways more about Grunty and his unrequited hidden love for his captain, Rootes, than it is about the loverbirds. The story is thus not only about tolerance (the loverbirds flee from homophobic Dirbanu to homophobic Earth), but also about desire, even if the relatively sympathetic portrayal of Grunty's sexuality is still figured as impossible either to satisfy or to speak aloud. It is also, perhaps ironically, about mutually sympathetic alliances between different types of queers, as Grunty sets the loverbirds free in the ship's lifeboat rather than leaving them to their doom. And finally, it is about the long-reaching ironies of making assumptions about which forms of sexuality are normal and which disgusting, as Dirbanu irrevocably rejects all contact with humans because the physical similarity of human males and females leads them to see humans as a queer race. In many respects, this story is both queerer and more contemplative about issues of sexuality than the canonical history of sf would suggest.

If there has then been a slowly burgeoning interest in the question of alternative sexualities within sf over the course of the last half century, it still remains for us to ask how queer theory, in particular, can illuminate the work being done in this area. One point needs to be made here: the purpose of applying queer theory to sf is not primarily to recuperate a gay and lesbian history of the field, although that is an important basis for any comprehensive study of sexuality in sf, so much as to examine the conceptual bases of *all* possible depictions of sexualities within sf. Queer theory also tends to be sceptical about epistemologies which see sexual orientation as a fixed identity, so that sf which describes bodies, genders, sexualities as fluid is much more in harmony with approaches that celebrate fluidity, liminality and other radical tactics for deconstructing the rigidity of binary identity categories. While some queer theorists recognize the strategic usefulness of identity politics for short-term legal and political gains, the real aim of queer theory is to make possible a future in which society is radically restructured in order to invalidate fixed identities and deconstruct the Cartesian binarisms which automatically value white over black, male over female and straight over gay.

John Varley is one sf writer who often imagines such a fluid future, one in which even the body becomes plastic and characteristics that we have traditionally believed to be fixed and immutable, such as biological sex, are as easily changed as one's hairstyle. 'Beatnik Bayou' (1980), for example, is partially about teen sexuality in a society where sexuality is subject to few regulations beyond consent and is as malleable and variable as the body itself. The same sociosexual discourses inform another of Varley's Luna stories, 'Picnic on Nearside' (1974), only in this case the teenaged Lunarians meet a very old man, a survivor of old Earth who has chosen to exile himself from Luna society. The revelation that the old man has never been a woman is as shocking to the teenagers as his obsession with incest – a word they have to look up – is incomprehensible.[15] Sexual and gender identities in Varley's stories are no longer a matter of discursive categories, but have become so fluid as to be almost purely performative, a notion supported by the exaggerated performances of femininity or masculinity amongst first-time sex changers.

Sexuality is also constructed as performative in Melissa Scott's queer cyberpunk novel, *Trouble and her Friends* (1994), where Trouble's ex-lover, Cerise, finds herself on the Net having virtual sex with a woman named Silk, who turns out to be the avatar of a teenaged boy. In this case, it is not the plasticity of the body but the limitless potential of virtual reality that breaks down the idea of fixed identity as a necessary or even as a desirable characteristic. In *Trouble*, the freedom of virtuality is emphasized by its contrast to the 'real' world, in which Trouble has 'always been on the outside, not quite of the community that polices the net, set apart by the brainworm, gender, and her choice of lovers'.[16] The rigidities of Trouble's reality have their echoes in the virtual world, but at the same time virtuality provides a place beyond identities based in our apprehensions of the physical body, of skin colour, biological sex and the unstable bodily markers that are expected to identify sexual orientation. Unlike Varley's celebration of the body's potentialities, however, cyberpunk's relationship to the physical body is notoriously troubled. The body is 'meat', yet even this disdain for corporeality can only work by envisaging a meeting place between body and mind, reality and virtuality. In this liminal space, subjectivities multiply and a teenage hacker can become beautiful leather-clad Silk, the sex between 'her' and Cerise as real as it is illusionary, a performance that lasts only as long as the machine code that translates and enables it.

The idea of performativity is one of the most useful analytical tools of queer theory for postmodern forms of sf, including cyberpunk. The theory of performativity draws predominantly on Judith Butler's assertion that all gender is a performance that is both involuntary and always to some extent imperfect, as we fail to live up to the discursive ideals of 'male' and 'female'. The same can be said to apply to sexuality. Having a notion of what 'gay' means, those subjects who identify as gay inevitably perform a type of gayness that is regulated by the discourses surrounding homosexuality. Although one can change the specifics of a given performance of sexual orientation, sexual orientation itself remains immutably something that one is constrained to perform. As a tool for the analysis of sexuality and gender in cyberpunk, performativity is perhaps obvious; however, it may be as useful to apply it to such richly textured postmodern works as Geoff Ryman's *The Child Garden* (1989), where performance itself, particularly of music and holographic opera, is highlighted at the same time that the protagonist, Milena, is unable to perform as an actor in pre-digested versions of Shakespeare. Ryman shows the limits of performativity in a world where only one interpretation of anything is possible, an interpretation that is already pre-programmed into every citizen's head by educational viruses. Ryman uses sf's ability to literalize metaphor to show performativity functioning at a level so extreme that it cannot help but be visible. *The Child Garden* is a world without options until Milena, the uninfectable, impossible lesbian, comes along to infect it with the possibility of getting the performance wrong.

Queer theory has only just started to provide new ways of looking at sf, one which suggests that sexuality is not merely peripheral, but absolutely central to the potential futures we may invent, as well as to our reflections on the present. In this sense, the application of queer theory to sf might take as its guideline Sedgwick's contention that 'an understanding of virtually any aspect of Western culture must be, not merely incomplete, but damaged in its central substance to the degree that it does not incorporate a critical analysis of modern homo/heterosexual definition'.[17] Indeed, given the coincidence between the history of sf and the history of modern sexuality, sf can hardly escape the influence of a culture in which epistemologies of sexuality have become so naturalized as to be invisible. Science fiction's task, often, is to make visible to us the unthinking assumptions that limit human potentiality; epistemologies of sexuality are just as blinding and just as important to the construction of any future society as are epistemologies of science. It is scarcely surprising then to find that sf and queer theory frequently share both a dystopian view of the present and a utopian hope for the future, a hope that it will be, at the very least, a place where we do not automatically kill what is different.

## NOTES

1. Eve Kosofsky Sedgwick, *The Epistemology of the Closet* (Berkeley: University of California Press, 1990), p. 22.
2. Theodore Sturgeon, 'The Sex Opposite', in Sturgeon, *E Pluribus Unicorn* (1951) (London: Panther, 1968), p. 127.
3. The term 'queer theory' was first used by Teresa de Lauretis for a conference at the University of California in 1989; for a useful overview, see Annamarie Jagose's *Queer Theory: An Introduction* (New York: New York University Press, 1996).
4. See, for example, Franz Rottensteiner's discussion of sex in sf in Rottensteiner, *The Science Fiction Book* (London: Thames and Hudson, 1975), pp. 116–17.
5. For a discussion of the various ways in which alternative sexuality may be introduced as a subject, see my 'Alien Cryptographies: The View from Queer', *Science-Fiction Studies* 26 (1999), pp. 1–22, at pp. 4–5.
6. Michel Foucault, *The History of Sexuality, Vol. 1: An Introduction* (New York: Vintage, 1990), p. 43.
7. Sedgwick, *Epistemology*, pp. 8–9.
8. Eric Garber and Lyn Paleo, *Uranian Worlds* (Boston: G. K. Hall, 1990), p. x.
9. Samuel R. Delany, 'Introduction' to *ibid.*, p. xx.
10. Keith Hartman, 'Sex, Guns, and Baptists', in Nicola Griffith and Stephen Pagel, eds., *Bending the Landscape: Science Fiction* (Woodstock: Overlock, 1998), pp. 13–25, at p. 14.
11. Graham Joyce and Peter F. Hamilton, 'Eat Reecebread', in Debbie Notkin, ed., *Flying Cups and Saucers* (Cambridge, MA: Edgewood, 1998), pp. 177–97.
12. Eleanor Arnason, *Ring of Swords* (New York: Tor, 1993), p. 79.

13. Samuel R. Delany, *Trouble on Triton* (published as *Triton*, 1976) (Middletown, CT: Wesleyan University Press, 1996), p. 254.
14. Garber and Paleo, *Uranian Worlds*, p. x. 'The World Well Lost' is to be found in Sturgeon's *E Pluribus Unicorn*, pp. 53–68.
15. John Varley, 'Beatnik Bayou' in *Picnic on Nearside* (New York: Berkley, 1980), pp. 146–81; 'Picnic on Nearside', *ibid.*, pp. 236–60.
16. Melissa Scott, *Trouble and Her Friends* (New York: Tor, 1994), p. 188.
17. Sedgwick, *Epistemology*, p. 1.

# 3

# SUB-GENRES AND THEMES

# 11

GWYNETH JONES

# The icons of science fiction

The feature that unites every kind of sf is the construction – in some sense – of a world other than our own. This may be another planet (or even another universe); or it may be a 'future world' in which conditions have changed in some dramatic way. But whatever new conditions or circumstances apply – alien invasion, Martian colonies, a permanent cure for the ageing process – the writer has to signal the changes, and the reader has to be able to understand the significance of these signals. Thus, the reading of an sf story is always an active process of translation.[1] What are we being told about the characters, the politics, the social conditions of the imagined world, through the medium of these bizarre artefacts, landscapes, relationships, industries and customs? The icons of sf are the signs which announce the genre, which warn the reader that this is a different world; and at the same time constitute that difference.

More than in any other fiction, in sf the imaginary setting is a major character in the story – and this fictional surface is held together by the highly foregrounded description of unreal objects, customs, kinships, fashions, that can be identified and decoded by the reader. The word 'icon' is derived from the Greek *eikon* – it means an image, but the term came into English usage via Byzantine art, where an 'ikon' is, specifically, a stylized representation of Christ or one of the saints. Similarly, an sf icon will represent something both supernatural (or at least other-worldly), artistically conventional (in that certain features are mandatory) and yet clearly belonging to the public domain. Just as Mary Shelley's Dr Frankenstein constructed the monster rather than 'inventing' him, it is probably fruitless to trace any of the icons of sf back to a single, original author. Vampires existed (widely) in folklore before Bram Stoker's *Dracula*, and mechanical men were known before the word 'robot' was first used in the sense that is now so familiar. Equally, since icons are culturally determined and to some degree each individual sf book or story is a culture, each book or story will have its own variant iconography (a differently designed robot, an idiosyncratic form of faster-than-light drive), to match the writer's particular intention. However, it is possible to identify, or to suggest, a core repertoire of these salient images, and examine their meaning – meaning which is available and relevant not only to sf readers, but to any consumer of twenty-first century folklore.

## Rockets, spaceships, space habitats, virtual environments

The rocket, with its upward thrusting phallic shape and dramatic flight, is an inevitable symbol of energy and escape, but a rocket is a weapon (first deployed on the battlefield in medieval China) as well as an innocent, spectacular firework. Though it was the sf dream of interplanetary travel that inspired Tsiolkovski, the seminal theorist of modern rocketry, theory became practical application only in the development of the German V-2 super-weapon. This ambivalent identity has been a vital feature of the rocket's career, in the real world and in sf. Thomas Pynchon's *Gravity's Rainbow* (1973), the American postwar novel which is a text of central significance to modern sf, weaves the story of this deadly icon, in the closing phases of the Second World War, into a rich and complex myth of origins: the rocket as both the climactic achievement and the embodied death wish of modern civilization. In *Gravity's Rainbow*, as the innocent adventurer, Tyrone Slothrop, pursues his quest for the ultimate device, we find the combination of hero-tale, technical specification and mystical speculation which is the great romance of classic sf: but also modern sf's insistence on conspiracy theory, seductive gadgets, brand-names, and the love-affair with ever more potent weaponry.

A rocket with a human payload is the ultimate image of *Gravity's Rainbow*,[2] and in the real world it is still impractical to launch anything into space except by sitting it on top of a giant V-2 stuffed with explosives, and, so to speak, lighting the blue touch-paper. In sf itself, however, the rocket as a symbol of escape to the stars has long been superseded. These days, planetary launches are rare in spacefaring sf; the whole struggle to leave Earth has usually been elided into the distant or recent past (Stephen Baxter's *Voyage* (1996), with its highly technical yet emotionally charged account of a first crewed flight to Mars, is a very interesting exception). The finned, phallic cone has been replaced by the spaceship. Designed not for experimental parabolas but for exploration, for freight and passenger transport and for long-term occupation, the spaceship (whether it carries colonists or invaders, or hides monsters in its secret depths) is an alternative, contained world in itself.

Postwar sf writers, grasping the barren prospects of our solar system and the immensity of the journey to any more hopeful landfall, quickly realized that travelling to the stars (even at the most fantastic speeds) would be a matter of years, or even many generations. Alexei Panshin's *Rite of Passage* (1968) is a rewarding example of the complete starship novel, in which social engineering, town planning and education schemes have equal status with the adventure story. Panshin's characters leave the ship for their initiation into the terrors of the unknown, but the assumption that danger lies in the abyss *outside* the spaceship's metal shell can be reversed to great effect. The nightmare scenario of the monster within can invoke an exquisite sense of vulnerability, as in Ridley Scott's 1979 movie *Alien* – foreshadowed as early as 1958 in a short story by Jerome Bixby, 'It – The Terror From Beyond'.

In Bruce Sterling's epic *Schismatrix* (1985), the fragility of space habitats is so terrifying that the use of weapons of mass destruction has become utterly taboo, even in a lawless and fragmented human future.[3] But in spite of that most celebrated of sf images – the fragile giant jewels, drifting in immense darkness, against a backdrop of pinprick diamonds – in the Kubrick film *2001*, the fictional spaceship is usually a place of refuge, security, stability. In C. J. Cherryh's Merchanter series the great ships that ply between habitable planets have a baroque feudal culture of their own, like privateers on the Spanish Main – the crew members stripped of any ties to the planet-bound by vast, time-distorting distances. Space 'stations', hubs where ships like these are serviced, become multi-layered cities, with exotic markets, zoning laws, class divisions, slums and parkland. Voyages may be so endless (as in Gene Wolfe's Book of the Long Sun series) that all notion of a destination is lost, and the ship's inhabitants remember their original purpose only in myth. Stories closer (notionally) to the foreseeable future reflect the military origins of real-world space flight. *Star Trek*'s Starship Enterprise may be read as 'a US navy nuclear submarine, cruising aimlessly around the Pacific, dispensing the morality of the Age of Liberalism at a vaguely doveish period in the Cold War';[4] and there are many variants on this naval, expeditionary theme. Even more realistically, the space habitat may become a giant shopping mall, which might as well be parked anywhere in suburbia. The ship can be a huge living organism (like Moya the Leviathan in the TV series *Farscape*), or a hollowed-out asteroid, as in my own novel *White Queen* (1991). Whatever shape the vessel takes it will be the locus for a drama of human relationships, an examination of ideas of conflict and dependence, recalling the medieval image of the Ship of Fools. The spaceship, forging its lonely way through a vast, inimical ocean, becomes a world like this one: a vulnerable and yet demanding closed environment, contradicting the rocket's promise of escape from our origins. The idea of escape from the human condition, by means of applied technology, has transmuted into a different form.

Can the virtual environment be an icon? Access to the virtual world has as yet no fixed, visual image attached, either in reality or in fiction. The nearest equivalent to the universally recognised finned cone, or the sleek gleaming shape of the starship, is the rather disgusting body-bag or vat of slime (as depicted in the definitive cybermovie *Matrix*) in which the cybernaut must be immersed, for a full virtual experience. In Pat Cadigan's intuitively satisfying (but equally disgusting) variant, people remove their eyeballs so that they can be plugged-in to the virtual via their optic nerves.[5] Other authors have found a modem-jack inserted into a hole in the back of the skull sufficient. In *Permutation City* (1995), Greg Egan's powerful treatment of virtual space as a colony-world, the cybernauts can, essentially, download their whole human personalities into the software avatars they have adopted in the world behind the screens, abandoning the 'real world' and their 'real bodies'. In my 1997 novel *Phoenix Café* I reversed the transaction, and had the virtual environments of my futuristic videogames prepared in the form of eye-drops loaded with molecular code. Your mind does not enter the virtual world, the virtual world enters your mind, and becomes an overlay on the everyday scene (which is possibly, currently, the sf idea closest to market-reality). Whatever mediation we choose, the persistence of the physical body, the 'meat'[6] that is left behind when we enter the seamless digital world, remains – linking this new concept to the ancient sf image of the super-potent but absurdly vulnerable disembodied brain. The debate will continue, as innerspace becomes – in sf as in the real world – something like the supplanter of the romance of galactic exploration and empire. But whatever kind of vessel we choose, what companions do we have with us, on this sf voyage?

## Robots, androids (and gynoids); cyborgs and aliens

A robot (from the Czech *robota*) is a worker. In Karol Čapek's play *R.U.R.* (1920), from which this name derives, mechanical men are created as workers, but become so competent that they supplant their masters. Perhaps the most visually definitive robot was Robby, the metal-box-bodied, goggle-eyed good servant in the 1956 film *Forbidden Planet*; but it was Isaac Asimov, in a series of story collections published between 1950 and 1977,[7] who developed the concept. The Three Laws of Robotics, the unbreakable code of ethics written into a Asimovian robot's 'positronic brain' have been so successful in fiction that they are worth quoting in full:

> 1. A robot may not injure a human being, or through inaction allow a human being to come to harm. 2. A robot must obey the orders given to it by a human being, except where such orders would conflict with the first law. 3. A robot must protect its own existence as long as such protection does not conflict with the first or second laws . . .

While real-world robotic devices proliferate, and the question of 'machine intelligence' (intelligent washing machines?) becomes blurred for us, Asimov's image of the machine as the *good servant* has an abiding charm, and the Three Laws have passed into received sf scripture. In *Divine Endurance* (1984), my first sf novel, Cho, a 'metagenetic gynoid', the perfect intelligent machine, becomes the unwitting nemesis of a remnant humanity by following Asimov's laws to the letter; and the grandmaster's message – *our machines are innocent but they may still destroy us* – forms the basis of a tragic love story. In Asimov's scenario the fact that the Three Laws are there to protect the humans from their mentally and physically superior creations was always clear. Robotic *goodness*, however, was the preferred image in liberal sf, becoming a theological romance in the legendary story by Anthony Boucher, 'The Quest for St Aquin'[8] – where a flawed and doubting priest is brought back to grace through the faith of his sentient mechanical steed. It took a renegade, anti-technophile sf writer, Philip K. Dick, to write with pity and conviction of the revolt of the 'replicants', in *Do Androids Dream Of Electric Sheep?*, now most famous as the inspiration of the Ridley Scott film *Blade Runner*.

The conviction (which has support from the neuroscience of robotics) that the perfected 'intelligent machine' will have a human or quasi-human form, raises obvious ethical questions. But though mechanical men, immediately read as an futuristic underclass ('gynoids' in post-*Divine Endurance* print fiction are invariably depicted as whores),[9] may resemble humans, they remain defined and devalued by their artificiality. A replicant, or 'andy', with an absurdly shortened lifespan, can be terminated without censure. A software-entity with a human personality, and more than human intelligence, can be legally subject to the Three Laws, and executed like a rebellious slave.[10] What is the ontological status of a genetically engineered biological human being, mass-manufactured to order? Or a being born human, who has elected to exchange some or all of her body parts for hardware, or to morph into a non-human body more suited to some alien environment? In the real world medical technology is now creating cyborgs – human beings entirely dependent on machine parts inserted into their bodies. In vitro fertilization techniques have blurred the line beween children created 'naturally', and children made to order; while the full humanity (or otherwise) of cloned human babies is a matter of serious debate. In sf these situations have been examined and re-examined, and the sf skill of active translation has allowed readers and writers to construe the apparently bizarre dilemmas of post-humanity as very familiar moral questions of social dominance, race and ethnicity, so that asking 'does a cloned baby have a soul?' is as obviously distasteful as asking the same about the child of a chattel-slave, in the nineteenth-century USA.

It may be already inevitable that the human race will fragment into the genetically rich and the genetically poor, or the biologically natural versus the bio-mechanically enhanced (a future history intensely documented in Nancy Kress's *Beggars in Spain* series of novels (1992–6), and the 1997 movie *GATTACA*). It may be inevitable that machine intelligence will become recognized as equal or superior to our own. It is by no means inevitable that the final transformation of the 'other beings' icon – the intelligent extraterrestrial – will ever cross over from fiction and twilight-zone delusion into fact. The career of 'aliens' in sf has reflected (as all sf concepts must) changes and developments in the real world. In the late nineteenth and early twentieth century there was sober, Darwinian speculation about life and ecology on other planets, with the sensational corrective of H. G. Wells's *The War of The Worlds* (1898). Aliens became competitors, and therefore our deadly enemies. In the chastened, exhausted years after the Second World War, and even more so in the 1960s, the decade of the Vietnam debacle and the Civil Rights Movement, peace was the message and aliens could be pitied, admired or defended, in print – though remaining monstrous invaders in the movies, battle providing better spectacle than trade missions. More recently, colourful (but conveniently humanoid) sf aliens – such as the aliens or demons in TV sci-fi and fantasy shows, such as *Star Trek*, *Buffy The Vampire Slayer* and *Angel* – have taken on a range of topical, dramatically useful roles: immigrants, ethnic minorities, underprivileged guest-workers, wily diplomatic opponents. But the scientific exploration of space offers little support, so far, to the sincere beliefs of ufologists and the hopes of SETI (the Search for Extraterrestrial Intelligence). Greg Egan, one of sf's most uncompromising and poetic realists, gives the sorry picture of our likely prospects in his latest novel *Schild's Ladder* (2002), where a young boy of the very far future, instead of having a spaceship land in his garden, finds a tiny patch of slime-mould that *might* be of genuine alien origin, and trembles in awe: 'When the lamplight finally returned the rainbow sheen he'd glimpsed from inside the building was unmistakable, an irregular gleaming patch of some filmy substance...Tchicaya approached and touched it with his fingertip. The substance was slightly sticky, and the film clung to his finger for a fraction of a millimetre as he pulled away...'[11]

Not exactly spectacular – but this colonized, terraformed planet will now have to be evacuated and become a nature reserve, because alien life, throughout the galactic empire, is so incredibly rare. As the great silence out there continues unbroken, actual 'aliens' may have to go the way of Martian canals and Venusian swamps, banished from our imagination. But the prospect of post-human speciation moves in to fill the vacated niche with an array of humanoid grotesques, and the far distant future will still provide a locus for stories of competition and conflict between widely divergent former colonies of earth. As long as there are other people around (especially if they look a little strange), the image of otherness provided by the term 'aliens' will survive, to fascinate and instruct us.

## Animals, vegetables and minerals

In the hierarchy of sf plausibility, technophile extrapolation from the here-and-now takes precedence. Martians who build (or once built, long ago) canals, like jungle-infested swamps on Venus, were dismissed by the arrival of improved information about the conditions on our neighbour planets. Equally, the status of a fully imagined alien ecology – somewhere, out there, far beyond our present reach – has been at times dubious. Isn't this just world-building fantasy, a kind of Narnia in sf clothing? But while the concept of an alien *person* allows us to discuss social, political and psychological permutations of human otherness, the alien planet, artefact, planet (or universe!) is equally vital. It is perhaps sf's greatest aesthetic gift, to both readers and writers, and brings us closest to experiencing the romance of scientific endeavour. It is important that the sense of wonder invoked, at coming face to face with the workings of the cosmos, should be freed as far as possible from the economic and political constraints of 'real' science, and it is no accident that some of the most beloved images of sf are enshrined in narratives of pure encounter. Arthur C. Clarke's *Rendezvous with Rama* (1973) is perhaps the most famous of these, where the fifty-kilometer-long alien artefact, or space probe, paying our system a glancing visit, remains almost entirely mysterious. In less ascetic versions of the same narrative, vanished aliens become intelligible, as in Frederik Pohl's remarkable *Gateway* (1979) and its sequels; or else it turns out that the archaeology of Elder-alien life (as in Jack McDevitt's *The Engines of God*, 1994, or Alastair Reynolds's *Revelation Space*, 2000), contains information that is urgently vital to all concerned. But the obligatory thriller plot seems a descent into the banal: the centre of these stories is a vastness, an inhuman majesty that cannot be reduced to human terms.

Real-world space exploration provides a convincing template for deep-space encounters: sf is at its least fictional here. The practice and theory of alien archaeology can be extrapolated, with little alteration, from the conditions in Egypt or Iraq, a hundred years ago. The most admired of *living* imagined worlds is still probably Frank Herbert's *Dune* (1965). The desert planet Arrakis is part of a galaxy-spanning human polity; but it is the arid terrain and its extraordinary wildlife that catches the reader's imagination, more than the fantasy power-politics of the plot. Roger Zelazny's *Lord of*

*Light* (1967), belonging to the same period, sf's Age of Liberalism, draws admiringly on Hindu mythology and the culture of India, in the same way as Herbert uses Islam and the desert Arabs; and Zelazny writes even more evocatively, though with less narrative strength: 'Near the city of Alundil there was a rich grove of blue-barked trees, having purple foliage like feathers. It was famous for its beauty and the shrinelike peace of its shade.'[12]

Reading those words, as a sixth-former in Manchester around 1970, I was instantly entranced. Generations of sf readers have been introduced, sometimes without knowing it, to the fabulous diversity of their own planet, by the alchemy of sf. As our world becomes more and more crowded, and ignorance is dispelled by the information revolution and the popularity of long-haul travel, sf's imagineers have become self-conscious about these borrowings.[13] Today you are likely to find an author openly declaring that the invented planet has been terraformed and reconstructed on purpose, as a kind of theme-park devoted to ethnic and cultural nostalgia, for example, in Orson Scott Card's Xenocide series, John Barnes's *A Million Open Doors* (1992), or Nalo Hopkinson's *Midnight Robber* (2000). Thus we can have a twentieth-century Caribbean-flavoured *quartier* of the human diaspora, just a dimension veil or two away (so to speak) from a recreation of 'medieval France'. But the most thrilling of imagined worlds are those that combine a high level of intuitive satisfaction as 'real' ecologies with an equally high degree of authorial meaning – a purpose in the work, other than faux-verisimilitude. Frank Herbert's *Dune* succeeds because the story of the desert planet is a story about scarcity, and the kind of human culture that scarcity produces; Herbert was, at the time, involved in environmental science and its fears. Sheri Tepper's *Grass* (1979), a imagined-ecology novel of the same calibre, uses the sf device of a planet without habitat or climate diversity to create a stunning pampas world, but here the meaning of the story is found in an ensemble of native animals with a remarkably coherent, thrilling and fearsome metamorphic life cycle. The denizens of *Grass* pass from an entirely animal larval stage, through a phase of callous, destructive and aggressive sentience, and struggle to reach a final, multi-dimensional imago almost beyond human comprehension. The close juxtaposition of a callous, destructive and aggressive culture of human expansion (humans are colonists of the pampas planet) points the same moral as Arthur C. Clarke's *Childhood's End* – the perennial admonition and promise of the genre. If sf were an education scheme, the report card for the human race would always read 'could do better'. But the sf audience will go on coming back for more, as long as the stubbornly aspirational message is wrapped in such an envelope of wonder, delight and playful invention.

## Mad scientists and damsels in distress

It is often said that sf is a genre devoid of convincing characterization. Whether or not they have the skill, sf writers do not have the space for deep and studied character development, because they are bound to foreground the imagined world, the action-adventure and the gadgets. There are some remarkable exceptions to this rule but it is true that sf relies, like the other popular fiction genres, on a set of stock figures, recognizable and emblematic as the characters of pantomime or the *Commedia dell'Arte*. There are countless hero-tales in sf; and many permutations of the basic romance of the young male adventurer. However, although plenty of sf heroes happen to be scientists, they usually, like Indiana Jones, display their sterling qualities outside their professional discipline. Gregory Benford's *Timescape* (1980), one of sf's few serious treatments of time travel, provides a rare exception, but this (like most real-life science) is an ensemble piece. Perhaps, ironically, the Faustian nature of scientific heroism is a difficult topic for the genre. Faust, the seeker after knowledge who challenges God and is destroyed when he makes a pact with the devil, is not the ideal central figure for a fiction designed to promote and celebrate Man's godlike dominion over the material world. The measured, exalted insanity of Mary Shelley's Dr Frankenstein, with his horrific project of creating life out of a collection of dismembered body parts, is the exception rather than the rule. A notable, and wonderfully crazed example, can be found in Greg Bear's *Blood Music* (1985), the early masterpiece of a writer who has become one of the genre's most respected apologists. Vergil Ulam, geek par excellence, has been ordered to destroy his colonies of intelligent lymphocytes (white blood cells engineered to possess self-awareness, and naturally supplied with a Darwinian drive to increase, multiply and take over the world). He just cannot do it.

> He held the syringe before his eyes for several minutes, knowing he was contemplating something rash. *Until now*, he addressed his creations mentally, *You've had it real easy . . . No severe test, no stress, no need to use what I gave you.*
> So what was he going to do? Put them to work in their natural environment? By injecting them into his body, he could smuggle them out of Genotron . . .[14]

Of course, Vergil commits this folly, and cataclysmic mayhem ensues.

In Ursula Le Guin's *The Dispossessed*, Shevek, an Einstein-like figure, provides a deeply thoughtful version of this story: the scientist viewed as a brilliant creative artist, forced by circumstance to confront the human meaning of his 'pure research'. When Shevek chooses, unilaterally, and in wartime, to make an extraordinary, momentous technology available to all humanity, the parallel with our own world is clear – but to many of the voices in *The Dispossessed*, Shevek appears as dangerously insane as Vergil Ulam. Shevek's decision costs lives, although not on the bio-catastrophe scale of *Blood Music's* scenario: but is all this loss justified by the birth of (in both cases) a whole new world? It is clear that to both Le Guin and Bear, the 'mad scientist' is not a bogeyman or a cartoon figure. He may be satisfying as a fictional character, but he also represents an idea, a discussion about the nature of responsibility, a topic for debate.

The topics of feminism and gender are discussed elsewhere in this volume, but an examination of sf's icons would be incomplete without some reference to that fabled sf cliché, the diaphanously clad damsel on the cover. There is an unavoidable subtext in the science fiction adventure. Hero-tales generally involve the hero being rewarded, after his trials, by gaining access – in some sense – to the desirable female. The male reader, at least, expected a taste of that reward from the original pulps, and was rarely disappointed. But the cover-art of pulp sf by no means relied on the sultry damsel to the extent that legend claims, and though feminism finds much to contend with in sf, the classic writers were often – according to their lights – positive and generous towards women. The scientist at the heart of Asimov's *I, Robot* stories is a female character. She may be presented in essentialist terms, as a frustrated mother to her machine-babies; but she is there.

One of the most striking developments in modern sf has been the emergence of the female-hero icon, who appears (like Joss Whedon's *Buffy the Vampire Slayer*, or Eidos's *Lara Croft*) to have captured the hearts of a generation of male writers. Critics have suggested that these potent young women have been appropriated by the male imagination, and are seen not as rivals but as permissive alter-egos[15] – tough and tooled-up on the outside, yet desirable and 'feminine' within. Intriguingly, the female-hero of Alastair Reynolds's recent and much-admired space opera, *Revelation Space* (2000), depicted in print as a bony, uncompromising, shaven-headed action-figure, appears on his website, with authorial approval, with a greatly enhanced cuteness quotient. Androgynous, childlike, culturally deracinated: lost in a hard-edged, grey-scale machine-made world in which (s)he is only tangential to the vast scheme of things, maybe Ilia Volyova is a very suitable candidate for the sf icon of our new century.[16]

## Traditions and challenges

In the twenty-first century, the other-worldly, sacred status of many of the genre's classic icons is rapidly changing. Rockets and space stations remain marginal to most people's lives, but hand-held global communicators (their eerie resemblance to the *Star Trek* version owing more to ergonomics than sf prescience) have passed into the mundane. Cyborgs, virtual environments, genetically engineered plants, animals and even humans, artificial intelligence, cataclysmic climate change, mind-reading machines, quantum computing – it seems as if almost every wild, innovative, sf plot device has been annexed by the everyday. At the same time, the most visual of popular print-fiction genres is challenged by ever more rapid developments in the entertainment media. Gone are the days when the B-movies could not hope to provide the same spectacular special effects, eye-kicks and entrancing false-realities that could be created by the reader's and the writer's inner eye. But an icon is meaning as well as spectacle, and there is a logic to the icons of sf that will always recall the reader of these signs to the printed page, and verbal rather than visual argument. These images of the future and of human desire deserve to be revisited, in their original forms. They may not be accurate technical drawings (the encroachment of reality generally reveals the absurdity of the science of sf) but they occupy a strange and very specific borderland. They are not drawn from nature, or invoked from the notional freedom of 'fantasy': they are the reasoned hybrids of imagination and the machine.

## NOTES

1. Gwyneth Jones, *Deconstructing the Starships* (Liverpool: Liverpool University Press, 1999), p. 6.
2. Thomas Pynchon, *Gravity's Rainbow* (London: Picador/Pan, 1975), pp. 758–60.
3. Bruce Sterling, *Schismatrix* (1985) (Harmondsworth: Penguin, 1986), pp. 79–80.
4. Jones, *Deconstructing the Starships*, p. 6.
5. Pat Cadigan, *Mindplayers* (New York: Bantam, 1987), p. 4.
6. William Gibson, *Neuromancer* (1984) (London: Grafton, 1985), p. 12.
7. Isaac Asimov, *I, Robot* (Hicksville, NY: Gnome Press, 1950); *The Rest of the Robots* (New York: Doubleday, 1964); *The Bicentennial Man* (New York: Doubleday, 1976).
8. Anthony Boucher, 'The Quest For St Aquin', in Raymond J. Healy, ed., *New Tales of Space and Time* (New York: Henry Holt, 1951).
9. See http://www.sorayama.net/Gynoids/gynoids.html/, for readers eighteen years and over only.
10. Melissa Scott, *Dreamships* (New York: Tor, 1992).
11. Greg Egan, *Schild's Ladder* (London: Gollancz, 2002), p. 70.
12. Roger Zelazny, *Lord of Light* (1967) (New York: Avon, 1969), p. 96.
13. Gwyneth Jones, 'Metempsychosis of the Machine', *Science-Fiction Studies* 24 (1977), p. 4
14. Greg Bear, *Blood Music* (1984) (London: Arrow, 1985), p. 24.
15. Carol J. Clover, *Men, Women and Chainsaws* (Princeton: Princeton University Press, 1992).
16. See http://members.tripod.com/~voxish/Home.html.

# 12

JOAN SLONCZEWSKI AND MICHAEL LEVY

# Science fiction and the life sciences

Since humans are innately biological, and since most sf concerns human beings or other biological life forms, sf writers inevitably make biological assumptions – if only the default assumptions that the planets their fictional space travellers visit will have adequate gravity, air and exotic natives with the right number of chromosomes to interbreed. Such crude assumptions are commonly taken for granted in so-called 'hard science' stories that focus on the physics of space travel or interstellar warfare. Over the past decade, however, writers more often have turned to biology as the 'hard science' frontier of the future. The quest for outer space has given way to the quest for the genome. The great adversary is no longer an alien superpower, but the enemies within – cancer, AIDS, and bio-weapons – as well as the accidental results of genetic manipulation, and our own lifestyle destroying our bio-sphere. The engineering challenge of the future is less a matter of machines replacing living organisms than of machines imitating life's complexity.

The early roots of biology in speculative fiction are well described in Pamela Sargent's thoughtful introduction to the anthology, *Bio-Futures* (1976).[1] In the nineteenth and early twentieth centuries, writers faced questions of biological change, intended or unintended, in human nature, or in our natural surroundings. The founding work, arguably the basis for all of sf since, is Mary Shelley's *Frankenstein* (1818). Dr Frankenstein attempts to usurp the power of Nature by creating life out of dead body parts, an idea extrapolated from known science of that era, the electrical stimulation of dead muscle. Frankenstein succeeds in creating life, but the result is a monster, a life-form undesirable by our 'natural' standard. Readers continue to enjoy the story today, though some wonder whether the 'monster' is really bad, or just foreign – different from its creator, as children can be different from their parents. Today's debate about human cloning raises remarkably similar issues: would a cloned child be 'bad', or simply different? Or, ironically, not 'different' enough?

Early sf treatments of biology were generally somewhat vague as to mechanisms, largely because advances in biology lagged behind the physical sciences until the discovery of DNA and the genetic code (building proteins based on DNA information). As late as the 1970s some scientists still argued that living systems were based on special 'vitalistic' or 'emergent' principles distinct from physical or chemical laws. Science fiction of that period reflects this ambivalence; for example, Frank Herbert's *Dune* (1966) portrays living ecosystems in mechanistic detail consistent with contemporary ecological science, yet the same book depicts people with extrasensory powers and memories of past lives that are inconsistent with fundamental science. In later decades, as medical research increasingly revealed the human body and mind as a physico-chemical system, sf shifted to 'cyberpunk' depictions of human-machine hybrids.

Over the past century, certain themes in sf related to biology have shown remarkable endurance up to the present. These include:

Intelligence and the brain. Increase, decrease or alteration of human intelligence or brain function fundamentally changes the nature of humanity.

Mutation and evolution. Mutation is the basis of all biological change, including nature's drama of evolution.

Genetic engineering. Genetic manipulation alters the physiology or behaviour of individuals, populations or the entire human race.

Sexuality and reproduction. Altered mechanisms of sex and reproduction change the nature of human relationships and restructure society.

Environment and biosphere. Endangered species and environments, indeed our entire biosphere, face destruction by human technology.

## Intelligence and the brain

A long-standing preoccupation of sf writers has been the nature of human intelligence, and its relationship to the physiology of the brain. Wells's *Time Machine* expresses pessimism regarding the survival of intelligence, but most writers of the early twentieth century aspired to enhance or transcend human brain-power. In J. D. Beresford's *The Hampdenshire Wonder* (1911), Olaf Stapledon's *Odd John* (1935), A. E. Van Vogt's *Slan* (1940; 1946) and other works, this increase in intelligence comes through natural evolution or mutation. In the film *Forbidden Planet* (1956), a member of an exploration team uses 'an IQ booster' to outsmart the evil scientist, but dies in the attempt to increase his brain-power. In Poul Anderson's *Brain Wave* (1954), as the Earth moves out of a radiation belt that has hitherto limited intelligence, causing animal IQs to increase to the level formerly achieved by developmentally disabled people, and the IQ of normal people to increase to super-genius levels, social disruption ensues. A more recent variation on this theme occurs in Vernor Vinge's *A Fire Upon the Deep* (1992), where some force innate to the galaxy controls the limits of intelligence, varying according to how far from the galactic core that intelligence evolves.

The Cold War and the Vietnam War led many writers back to pessimism regarding the value of human intelligence. Michael Crichton's *The Andromeda Strain* (1969) depicts the errors of America's brightest medical scientists trying to fight a deadly plague from outer space. Crichton concludes with a remarkable essay on the human brain as a parasite, draining more than its share of blood flow while leading us to inevitable blunders. A similar sense of the uselessness of brain-power drives Kurt Vonnegut's *Galápagos* (1985). In this brilliant updating of *The Time Machine*, the self-destruction of the human race leaves only a handful of survivors on an isolated island where their intelligence no longer contributes to survival. In the absence of natural selection for intelligent offspring, degenerative evolution occurs, and the humans evolve into mindless sea creatures. The mechanisms of genetic selection and evolution are depicted with textbook accuracy, while the politics and moral conventions of the 'Star Wars' era are dissected with savage irony.

The relationship between the human mind and the physiology of the brain has been a common theme in sf. Until the 1970s, how the brain functioned was largely unknown and major institutions such as Duke University supported research into so-called extrasensory perception (ESP), phenomena that supposedly existed outside testable science. Part of this interest in psychic phenomena grew out of the popularity of such late nineteenth and early twentieth century occultists as H. P. Blavatsky and Charles Fort, and found expression in such novels as J. D. Beresford's *The Hampdenshire Wonder*, A. E. Van Vogt's *Slan,* Theodore Sturgeon's *More Than Human* (1953), and Joanna Russ's *And Chaos Died* (1970). Even a writer as scientifically based as Frank Herbert postulated extrasensory perception and supernatural powers in novels such as *Dune* (1965) and *The Dosadi Experiment* (1977). Although ESP still turns up in latter-day pulp adventure fiction and film, in *Star Wars* for example, it is relatively rare in contemporary hard sf.

As physical and chemical imaging techniques have revealed the brain's inner workings, sf writers have gone beyond the largely discredited notion of ESP to explore the biochemical frontiers of the brain. For example, Nancy Kress's *Beggars in Spain* (1993) and its sequels depict a class of humans genetically modified for brain function without sleep (a possibility that sleep researchers are exploring). Orson Scott Card in *Xenocide* (1991) and Vernor Vinge in *A Deepness in the Sky* (1999) consider the possibility of altering the human brain to induce obsessive compulsive disorder, creating highly talented workers who think only of the job at hand. In *Nekropolis* (2001) Maureen McHugh postulates a process whereby employees might be emotionally addicted to their employers, thus ensuring loyalty, and in *Queen of Angels* (1990) and *Slant* (1997) Greg Bear introduces a future America in which citizens routinely receive biochemical therapy to improve their mental stability. Kress's story 'The Flowers of Aulit Prison' (1996), and its sequel *Probability Moon* (2000), take a familiar sf theme of individuals with externally linked minds, but explains this based on an airborne chemical neurotransmitter. Joan Slonczewski's *Brain Plague* (2001) depicts microbial manipulation of the neurotransmitter dopamine to control human pleasure, based on current knowledge of molecular pathways in the brain.

## Mutation and evolution

Mutation, the ultimate mode of biological change, is an enduring theme in sf. Mutation leads to evolution, a principle of central importance to sf. The earliest writers to use that concept, particularly in France, were influenced as much by Lamarck and Henri Bergson as by Darwin: for example the astronomer Camille Flammarion's *La Fin du monde* (1893–4), translated as *Omega: The Last Days of the World*, and J.-H. Rosny aîné's prehistoric fantasy *La Guerre du feu* (1909), which was made into a 1981 film, *Quest for Fire*. As is so often the case, however, H. G. Wells, and particularly his *The Time Machine*, with its downbeat relatively near-future depiction of humanity evolved into two hostile sub-species, remains the classic of the theme. Wells accurately depicts the result of natural selection in terms of the evolution of large eyes in the dimly lit underground, and the degenerative evolution of the Eloi. He fails, however, to distinguish between genetic and social evolution, a crucial distinction that became clear later with the discovery of DNA.

*The Time Machine* has itself provoked several notable sequels, including David Lake's *The Man Who Loved Morlocks* (1981) and, more recently, Stephen Baxter's *The Time Ships* (1995), both of which argue forcefully against Wells's pessimism, and indeed turn the Morlocks into near-utopians. Although Wells was writing as much about class differences as about evolution when he described his Morlocks and Eloi, the novel popularized the idea that different species of humanity would be unable to coexist peacefully. Early examples of this theme have already been discussed above, including such tales as Stapledon's *Odd John* and Van Vogt's *Slan*. More recent examples of this theme are found in Greg Bear's *Darwin's Radio* (1999) and Octavia Butler's Xenogenesis trilogy (1987–9). Vonnegut's *Galápagos* echoes Wells's fear that the human brain may ultimately find itself useless and give way to degenerative evolution.

The idea that some key mutation might cause sudden evolutionary change, that entire new species might come into existence practically overnight, has always been popular. John Taine's evolutionary fantasies, *The Iron Star* (1930) and *The Seeds of Life* (1931), were important early examples of this idea. Recently, with the increasingly powerful arguments being promulgated by Stephen J. Gould and others for the concept of punctuated evolution, the theory that some changes can occur in a very short time frame, has gained renewed interest and has been used by a number of sf writers. Current examples include Bear's *Darwin's Radio* (1999), in which viral DNA hidden in non-coding sequences of the human genome (so-called junk DNA) holds a previously unguessed purpose, the sudden evolution of a new human species; and Greg Egan's *Teranesia* (1999), in which an unexplained mutation among the butterflies on a tropical island is the first hint that our world is about to be transformed.

The 'sudden change' stories, however, generally miss the point that even 'punctuated equilibrium' requires natural selection, including the deaths of numerous 'less fit' individuals, and takes many successive steps to generate true species divergence. Furthermore, they and other alien-ecosystem stories generally fail to depict the divergence of many related forms of life, instead of one or two; as a famous example, Herbert's *Dune* depicts only one species of desert-adapted sandworm. Multiple species divergence is depicted, however, in Crichton's *Jurassic Park* (1990) (many dinosaur species), Slonczewski's *A Door into Ocean* (1986) (various 'cephaglobinids', related to squid and octopus) and Slonczewski's *The Children Star* (1998), in which the entire ecosystem consists of animals, plants and microbes with a ring-shaped body plan. In other variations on this theme, Robert Charles Wilson, in *Darwinia* (1998), creates a modern Europe whose entire ecology has been replaced by life-forms from a wildly divergent evolution and Greg Bear, in *Legacy* (1995), postulates an alien world where the ecology of each continent consists of one living organism, called an 'ecos', which differentiates its various 'scions' to fill every available niche. In *Chaga* (1995, published in the USA as *Evolution's Shore*), Ian McDonald depicts the spread of a complex alien ecology across Africa and its gradual co-opting of terrestrial life-forms.

The spread and mutation of microbial life-forms, often deadly plagues, has been a theme since Wells's *War of the Worlds* (1898) in which, ironically, a plague from Earth saves humans from invading Martians. In most plague stories humans do not fare so well. One exceptionally well-done portrayal of plague, from the standpoint of medicine and character, is *Doomsday Book* by Connie Willis (1992). Time travellers accidentally visit the period of the Black Death, where they find that even their modern medical knowledge cannot save people of the fourteenth century from the scourge. Another is Kim Stanley Robinson's *The Years of Rice and Salt* (2002), which postulates a more virulent Black Death, one that kills 99 per cent of the population of Europe. Perhaps the most famous plague story is Michael Crichton's *The Andromeda Strain* (1969; filmed 1970) in which an extraterrestrial microbe kills nearly all its victims until it mutates into a form that grows outside humans. This scenario, while improbably rapid, does reflect the natural course of plague epidemiology, in that deadly pathogens tend to evolve into less virulent strains that keep their hosts alive longer.

In *Starfish* (1999) and *Maelstrom* (2001), Peter Watts depicts the sudden release of a primordial microbe from its limited ecological niche in a deep sea vent, due to human attempts to harness geothermal energy, and the horrific effect this has on all other terrestrial life. In *The Secret of Life* (2001) by Paul McAuley a similarly destructive life-form is brought back from Mars. Other writers have invented genetically engineered plagues, for example Stephen King in *The Stand* (1978), Frank Herbert in *The White Plague* (1982) and Geoff Ryman in *The Child Garden* (1989). More recently, Kathleen Ann Goonan in *Queen City Jazz* (1994) and its sequels has depicted genetically engineered plagues that have radically transformed life on Earth.

Several recent sf writers have gone so far as to blur the distinction between biological and artificial life-forms. Harking back to Greg Bear's seminal work *Blood Music* (1985), both Wil McCarthy, in *Bloom* (1998) and Linda Nagata in *Limits of Vision* (2001) postulate the creation of artificial life-forms that can evolve and differentiate much more quickly than can biological species. In McCarthy's novel, these 'mycora' take over the entire inner solar system, constantly creating new forms as needed, while unchanged humanity maintains a precarious toehold among the asteroids and the moons of Jupiter. Slonczewski's *Brain Plague* (2001) depicts intelligent microbes that manipulate nanotech devices while inhabiting the human circulatory system. As in *War of the Worlds*, however, these microbes reveal unexpected possible benefits for humankind.

A sinister extension of the plague theme involves biological warfare and bio-terrorism. In *The Andromeda Strain*, Crichton speculates that the deadly microbe from outer space may actually be a bio-weapon engineered by the government during the Cold War and released by accident. This could explain why the strain mutated so fast – it was engineered to become harmless after its deadly mission was complete. In Chelsea Quinn Yarbro's *Time of the Fourth Horseman* (1976) plagues are intentionally released upon the world in a wrong-headed attempt to deal with overpopulation. More recently, in Richard Preston's *The Cobra Event* (1997), a bio-terrorist creates a virus that induces the horrible self-mutilating symptoms of Lesch-Nyhan syndrome. The real-life anthrax scare of 2001 will surely inspire even more of this genre. In fact, continuing public concern about both biological warfare and emerging diseases, fuelled by such non-fiction best-sellers as Preston's own *The Hot Zone* (1994) and Laurie Garrett's *The Coming Plague* (1994), has already triggered the production of any number of biologically based, borderline-sf thrillers, in both book and movie format, for example the film *Outbreak* (1995), based on an earlier Robin Cook novel, and Charles Pellegrino's eco-thriller *Dust* (1998).

## Genetic engineering

The manipulation of mutation and evolution by humans is genetic engineering, once a fearful, undefined prospect, now a multibillion-dollar industry. The accumulating advances of the last half-century have found expression in sf, for example Janet Kagan's *Mirabile* (1991), which concerns genetically engineered animals (including Frankenswine) that hide the genomes of extinct species in the non-functional portions of their DNA. The culminating novel of gene technology is Crichton's *Jurassic Park* (1991, filmed 1993), about the cloning of dinosaurs based on minute quantities of DNA extracted from blood-sucking insects fossilized in amber. While at the time of writing the cloning of extinct creatures remains impossible, the use of the DNA detection methods shown in *Jurassic Park* is now a routine part of forensic biology and archaeology; and human cloning is a real possibility. Although cloning has a long history in sf, having been used with little or no serious scientific support by A. E. van Vogt in *The World of Null-A* (1948), among other early works, it has received more realistic depictions in recent years in such novels as Pamela Sargent's *Cloned Lives* (1976), Kate Wilhelm's *Where Late the Sweet Birds Sang* (1976) and, perhaps most impressively, in C. J. Cherryh's *Cyteen* (1988). More recently Robert Sawyer's *Frameshift* (1997) depicts an attempt to clone a Neanderthal.

The promise of the biotechnology revolution, however, has led to expectations that will not be fulfilled for many years. One concern is the expense of the new technologies: will they lead to a society of genetic haves and have-nots? The film *GATTACA* (1997) boldly explores what might happen if society took 'DNA perfection' too far, by reading the sequence of every individual's genome to determine their place in life. Slonczewski's *Daughter of Elysium* (1993) explores what a world might look like in which some people age and die, whereas others are engineered to live seemingly for ever. Many books, including Bruce Sterling's *Holy Fire* (1996), Brian Stableford's *Inherit the Earth* (1998) and its sequels, and Ken MacLeod's *Cosmonaut Keep* (2000) and its sequels, explore similar themes, while Sterling's *Distraction* (1998) turns a satirical eye on the near-future political complexities involved in genetic engineering.

The genetic technology that has led us to the threshold of cloning human beings has also spun off more esoteric technologies, such as the culturing of embryonic stem cells, which may enable the generation of artificial organs. The insertion of adult chromosomes into stem cells – in effect, cloning a person into tissue culture – could theoretically mean an inexhaustible supply of future organs. Yet such technology brings us perilously close to cloning babies for their parts. Science fiction is full of stories about harvesting humans and clones for their parts. Larry Niven has frequently written on this theme, beginning with 'The Jigsaw Man' (1967) and 'The Organleggers' (1969), envisioning that the availability of such a technology would lend itself both, outside the law, to a new and hideous form of bootlegging, and, inside the law, to new sorts of sentences for criminals. The idea soon moved into the realm of the mainstream thriller, most famously in Robin Cook's *Coma* (1977), in which patients undergoing minor surgery are kept in a comatose state to harvest their organs for transplantation. In a more recent variation on this theme, Michael Marshall Smith's *Spares* (1997), the rich clone themselves and keep their extra bodies in what are essentially prisons, gradually removing spare parts as needed.

## Sexuality and reproduction

The psychological aspects of sexuality are handled in great detail by Peter Nicholls in his entry on 'Sex' in *The Encyclopedia of Science Fiction*, but the biological side of this topic is of equal interest. From the very beginning sf writers have been fascinated by the depiction of new ways to create human life. In *Frankenstein* Mary Shelley postulates the possibility of sewing together human body parts and using lightning to jump-start that dead organic material. Directly or indirectly descended from her novel are hundreds, perhaps thousands, of sf stories that involve the creation of androids, cyborgs, clones and other artificial but organic human life-forms, from the title character of the film *The Terminator* (1984) to Marge Piercy's more emotionally complex golem in *He, She and It* (1991), the 'dolls' of Paul McAuley's *Fairyland* (1995) or Oscar Valparaiso, the politician-clone of Sterling's *Distraction*. In *Brave New World* (1932) Aldous Huxley created an entire civilization in which sex and reproduction have been completely separated.

Babies are born out of artificial wombs following a gestation period during which they have been carefully prepared to accept their future careers. This concept has seen more recent variations in the work of Marge Piercy, Lois McMaster Bujold and Octavia Butler. In her Vorkosigan series, Bujold postulates an entire galaxy-spanning civilization where artificial wombs are commonplace and where genetic material, suitably tailored to the needs of the customer, is easily purchased. In her *Ethan of Athos* (1986) she describes an entire planet whose homosexual society uses artificial wombs as the exclusive means of reproduction. Butler, in her Xenogenesis trilogy, beginning with *Dawn* (1987), goes one step further, describing an alien race which has specifically evolved to combine its own DNA with that of other species, thereby being able to create new, tailored life-forms without the need for technological assistance.

Although earlier writers, such as Theodore Sturgeon in *Venus Plus-X* (1960), had toyed with the idea of making basic changes in the human body structure and particularly in the means of sexual reproduction (some of them misogynistic, such as L. Sprague de Camp's 1951 *Rogue Queen* with its matriarchal hive society), most of the more interesting variations in the depiction of physical human sexuality are an outgrowth of the women's movement and the increased participation of women in sf. Ursula K. Le Guin's *The Left Hand of Darkness* (1969), set on a planet where in the prehistoric past an alien race had manipulated human DNA to make its inhabitants functional hermaphrodites, is perhaps the most important book of this sort. Also significant, however, is philosopher Shulamith Firestone's treatise *The Dialectics of Sex* (1970), which describes a number of feminist/utopian alternatives to our world and which directly or indirectly influenced such novels as Suzy McKee Charnas's *Walk to the Edge of the World* (1974), Joanna Russ's *The Female Man* (1975), Marge Piercy's *Woman on the Edge of Time* (1976) and Samuel Delany's *Triton* (1976). The Russ and Delany novels postulate cultures in which technology makes possible the reassignment of basic biological roles such as breast-feeding. In Piercy's novel, which was heavily indebted to Firestone, artificial wombs are used to free women for other work. Building on the work of Charlotte Perkins Gilman, above all her *Herland* (1915), and other earlier feminist writers, Charnas, in *Walk to the Edge of the World*, *Motherlines* (1978) and two much later sequels, creates a ruined world where some women, the descendants of an ancient scientific experiment, reproduce parthenogenetically, without the aid of men, using horse sperm to trigger but not actively participate in reproduction. James Tiptree, Jr uses a similar concept in the classic short story 'Houston, Houston, Do You Read?' (1977). More recent writers, such as Joan Slonczewski in *Daughter of Elysium* (1993) and Carolyn Ives Gilman in *Halfway Human*

(1998), have continued to explore possible physical variations in human sexuality.

A theme related to reproduction and life cycles is parasitism. The enduring popularity of the *Alien* series of films attests to the intense fascination of this horrifying phenomenon – when humans are the ones parasitized by an alien creature. The first film, *Alien* (Ridley Scott, 1979), does a particularly nice job of illustrating the actual principles of biological parasitism – insertion of the egg into an unwilling or unknowing host, feeding of the larva within the host's helpless body, then unthinking destruction of the host upon the creature's exit. A more subtle relationship between host and parasite is that shown in Octavia Butler's award-winning story 'Bloodchild' (1984). In this case, an insectoid alien requires human hosts for its brood, but attempts to feed the host and ensure its survival after the ordeal. Critics have suggested that both these works indirectly comment on the idea of 'male pregnancy', that is to say, how would we think of pregnancy if it happened to men?

## Environment and biosphere

Since the publication of Rachel Carson's *Silent Spring* (1962), and the awakening of the environmental movement, sf writers have confronted the dilemma of the effects of human beings on our biosphere. The most stark cases have been in the genre of post-apocalyptic novels, such as Nevil Shute's *On the Beach* (1957), or Russell Hoban's *Riddley Walker* (1980), or in novels predicting impending environmental collapse, such as David Brin's *Earth* (1990), and Dennis Danvers's *The Fourth World* (2000). In other cases, environmental concern has led to large-scale depictions of entire planets and multiple societies grappling with the problem of 'terraforming', that is, of how much change, intended or otherwise, to inflict on a biosphere to bend it to human needs.

The first planetary ecology novel on a grand scale was Frank Herbert's *Dune* (1965), a book so large and complex that it was rejected by sixteen publishers before it became a best-seller. *Dune* depicts several different cultures and political groups in their attempt to control the desert planet Arrakis, where a unique ecosystem has evolved to survive with minimal water. The ecosystem with its food web is depicted in intriguing detail, including the complex life cycle of the sandworm which produces the unique psychotropic 'spice'. The Fremen, people native to Arrakis, face the dilemma of terraforming the planet to bring water, while avoiding extinction of the sandworms that product the invaluable spice. Ahead of its time, *Dune* foreshadows the agonizing struggles of the future between near-term utilization and long-term preservation of natural resources.

The success of *Dune* enabled the publication of other epic novels of world-building, such as Slonczewski's *A Door into Ocean* (1986), perhaps the most complex ecosystem that has been presented in fiction. *Ocean* in some ways is a direct answer to *Dune*: a world whose central problem is not lack of water, but lack of land. The ecosystem of the ocean world Shora features a full range of organisms, including producers, primary and secondary consumers and symbiotic microbes. Evolutionary divergence is shown among the diverse species of 'cephaglobinid', a squid-like life-form. Where *Dune* foreshadows ecological disruption, *Ocean* illustrates the disruptive dynamic: removal of one species, the monster seaswallowers, perturbs population of species all along the food chain. The people of Shora, who call themselves 'Sharers', claim to resist terraforming their planet, preferring even to be eaten alive by predators rather than harm the balance of nature. Yet the Sharers are in fact advanced genetic engineers, actively regulating the populations of many species. Thus their role is ambiguous: are they truly non-disruptive participants in their ecosystem, or are they the ultimate genetic regulators of their world? In our third millennium, environmental protectors increasingly find themselves forced into the latter role, reluctant managers of our ever-shrinking biosphere.

A book that brought terraforming closer to home (or at least back to our solar system) is Kim Stanley Robinson's *Red Mars* (1992). *Red Mars* arguably presents the most compelling depiction of the Martian landscape ever written. The frigid, dry landscape with its towering volcanoes and deep canyons gives way to colonization by the first living organisms: microbes resistant to cold and cosmic radiation, including species such as cyanobacteria, which provide oxygen for the atmosphere. The human colonists discuss extensively the merits of terraforming: the value of leaving Martian geology intact; the need for scientifically controlled management, to enable large-scale human habitation; and the political view that planetary change is inevitable and uncontrollable. In 1998 Robinson made the dangers of accidental terraforming even more compelling in his novel *Antarctica,* which depicts the near destruction of that continent's ecology due to global warming and other human-related activities.

Where is biological sf headed in the new millennium, as daily headlines on human cloning and global warming outdate our fiction? Ironically, works intended as pessimistic, such as *Jurassic Park*, have had the actual effect of inspiring a generation of optimistic scientists: gene cloners, the pioneers of biotechnology, clone stem cells to cure aging, while a new breed of techno-ecologists model greenhouse-gas emissions and mount sophisticated political campaigns to rescue our biosphere from ourselves. An updated 'Franken-stein' monster, portrayed in the *X-Files* episode 'Postmodern Prometheus', is generated by gene technology based on contemporary experiments on the fruit fly. After much mayhem, the irrepressible FBI duo liberate the monster to dance in a nightclub. In post-millennial sf, the band plays on for genetic engineers, with our breakthroughs in human cloning and stem cell research. Yet it also leaves us fearful of biological warfare, and wondering how our moral traditions of the past millennia will survive the technological challenges of this one.

## NOTE

1. Pamela Sargent, ed., *Bio-futures* (New York: Vintage, 1976), pp. xi–xxxv.

# 13

### KATHRYN CRAMER

# Hard science fiction

### Knowing it when we see it

Hard science fiction, the most science-oriented sf, enjoys greater popularity with readers and writers than with critics. Less criticism is written on hard sf than on many other aspects of sf. What criticism exists tends to try to define it compactly, thus making it easier to study retrospectively. What critics usually exclude from the sub-genre either plays too loosely with the facts, or lacks the proper attitude. (The latter is usually considered the more serious transgression.)

Sf's community of writers, readers and editors resists defining genres and sub-genres. In 1999, long-time *Analog* editor Stanley Schmidt, heir to John W. Campbell's job, remarked:

> Lately I've been saying I'd like the term 'Hard SF' to go away. Too many people use it to mean something much narrower than what I mean by it...science fiction is simply fiction in which some element of speculation plays such an essential and integral role that it can't be removed without making the story collapse, and in which the author has made a reasonable effort to make the speculative element as plausible as possible. Anything that doesn't meet those requirements is not science fiction at all, as far as I'm concerned, so there's no need for a separate term like 'Hard SF' to distinguish it from 'other' kinds of sf.[1]

The anti-definition/boundary sentiment is widespread, partly because definitions and genre boundaries are often seen as publisher's impositions of marketing categories on writers' creativity; and, as in Schmidt's case, to editors and publishers, they can seem like unnecessary constraints imposed by the audience or the distribution system.

Also, as Schmidt says, to consider hard sf as a separate sub-genre presents definitional problems. Unlike other sub-genres, such as cyberpunk or feminist sf, that branched off from sf in a specialized political or aesthetic departure from the norm, hard sf began undifferentiated from sf as a whole. Only in the late 1950s was there a felt need to name it. Nonetheless, by studying hard sf, we implicitly accept the need of a sub-genre and its accompanying baggage.

Since a literary genre is a form of conversation among writers, one useful approach is to find writers who say they are writing hard sf and see what they do and say about it. This means including writers who seem out of place, have a bad attitude (that is, who display inadequate faith in and enthusiasm for science and technology) or choose unorthodox tactics for yoking the science to the fiction. This approach occasionally enrages hard sf purists, as it results in a more sprawling sub-genre.[2] However, it more faithfully reproduces the range of literary activities going on in hard sf. The body of interviews with hard sf writers and also the occasional essays by these writers comprises one of the most useful secondary sources on hard sf. Many of these interviews were published in *Locus* over the past twenty years; a growing number appear on authors' websites.[3] If one scours interviews and essays for what these writers think they are doing, it quickly becomes apparent that they do not agree on what hard sf is or ought to be, nor on how to do it. This disagreement is very fertile ground for a growing literature.

Another rule of thumb for studying hard sf is that it is important to know the history of the motifs used – the main element, idea, theme or subject to be elaborated on or developed. There is something like scientific refereeing going on in hard sf, and so it is often necessary to know the other works with which a work is in dialogue. As Gregory Benford remarks, 'In my experience, writers of "the hard stuff" . . . hold in common the internationalist idealism of scientific bodies, and in their free trading of ideas often behave like scientists.'[4] Sometimes a motif appears in many works published around the same time because the topic is in the air, as with the many hard sf novels about Mars in the 1990s, which followed the first President Bush's pronouncement about a manned Mars mission in the twenty-first century; in other instances, for example Allen Steele's *Chronospace* (2001) which is in argument with previous time travel sf, a discussion is in progress. To fail to follow the thread of motifs is to be deaf to an important part of the sub-genre conversation.

So if the sub-genre is a contentious conversation in constant flux, how do we avoid solipsistic definitions that amount to knowing it when one sees it? We return to a modified conventional wisdom for our definition: a work of sf is hard sf if a relationship to and knowledge of science and technology is central to the work. Such works are usually characterized by attitudes found in previous examples of hard sf, but may instead be characterized by attitudes in opposition to or in argument or dialogue with such attitudes.

The primary characteristic for defining a work as hard sf is its relationship with science.

In 'Hard Science Fiction', David Hartwell enumerates criteria for recognizing hard sf: (1) 'Hard SF is about the beauty of truth...about the emotional experience of describing and confronting what is scientifically true.' (2) 'Hard SF feels authentic to the experienced reader when the way things work in the story is scientifically plausible.' (3) 'Hard SF relies, at some point in the story, on expository prose rather than literary prose, prose aimed at describing the nature of its particular reality.' (4) 'Hard SF relies on scientific knowledge external to the story.' And (5) 'Hard SF achieves its characteristic affect essentially through informing, by being, in fact, didactic.'[5]

Also, as I have remarked elsewhere,[6] when scientific ideas and formulations are invoked in a text that does not make use of mathematics in appropriate amounts, the text relies upon other texts that do. Before science can be incorporated into hard sf, it must be stripped of its mathematical bones, so that – no matter how accurate the text – science is used as a mythology. What science gives to hard sf is a body of metaphor that provides the illusion of both realism and rationalism.

By reputation, hard sf is science fiction that gets its science right and has a certain hard-nosed attitude.[7] Its plots and backgrounds are in the tradition of Hal Clement's *Mission of Gravity* (1953), its attitudes in the tradition of Robert A. Heinlein.

Gregory Benford remarks that hard sf 'sticks to *facts*...but can play fast and loose with theory as it likes'.[8] The author need not think said theory is likely to be true; only that it should not compromise fidelity to facts for purposes of narrative drama or, if it does, that this should happen in such a way that the reader does not much notice. Two of Benford's stories that are careful with facts and high-handed with theoretical speculation are 'Matter's End', in which a Hindu physics cult turns out to be right about quantum mechanics, and 'Anomalies', concerning a mathematical correction which propagates through the universe, making changes as it goes.[9] While not the sole tactic by which science is incorporated into what we recognize as hard sf, this is the most often discussed.

By reputation, hard sf is Campbellian, in the mould of the fiction published and promoted by John W. Campbell[10] (an idealized Campbell, not the real man who was taken in by hokey ideas such as extrasensory perception and L. Ron Hubbard's Dianetics). Hard sf stakes an implicit claim to being apolitical. In hard sf, when politicians appear at all, they are usually ignorant fools or outright villains, reflecting the experiences of actual working scientists.

The works of Hal Clement, for example, are almost entirely apolitical, in that he disdains political discourse for scientific discourse.

The most frequently discussed example of the hard sf attitude is Tom Godwin's controversial story 'The Cold Equations' (1954), in which the girl stowaway is ejected out the airlock 'because the lives of many depend on it'.[11] The Campbellian moral is that the universe does not furnish happy endings just because we want them. This attitude is embodied by a tough, pragmatic, (usually) masculine narrative voice. But it is also futuristic and often utopian, and therefore a bit fanciful. These aspects are expected to pair up naturally: the attitude arising from scientific accuracy; the scientific and technological accuracy arising from the proper attitude. However, overfocusing on attitude not only ejects most of the women writers from the sub-genre,[12] but also distracts us from discovering the virtues crucial to an appreciation of hard sf.

Strict application of hard sf's traditional definitions excludes more hard sf than it includes. Not only do 'facts' age badly, but often the most memorable stories bend more than just theory to their purposes. And the hard sf attitude can be stripped of its scientific underpinnings until what remains is fetishism – a love of hardware for its own sake, especially military hardware – and the hard-nosed Ayn Rand voice that we now identify as libertarian. More importantly, many fine examples of hard sf either deploy science unconventionally or lack that hard sf attitude. Not only does the strict-constructionist definition exclude the likes of Ursula K. Le Guin even at her most ethnographic (as in *Always Coming Home*, 1985), but as Tom Shippey points out, if applied honestly, it also requires that we kick out Isaac Asimov despite his claim to write hard sf and a strict-constructionist critical consensus that he belongs in the club.[13]

Complicating matters further, authors are not uniform within their own bodies of work as to how they use science and technology, nor are they consistent in the attitudes of their narrative voices. A major reason for critics to define genre boundaries is to examine the games writers play with them. Even among the most clear-cut members of the club, there can usually be found individual works that play subversive games with the supposed boundaries of hard sf or in some other way transgresses them within the author's body of work. Genre boundaries matter in large part because they are an object for collective artistic innovation.

The term 'hard sf' is used similarly to 'Golden Age sf' and has always been nostalgic, referring to a lost era of 'real sf'.[14] But through its connection to contemporary science, itself a moving target, hard sf as a literature has remained a difficult target for critical examination.

## Finding the science in hard science fiction

Hard sf derives virtues from its unique relationship with science. In an appendix to *The Ascent of Wonder*, David Hartwell and I sorted stories into categories by the primary manner in which science is used.[15] Arthur C. Clarke's 'Transit of Earth' (1971) and Poul Anderson's 'Kyrie' (1969) both use science's imagery: Clarke to refute the New Wave, specifically J. G. Ballard's dying astronaut stories such as 'The Cage of Sand' (1963), by demonstrating the proper attitude towards planetary exploration; and Anderson by using a black hole as a device to literalize a piece of Christian theology. Both Greg Bear's 'Tangents' (1986) and Vernor Vinge's 'Bookworm, Run!' (1966) use their scientific concepts in the service of characterization: Bear's protagonist is a bright boy who does not really fit in and so retreats to the fourth dimension; Vinge's protagonist is a technologically augmented chimpanzee. Both stories use scientific and technological concepts to portray the predicament of the too-smart kid. Rudy Rucker's 'Message Found in a Copy of Flatland' (1983) and Gregory Benford's 'Relativistic Effects' (1982) are set in two very different scientifically generated places; the science underlying the setting allows the story to exist. The literary point of view in Ursula K. Le Guin's 'Author of the Acacia Seeds' (1974) is an anthropological report written by an ant. And in Henry Kuttner and C. L. Moore's 'Mimsy Were the Borogroves' (1943), contrasting characters' points of view drive the plot of the story: some characters perceive more physical dimensions than others. In Frederik Pohl's 'Day Million' (1966), the accelerated narrative pace points towards a future of accelerating change.

Bob Shaw's 'Light of Other Days' (1966) is a big-idea story: light takes years to get through Shaw's slow glass, allowing the viewer looking through, in effect, to see into the past. (It will not work. But Shaw's story-telling carries us past that.) Finally there are the problem-solving hard sf stories which focus on plot, such as Larry Niven's 'The Hole Man' (1973), concerning a murder in which the murder weapon is a quantum black hole (a now-discarded scientific idea), and Edgar Allen Poe's 'A Descent into the Maelstrom' (1841), in which the protagonist uses scientific knowledge to save himself from being swallowed by a whirlpool. Big-idea stories and problem-solving stories are the easiest to identify taxonomically and are in the purist or conservative view the only 'real' hard sf.

Comparing and contrasting stories that use similar strategies of appropriating science for fiction, but to very different effect, could yield interesting criticism on hard sf. But since critics rarely consider initial strategies employed, such articles are rare. However, as one can see, the possibilities have not been lost on the writers themselves.

In 1986, David Brin remarked on an abundance of sf convention panels on the topic 'Is hard sf dead or dying?', on whether hard sf's source of material was 'mined out': 'Scientific SF – the hard SF having to do with the very nature of reality – may be entering an era of hard times. It is a common truism that there will never be a dearth of good and original new ideas. But is it wise to count on a truism to be true?'[16] In 1994, Brian Stableford suggested that even the availability of ideas may not be sufficient to keep hard sf alive.[17]

But in 2003, hard sf is in wonderful shape. Is this merely because the truism remains true? Or are other forces at work? Certainly, to some extent the truism holds good. The rise of the Internet and other communications technologies as a social force and the rapid progress in the biological and information sciences and in astronomy, resulted in an explosion of good stuff to write about and writers met the challenge: Greg Egan's 'Wang's Carpet' (1995) (most memorable for the image of a naturally occurring computer program in which exists virtual life) and 'Reasons to Be Cheerful' (1997) (in which the protagonist is given the technological means to choose what gives him pleasure); Joan Slonczewski's 'Microbe' (1995) (where she takes an existing form of DNA, the toroidal chromosomes of prokaryotes, and extrapolates a whole cultivated world in which all niches are filled by organisms of that type); Paul McAuley's 'Gene Wars' (1991) (a dystopia: the biotech revolution leads to a rate of social change like that in Pohl's 'Day Million', 1966); and Vernor Vinge's 'Fast Times at Fairmont High' (2001) (the information revolution run amok in high school).[18]

Also, as Stephen Baxter observes, hard sf has digested the more disheartening findings of planetary exploration, and has begun to appreciate the planets as they actually are (rather than as we had hoped they might be):

> The Moon turned out to be dead and dull, spaceflight there was difficult and a bore, Mars is almost inaccessible to us right now and sterilized by ultraviolet anyhow, Venus is a hellhole. We've learned all this in the last couple of decades, and it shattered a lot of fond illusions. Did you know that the first Mars probe, Mariner 4, was sent over a part of Mars where canals were expected? . . . the craters were a hell of a shock. And the Soviet's first Venus probe was equipped to float in the oceans there. Now we've worked through all that, to some extent.[19]

Leading the planetary charge, Kim Stanley Robinson mined his 1985 novella 'Green Mars' for what became his Mars trilogy – *Red Mars* (1992), *Green Mars* (1994), *Blue Mars* (1996) – and a collection, *The Martians* (1999). Robinson injects large doses of communitarian political discussion, but also intensifies the overt science and portrays scientists at work, and (like Arthur C. Clarke) evocatively describes the natural landscape of his planetary setting. Robinson's Mars books were among the first in what became a wave of Mars exploration books: *Moving Mars* (1993) by Greg Bear, *Mars* by Ben Bova (1992), *Mars Crossing* (2000) by Geoffrey A. Landis and others.

When it was more fashionable to explore virtuality, Robinson remained steadfastly loyal to actuality as the true origin of stories. Rather than exploring the multi-layered virtual worlds and uploaded minds, he imagined how people would get along if they colonized Mars; not the sf trope Mars, the easily habitable planet, in the tradition of Edgar Rice Burroughs's Barsoom series, Stanley G. Weinbaum's 'A Martian Odyssey' (1934), Ray Bradbury's *Martian Chronicles* (1950) or for that matter, Philip K. Dick's *Martian Timeslip* (1964), but the real place. While to some extent, Robinson's approach to Mars comes out of Clement's *Mission of Gravity* (1953), his approach is less world-building than a faith in powerful settings to tell powerful stories. New tales of planetary exploration are characteristic of the revival of hard sf in North America in the 1990s.

Another change in hard sf came through the magazines. It is one over which the British sf magazine *Interzone* has had more influence than the old American standard, *Analog*, and that is a shift in attitude, or more precisely, politics.

### Politics and hard science fiction

Hard sf is receptive to a variety of sciences, but its literary tactics and attitude seem most suited to physics and astronomy, disciplines operating on a grand scale. Dealing as they do with the fundamentals of the universe, these are superficially the purest of the sciences, but have been irretrievably politicized by the march of twentieth-century history: a rocket is not just transportation to the moon, but also an instrument of mass destruction. The political elements that unify hard sf are the advocacy of space travel; the elements that divide are those of military policy. Despite its divisiveness, military policy provides a nearly irresistible lure for hard sf writers, especially American writers, namely, the seductive possibility of a technological fix for the problem of nuclear arms, the possibility that the nuclear genie might somehow be stuffed back in its bottle.

In the early 1980s, Jerry Pournelle called together Robert A. Heinlein, Gregory Benford, Poul Anderson, Larry Niven, Dean Ing and others to form an official science advisory committee, Citizen's Advisory Council on National Space Policy, to advise then President Ronald Reagan, and promoted the Strategic Defense Initiative (SDI; called 'Star Wars' by the press). As Greg Bear told the story in his 2001 WorldCon Guest of Honour Speech,

'Science fiction writers helped the rocket scientists elucidate their vision and clarified it. They put it together in prose that Ronald Reagan could understand, and Ronald Reagan, who read science fiction, said "Why not?"'

Gregory Benford has discussed the political schisms within hard sf that resulted from the Council's advocacy of SDI.[20] Arthur C. Clarke and Robert A. Heinlein had a falling-out at a meeting of the Council because Clarke suggested SDI was a bad idea – this moment symbolizes the developing divide between US and UK hard sf in the 1980s, of the consequences of the right-wing politicization of American hard sf that began in the 1970s. There was a divide among US writers too: Isaac Asimov resigned from the board of governors of the L-5 Society, a pro-space lobbying group, because the organization would not oppose SDI. H. Bruce Franklin discusses sf's influence on US military policy for the several decades leading up to these events in his book *War Stars* (1988).

Print literature took a parallel course with similarly divisive results. Editor Jim Baen – first at Tor Books and, by 1984, at his own company, Baen Books – published and promoted right-wing, militaristic hard sf and space opera. Jerry Pournelle's There Will Be War anthology series is the touchstone for this type of publishing: 'hard SF evolved into right wing power fantasies about military hardware, men killing things with big machines'.[21] By 1995, Baen Books went so far to publish *1945*, a collaboration between sf writer William Forstchen and arch-conservative Speaker-of-the-House Newt Gingrich about super-weapons and the Third Reich.

The politics of *Analog* were a bit milder: by the mid-1980s they had become codified as a technologically optimistic libertarianism. *Analog*'s outlook is so rosy now that one wonders whether Godwin's 'The Cold Equations' (1954) would be accepted for publication there today. If, indeed, it was once paradigmatic of the Campbellian strain of hard sf,[22] it is no longer.

The most generalized symptom of the reactions against the politicization of hard sf was a sense that good writers were turning away from the subgenre and that its continued existence was in peril. However, some writers and editors became more proactive, trying to wrestle hard sf back into what they considered the proper shape.

In the early 1980s Bruce Sterling became the centre of a literary duststorm by publishing the fanzine *Cheap Truth* under the pseudonym Vincent Omniaveritas.[23] The first issue was mainly an attack on fantasy: 'As American SF lies in a reptilian torpor, its small, squishy cousin, Fantasy, creeps gecko-like across the bookstands.' For four or five issues, Sterling attacked fiction he found irritating and praised a variety of books with descriptions like: *Past Master* by R. A. Lafferty, 'His most decipherable SF novel', or *A World Out of Time* by Larry Niven, 'Heartening indication that Niven may escape total artistic collapse.' Eventually, Sterling came round to the rhetoric he is known for and *Cheap Truth* evolved into the propaganda organ for the movement later known as cyberpunk. When laying out *Cheap Truth 6*, he took a pair of scissors to a photocopy of David Pringle and Colin Greenland's editorial in *Interzone* 8 (Summer 1984), which read:

> Last issue we described *Interzone* as a magazine of *radical* science fiction and fantasy. Now we should like to go further and outline (however hazily) a type of story that we want to see much more of in this magazine: the *radical, hard SF* story. We wish to publish more fiction which takes its inspiration from science, and which uses the language of science in a creative way. It may be fantastic, surrealistic, 'illogical', but in order to be radical *hard* SF it should explore in some fashion the perspectives opened up by contemporary science and technology. Some would argue that the new electronic gadgetry is displacing the printed word – if so, writers should fight back, using guerrilla tactics as necessary and infiltrating the territory of the enemy.

At the time, Sterling was one of only a handful of US subscribers to *Interzone* and set out to spread this gospel in the US. The editorial for the sixth issue of *Cheap Truth*, created using rubber cement and Burroughsian cut-up technique, read:

> EDITORIAL. radical, hard SF
> seeing signs that something new is imminent –
> new fiction from the bounty of new technology.
> /// the perspectives opened up by contemporary science fight back, using guerilla tactics
> new information systems f/a/s/h/i/o/n that new science fiction
> for the *electronic age*

Thus, in the US, 'radical hard SF' was an early name for the movement later christened 'cyberpunk'. Within a few years, cyberpunk was characterized by a particular attitude, specific literary furniture and a fetish for new technology, but early on – in Sterling's vision – it involved reinventing hard sf. Of those writers identified with early cyberpunk to whom the term stuck, Sterling is the one most interested in science as such and only he and Rudy Rucker have a continuing interest in hard sf.

Meanwhile, *Interzone* was more successful at hard sf's radical reform, nurturing the early careers of a number of writers who led hard sf to its current state of health, most notably the British writers Stephen Baxter and Paul McAuley, and the Australian, Greg Egan. Stephen Baxter represents a return to the hard sf's apolitical mode, with its contempt for bureaucrats and advocacy of space exploration.

In contrast, Paul McAuley labels himself a writer of radical hard sf, defined as:

> SF rooted in the core traditions of SF but also surfing the wave of the present, with rounded characters, bleeding edge science, an attempt to convey the complexity of a world or worlds. It's a reaction to the trad SF approach of filtering the future through One Big Change – nanotechnology, immortality, biotech. If there's one thing we've learnt from the twentieth century, it's that change is continuous and is advancing on a thousand different fronts.[24]

Greg Egan was one of the most innovative and controversial hard sf writers of the 1990s. He says in an interview: 'what happens in my novels is that the border between science and metaphysics shifts: issues that originally seemed completely metaphysical, completely beyond the realms of scientific enquiry, actually become part of physics. I'm writing about extending science into territory that was once believed to be metaphysical, not about abandoning or "transcending" science at all.'[25] The new flowering of hard sf provides many opportunities for critical examination. Older forms of hard sf continue to appear alongside the new, resulting in a rich, diverse sub-genre. We are in the second stage of this flowering as readers and writers rush to update their scientific currency under pressure of rapid scientific and technological change.

## NOTES

1. Interview with Stanley Schmidt by Jaime Blashke. SF Site, http://www.sfsite.com/07a/sts84.htm.
2. Of this approach in David G. Hartwell and Kathryn Cramer, eds., *The Ascent of Wonder* (New York: Tor, 1994), David Samuelson complains in 'A Softening of the Hard-SF Concept', at p. 409, that '[it] deprecate[s] the real thing, watering it down so much as to virtually destroy any generic consistency'.
3. Alastair Reynolds links to the websites of many hard sf writers plus an essay of his own at members.tripod.com/~voxish/sf_hard_authors.html.
4. Gregory Benford, 'Real Science, Imaginary Worlds', in Hartwell and Cramer, eds., *The Ascent of Wonder*, p. 16.
5. David G. Hartwell, 'Hard Science Fiction', in Hartwell and Cramer, eds., *The Ascent of Wonder*, pp. 30–4.
6. Cramer, 'Science Fiction and the Adventures of the Spherical Cow', *The New York Review of Science Fiction* 1 (September 1988), pp. 1, 3–5.
7. See, for example, George Slusser and Eric Rabkin: 'The method . . . of the hard science fiction story is logical, the means technological, and the result . . . objective and cold': Introduction to Slusser and Rabkin, eds., *Hard Science Fiction* (Carbondale: Southern Illinois University Press, 1986), p. vii.
8. Benford, 'Real Science, Imaginary Worlds', p. 16.

9. 'Matter's End', in Lou Aronica *et al.*, eds., *Full Spectrum 3* (New York: Bantam Spectra, 1991); 'Anomalies', in Al Sarrantonio, ed., *Redshift* (New York: Roc, 2001).
10. Gary Westfahl, *Cosmic Engineers* (Westport, CT: Greenwood, 1996), p. 9.
11. Godwin's story has been reprinted many times, including in Hartwell and Cramer, eds., *The Ascent of Wonder*. Arguments over the story's interpretation raged in *NYRSF* for several years, from no. 64 (December 1993); contributors included John Kessel, Damon Knight, Algis Budrys, Brian Stableford, Sam Moskowitz, David Drake and Michael Swanwick.
12. In the introduction to the hard sf issue of *Science-Fiction Studies*, David Samuelson claims 'C. J. Cherryh may be the only woman to find writing hard sf congenial', but remarks that 'backgrounds in science inform' the works of several women writers including Joan Slonczewski: *Science-Fiction Studies* 20 (1993), p. 146.
13. Tom Shippey, review of Westfahl's *Cosmic Engineers*, in *NYRSF* 97 (September 1996), p. 4.
14. Use of the term 'hard science fiction' dates back at least as far as November 1957, when P. Schuyler Miller used it in the introductory essay leading off one of his 'Reference Library' columns in *Astounding*. See Brian Stableford, 'The Last Chocolate Bar and the Majesty of Truth', *NYRSF* 71 (July 1994), p. 1.
15. Our categories are drawn from E. M. Forster's *Aspects of the Novel*, modifying where appropriate: see Hartwell and Cramer, eds., *The Ascent of Wonder*, pp. 989–90.
16. David Brin, 'Running Out of Speculative Niches: A Crisis for Hard SF?', in Slusser and Rabkin, eds., *Hard Science Fiction*, p. 13.
17. Stableford, 'The Last Chocolate Bar', p. 16.
18. Stories reprinted in Hartwell and Cramer, *The Hard SF Renaissance* (New York: Tor, 2003).
19. Interview with Stephen Baxter, 1995, at http://www.sam.math.ethz.ch/~pkeller/BAXTER/Interview.html.
20. Benford, 'Old Legends', in Greg Bear and Martin H. Greenberg, eds., *New Legends* (New York: Tor, 1995), pp. 279–80.
21. Cramer, 'On Science and Science Fiction', in Hartwell and Cramer, eds., *The Ascent of Wonder*, p. 26.
22. In *Cosmic Engineers*, p. 81, Westfahl questions whether it was ever truly the paradigm.
23. Back issues of *Cheap Truth* are posted at http://www.io.com/~ftp/usr/shiva/SMOF-BBS/cheap.truth.
24. 'Hard Science, Radical Imagination', interview with Paul J. McAuley by Nick Gevers, *InfinityPlus*, 1991, http://www.iplus.zetnet.co.uk/nonfiction/intpmca.htm.
25. 'The Way Things Are', interview with Greg Egan by Carlos Pavón, First published in Spanish in *Gigamesh*, July 1998, and reprinted at http://www.netspace.net.au/~gregegan/INTERVIEWS/Interviews.html#noise.

# 14

GARY WESTFAHL

# Space opera

Space opera is the most common, and least respected, form of science fiction. Its popularity in magazines of the 1920s and 1930s helped establish science fiction as a genre, and it continues to find appreciative readers, even while scorned by learned commentators. To many, space opera is synonymous with sf, and to this day, average citizens asked to define sf might respond, 'You know, the *Star Trek*, *Star Wars* stuff', which is to say, space opera. Still, although chastised for lacking merit and damaging the reputation of sf, space opera has endured, evolved and grown, so that sophisticated writers and scholars increasingly look to the form with bemused affection, or even genuine admiration.

Despite signs of changing attitudes, space opera has garnered little critical attention; only a few scholars have attempted anything resembling a rigorous definition.[1] Necessarily, anyone discussing the nature, parameters and history of space opera at length breaks new ground.

Wilson Tucker's pioneering 1941 definition provides a useful framework for describing the subgenre: 'In these hectic days of phrase-coining, we offer one. Westerns are called "horse operas", the morning housewife tear-jerkers are called "soap operas". For the hacky, grinding, stinking, outworn space-ship yarn, or world-saving for that matter, we offer "space opera".'[2] Tucker suggests that three characteristics define space opera.

First, space opera involves a 'space-ship': like the nautical fiction from which it borrows terminology and tropes, space opera depicts journeys through uncharted realms in vessels bringing humans into contact with the mysterious stuff separating their safe harbours. Even narratives occurring on the surfaces of alien planets must have nearby spaceports, creating the possibilities of departures to or arrivals from other worlds. Stories on worlds without access to space travel, or stories featuring travel to other planets by mystical means, are better termed planetary romances.[3]

Second, space opera is a 'yarn' – an exciting adventure story. Typically positing a universe filled with human or alien spacefarers – some hostile, some friendly – space opera is a literature of conflicts, usually with violent resolutions. In the year Tucker coined 'space opera', a letter in *Astounding Science-Fiction* described E. E. 'Doc' Smith's stories as 'scientific melodrama', epitomizing this aspect of the sub-genre,[4] and while some scholars laud the sub-genre for breathtaking visions of the cosmos, most emphasize that space opera is 'heady, escapist stuff' and 'pure entertainment', lacking a serious purpose.[5]

Third, space opera tends to become 'hacky, grinding, stinking, outworn'; like westerns and domestic dramas, it often succumbs to formulaic plots and mediocrity. Almost any well-received space opera generates sequels; many spawn endless adventures involving the same characters in similar situations; even stories not in sequences may closely resemble innumerable predecessors. As early as 1932, Hugo Gernsback or an editor announced impatience with 'A plot . . . that simply relates a war between two planets, with a lot of rays and bloodshed';[6] and Tucker significantly christened the form while criticizing its staleness and abysmal quality. To remain at the forefront of science fiction, which esteems freshness and originality, space opera must continually reinvent itself. So, as one form of space opera falls out of favour and migrates to less prestigious venues – juveniles, films, television, comic books, cartoons, video games – another, improved form of space opera emerges for discriminating readers.

The origins of space opera are disputed, since space adventures preceded the sf magazines, and commentators label texts such as Garrett P. Serviss's *Edison's Conquest of Mars* (1898), Robert W. Cole's *The Struggle for Empire* (1900) and George Griffith's *A Honeymoon in Space* (1901) progenitors of the form. However, the work that first established and popularized space opera was unquestionably Smith's *The Skylark of Space* (1928). He began the story in 1915, collaborating with a friend's wife, Lee Hawkins Garby, recruited to handle the romantic elements and originally credited as co-author; yet her contributions were minimal, and Smith eventually finished the novel by himself, perhaps anticipating that his readers would not demand sensitive portrayals of men and women in love. After numerous rejections, Smith's story found a home in the sf magazine *Amazing Stories*, where it was met with tremendous enthusiasm.

Modern readers may find the novel unimpressive, with many pages devoted to shenanigans on Earth, interminable scientific double-talk and clumsy dialogue, but some passages convey the excitement of stories about spaceships hurtling into the unknown. Consider the scene when villainous DuQuesne, who inaugurates human space travel by being catapulted with three passengers thousands of light years from Earth, finds his ship running out of fuel and falling toward a 'dead star' – arguably the first crisis to afflict characters in space opera:

> Thus time wore on – Perkins dead; Margaret unconscious; Dorothy lying in her seat, her thoughts a formless prayer, buoyed only by her faith in God and in her lover; DuQuesne self-possessed, smoking innumerable cigarettes, his keen mind at grips with its most desperate problem, grimly fighting until the very last instant of life – while the powerless spaceship fell with an appalling velocity, and faster and yet faster, toward that cold and desolate monster of the heavens.[7]

Rescued by Dorothy's lover Seaton and friend Crane, the humans journey to the planet Osnome, where they intervene in a conflict between a peaceful nation and its aggressive enemy. With such thrills available in space adventures, readers lacked enthusiasm for tales of scientists in laboratories and demanded more of what Gernsback called 'interplanetary stories'[8] – which soon appeared, including two sequels to *The Skylark of Space*.

The 1930s proved the golden age of classic space opera, with stories ranging across a broad spectrum. At one extreme, stories about the solar system of the near future, positing only modest scientific advances, resembled nautical literature, detective fiction or westerns. Space pirates preyed upon passenger liners; interplanetary agents chased outlaws to uncharted moons; prospectors searched for asteroids of gold. These works might occasionally command attention – such as Ross Rocklynne's stories about a policeman pursuing a criminal that placed the friendly adversaries in intriguing scientific traps, such as the 'Center of Gravity' of a huge hollow sphere or the surface of a frictionless concave mirror[9] – but despite their numbers these stories are rarely appreciated or anthologized. Still, they served an important purpose: since space was a relatively new setting for fiction, a literary frontier as it were, writers sensibly used familiar storylines from genres dealing with frontiers, such as the ocean, criminal underworld and Wild West, to introduce the universe to readers in reassuring fashion and blaze a trail for works that would display more imagination.

Moving along the spectrum, one finds more ambitious stories, often reminiscent of future-war novels, with menacing aliens from nearby planets – usually humanoid in appearance but exotically hued or resembling loathsome creatures – battling humanity, possibly aided by nicer, more attractive aliens. With mighty forces in play, entire planets might be destroyed or moved – as in Leslie F. Stone's 'The Fall of Mercury' (1935), where a benevolent Saturnian helps humans defeat malevolent Mercurians by hurling their planet into the Sun. Such stories more frequently appear in nostalgic anthologies, since they reflect the 'sense of wonder' said to define sf. In Jack Williamson's 'Born of the Sun' (1934), for example, people escape from Earth in a space ark when they learn our world is only an egg, with a gigantic creature about to hatch from and destroy it.

At the far end of the spectrum, stories such as Smith's extended into the galaxy and beyond, featuring heroic geniuses who, facing vast alien empires, develop more and more powerful super-scientific weapons. In one series inspired by Smith's Skylark novels, John W. Campbell, Jr's Arcot, Wade and Morey stories, heroes progress from adventures in Earth's atmosphere to voyages across the universe by means of 'cosmic power', the ability to accomplish anything with a single thought, which eliminates prospects for conflict and ends the series.[10] While such stories can fall victim to sheer excess, a more carefully structured epic of this kind, Smith's Lensmen series, represents the crowning achievement of classic space opera. In the first of six volumes grandiosely entitled 'The History of Civilization', Smith begins by saying, 'Two thousand million or so years ago two galaxies were colliding,'[11] and proceeds to describe the ensuing war between those galaxies' races, the virtuous Arisians and evil Eddorians, which is eventually joined by humanity. Kimball Kinnison becomes one of many heroes with a 'Lens' of immense powers employed against allies of Eddore until, in a final confrontation, the Eddorians are defeated by Kinnison's children. Continually in print and adapted as an animated film, this thrilling series has significantly influenced innumerable literary and cinematic space operas, including George Lucas's Star Wars films.

Despite the accomplishments of Smith and contemporaries such as Campbell, Williamson, Ray Cummings and Clifford D. Simak, the most prolific and prominent writer of classic space operas was Edmond Hamilton. Particularly fond of stories involving planets being threatened or blown to pieces, Hamilton earned the epithets 'World-Saver' and 'World-Wrecker', and the reference to 'world-saving' in Tucker's definition suggests that Hamilton was his principal target. Yet Hamilton proved capable of producing more subdued, wistful varieties of space opera, such as 'The Dead Planet' (1946), where space explorers hear the holographic testimony of a long-dead alien civilization that sacrificed itself to save the galaxy; finally, we learn those aliens were in fact the human race. Hamilton also crafted the first space opera franchise, Captain Future, a magazine said to prefigure Star Trek in describing the exploits of a spaceship captain and his crew – a robot, android and disembodied brain.

Space operas quickly made the transition to visual media: two Earth-bound stories about a man who hibernates for centuries and awakens in a future America conquered by Asians[12] inspired a comic strip, Buck Rogers, which ventured into space along with another comic strip, *Flash Gordon*; these became the basis for four film serials between 1936 and 1940. Hampered by inadequate special effects, these films portrayed space travel only fleetingly, with crude model spaceships, otherwise limiting the action to planetary surfaces and spaceship interiors, like early television series that mimicked these serials such as *Captain Video* (1949–56) and *Tom Corbett, Space Cadet* (1950–5). Science fiction films of the 1950s offered better effects, with *This Island Earth* (1955), *Forbidden Planet* (1956) and *It! The Terror from Beyond Space* (1958) qualifying as most reminiscent of space opera, but further advances in this area were needed before space opera could blossom on the screen. Since comic books faced no such limitations, extravagant space heroes such as Adam Strange, Captain Comet, Space Ranger, Star Hawkins and the Star Rovers emerged as readers' favourites.

Even as classic space opera found new audiences in newspapers, theatres, television and comics, it was being abandoned by sf magazines, where Campbell, now a major editor, promoted more mature approaches to the genre. Space opera had focused on conquering the universe; but after conquest, new questions arise, such as how to govern the universe or how to make a living in the universe, and writers such as Isaac Asimov and Robert A. Heinlein were addressing these issues in stories that captivated readers not with derring-do but with thoughtful discussions and imaginative portrayals of future prospects. Further, postwar programmes designed to send humans into orbit appeared to demand more realistic stories about space pioneers to inform and promote such initiatives, such as Arthur C. Clarke's *Prelude to Space* (1951). Providing these important social and scientific speculations, Asimov, Heinlein, Clarke and similar-minded authors would recoil at suggestions that their works were merely space operas. Planetary romances and classic space operas still flourished in less prominent magazines of the 1940s and 1950s such as *Planet Stories*, and distinctive practitioners could still make an impression – like Leigh Brackett and A. E. van Vogt in the 1940s, and Alfred Bester and Cordwainer Smith in the 1950s. Yet the dominant voice of sf increasingly sounded practical, worldly-wise and antithetical to space opera.

However, one type of story nurtured in this new atmosphere belongs to the sub-genre. In settled regions of space, with worlds functioning either as independent principalities or fiefdoms of larger empires, new sorts of adventurers could seek rewards, such as profitable bargains or advantageous alliances, on remote planets. While physical strength might be required, these heroes would also need to be eloquent, diplomatic and vigilant while negotiating their way through alien societies filled with shady merchants and corrupt officials. Because tales of intrigues in imaginary European nations are called Ruritanian romances, one might call these stories Ruritanian space opera, especially since they frequently borrow the trappings of medieval or early modern Europe for planetary cultures (though the suggested alternative 'space operetta' is tempting).[13]

Seemingly as inconsequential as stories about space pirates, Ruritanian space operas were distinguished by a sophisticated, ironic style and vivid descriptive detail. Jack Vance's Magnus Ridolph is representative of the charming rogues in these adventures, and opening paragraphs from 'The King of Thieves' suggest how engaging they might be:

> 'There's much wealth to be found here on Moritaba,' said the purser wistfully. 'There's wonderful leathers, there's rare hardwoods – and have you seen the coral? It's purple-red and it glows with the fires of the damned! But . . . Nobody cares for anything but telex – and that's what they never find. Old Kanditter, the King of Thieves, is too smart for 'em.'
>
> Magnus Ridolph . . . sauntered to the port, looked out toward Moritaba.
>
> Gollabolla, chief city of the planet, huddled between a mountain and a swamp. There were a Commonwealth Control office, a Uni-Culture Mission, a general store, a school, a number of dwellings, all built of corrugated metal on piles of native wood and connected by rickety catwalks.
>
> Magnus Ridolph found the view picturesque in the abstract, oppressive in the immediate.

On a world where everyone carries all their belongings around to avoid virulent thievery, Ridolph employs 'near-gaseous creatures' from another planet to steal the crown from the King of Thieves, making himself King and outmanoeuvring a duplicitous rival for rich profits from mining telex crystals.[14] Along with similar stories, Vance also wrote a novel entitled *Space Opera* (1965), actually about an opera company travelling through space.

Another master of these stories, Poul Anderson, created two popular heroes: Nicholas van Rijn, a merchant in an era of galactic expansion under the Polesotechnic League, and Ensign Dominic Flandry, who centuries later works for the Terran Empire that supplanted the League. (Anderson also merits attention for writing the most literally medieval space opera, *The High Crusade*, 1960, where alien invaders of fourteenth-century England are defeated by Sir Roger de Tourneville's knights, who commandeer their spaceship to establish a chivalrous, Christian galactic empire.) The most ubiquitous Ruritarian adventurer, however, is Keith Laumer's indefatigable diplomat Jaime Retief, who in dozens of stories and novels resolves complex disputes on disparate worlds. An especially Ruritanian story, 'The Prince and the Pirate' (1964), features a dinosaur hunt precisely similar to an English fox hunt before Retief is tossed in a dungeon. Ignored by scholars and mainstream readers, these characters were cherished by fans, who eagerly awaited each new addition to their series.

The peripatetic heroes of Ruritanian space opera were typically traders, spies and diplomats, but other professions were represented, including Vance's opera singers; Frank Belknap Long's mystery-solving botanist, John Carstairs; the handymen of Robert Sheckley's AAA Ace Interplanetary Decontamination Service; and more recently, Sheila Finch's Guild of Xenolinguists. A noteworthy sub-category is spacefaring doctors; while Murray Leinster produced several Med Service stories, the master of medical science fiction was James White, whose physicians, based on a huge space station, Sector Twelve General Hospital, treated a dizzying variety of ailing aliens in stories spanning four decades.

In the 1960s, a new generation of writers generally eschewed space opera, though they were occasionally willing to make fun of it – engendering a new form, satirical space opera. Perhaps the earliest works of this kind are Harry Harrison's novels featuring Slippery Jim diGriz, the Stainless Steel Rat, an interstellar policeman who resembled his Ruritanian predecessors but inspired more tongue-in-cheek humour. Brian W. Aldiss especially enjoyed a scene in *The Stainless Steel Rat* (1961) when diGriz encounters a coal-driven robot on a backwards planet.[15] Even more openly satirical were Harrison's *Bill, the Galactic Hero* (1965) and *Star Smashers of the Galaxy Rangers* (1973). Around the same time, in Poland, Stanislaw Lem's stories about space travellers Ijon Tichy and Pirx the Pilot humorously critiqued Western space operas.[16] After assembling a collection of space-opera stories, Aldiss offered his own lighthearted take on such adventurings, *The Eighty-Minute Hour* (1974), and a passage from a vignette he anthologized, Robert Sheckley's 'Zirn Left Unguarded, the Jenghik Palace in Flames, Jon Westerley Dead' (1972), summarizes everything ripe for lampooning in both classic and Ruritanian space opera:

> The reptilian forces of Megenth, long quiescent, suddenly began to expand due to the serum given them by Charles Engstrom, the power-crazed telepath. Jon Westerley was hastily recalled from his secret mission to Angos II. Westerley had the supreme misfortune of materializing within a ring of Black Force, due to the inadvertent treachery of Ocpetis Marn, his faithful Mnerian companion, who had, unknown to Westerley, been trapped in the Hall of Floating Mirrors, and his mind taken over by the renegade Santhis, leader of the Entropy Guild.[17]

The outstanding example of satirical space opera was Douglas Adams's *The Hitchhiker's Guide to the Galaxy*, which appeared as a BBC radio series (1978), a trilogy of books (1979–82) and a BBC television series (1981). Adams's success demonstrated that space opera was becoming part of popular culture, its tropes fair game for good-natured jokes; so it is that Earth is destroyed not by malevolent design but as an inadvertent side effect of the construction of an interstellar highway, and alien Vogons are feared not for their awesome weaponry but for their terrible poetry. The BBC television series *Red Dwarf* (1988–99) played with space opera conventions with equal effectiveness.

Despite sporadic satires, the most conspicuous development in space opera since the 1960s, the series *Star Trek* (1966–9) and its successors, traversed space in complete earnestness. To sf readers, the first series seemed little more than a compendium of shopworn plots from old stories, reflecting the influence of both classic space opera (in episodes featuring space battles such as 'Balance of Terror' and 'The Doomsday Machine') and Ruritanian space opera (in episodes involving diplomatic intrigues such as 'Journey to Babel' and 'Elayn of Troyius'). Yet *Star Trek* contributed something new to space opera – the subject matter and sensibility of the romance novel. It was not simply the recurring subplot involving Nurse Chapel's unrequited love for Spock, nor the several episodes where male stars fell in love with attractive women; rather, it was the strong personal bond between Kirk, Spock and McCoy that transcended the bantering, locker-room camaraderie previously characteristic of space opera (though fan-produced 'slash fiction' went even further, projecting a homosexual relationship between Kirk and Spock). It is as if Smith's original plan to combine masculine scientific adventures with Garby's feminine romantic touches had finally been realized. Arguably, in fact, *Star Trek* borrowed its deep structure from the classic triangle of the romance novel, with Kirk the impetuous heroine torn between McCoy, the stolid boy next door, and Spock, the dark mysterious stranger.[18]

Even if one rejects such interpretations, *Star Trek* projected enough of the ambience of a romance novel to warrant the label of romantic space opera, and this helped to make *Star Trek* the first form of space opera to attract a significant female audience, contributing to its astounding longevity in television, films, merchandise and numerous *Star Trek* novels – all qualifying as space operas – that absorbed or replaced the run-of-the-mill space operas of previous decades. And, as if eager to attract female *Star Trek* fans seeking new diversions, writers after 1980 increasingly made women the heroes of space adventures. Anxious to show they were just as tough as male counterparts, these women also betrayed their softer sides in a manner reminiscent of the romantic space opera of *Star Trek*. The opening lines of Dana Stabenow's *Second Star* (1991) epitomize this combination of bravado and tenderness: 'My full name is Esther Natasha Svensdotter but if you want to live you'll call me Star. Star is what Esther means, it was the first word I ever said, and when I'm feeling romantic, I like to say that among the stars is where I live.'[19] Others such as Melisa C. Michaels's Skyrider, Chris Claremont's Nicole Shea, and S. L. Viehl's StarDoc joined Star Svensdotter as the new female champions of space opera, but its major woman warrior was David Weber's Honor Harrington, who in several novels re-fought the Napoleonic Wars in space with zeal and panache.[20]

In contrast to *Star Trek*, *Star Wars* (1977) was less mature and innovative as sf: it was a straightforward transcription of old epics about heroic rebels opposing cruel space empires. Still, the exotic aliens, humanoid robots and duelling starships of space opera had never looked so impressive, delighting long-time fans as a pulp magazine brought to life. *Star Wars* engendered various successors, including inferior imitations such as *The Black Hole* (1979), *Starcrash* (1979), *Battle beyond the Stars* (1980) and television series *Battlestar Galactica* (1978–9) and *Buck Rogers in the Twenty-Fifth Century* (1979–81); Lucas's sequels, *The Empire Strikes Back* (1980), *Return of the Jedi* (1983), *The Phantom Menace* (1999) and *Attack of the Clones* (2002); and the distinctive but equally stylish *Alien* (1979), which has spawned three sequels to date.

*Star Wars* further played a role in bringing space opera into a new medium – video games – since its space battles inspired the pioneering game Space Invaders, which like the similar Galaga required players to blast un-ending armadas of enemy spaceships out of the sky to earn high scores. Video and computer games with more sophisticated narrative frameworks and visuals later appeared, including adaptations of *Star Wars* and *Star Trek*. An sf counterpart to the popular role-playing game Dungeons and Dragons emerged, appropriately named Space Opera, and it became popular as well; indeed, websites located by Internet searches for 'space opera' will most likely discuss that game, not the sub-genre. Other visual offshoots of *Star Wars* in-clude the space operas of Japanese anime, such as the Gundam Mobile Suit series, that brought an American response in the animated film *Titan A. E.* (2000).

Turning to the recent literature of space opera, one finds innumerable nov-els based on franchised universes alongside more respected works by writers such as Greg Bear, Gregory Benford, David Brin and Larry Niven. However, C. J. Cherryh and Lois McMaster Bujold have been the most noteworthy new creators of traditional space opera, garnering large sales and major awards for series of novels set in richly elaborated future universes. Cherryh describes a region of space where Earth, the domineering Union and the loosely struc-tured Alliance vie for power and influence; Bujold's Miles Vorkosigan novels chronicle the adventures of a dwarfish but engaging soldier and diplomat.

These authors' novels are blends of classic, Ruritanian and romantic space opera, with wars in space balanced by a nuanced understanding of politics and persuasive attentiveness to personal relationships.

If a new form of space opera is developing, it is represented by the texts occasionally termed postmodern space operas. One might provisionally characterize these works by listing some common, but not universal, features. Stories aspire to the epic scope of classic space opera but may be tempered by a hard-edged cynicism, deeper than the self-serving pragmatism of Ruritanian space opera, or even grave pessimism about humanity's future. Instead of featuring only humans and humanoid aliens, authors embrace extreme variety in forms of intelligent life – humans, aliens, machines or combinations thereof – crafted by evolution, technology or bioengineering. Other heresies include a universe where humans are not dominant, means of transportation other than starships, a rich texture of literary and cultural allusions and an overtly serious intent juxtaposed with a lingering aura of escapist adventure. Whether such traits make these works 'postmodern' as scholars define the word is problematic – 'postmodern' may serve primarily as a fashionable synonym for 'sophisticated' – and another term to describe this embryonic form may emerge.

Works associated with postmodern space opera suggest the variety of ideas and approaches being explored. In Bruce Sterling's *Schismatrix* (1985) and *Schismatrix Plus* (1996), Mechanists seeking to transform humanity by technology struggle with Shapers who champion bio-engineering. Michael Swanwick's *Vacuum Flowers* (1987) features rebellious spacefarers, able to create and implant new personalities in themselves, battling the hive-mind that controls Earth. Dan Simmons's Hyperion series – *Hyperion* (1989), *The Fall of Hyperion* (1990), *Endymion* (1996) and *The Rise of Endymion* (1997) – envisions a galactic government united by miraculous teleportation that destroys this wonderful tool to rescue humans from insidious artificial intelligences. Colin Greenland's Plenty trilogy – *Take Back Plenty* (1990), *Seasons of Plenty* (1995) and *Mother of Plenty* (1998) – depicts a female adventurer who commandeers a vast alien spaceship and ventures into the cosmos, while John Clute's *Appleseed* (2001) offers a densely written portrait of a universe where a travelling merchant encounters artificial intelligences ('Made Minds') and godlike aliens.

However, Iain M. Banks's Culture novels are those most frequently described as postmodern space opera.[21] The first Culture novel, *Consider Phlebas* (1987), reads much like rousing space opera along standard lines, as a shapeshifting agent for reptilian Idirans works to retrieve a stranded artificial intelligence developed by the Culture, a seemingly utopian space empire dominated by such Minds. Yet the novel's title, taken from a stanza of T. S. Eliot's *The Waste Land* describing a corpse in a whirlpool, suggests a underlying grimness: the sense that humanity will never hold its own against superior machine intelligences, that their millennia of effort will culminate in failure, perhaps that space opera itself, founded on expansive optimism about the future, faces extinction in light of these sobering realizations.

Novels such as these, rather than culminations of space opera's glorious traditions, might be interpreted as harbingers of the sub-genre's exhaustion. Some writers may feel that way, as indicated by the elegiac tone of not only Banks's series but also the Hyperion novels and *Appleseed*. For all the creativity poured into postmodern space operas, they may resultingly exude the aura of exercises, brilliantly accomplished but lacking the fervent conviction regarding humanity's manifest destiny in the cosmos that distinguished classic space opera.

Yet postmodern space opera remains relatively new, capable of further evolution towards its own sort of conviction, and with readers still clamouring for traditional space operas and talented writers pushing the boundaries of the sub-genre, proclaiming the death of space opera would be premature. Between the time space opera emerged in the magazines and today, science fiction has linked itself to many sobering responsibilities – guiding scientists, preparing citizens for the future, analysing social problems and emulating literary masterpieces – and works that have visibly addressed such goals have received most of the attention, while seemingly frivolous space operas, committed only to presenting exciting adventures, have been overlooked. However, though earlier writers seeking respect disliked the label of space opera, the outstanding writers of today willingly embrace it. Perhaps science fiction is coming full circle, tacitly acknowledging the true frivolity of its portentous agendas while freshly appreciating the importance and dignity of the 'pure entertainment' that space opera in all its forms provides.

## NOTES

1. See Patricia Monk, '"Not Just Cosmic Skullduggery"', *Extrapolation* 33 (1992), pp. 295–316; Gary Westfahl, 'Beyond Logic and Literacy', *Extrapolation* 35 (1994), pp. 176–88; and Westfahl, ed., *Space and Beyond* (Westport, CT: Greenwood, 2000), especially David Pringle's contribution 'What Is This Thing Called Space Opera?' (pp. 35–47), which was immensely helpful in writing this chapter.
2. Wilson Tucker, writing as Bob Tucker, 'Depts of the Interior' [*sic*], *Le Zombie* (January 1941), p. 8.
3. See John Clute, 'Planetary Romance', in John Clute and Peter Nicholls, eds., *Encyclopedia of Science Fiction* (London: Orbit, 1993), pp. 934–6.
4. Stilson Wray, letter, 'Brass Tacks', *Astounding Science-Fiction* (May 1941), p. 129.

5. Brian W. Aldiss, 'Introduction', in Aldiss, ed., *Space Opera: An Anthology of Way-Back-When Futures* (Garden City, NY: Doubleday & Company, 1974), p. xi; and Terry Carr, 'Introduction', in Carr, ed., *Planets of Wonder: A Treasury of Space Opera* (Nashville and New York: Thomas Nelson, 1976), p. 10.
6. 'Wanted: Still More Plots', *Wonder Stories Quarterly* (Summer 1932), p. 437.
7. E. E. 'Doc' Smith, *The Skylark of Space* (1928) (New York: Pyramid, 1962), p. 70.
8. Hugo Gernsback, 'Good News for Our Readers', *Wonder Stories Quarterly* (Fall 1932), p. 5.
9. Stories referenced are Rocklynne's 'At the Center of Gravity' (1936) and 'The Men and the Mirror' (1938).
10. The Arcot, Wade and Morey stories were published as *The Black Star Passes* (Reading, PA: Fantasy Press, 1953), *Islands of Space* (Reading, PA: Fantasy Press, 1957) and *Invaders from the Infinite* (Reading, PA: Fantasy Press, 1961).
11. E. E. 'Doc' Smith, *Triplanetary* (1948) (New York: Pyramid, 1965), p. 11; novel (without this opening passage) first published in *Amazing Stories* in 1934.
12. Philip Francis Nowlan's 'Armageddon 2419 A. D.', *Amazing* (1928) and 'The Airlords of Han', *Amazing* (1929).
13. Pringle, 'Space Opera', p. 40.
14. Jack Vance, 'The King of Thieves' (1949), reprinted in Vance, *The Many Worlds of Magnus Ridolph* (New York: Ace, 1966), pp. 82–3, 100.
15. Brian W. Aldiss with David Wingrove, *Trillion Year Spree* (London: Gollancz, 1986), pp. 319–20.
16. Available in English in *The Star Diaries* (New York: Seabury/Continuum, 1976), *Memoirs of a Space Traveler: Further Reminiscences of Ijon Tichy* (New York: Harcourt Brace Jovanovich, 1982), *Tales of Pirx the Pilot* (New York: Harcourt Brace Jovanovich, 1980), and *More Tales of Pirx the Pilot* (New York: Harcourt Brace Jovanovich, 1982).
17. Robert Sheckley, 'Zirn Left Unguarded, the Jenghik Palace in Flames, Jon Westerley Dead', in Aldiss, ed., *Space Opera*, p. 7.
18. See Westfahl, 'Where No Market Has Gone Before', *Extrapolation* 37 (1996) pp. 291–301.
19. Dana Stabenow, *Second Star* (New York: Ace, 1991), p. 1.
20. Skyrider Melacha Rendell first appeared in Michaels's *Skirmish* (New York: Tor, 1985); Nicole Shea in Claremont's *FirstFlight* (New York: Ace, 1987); StarDoc Cherijo Grey Veil in Viehl's *StarDoc* (New York: Penguin/Roc 2000); and Honor Harrington in Weber's *On Basilisk Station* (New York: Baen, 1993).
21. Culture novels to date are Banks's *Consider Phlebas* (Basingstoke: Macmillan, 1987), *The Player of Games* (Basingstoke: Macmillan, 1988), *The State of the Art* (London: Orbit, 1989), *Use of Weapons* (London: Orbit, 1990), *Excession* (London: Orbit, 1996), *Inversions* (London: Orbit, 1998) and *Look to Windward* (London: Little, Brown/Orbit, 2000).

# 15

ANDY DUNCAN

# Alternate history

'Alternate history' – or, as grammatical purists call it, 'alternative history' – is an inaccurate but common label for a small but intriguing body of literature. An alternate history is not a history at all, but a work of fiction in which history as we know it is changed for dramatic and often ironic effect.

Often an alternate history dramatizes the moment of divergence from the historical record, as well as the consequences of that divergence. Such a story or novel might seem at first to be a work of traditional historical fiction, in which invented characters and events are woven into the known tapestry of history, but the alteration announces itself quickly, usually in the first few pages.

An example is 'The Lucky Strike' by Kim Stanley Robinson (1984), which begins:

> War breeds strange pastimes. In July of 1945 on Tinian Island in the North Pacific, Captain Frank January had taken to piling pebble cairns on the crown of Mount Lasso – one pebble for each B-29 takeoff, one cairn for each mission. The largest cairn had four hundred stones in it. It was a mindless pastime, but so was poker.[1]

For several pages, the fictional adventures of Captain January seem to have a nonfictional backdrop, for the setting meshes with the reader's knowledge, however vague, of the closing months of the Second World War, as US forces in the Pacific ready atom bombs to drop on Japan. Then comes a spectacular moment of divergence, as the horrified January watches a plane in trouble:

> Maybe he was trying for the short runway on the south half of the island. But Tinian was too small, the plane too heavy ... It exploded in a bloom of fire. By the time the sound of the explosion struck them they knew no one in the plane had survived ... 'He was going to name the plane after his mother,' Scholes said to the ground. 'He told me that just this morning. He was going to call it *Enola Gay*.'[2]

The crash of the *Enola Gay* is the story's moment of divergence, the fork in the road, the signal that 'The Lucky Strike' is not historical fiction but alternate history. In history as we know it – which many readers of alternate history would call 'our timeline' – *Enola Gay* was the aeroplane that dropped the atom bomb on Hiroshima. Clearly, that cannot happen in Captain January's timeline. Instead, the bomb mission passes to January and his crew, aboard the aeroplane nicknamed *The Lucky Strike*. Now the reader, led down this 'road not taken', is in suspense not only about what happens to Captain January, but also about what happens to the bomb, to Hiroshima, to the war, to the world. An alternate history presumes a reader's interest not only in how its focal characters change and develop, but in how their world changes and develops as well.

Alternate histories do not always dramatize their moments of divergence, however. Often the story or novel begins many years after that moment has occurred. The reader is immediately in a different world, so that a pleasure of the reading becomes the discovery not only of what *will* happen but also of what *already* happened, to make this 'alternate world' the way it is.

An example is 'The Signaller' by Keith Roberts (1966), in which young Rafe Bigland lies in the grass for hours watching the neighbourhood semaphore station at work:

> Very high it was, on its pole on top of its hill; the faint wooden clattering it made fell remote from the blueness of the summer sky...It was talking, he knew that without a doubt; whispering and clacking, giving messages and taking them from the others in the lines, the great lines that stretched across England everywhere you could think, every direction you could see.[3]

The story depicts Rafe's apprenticeship in the Guild of Signallers, and what happens to him, but it simultaneously introduces the reader to a strange twentieth-century England. Rapid long-distance communication is possible only by semaphore because radio is unknown. Church and state are one, and a rigid, dogmatic Catholicism is enforced nationwide not only by priests but by soldiers and Inquisitors. The economy is dominated by medieval trade guilds, and the capital is still known as Londinium. For in the timeline of 'The Signaller', the reader gradually understands, the Spanish Armada conquered England in the name of the Pope in 1588 and ended not only the English Reformation but the English Renaissance as well. Roberts later incorporated 'The Signaller' and related stories into the novel *Pavane* (1968), which many consider the best novel of alternate history.

That 'The Lucky Strike' and 'The Signaller' are alternate histories is indisputable; whether they are also sf is a more complex question. Many sf writers have written alternate histories, and many sf magazines and publishing houses have published them, but a lot of alternate history has been published outside the genre as well. Certainly the growing number of social scientists who publish 'counterfactual' essays in sober-sided university-press volumes such as *Counterfactual Thought Experiments in World Politics*, edited by Philip E. Tetlock and Aaron Belkin (1996), have not swollen the ranks of the Science Fiction and Fantasy Writers of America. Yet John W. Campbell Jr, the longtime editor of *Astounding* whose influence is central in the development of US sf, liked to think of the stories he published, too, as thought experiments, and historian Niall Ferguson sounds very like a sf writer when he tells The *New York Times* that 'counterfactualists' seek 'to recapture the chaotic nature of experience' and demonstrate 'that there are no certain outcomes'.[4] Both sf and alternate history are literatures of change, of possibilities, of uncertainties.

Harry Turtledove, today's most popular author of alternate history – and, incidentally, a SFWA member in good standing – well articulates the link between the genres:

> Establishing the historical breakpoint . . . is only half the game of writing alternate history. The other half, and to me the more interesting one, is imagining what would spring from the proposed change. It is in that second half of the game that science fiction and alternate history come together. Both seek to extrapolate logically a change in the world as we know it. Most forms of science fiction posit a change in the present or nearer future and imagine its effect on the more distant future. Alternate history, on the other hand, imagines a change in the more distant past and examines its consequences for the nearer past and the present. The technique is the same in both cases; the difference lies in where in time it is applied.[5]

Whether they dramatize the moment of change or merely the consequences of that moment, alternate histories such as 'The Lucky Strike' and 'The Signaller' might be called 'pure' or 'core' alternate histories. They depict self-contained timelines that intersect with ours only in the reader's mind, and they rely little, if at all, on overt elements of sf or fantasy.

Some of these alternate histories depict bloody and chaotic disruptions in history as we know it. 'Dispatches from the Revolution' by Pat Cadigan (1991) is told as a series of fragmented documents looking back at the 1968 Democratic National Convention in Chicago, where – in the timeline of this story – President Lyndon Johnson and all the Democratic presidential candidates were killed. Martial law was declared, the election was never held and thirty years later, civil rights apparently no longer exist. Each fragment carries a stark label implying it was seized as evidence: 'Papers found in a hastily vacated room in an Ecuadorian flophouse by occupying American forces during the third South American War, October 13, 1998.'[6] Similar in theme but very different in tone and execution, 'The Summer Isles' by Ian R. MacLeod (1998) is set in a Britain that became a fascist dictatorship after losing World War I, a Britain in the process of shipping its Jews via cattle car to the sinister title destination. MacLeod's protagonist, a dying, somewhat hapless Oxford don in mourning for a lost love but determined to perform one last, perhaps futile, act of protest, resembles the protagonist of another British anti-fascist parable, *Nineteen Eighty-Four* by George Orwell.

Other alternate histories, however, are more playful, focusing on quieter, sometimes puckish alterations. The comic 'Ike at the Mike' by Howard Waldrop (1986) gives us Dwight Eisenhower and George S. Patton as famed jazz musicians and Elvis Presley as a US senator. In 'The Undiscovered' by William Sanders (1997), a celebrated Elizabethan playwright voyages to the New World and winds up living the rest of his life among the Cherokees, where 'Spearshaker' writes a most cross-cultural play indeed: 'Once there was a great war chief who was killed by his own brother.'[7] 'The Franchise' by John Kessel (1993) is a baseball story about the World Series showdown between a celebrated pitcher and an underdog batter. They are Fidel Castro and George Herbert Walker Bush, who in this timeline have forsaken politics for baseball – at least temporarily, for Castro's brother and Bush's father, like implacable embodiments of History itself, have ambitious other plans for the young men. 'Dori Bangs' by Bruce Sterling (1989) takes two real-life heroes of the US counter-culture, the cartoonist Dori Seda and the rock critic Lester Bangs, and allows them to fall in love with one another, get married and live much longer lives than our timeline afforded them. The ripple effect on the wider world is minimal. The subtlest alternate history of all may be another John Kessel story, 'Buffalo' (1991), which imagines only a brief, poignant meeting between Kessel's father, a fervent fan of H. G. Wells, and the great Wells himself: 'This is the story of their encounter,' the story boldly begins, 'which never took place.'[8]

Most alternate histories, however, are presented on a grander scale, and they tend to depict dystopias, bad societies that might have been. Hence the appeal of two questions around which many alternate histories have been written: 'What if Hitler had won?' and 'What if the Confederacy had won?' The best of both worlds, so to speak, were written at mid-century. The Hugo Award-winning *The Man in the High Castle* by Philip K. Dick (1962) is a thoughtful and thorough examination of several 'ordinary' Americans – a shady antiques dealer, a judo instructor, a truck driver – living on a Japanese-occupied West Coast (the Germans hold the East). As is common in Dick's novels, the reality of this alternate world is ultimately called into question – but, then, so is the reality of ours. *Bring the Jubilee* by Ward Moore (1953) is the story of Hodge Backmaker, a young man without prospects in an economically devastated 1940s United States, which never recovered from its abject surrender to the Confederacy in 1864. Hodge allies uneasily with the wild-eyed veterans of the Grand Army of the Republic (now a terrorist organization), befriends a Haitian diplomat, has several tormented love affairs and finds eventual refuge in an agrarian enclave of scholars. The novel is unusual among alternate histories for its rueful, self-mocking narration and its bursts of eroticism.

*Bring the Jubilee* is less unusual in that it is partially, if belatedly, a time-travel story. Many alternate histories make explicit the comparisons between real and fictional timelines by intersecting one with another through some sf mechanism, most commonly time travel. An early example is *A Connecticut Yankee in King Arthur's Court* by Mark Twain (1889), in which the pragmatic title character finds himself in Camelot and sets about modernizing the place. He exposes Merlin as a mumbling fraud, persuades the knights to switch from horses to bicycles and launches an industrial economy based on factories and electricity. All this meddling, however, leads to devastation and slaughter. The novel's brief prologue and epilogue, in which the Yankee tells his story to a recognizable Mark Twain in a recognizable Victorian England, imply that this Arthurian misadventure – assuming it really happened, and was not all in the Yankee's head – caused no long-term disruption in the timeline. But the novel vividly depicts a past, at least, changed for the worse, a very alternate history indeed.

Since Twain's Yankee, countless fictional time travellers have gone into the past to consciously or unconsciously, successfully or unsuccessfully, change the course of history. For example, in *Lest Darkness Fall* by L. Sprague de Camp (1941), the resourceful twentieth-century archaeologist Martin Padway, upon finding himself in sixth-century Rome, introduces the printing press, Arabic numerals and Copernican astronomy in an apparently successful attempt to prevent the Dark Ages.

As befits its more optimistic author, de Camp's novel has a far more upbeat, less ambiguous conclusion than Twain's:

> There was a semaphore telegraph system running the length and breadth of Italy, some day to be replaced by a true electric telegraph, if he could find time for the necessary experiments. There was a public letter post about to be set up. There were presses in Florence and Rome and Naples pouring out books and pamphlets and newspapers. Whatever happened to him, these things would go on. They'd become too well rooted to be destroyed by accident. History had, without question, been changed. Darkness would not fall.[9]

A much later story, 'Mozart in Mirrorshades' by Lewis Shiner and Bruce Sterling (1985), can be read as a spoof of the long fictional tradition of meddling time travellers. In the story, greedy entrepreneurs discover they can change the past without suffering any consequences in their own timeline. They proceed to make a fortune looting, bilking and buying their ancestors – and, in the process, casually creating, exploiting, then discarding one alternate history after another, like so many paper cups. 'You didn't sign up for a time-travel project,' muses the protagonist, Rice, 'unless you had a taste for incongruity,'[10] and Rice's creators indulge that taste with sentences such as: 'Marie Antoinette sprawled across the bed's expanse of pink satin, wearing a scrap of black-lace underwear and leafing through an issue of *Vogue*.'[11]

Although time travel is the most common sf mechanism for rationalizing an alternate history, other mechanisms exist as well. Many stories and novels presume that more than one 'parallel world' with divergent histories can co-exist, so that characters can purposefully or accidentally travel, or 'timeslip', from one timeline to another, like a commuter switching trains.

For example, 'He Walked Around the Horses' by H. Beam Piper (1948) uses a timeslip to explain a mysterious actual event summarized in the story's prologue:

> In November, 1809, an Englishman named Benjamin Bathurst vanished, inexplicably and utterly. He was *en route* to Hamburg from Vienna, where he had been serving as his Government's envoy to the court of what Napoleon had left of the Austrian Empire. At an inn in Perleburg, in Prussia, while examining a change of horses for his coach, he casually stepped out of sight of his secretary and his valet. He was not seen to leave the inn yard. He was not seen again, ever. At least, not in this continuum...'[12]

The ensuing story, told as a series of letters between mystified bureaucrats, makes clear that on the other side of the horses, Bathurst timeslipped into an alternate 1809 Europe in which the American Revolution failed and the French Revolution never materialized, leaving the French monarchy in place and Napoleon a lowly if brilliant artillery commander loyal to his king. The stranded Bathurst's last days are unhappy ones, and his odd appearance remains an enigma in *that* world just as his odd *dis*appearance remains an enigma in *this* one.

Other fiction writers have created Bathursts wholesale, in a sense, by imagining large-scale timeslips that affect many people, not just one. For example, in 'Sidewise in Time' by Murray Leinster (1934), a 'time storm' jumbles together many parallel Earths, wreaking havoc as the unwary wander into neighbouring territories governed by very different historical norms – a

Russian San Francisco, a Roman province of Virginia, a twentieth-century Confederacy.

Related to the timeslip story is the 'time loop' story, a very personal sort of alternate history in which a part of the protagonist's life repeats itself, with variations. The best example is the World Fantasy Award-winning novel *Replay* by Ken Grimwood (1986), which begins in 1988 with the sudden heart-attack death of forty-three-year-old Jeff Winston. Though he dies in the first sentence, Winston is the novel's protagonist; he awakens from death to find himself in 1963, age eighteen, in his college dorm room, but with all the memories of the twenty-five years yet to come. He makes many different choices this time around, makes himself a richer and more satisfied man, yet dies once more at age forty-three – and wakes up young again, now with the memories of *two* lifetimes. As the increasingly complex novel unfolds, Winston's life continues to 'replay', over and over again, as he experiences every possible alternate timeline in his power to create, even ones that end with his suicide.

Other alternate histories dramatize more than one timeline while denying the protagonists any awareness of their parallel selves. For example, 'US' by Howard Waldrop (1998) imagines three different lives for Charles Lindbergh Jr, son of the famed transatlantic aviator. In one, the son becomes an Apollo astronaut; in another, an avant-garde pop artist; in another, a small-town eccentric, forgotten by the wider world. These stories are bracketed by vignettes reminding the reader that in our own timeline, Charles Lindbergh Jr was killed as a toddler in a botched kidnap attempt. The cumulative effect of the four parallel stories, each quite low-key in its own right, is quite moving, and the umbrella title invites the reader to seek a broader meaning.

Many recent writers of alternate history, taking advantage of the genre's growing popularity among readers of sf and fantasy, incorporate into their books any number of genre elements, from dragons to space travel; some have expanded into the popular multi-volume format as well. In the four-volume Worldwar series by Harry Turtledove (1994–6), World War II is interrupted by alien invaders armed with nuclear weapons; Axis and Allies must unite to fight the common threat. In the four-volume (to date) Tales of Alvin Maker series by Orson Scott Card, which begins with the World Fantasy Award-winning story 'Hatrack River' (1986) and the novel *Seventh Son* (1987), Europeans with magical 'talents,' facing persecution for their powers, have immigrated in great numbers to the frontier of colonial America, there to collide with the magic of the native peoples.

Despite the boom in sf cinema since *Star Wars* (1977) and the ongoing popularity of movies with historical (or at least quasi-historical) settings such as *Gladiator* (2000), movie-makers so far seem uninterested in alternate history. An exception, *It Happened Here* (1966), written and directed by Kevin Brownlow and Andrew Mollo, depicts in documentary fashion a successful Nazi invasion of Britain, but that was such a low-budget effort as to be virtually a home movie. Much more popular among mainstream filmmakers, because of its potential for race-against-time action, is the theme of time travellers altering history, as seen in the successful *Back to the Future* trilogy (1985–90) and many *Star Trek* instalments, including the celebrated TV episode 'The City on the Edge of Forever' (1967) and the movie *Star Trek: First Contact* (1996). But the alteration depicted in these adventures is invariably short-lived, as the heroes put history to rights again.

More interestingly, two movies released in 1998, the same year 'US' was published – *Sliding Doors*, written and directed by Peter Howitt, and *Run Lola Run*, written and directed by Tom Tykwer – similarly dramatize parallel outcomes for their busy protagonists. In discussing *Run Lola Run*, film critic Roger Ebert argues that such stories are inherently cinematic: 'Film is ideal for showing alternate and parallel time lines. It's literal; we see Lola running, and so we accept her reality, even though the streets she runs through and the people she meets are altered in each story.'[13] The following year, a time loop was the subject of 'Monday', a memorable episode of television's *The X-Files*, but the best time-loop movie remains *Groundhog Day* (1993), directed by Harold Ramis and written by Ramis and Danny Rubin, which echoes the theme of *Replay* as a TV weatherman works through infinite repetitions of the same February 2 on his way to enlightenment.

The theme of many alternate histories is neatly summarized in a Gregory Benford story title: 'We Could Do Worse'. However unsettling these visions, their effect is reassuring; they make readers feel better about their own time-line, however troubled it may be. Indeed, too much alternate history seems to echo the character Pangloss in Voltaire's satire *Candide* (1759), who keeps repeating, 'This is the best of all possible worlds', despite abundant evidence to the contrary.[14]

Like popular history in general, alternate history also suffers from militarism – a fixation on war as the instrument of historical change – and from the flawed assertion of historian Thomas Carlyle in 1841: 'The history of the world is but the biography of great men.'[15] Both trends are evident in a popular anthology series that includes *Alternate Warriors* (1993), *Alternate Tyrants* (1997) and *Alternate Generals* (1998) – ultimately formulaic volumes that nevertheless include some effective stories. That peace is as fateful as war, that the everyday lives of you and me are as crucial to history as the lives of Napoleon and Hitler, is too often overlooked by the writer of alternate history.

Why should this be? Some writers of alternate history, one supposes, are indeed militarists and do indeed agree with Carlyle. Historian Niall Ferguson finds the counterfactual enterprise necessarily right-wing, 'anti-Marxist', in its emphasis on individualism rather than on predestined struggles between economic classes.[16] Yet many writers of alternate history are leftists. A better answer lies in the simple fact that the effectiveness of an alternate history depends on the reader's understanding that there *is* an alteration.

The one invariable rule of alternate history is that the difference between the fictional timeline and the real one must be obvious to the reader. An alternate history about, say, nineteenth-century Chinese immigration to California would be harder to write than an alternate history about the outcome of the American Civil War because so many fewer readers know anything about it. For this reason the alternate history, Isaac Asimov once wrote, is

> a type of story few are able to handle convincingly. You have to know the times, and not only be able to present them clearly and plausibly, but you must trace the consequences of some small change and make that clear and plausible, too. Although I've written numerous books of history, I would have no faith in my own ability to perform the task, and have never done a story of this kind, nor do I intend ever to do one.[17]

Small wonder that so many writers have concentrated on the American Civil War, the Second World War and other well-known cataclysms, and on such fairly resonant historical figures as Lincoln and Churchill, in writing their alternate histories. But countless sf novels have been written about obscure scientific principles, properly explained, and more alternate histories eventually will follow their example and explore new ground – new *old* ground, that is.

The best alternate histories, including many of those mentioned above, focus not on battle manoeuvres but on the daily strivings of individual human beings – any of whom *might have* existed, had things gone differently. Their strange half-life in the reader's mind is more poignant, somehow, than the lives of other fictional characters, since we, too, create and destroy alternate versions of ourselves through our actions every day. The most heartfelt expression of the necessity, and futility, of this odd genre is by Bruce Sterling at the conclusion of 'Dori Bangs':

> Dori Seda never met Lester Bangs. Two simple real-life acts of human caring, at the proper moment, might have saved them both; but when those moments came, they had no one, not even each other. And so they went down into

darkness, like skaters, breaking through the hard bright shiny surface of our true-facts world. Today I made this white paper dream to cover the holes they left.[18]

At its best, the alternate history reminds us that we all change the world.

## NOTES

1. Kim Stanley Robinson, 'The Lucky Strike', in Martin H. Greenberg, ed., *The Way It Wasn't: Great Science Fiction Stories of Alternate History* (New York: Citadel Twilight-Carol, 1996), p. 320.
2. *Ibid.*, pp. 324–5.
3. Keith Roberts, 'The Signaller', in *Pavane* (1968) (Harmondsworth: Penguin, 1984), pp. 55–6.
4. William H. Honan, 'Historians Warming to Games of "What If?"', *New York Times*, 7 January 1998.
5. Harry Turtledove, 'Introduction', in MacKinlay Kantor, *If the South Had Won the Civil War* (New York: Forge, 2001), pp. 7–8.
6. Pat Cadigan, 'Dispatches from the Revolution', in Gardner Dozois, ed., *The Year's Best Science Fiction: 9th Annual Collection* (New York: St Martin's, 1992), p. 230.
7. William Sanders, 'The Undiscovered', in Gardner Dozois, ed., *The Year's Best Science Fiction: 15th Annual Collection* (New York: St Martin's, 1998), p. 238.
8. John Kessel, 'Buffalo', in his *The Pure Product* (New York: Tor, 1997), p. 282.
9. L. Sprague de Camp, *Lest Darkness Fall* (1941) (New York: Del Rey-Ballantine, 1974), p. 208.
10. Bruce Sterling and Lewis Shiner, 'Mozart in Mirrorshades', in Sterling, ed., *Mirrorshades: The Cyberpunk Anthology* (New York: Arbor House, 1986), p. 223.
11. *Ibid.*, 'Mozart', p. 231.
12. H. Beam Piper, 'He Walked Around the Horses', in Isaac Asimov and Martin H. Greenberg, eds., *Isaac Asimov Presents the Great SF Stories 10 (1948)* (New York: DAW, 1983), p. 28.
13. Roger Ebert, review of *Run Lola Run*, written and directed by Tom Tykwer, *Chicago Sun-Times: Electronic Edition* 1999 http://www.suntimes.com/ebert/ebert_reviews/1999/07/070203.html.
14. Voltaire, *Candide*, 1759, *The Best of All Possible Worlds?*, ed. Eric Jonas, 1999 http://www.ericjonas.com/features/candide/fulltext/default.asp.
15. Thomas Carlyle, *Of Heroes and Hero Worship*, 1841, *Project Gutenberg*, ed. Ron Burkey, November 1997, 9 June 2002, ftp://ftp.ibiblio.org/pub/docs/books/gutenberg/etext97/heros10.txt.
16. Honan, 'Historians Warming'.
17. Isaac Asimov, 'Introduction' to 'He Walked Around the Horses', p. 28.
18. Bruce Sterling, 'Dori Bangs', *Globalhead* (1992) (New York: Bantam Spectra, 1994), pp. 338–9.

# 16

EDWARD JAMES

# Utopias and anti-utopias

It is sometimes said that the ability of the writer to imagine a better place in which to live died in the course of the twentieth century, extinguished by the horrors of total war, of genocide and of totalitarianism. The genre of utopia, created unwittingly by Sir Thomas More when he published *Utopia* in 1516, died when idealism perished, a victim to twentieth-century pessimism and cynicism. It is the contention of this chapter that utopia has not disappeared; it has merely mutated, within the field of sf, into something very different from the classic utopia.

Hoda M. Zaki, whose *Phoenix Renewed* (1988) is the only published monograph on sf utopias, was on the point of recognizing this, although she failed; as a political scientist, she was still looking in vain for the classic utopia. She concluded that 'the disappearance of utopian literature in the twentieth century is surprising' and 'an issue with serious implications for the entire body politics'. Her study was based on the nineteen novels which had won the Nebula Award between 1965 and 1982. Almost all these novels had utopian elements, she concluded, but none of them were actual utopias: although many of those novels offered critiques of the contemporary world, none of them offered the necessary coherent account of a superior and desirable alternative in the future. Modern sf thus had no utopias to offer, but only 'tantalizing fragments in the utopian tradition'.[1] However, one can use the same evidence to suggest something quite different: if almost all the novels had utopian elements, this is a demonstration of the profound way in which utopianism has permeated sf. These 'tantalizing fragments' are what help make sf not only an important part of the utopian genre, but a part which is moving that genre in very new directions.

We need to understand what science fiction is reacting against. In the numerous versions of the classic utopia in the centuries succeeding Thomas More's *Utopia* (1516), we have a traveller, perhaps with a small number of companions, who lands on a remote island or undiscovered continent; in more recent versions this is another planet, or the future. He (it is almost invariably 'he') is welcomed by the locals, who are usually eager to show off their society to him. Very soon he meets an older man, who will spend much of the rest of the book lecturing to him about the delights of this society. Sometimes the visitor will respond by pointing out the contrasts between the institutions of this ideal society and those of his own home; in most cases, however, readers will be left to pick these out themselves.

The framework of these ideal societies developed over the years. More's utopian society, not accidentally, is like a Benedictine monastery, although with both men and women and without the celibacy. All his utopians wear monastic habits, and eat and work together communally; all work for the common good; all watch each other closely for signs of disobedience. More was a Catholic; he believed that original sin had to be restrained by strict laws. By the later nineteenth century, however, most utopias offered varieties of socialism. For the followers of nineteenth-century utopianists such as Charles Fourier and Robert Owen, men were not inherently wicked; they were naturally good, and that goodness would show through once the distorting effects introduced by capitalism were removed.

Whether the utopia was Catholic, Protestant or socialist, however, its distinguishing characteristics were remarkably similar. Communal activities within small village-style communities were crucial. Most utopias eliminated money and private property, thus at one stroke removing greed, theft, jealousy and most causes of civil strife. Reason and good will would be sufficient to provide peace and harmony within the community; utopian writers were almost unanimous in eliminating the parasitic occupation of lawyer, and from the nineteenth century onwards it was common to regard priests as little better than lawyers: both groups claimed to bring reconciliation and peace, but in fact promoted disinformation, disharmony and self-interest. Authors offered ingenious ways to promote happiness and contentment in their utopias, by offering job satisfaction in various ways, and great freedom for the individual.

In the twentieth century, such utopian visions were attacked from two directions: by those who argue that in reality many such utopias would turn out to be 'dystopias', that is, oppressive societies, either because of the tyranny of the 'perfect' system over the will of the individual, or because of the difficulty of stopping individuals or elites from imposing authority over the majority, or, indeed, over minorities. Critics of utopia usually assume that the author is producing a risibly impractical blueprint for a future society rather than (in most cases) a trenchant critique of contemporary institutions in fictional form. But such criticism is made easier by associating utopianism with socialism and communism, and thus with the Soviet bloc; and most sf writers have concluded that capitalism, for all its flaws, offers more freedom than totalitarianism. But even the naive capitalist utopias of early sf, where advanced technology brings happiness to all, can be shown as having their sinister side. In William Gibson's anti-utopian story 'The Gernsback Continuum' (1981) the protagonist experiences a vision of an alternate 1980s as envisaged in the pulp sf magazines of the 1930s, a world 'with all the sinister fruitiness of Hitler Youth propaganda', with its smug, white inhabitants. When he gets back to 'the human near-dystopia we live in', a newspaper-seller says, 'Hell of a world we live in, huh? . . . But it could be worse, huh?' and he replies, 'That's right. Or even worse, it could be perfect.'[2] The protagonist would have sympathised with the far-future narrator of Cordwainer Smith's 'Alpha Ralpha Boulevard' (1961), who writes of the first years of the Rediscovery of Man, when 'everywhere, men and women worked with a wild will to build a more imperfect world'.[3] If sf writers find self-styled utopias, they must destroy them, acting like one of Somtow Sucharitkul's Inquestors, rulers of a Galactic civilization whose main task is to destroy utopias. 'The breaking of joy is the beginning of wisdom' goes their Covenant. In 'The Thirteenth Utopia', Sucharitkul's first story, Inquestor Ton Davaryush destroys twelve flawed utopias, but then finds a society which, thanks to its symbiotic relationship with its sun, seems to be a genuine utopia: something he has been taught is impossible.[4]

The classic sf objections to utopia are expressed by Arthur C. Clarke in two of his most famous novels: *Childhood's End* (1953) and *The City and the Stars* (1956). In both he describes a classic utopia, and then shows it as fatally flawed. In the apocalyptic ending of *Childhood's End*, Earth is destroyed, along with most of its population, but the energy thus unleashed is used by the psychically gifted children of men to become pure Mind. In the course of the novel Clarke expounds one of the most detailed and attractive utopian futures to be found in the whole of the sf genre. But it is a dead end: there is boredom; there is 'the virtual end of creative art'.[5] The utopian end in the novel is not the creation of an ideal society on Earth, but humanity rising from its cradle on Earth, evolving into something else. In *The City and the Stars* the inhabitants of Diaspar ('Paradise') 'were, perhaps, as contented as any race the world had known, and after their fashion they were happy';[6] there is no disease, no crime, no poverty, no conflict, no material want, and the inhabitants have an almost magical ability to control their environment. Yet the protagonist Alvin, and Clarke, regard their existence as 'futile':[7] apparently because it is man's destiny to be curious and to learn more about (that is, dominate) the world around him. That this is possibly a culturally specific notion is not acknowledged: nor is it recognized that it does not necessarily suit the psychologies of the vast majority of those in Diaspar, who have been conditioned to accept their situation even more effectively than Clarke and his contemporaries have been conditioned to accept theirs. Alvin breaks apart this 'utopia', by forcing it out of its isolation; the future, it is implied, will be in outward expansion and the winning of the stars: the true destiny of Mankind.

It is not just the idea of 'perfection' which the sf writer objects to: it is the feeling that the utopian writer is aiming for a largely static society. There may be a gentle progression towards even more perfect systems; but there is a denial of adventure, of risk-taking, of the expanding of spatial or technological horizons. 'Maybe we weren't made for Paradise', Captain Kirk muses at the end of 'This Side of Paradise', a *Star Trek* episode from 1967. 'Maybe we were meant to fight our way through . . . Maybe we can't stroll to the sound of the lute – we must march to the sound of drums.' It is not just that sf authors are wedded to change, but that utopia is rejected in favour of continued struggle and progress. In one sense the project of twentieth-century sf writers is antithetic to the classic utopia; but, as I shall argue, this in itself may be a form of utopianism, which we may call 'technological utopianism'.[8]

The other objection to the classic utopia as a form rests on purely literary grounds. Most classic utopias fall far short of the standards expected of a novelist. Characterization is often non-existent: the protagonists merely fulfil their necessary roles, as visitor-listener, as utopian-lecturer or as token female. Large amounts of the utopian 'novel' can be taken up with what sf writers have called 'info-dump', where one character painstakingly explains the details of his world. The plot development is perfunctory: once the visitor has arrived, he is shown or merely told about one aspect of the society after another. By definition, there is no conflict in utopia; for a writer in popular fiction, brought up to believe that conflict is the essence of a plot, this is a problem. An achieved utopia may offer no fictional excitement; but the perpetual and unending struggle for a better world offers plenty of plot opportunities.

On the one hand, sf writers are hostile towards utopia; on the other hand, we find the editor John W. Campbell writing to Eric Frank Russell that 'The one thing that science-fictioneers have in common is a genuine and deep desire to create a better world.'[9] There is no contradiction there. 'A better world' is not the same as 'an ideal world'. A better world could be achieved by 'science-fictioneers' mostly through education about science, but also through the presentation of alternate possibilities. Most of those alternate possibilities are about technological rather than political revolution: the construction of constitutions and political arrangements, the staple of classic utopia, have little appeal for most sf writers. There have been some exceptions, however, and I am going to look at three, from very different generations: Eric Frank Russell, Mack Reynolds and Kim Stanley Robinson.

Russell was English, although he adopted the American idiom so well for his fiction, much of which was published in Campbell's *Astounding*, that many of his readers never realized it. Many of his stories dabbled with anarchist ideas, but perhaps his most typical was '. . . And Then There Were None', a novella published in *Astounding* in June 1951, and later incorporated into the fix-up *The Great Explosion* (1962).[10] Russell's anti-authoritarian imagination here envisages the clash between military bureaucrats, investigating lost Earth colony planets, and the Gands, whose political philosophy is derived from anarchism, via Tolstoy and Gandhi. Their attitude to authority is summed up in the acronym F. I. W. ('Freedom – I Won't'), and their society operates without leaders of any kind (which causes problems when the military command utter the familiar lines 'Take me to your leader'). As in the classic utopia, there is no private property, and no money. The economy operates by individuals exchanging services with each other; 'laying an ob' (obligation) on someone: A doing a service for B, so that B would have to kill the ob by doing a service for A. Cooperation between equals and the denial of anyone's right to hold authority over another are the two main principles of Gand society. They are horrified by the military mind: the wearing of uniforms and the taking of orders are both repulsive to them. But their society proves too much of an attraction to the ship's crew; they desert one by one, until the commanding officer himself gives in to the inevitable . . . and then there were none.

Russell's ventures into political exploration, always tinged with humour, were minor compared to the work of Mack Reynolds, once voted most popular sf writer by the readers of *Galaxy* and *If* magazines and probably the most prolific utopian writer of all time. Between 1972 and his death in 1983 he wrote over a dozen works which are self-conscious utopian novels, and numerous short stories connected with the same project. As a lifelong socialist, he was unusual among American sf writers, and one of his aims was to make Americans realize that socialism had once had a significant American following: *Looking Backward, From the Year 2000* (1973) and *Equality in the Year 2000* (1977) were both updates of Edward Bellamy's *Looking Backward, 2000–1887* (1888) and *Equality* (1897).

Bellamy's *Looking Backward* was undoubtedly the most influential of all American utopias: it not only became a best-seller, but inspired the creation of a political party. Its premise was very science-fictional: a wealthy Bostonian, Julian West, is mesmerized, and by a serious of implausible accidents is still alive in the year 2000, when he is discovered and awakened. Much of the novel consists of lectures by his guide, Dr Leete, about the wonders of Boston in the last year of the twentieth century. It is a place of universal equality of income, where all work in the Industrial Army until a peaceful and prosperous retirement at the age of forty-five. Bellamy stresses efficiency: eating in communal dining rooms, and buying clothes in department stores, are efficient, as well as fostering feelings of community. The dangerous individualism of the nineteenth century is summed up by a painting of people walking out in the rain, each under their own umbrella; Bostonians in 2000 are all protected by awnings over the sidewalks.

Mack Reynolds gave Bellamy new currency, by setting him in a realistic future, at the end of the twentieth century or shortly afterwards. He kept many of Bellamy's ideas, notably the idea of universal equality of income; indeed, he 'used various of his passages all but verbatim'.[11] But in Reynolds's AD 2000 there can be no Industrial Army; indeed, the problem for Reynolds is how to cope with mass unemployment. Industrial efficiency and in particular the greater use of automation mean that only a small number of administrators and engineers are needed to provide food and manufactured goods enough for all. If all live in relative comfort on Guaranteed Annual Income (also known as Negative Income Tax), without having to work for a living, can people achieve happiness? This was a problem Reynolds explored again and again, from different angles, in other utopian novels which he set either in a near future America, such as *Commune 2000 AD* (1974), or else on space habitats, such as *Lagrange Five* (1979). Space habitats, in the real world of the early 1970s, were being boosted by some American space enthusiasts as the High Frontier, the next place for American expansion: the L5 Society, indeed, still promotes the possibilities of a habitat at one of the stable points in the Earth–Moon gravitational system named after the eighteenth-century mathematician Lagrange.[12]

It is interesting that Reynolds, despite his enthusiasm for Bellamy-style socialism and for the traditional utopia, nevertheless accepted some of the critique of utopia from his fellow sf writers. Once utopia had been achieved, what then? Utopia in the classic sense of the absence of want, injustice, inequality and conflict, will have its own problems. One is the excess of leisure in a post-industrial society: is there any way of dealing with that apart from some modern equivalent of bread and circuses? The modern equivalent might not be so different from the Roman imperial version, as Reynolds suggested in *Time Gladiator* (1966). The second problem would be that of preventing new undemocratic elites seeking power for themselves in utopia: this is something Reynolds discussed in *After Some Tomorrow* (1967), *Rolltown* (1976) and elsewhere. And thirdly there is the question of the necessity for progress and for goals. In *After Utopia* (1977), the

Dr Leete figure explains to Tracy Cogswell, the visitor from the past, that they have achieved everything any utopian could have wished for: 'Democracy in its most ultimate form. Abundance for all. The end of strife between nations, races and, for all practical purposes, between individuals.'[13] And the species is dying for lack of goals and direction. Cogswell decides to manufacture the idea of an alien threat, 'to unite the race, to put it back on the road to progress and expansion'.[14] It is a plot motif used by other sf writers, and used by Reynolds himself in novels such as *Galactic Medal of Honor* (1976) and *Space Visitor* (1977). But Reynolds also uses another standard sf device to break free from what is regarded as the stasis of utopia: pushing the frontiers out into the solar system and beyond. At the end of *Chaos in Lagrangia* (1984), the more ambitious and therefore discontented inhabitants of Reynolds's space habitat are planning to go to the stars in a generation ship – like the people in Heinlein's 'Universe' (1941), as a teenage sf fan in the book points out.

Reynolds's utopian novels were mostly written in the 1970s, coinciding with the appearance of a number of much more critically acclaimed sf utopias. The revival of sf utopias in the 1970s was largely a result of the re-emergence of feminism in the later 1960s, although the contribution of the Civil Rights movement, the New Left, the ecological movement, the anti-war protests of the early 1970s and the emerging gay and lesbian movements were all significant as well. When Tom Moylan discusses these novels in his book *Demand the Impossible* (1986), he concentrates on four: Ursula K. Le Guin's *The Dispossessed* (1974), Joanna Russ's *The Female Man* (1975), Samuel R. Delany's *Triton* (1976) (now republished as *Trouble on Triton*) and Marge Piercy's *Woman on the Edge of Time* (1976). He calls these novels 'critical utopias': the authors were all aware of the dangers of presenting a utopian blueprint, and used their novels to criticize not only the society within which they wrote, but also the possible utopian alternatives. Moylan does not include Reynolds in his discussion, but perhaps he should have done: Reynolds's too were 'critical utopias', responding to some of the same concerns of the 1970s.

The four books discussed by Moylan have received more critical comment than any other modern utopian novels. Le Guin's novel is an exploration of the problems of constructing a genuinely anarchist society, through the struggles for intellectual freedom by Shevek, a theoretical physicist whose discoveries threaten to tear down the walls with which the utopians of Anarres protect their society. Russ's is a richly comic discussion of four different women, or the same woman as she might have been in four different societies; the all-female society of Whileaway, which shares numerous features with classic utopias, is compared with three dystopias (one being our own 1970s). Delany's book, which, borrowing a term from Foucault, he calls 'an ambiguous heterotopia', is a bold attempt to show how a society which caters to all kinds of cultural and sexual desires might be possible, thus meeting head-on the standard criticism of utopia that it is uniform and unwelcoming of diversity. Piercy looks at the dystopic world of Connie, a poor Hispanic woman locked up in a mental hospital, and at her visions of (or possibly 'real' connection to) a future Massachusetts, where barriers between race, class and gender have been largely eliminated.

Some of the consciously utopian novels of the last three decades of the century arose out of single issues: concern for the environment in Ernest Callenbach's *Ecotopia* (1975), or concern for gender relations in Pamela Sargent's *The Shore of Women* (1986) and Sheri S. Tepper's *The Gate to Women's Country* (1988). A few writers have written more than one text which could be considered utopian, including the Scottish writers Iain M. Banks (the Culture novels) and Ken MacLeod (the Fall Revolution novels). But the best-known sf writer consciously to contribute to the genre is Kim Stanley Robinson. His *Pacific Edge* (1990) postulates the emergence by the mid twenty-first century of a utopian society based on utopian ideals which has grown out of environmental and other legislative reforms begun in our century, while his Mars trilogy, possibly the greatest achievement of American sf in the 1990s, always keeps the utopian possibilities of planetary colonization in mind. Throughout the three long novels there are debates about how to create a new society on Mars which will avoid the failures of Earth societies, and these culminate in *Blue Mars* (1996), which describes the creation of a utopian constitution for the newly terraformed planet.[15] As one might expect from a 1990s constitution, it includes not only a set of political arrangements, but also a list of human rights and of human obligations, and a list of the rights of the Martian landscape.

All these texts are recognizable utopias, even though they may be posing more questions than presenting solutions. But numerous other scenarios presented in sf present future utopias as a natural result of human progress. Clarke, who, as we have seen, decried the classic utopia back in the 1950s, in the 1990s presented us with a near-utopia in *3001: The Final Odyssey* (1997), in which many psychopathologies of the twentieth century (including religious belief) have been eliminated. Most of Clarke's novels from the 1970s onwards show his belief in the continuing state of social progress, alongside scientific progress and the expansion of humanity beyond its home planet.

The state of dynamism itself – the expansion of the human race along with the expansion of its horizons and potentials – is itself a potentially utopian state. But the sf writer's urge to change the nature of utopianism does not stop there. The traditional utopia is about envisioning ways in which human society might be reorganized on earth. Its mechanisms are legislation, education or institutional changes, occasionally changes in technology or environmental management. But the sf writer has not been prepared to accept such a limited view of human development. Why should we not use technology to remove drudgery, and to provide all material needs? The medieval peasant's dream of Cockaigne where cooked birds fly into one's mouth and the streams flow with wine is, *mutatus mutandis*, the world of *Star Trek*'s Captain Picard, whose mug of Earl Grey materializes in front of him when he tells the computer what he wants. More recently, sf writers have suggested the utopian possibilities of nanotechnology (machines at the molecular level), which illustrate Clarke's dictum that 'any sufficiently advanced technology will be indistinguishable from magic': miniature machines can create, and cure, as if miraculously. The traditional utopia takes limited resources as a given; nowadays, in post-scarcity futures such as those of Iain M. Banks's Culture series, that need not be taken for granted. The traditional utopia takes the human condition as a given, and hopes to make the human fit into utopia by legislation and education; the modern form of utopia regards a more perfect society to be the result of evolution and technology.

There are more profound questions that the sf writer has asked, which never occurred to the utopian writers of a century earlier. Why should human physiology or psychology remain the same? Would what human beings recognize as utopia a millennium from now be recognizable as utopia for us at all? Greg Bear, in *Blood Music* (1984), called by its publicists 'the *Childhood's End* for the 1980s', ironically imagines 'utopia', the end of human conflict and the coming of perfect harmony and understanding, through the swallowing up of all humanity into one giant organism (created accidentally in the laboratory by a scientist nerd); Frederik Pohl in *Jem: The Making of a Utopia* (1979) imagines human colonists on another planet creating 'utopia' by losing, or changing, their humanity, joining in symbiosis with indigenous life-forms. Sheri S. Tepper, many of whose novels from the late 1980s onwards have described the victory of human freedom in the face of oppression, particularly patriarchal oppression, shows in *Raising the Stones* (1990) and *Sideshow* (1992) a utopian society arising from a symbiosis with a fungus which promotes human feelings of empathy, 'a communication net that lets you in on how the intelligences around you feel and what they think and know'. After decades of enquiry into the Great Question, the Ultimate Destiny of Man, they realize that this destiny is 'to stop being only man', and they joke that the new Great Question is going to be 'What shall we become now we are no longer Man?'[16]

There are numerous themes of modern sf which should probably be re-garded as part of the utopian project. Back in the 1950s, for instance, there was serious scientific work on telepathy and other forms of ESP, most famously by J. B. Rhine at Duke University, and therefore speculation along these lines was justified as science and not fantasy. What kind of society might emerge if all thoughts were open to all and perfect harmony and un-derstanding – the goal of utopian writers since More – could be achieved? Some questions are still with us. What could be achieved if medical and biological science made improvements to the human body: eliminating dis-ease, or creating something approaching immortality? What about possible changes in the human body, to be brought about by cyborgization (the min-gling of human and machine/computer)? When one imagines such changes, it is possible to think of just as many dystopian outcomes as utopian ones. Universal telepathy might bring mental harmony; it might bring political control and the end of privacy. Immortality might extend the human propen-sity for growth and development; it might bring boredom, mental instability or dangerous over-population.

The unasked but essential question in most utopian novels – 'what is the meaning of life?' or 'what is the destiny of man?' – is a question raised by almost no one these days apart from theologians and sf writers. It is the ultimate, unanswerable, question. After thinking about the question for six days and nights in Le Guin's *The Left Hand of Darkness* (1969), 'all the Celibates were catatonic, [and] the Zanies were dead'.[17] Science fiction writers, by asking such unanswerable questions, have extended the horizons of utopia, and helped to acclimatize it to a world in which the future has so many more possibilities and uncertainties than Sir Thomas More could ever have imagined.

## NOTES

1. Hoda M. Zaki, *Phoenix Renewed* (Mercer Island, WA: Starmont, 1988), pp. 112, 113.
2. William Gibson, 'The Gernsback Continuum' (1981), cited from Gibson, *Burning Chrome* London: Grafton, 1988), pp. 47 and 50. I have put this story in its context among 'anti-utopias' in 'Even Worse, It Could Be Perfect' (see below, p. 283).
3. Cordwainer Smith, 'Alpha Ralpha Boulevard' (1961), in Smith, *The Rediscovery of Man* (London: Gollancz, 1988), pp. 283–314, at p. 284.
4. First published in *Analog* (April 1979), pp. 144–64, this story was incorporated into the first of four Inquestor novels, *Light on the Sound* (New York: Bantam, 1986).
5. Arthur C. Clarke, *Childhood's End* (1953) (London: Pan, 1956), p. 64.
6. Clarke, *The City and the Stars* (1956) (London: Corgi, 1957), p. 70.
7. *Ibid.*, p. 34.

8. A term used by Segal in *Technological Utopianism in American Culture* (Chicago: Chicago University Press, 1985), a study of the optimistic reliance in the USA on technology for social improvement.
9. Letter of 30 November 1952: Eric Frank Russell archive, Science Fiction Foundation collection, University of Liverpool.
10. For a discussion of these stories, see my 'A "Double-Dyed Distilled Detractor"', *Anarchist Studies* 7 (1999), pp. 155–70.
11. Mack Reynolds, *Looking Backward, From the Year 2000* (New York: Ace, 1973), introduction, p. 4.
12. On the space station or habitat as a locale for utopia, see the index to Westfahl, *Islands in the Sky* (San Bernadino, CA: Borgo Press, 1996).
13. Reynolds, *After Utopia* (New York: Ace, 1977), pp. 53–5.
14. *Ibid.*, p. 250.
15. The constitution itself is printed, with some commentary, in Robinson, *The Martians* (London: Voyager, 1999), pp. 226–39.
16. Sheri S. Tepper, *Sideshow* (1992) (New York: Bantam, 1993), pp. 420, 478, 480.
17. Le Guin, *The Left Hand of Darkness* (1969) (London: Panther, 1973), p. 62.

# 17

KEN MACLEOD

# Politics and science fiction

There are no politics in Utopia; as in its neighbour Dystopia, the government of people has been replaced by the administration of things. To many observers, this state of affairs implies anything but freedom. It is the absence of political debate, as much as the absence of privacy and the relentless presence of morality, that makes the communism of Anarres, in Ursula Le Guin's anarchist classic *The Dispossessed* (1974), so oppressive. When her hero Shevek finds himself in conflict with aspects of his society he has no forum in which to express it, no way to find like-minded individuals with whom he might find common ground; instead, his conflicts become conflicts with *other individuals*. He is as isolated as any dissident in a totalitarian state.

For a Western tradition of political thought which begins with Aristotle and continues through such diverse philosophers as the conservative Edmund Burke, the radical Thomas Paine, the liberal Lord Macaulay, the communist Antonio Gramsci, the socialist Tony Polan and the social democrat Bernard Crick, politics provides the forum to which free people – not always, of course, a majority of the adult populace – bring their conflicts of collective interest for peaceful resolution. For most of these thinkers the forum is as central an institution of a free society as the market and the court of law, and the interaction of politics, economics and justice is the substance of public life.

Politics in this sense occupies two areas within sf distinct from utopia or dystopia: in stories that take into account, or have as their theme, the political process itself; and in stories in whose setting or plot the consequences of a particular political philosophy are examined. In sf the former is the less common. Politics, as one of the practical arts – of coalition and compromise, conflict and coercion – requires a different frame of mind and set of priorities to that of most sf readers and writers, whose characteristic ways of thinking are economic, technical and scientific. In the words of Macaulay, 'Logic admits of no compromise. The essence of politics is compromise.'[1] The characteristic sf cast of mind is inclined to the logical and uncompromising. The consequent 'engineering mentality', or an apolitical mentality in general, is, however, well equipped to dramatize political philosophy, by thought experiments which take ideologies to uncompromisingly logical conclusions. In the dystopian tradition the exemplar in this respect is George Orwell. Orwell's interest in, and aptitude for, politics as a practical art were negligible, but his interest in, and imaginative grasp of, the implications of political philosophies were deep. What he said in a sentence about the potentially repressive underside of the anarchist ideal summarizes most of the message of Le Guin's *The Dispossessed*.

Science fiction is essentially the literature of progress, and the political philosophy of sf is essentially liberal. Much, though as we shall see not all, of the most popular and enduring sf is firmly within the Western liberal current: the historically very recent idea that the increase of human power over the rest of nature through the growth of knowledge and industry is possible and desirable, and that freedom – political liberty, personal autonomy, free thought and the free exchange of goods – is desirable in itself and as a means to that end. 'To increase the power of man over nature and abolish the power of man over man' was a formulation of the social good on which the Bolshevik Leon Trotsky and the liberal John Dewey could agree, in the midst of a passionate disagreement over morals. The link between civic freedom and scientific progress is conceptually as well as empirically close. Douglas Adams encapsulated the scientific attitude as 'Any idea is there to be attacked.'[2] A like iconoclasm in political and social matters is its extension and precondition. This view is not only recent, but rare. Its global hegemony seemed assured after the Fall of the Wall; less so, after the Fall of the Towers.

The central political voice in genre sf is that of Robert A. Heinlein. To recognize this is not necessarily to agree with his views. Sociology has been described as a dialogue with Marx; the political strand in sf can be described as a dialogue with Heinlein. This dialogue, however, has not been conducted through sf texts. Gordon R. Dickson's *Naked to the Stars* (1961), an obvious rejoinder to *Starship Troopers*, is a rare exception (and worth seeking out). Heinlein's influence has, rather, worked on generations of readers, some of whom have gone on to become writers. Heinlein's liberalism (in the above sense) is fairly consistent, as is his movement from democratic to elitist formulations of it. His earlier works show a faith in 'the common man'; his later, in the competent man. His works include some that are sensitive to the realities of politics, and some that decidedly are not, but which do embody the imaginative exposition of a political philosophy. The best example of the former is *Double Star*; of the latter, *Starship Troopers*. One that attempts to do both, and fails to do either, is *The Moon is a Harsh Mistress*. Heinlein's '"If This Goes On –"' (1940) deals with a revolt against a future American theocracy. The hero, John Lyle, joins the underground revolutionary Cabal (which is, amusingly enough, nothing other than the Freemasons) and gets the chance to read uncensored history for the first time. While the revolutionary politics is a typical Heinleinian top-down conspiracy, the validity of democratic politics is affirmed:

> I had trouble at first in admitting the possibility of what I read; I think perhaps of all the things a police state can do to its citizens, distorting history is possibly the most pernicious. For example, I learned for the first time that the United States had not been ruled by a bloodthirsty emissary of Satan before the First Prophet arose in his wrath and cast him out – but had been a community of free men, deciding their own affairs by peaceful consent. I don't mean that the first republic had been a scriptural paradise, but it hadn't been anything like what I had learned in school.[3]

*Double Star* (1956) is unusual in sf in that it presents sympathetically and realistically – plot shenanigans aside – the workings of a parliamentary democracy. Even more unusually, the democracy in question is a constitutional monarchy on the Westminster model, which has expanded from the Dutch Empire to encompass the solar system. It is unlikely to be accidental that the Emperor shares the name and house of another Willem – William of Orange. The political formation issuing from Britain's Glorious Revolution of 1688 has proven capable of repeated and essentially emancipatory reforms which – along with the vast increases in both civil and military production which it stimulated and shielded – have enabled it to endure for centuries and replicate across the globe. In view of this Darwinian success it is therefore not as implausible as it may at first seem that a future solar commonwealth might trace the descent, with modification, of its political institutions to those of the Empire on which the sun never set. The novel's Willem is a much more ceremonial figure than his namesake, and it is his First Minister who has the daunting task of the inclusion of extraterrestrials as Imperial citizens. The plot's occasional absurd devices need not detain us: what endures from the book is the transformation and political awakening of its protagonist, the sense of politics as process, and the experience – so frequent in life, and so rare in sf – of waiting as the results of a closely contested election come in. The book ends with a ringing libertarian statement which, unlike so many in Heinlein, is not vitiated by elitism and solipsism.

Heinlein's far more widely and passionately discussed *Starship Troopers* (1959) provides a striking contrast. Instead of the peaceful association of intelligent beings who share a common moral frame whatever their bodily form, celebrated in *Double Star*, there is a pseudo-Darwinian rationale for an endless inter-species Hobbesian war of all against all. Instead of an imagined enlargement of a political system achieved by happy accident and tested by history, there is a new political order which has emerged literally from the ruins of our present civilization in the Third World War. From small beginnings as a vigilante gang of discharged veterans in Aberdeen, a form of democracy in which only veterans have the vote has spread to the stars. If 'the franchise is force, naked and raw, the Power of the Rods and the Ax', as Heinlein's mouthpiece character Major Reid argues,[4] then it is only just that it should be reserved to those who have shown themselves willing to risk their lives in its employ. Political power comes out of the barrel of a gun, and only those who have volunteered to be at both ends of the gun are morally fit to participate in its aim. They have shown they will put their lives on the line for the greater good. This is the sole civic virtue attributed to them. These arguments are ultimately and avowedly irrelevant: the system's justification is that 'it works' – by authorial fiat. The virtues of the system of veterans' franchise are the engineering virtues of symmetry and rigour, underpinned by conformity to a calculus of moral equations which is (wisely) never shown on the page. For a book where civics infodumps and accounts of brutal boot-camp training far outweigh the thin and tensionless combat scenes, *Starship Troopers* is an oddly compelling read. The system it defends is far from the fascism it is sometimes accused of. Anyone who can understand the oath may serve, regardless of their other attributes or abilities. The civilian society which this political system secures is one without wars within the human species, with lots of personal freedom, where almost everyone is reasonably well off, and people who despise the government can do so openly and fearlessly. The book's effect may be analogously benign. Far more of its readers must have been stimulated by it to take an interest in political and moral philosophy than have been converted to that advocated in the text.

The work of Heinlein's which has had a more direct, if small, political effect – through its influence on David Friedman and other theorists of anarcho-capitalism, a significant minority strand in modern libertarianism – is *The Moon is a Harsh Mistress* (1966). What is not immediately evident is that the book's hero and narrator is, albeit unwittingly, the villain of the piece. The carefully plotted revolution in a Lunar penal colony – in the name of free trade with Earth – establishes a democratic state and destroys the capitalist anarchy which the colonists already enjoyed under the Warden's distant rule. They had liberty already, had they but known it, and by the end there is nothing for a good libertarian to do but move out to the new frontier of the asteroid belt. Just why this reversal is obscure points up the two main weaknesses of the book. The first is that the system in which Manny, the narrator, is born is shown in action only fleetingly and incidentally: the key scene, where Manny acts as impromptu but legitimate judge – in a potentially capital case, at that – and forms a jury from the drinkers in a bar, can easily pass by as local colour, and the obvious objections to such frontier justice as the basis of a stable way of life are never seriously addressed. Instead they are dismissed in another offhand display of pseudo-Darwinian authorial legerdemain: those who abuse the system sooner or later find themselves outside an airlock without a pressure-suit. The second is that the revolutionary conspiracy whose progress is the spine of the story is run as a process of top-down manipulation. Heinlein's mouthpiece character, Professor LaPaz, attributes this technique to Lenin's Bolshevik party – a serious misreading of the October Revolution. Without the tumultuous feedback of an insurgent democracy of workers' councils, the Bolsheviks would have been as isolated as many of their emulators found themselves. Likewise, the party itself could not have been prepared for revolutionary action without the preceding decades of factional strife. The 'Fifth International' which provides Heinlein's conspirators with their initial cadre and milieu is too ideologically diverse – virtually spanning the visible political spectrum – to be credible as a potential vanguard.

A more persuasive portrayal of revolutionary politics can be found in Robert Silverberg's *Hawksbill Station* (1968). A decade after Silverberg's protagonist is forced into underground activism by a fascist coup in the USA, he finds that the revolution for which he and his comrades are working has faded from his mind: being a revolutionary has become what he does from day to day. There's always another leaflet to write, another contact to make, another slogan to spray-bomb. With similar realism, the eventual overthrow of the dictatorship takes the revolutionaries by surprise.

For readers and writers in the late twentieth- and early twenty-first centuries, popular revolution has become a familiar television image. The jubilant, implacable crowd in Republic Square, the parliament building in flames, the snowstorm of secret police files drifting from the broken windows of the Ministry of the Interior, the armed students reading the news in the national television studio . . . these have become sights as commonplace as the default night-vision image of recent wars: the sinister green glare of cruise missiles exploding over some hapless capital in the Third or Second World.

This demystification and familiarization of insurrection has affected its portrayal in sf. In the first half of the 1990s, Peter F. Hamilton's *Mindstar Rising* (1993) and my own *The Star Fraction* (1995) both placed in the back-stories of their future Britain a left-wing republican regime overthrown in a popular counter-revolution; in both cases the imagery of the Eastern European uprisings is obvious. Hamilton's Greg Mandel books, of which *Mindstar Rising* is the first, have as their implicit political viewpoint a moderate patriotic conservatism which, in its distance from left-wing 'common sense' and libertarian radicalism alike, is as unusual (for sf) as it is honourable.

A surprising exception to the influence of recent, and real, revolutions can be seen in the political high point of 1990s sf, Kim Stanley Robinson's Mars trilogy (1992–6); surprising, because the work is as much about revolution as it is about terraforming. Here the Red Planet is a literal new world in which new societies tumble over each other in a series of revolutions, even as the landscape is transformed. Nevertheless, Robinson's political imagination seems stunned by the failures of existing socialisms. An early and interesting advocacy of communism – in its original sense of voluntary labour and free access to goods – as an extension of the lifestyle of the scientific community is not followed up. Instead the eventual Martian Congress adopts an economic system which is not so much a free socialism as a fettered capitalism. The most hopeful legacy of the East European regimes was the manner of their passing – through mass, peaceful, popular protest – but this is nowhere reflected in the trilogy. Robinson's images of a revolutionary process draw instead on a 1960s New Left model, of mass discussion backed up by sabotage and guerrilla warfare. The mass discussions are given in realistically exhausting detail.

None of this detracts from Robinson's broader achievements, in making Mars for the first time in sf a *land*, a world in its own right in which the names on the map acquire an historical as well as *areographical* resonance as the story unfolds; and in projecting a future in which a succession of political forms are not only (as Marx said of the Paris Commune's radical democracy) 'at last discovered' but to an extent invented, foreseen and worked towards, as increasingly ample venues 'under which to work out the economical emancipation of labour';[5] until eventually, in the solar system as a whole, revolution becomes permanent.

In the state-socialist countries of the USSR and Eastern Europe, sf had an inescapably political role, often critical of its society in ways as obscure to Western readers even now as it was at the time to the censors. In a society whose ideological justification was utopian and future-oriented, the relationship between the political establishment and sf was necessarily fraught. The iconic salience of space exploration, combined with the perceived status of cosmonauts as a specialized (and privileged) fraction of the working class – an orbital labour aristocracy – doubtless contributed to the distinctive tone of Soviet sf, in which the cosmic environment – hostile or benign – is treated with the same intimacy as terrestrial nature. The fantastic unconscious of the Space Age is arguably the UFO phenomenon, and here too the Soviet combination of official denial with covert investigation and popular fascination carried a different emotional and symbolic freight to that of its

Western counterpart. An analysis of these different but intricately related forms of reflection on the non-human world and the future in the Soviet bloc is overdue.

Turning from politics as process to polity as outcome, the great glaring exception to sf's broadly liberal consensus can be found in Frank Herbert's *Dune* (1965) and its sequels. The institutions of Herbert's galaxy are based on those of the Ottoman Empire, within which model the use of European feudal nomenclature is deeply misleading. His planetary viceroys are called dukes, and their domains fiefs, where satrap and satrapy would be the un-varnished truth. Here the link between freedom and progress is confirmed in the negative. Progress has long since been halted by the Butlerian Jihad (a witty refererence to Samuel Butler's *Erewhon*, 1872), which destroyed all computers and whose stricture against making 'a machine in the likeness of a human mind' is still rigorously kept.[6] Politics and religion are devoted to mass manipulation. The only progress that remains is evolutionary, and is achieved by the secret long-term breeding programme of the Bene Gesserit sisterhood and by the random mixing of genes in the bloody tsunami of the jihad. No world less congenial to the values implicit in most sf has been presented on such a scale, and with such hermetic absence of intratextual criticism.

A more troubling exception to the generally progressive spirit of sf might appear to be feminist sf. Some of it does indeed turn its back on progress and the conquest of the universe as a typically male power fantasy – and to that extent, and perhaps for that reason, it has isolated itself from all but a few sf readers. But not all feminist sf, even of the most radical kind, takes that view. Joanna Russ's *The Female Man* (1975) carries a militant message of progress even in its title. That the English word for the human species and the word for the male sex is the same, with its implied exclusion of half the human race from the achievements ascribed to all of it – 'man's conquest of space', and so on – is an old problem. While some feminist writers have responded by repudiating the achievements, Russ stakes a claim on all of them for women. Women can be Man, without being men. Russ makes a passionate claim for freedom and achievement. That there are no men in her imagined future world of Whileaway is literally a biological accident – the women of that world do all the things women do, and all the things men do, including industrializing the Earth and exploring the universe.

A dialectical trope of sf is the notion of imperial expansion as the vehicle of escape: if empire begins by extending the reach of oppression, it ends by undermining it. A galactic empire has been a staple of sf since Asimov's Foundation trilogy, and his Roman original and its parabolic trajectory has provided the template for many a tale of decline and fall, and of post-imperial diversity analogous to the rise of feudalism and capitalism in Europe. That a genuinely feudal polity is not a limitless despotism is a point underlined by Lois MacMaster Bujold's Vorkosigan series. Her Barrayar has emerged from centuries of isolation as a galactic anachronism, with an emperor and his counts and their armsmen, and the gradual transition from a politics conducted by baronial war and dynastic coup to one in which the holders of a still-restricted franchise have to take into account the views and interests of an increasingly self-assertive citizenry provides the milieu for her maturing hero's adventures and intrigues. Other possible orders – the eugenic human topiary of Cetaganda, the social-democratic brave new world of Beta Colony, the anarcho-capitalist tyranny of Jackson's Whole – are sharply limned and deftly satirized.

If freedom is the engine of progress, as liberalism and with it most sf affirm, the possibility seems to arise of escaping the political realm altogether through an individual or voluntarily communal autonomy enabled by interstellar distance or technological self-sufficiency. Poul Anderson's 'The Last of the Deliverers'[7] is set in a future where cheap, small fusion power plants have made possible a radical decentralization of population and power into small and largely self-sufficient communities. The confrontation between the last communist and the last enthusiast for capitalism, on which the story turns, is given added bite by its ending, in which it becomes apparent that the passing of class struggle and the state has not been the end of conflict, or even of 'self-evident' ideological blind-spots.

In its most moderate form this physical realization of autonomy is an extension of pluralism, as in Peter F. Hamilton's Night's Dawn trilogy (1996–9), which portrays with panache a diverse interstellar order within a capitalist framework. His pluralistic Confederation is a worthy competitor to Empire, Federation and Culture.

A further development of pluralism was shown in Eric Frank Russell's fix-up *The Great Explosion* (1962), in which scores of scattered colonies are being corralled into Earth's bureaucratic empire, with mixed success. In the collection's culminating story, '. . . And Then There Were None', one particular shipload of bureaucrats and their increasingly mutinous crew confront a highly individualistic anarchy whose 'secret weapon' of Gandhian disobedience is both operating principle (if co-operation is voluntary, its withdrawal is an effective means of enforcement) and revolutionary strategy.

A less idealistic withdrawal of consent is through tax evasion, or indulgence in prohibited entertainment, sex and drugs. In Cyril Kornbluth's *The Syndic* (1953) finance capitalism and the welfare state have collapsed under the strain of competing with their black-market rival: far from the State abolishing the family, the Family has abolished the state.

The suspicion that the state is a vehicle for activities no less self-seeking than those of corporations or criminal gangs has seeped into the ground-water of US culture since the first Kennedy assassination. In this context of popular paranoia Robert Shea's and Robert Anton Wilson's *Illuminatus!* (1975) trilogy works as a parable to impart a subtler insight. The reader is introduced to a succession of conspiracy theories, each of which explodes the previous one by revealing, behind the secret masters, other masters more secret still. Behind the Bilderbergers, Trilateralists and other usual suspects we find the Freemasons, behind them the Illuminati, behind them the Templars, the Cathars, the Gnostics . . . by the time the ultimate manipulator of events is exposed as a Lovecraftian monster in the pre-Cambrian epoch, the reader has long since got the point (a point similarly made, though perhaps less self-consciously, by the labyrinthine elaborations of *The X-Files*, and entirely consciously in Umberto Eco's *Foucault's Pendulum* (1989)): that such conspiracy theories serve to deflect attention from the quite visible holders of, and contenders for, political power.

The extremism of pluralism is anarchy. The closest analogy to a functioning anarchy in everyday experience is the Internet, and this analogy has been explored and not yet exhausted in recent sf. Neal Stephenson's *Snow Crash* (1992) has the US government reduced to a gang among gangs, printing trillion-dollar bills ('Reagans') as small change. It reflects vividly the freewheeling ethos of the Internet's pioneering years, when mutually hostile 'online communities' of researchers, libertarians, anarchists, labour and human-rights activists, Holocaust revisionists and pornographers found common cause in evading censorship. A cynical saying in the geek culture of programming is 'If you document a bug, it's a feature' and Stephenson gleefully takes this approach to some obvious objections to anarchy: unstable individuals with personal nuclear weapons are dealt with by . . . extreme politeness. With Greater Hong Kong as a chain of motorway service areas, the Mafia as pizza delivery franchise ('You have a friend in the Family') and the whites-only enclaves of New South Africa brandishing their bazookas, the anarchy of cyberspace has been mapped on to the dismembered body of the state. That a stateless society can, as Thomas Hobbes warned, become riven by mutual warfare is not always seen as a decisive objection to it. The war of all against all provides endless options to love or leave. At worst one can keep running: happiness, as Hobbes also said, is to go forward.

Vernor Vinge's *A Fire Upon the Deep* (1992) uses the Internet not only as the model for his galactic communications web, the 'Net of a Million Lies', but also for the galactic society of societies. Vinge radically flattens the distinction between public and private associations. For him, anarchism is not a programme; rather, anarchy is a description of the existing state of affairs.

There are in his world statists, but no states, in the sense of authorities whose claim to legitimacy can be upheld or attacked. For Vinge, as for the political philosopher Robert Paul Wolff, there simply is no legitimate authority.[8] It's turtles, all the way down – or pretenders, all the way up. Neither humanity nor its successors nor its superiors ever emerge from the state of nature, and they never have, and never can. There is no overall hegemon, no final court of appeal and to all appearances, no God. There are indeed gods – in Vinge's universe theology is an applied science – but these superhuman but not super-natural beings are themselves in the state of nature, more pandaemonium than pantheon. Powers and Perversions and 'Powers beyond the Powers' make the 'appeal to Heaven' a literal possibility, albeit too dangerous for all but the very last resort. Vinge thus accomplishes for political philosophy what Heinlein achieved for world-building: the economical avoidance of ex-plication, by what is taken for granted. In Vinge's works, unlike Heinlein's, few authorial spokesmen dilate.

What makes the Internet so attractive as a model of anarchic co-operation is that it vastly extends both private initiative and public space. Communal utopias are paradoxically, and endemically, deficient in their provision for public debate. My own, the Solar Union of *The Cassini Division* (1998), is no exception. In my other Fall Revolution books I have explored other problems of anarchy: in *The Star Fraction* (1995), the conflict between community and individual autonomy; in *The Stone Canal* (1996) that between inequality and liberty; and in *The Sky Road* (1999), those between legality and humanity, and between stability and progress. In all of them I have used – perhaps over-used – the real Fourth International (seedbed of most of the sects on the British far Left) as a model of revolutionary politics. The obscurity of this inspiration is admittedly paralleled by its levity. Nonetheless, I am confident that any story set in the near future – say, the remainder of the twenty-first century – gains realism and relevance from a recognition that the 'epoch of wars and revolutions' is far from over.

The future of political themes in sf is to some extent dependent on po-litical developments in the real world, which at the time of writing are in considerable flux. The post-political future adumbrated in 1980s cyberpunk, where government is irrelevant in the face of the corporate power wielded by zaibatsus and policed by their ninja hitmen, seems like a vision tuned to a dead channel. Writers such as Bruce Sterling, Paul McAuley and Alastair Reynolds have shown new political issues and alignments emerging from new technological possibilities in the areas of life-extension and other forms of human self-modification. Their Mechanists and Shapers, Demarchists and Radical Primitives point towards a postmodern and indeed posthuman po-litical field not polarized by the issues of liberty and authority which have preoccupied the Western tradition I referred to at the outset. They suggest that collective disagreements can be debated, and that political engagement can exist, without public or private coercion. In doing so they ably carry forward the most subversive message in sf: that humanity or its successors may yet outlive the state.

## NOTES

1. Thomas Macaulay, *The History of England*, vol. ii, ch.10 (Everyman edn, London, J. M. Dent, 1906), p. 184.
2. Douglas Adams, in 'an impromptu speech in 1998', quoted in Richard Dawkins, 'Time to Stand Up', *The Freethinker* 122:1 (January 2002), p. 8.
3. Robert A. Heinlein, '"If This Goes On –"' (1940), in Heinlein, *The Past Through Tomorrow* (1967) (New York: Ace, 1987), pp. 498–9.
4. Heinlein, *Starship Troopers* (1959) (London: NEL, 1970), p. 155.
5. Karl Marx, 'The Civil War in France: Address of the General Council', in D. Fernbach, ed., *The First International and After* (Harmondsworth: Penguin, 1974), p. 212.
6. Frank Herbert, *Dune* (London: New English Library, 1977), pp. 495–6.
7. Poul Anderson, 'The Last of the Deliverers' (1958) in Harry Harrison, ed., *Back-drop of Stars* (1968) (London: NEL, 1975), pp. 27–40.
8. See Robert Paul Wolff's *In Defense of Anarchism* (New York: Harper and Row, 1970).

# 18

HELEN MERRICK

# Gender in science fiction

Traditionally, sf has been considered a predominantly masculine field which, through its focus on science and technology, 'naturally' excludes women and by implication, considerations of gender. To varying degrees over its history, sf has in fact functioned as an enormously fertile environment for the exploration of sociocultural understandings of gender. My use of the rather slippery term 'gender' here refers to the socially constructed attributes and 'performed' roles that are mapped on to biologically sexed bodies in historically and culturally specific ways. Rather than a comprehensive account of representations of masculinity and femininity, this chapter explores sf's potential to engage with gender issues, highlighting texts that have served to disrupt or challenge normative cultural understandings.[1]

Despite populist notions of the overwhelmingly masculinist nature of sf, the problematic spaces signaled by 'gender' are crucial to sf imaginings. The presence of 'Woman' – whether actual, threatened or symbolically represented (through the alien, or 'mother Earth' for example) – reflects cultural anxieties about a range of 'Others' immanent in even the most scientifically pure, technically focused sf. The series of 'self/other' dichotomies suggested by 'gender', such as human/alien, nature/technology, and organic/inorganic, are also a central (although often unacknowledged) facet of the scientific culture informing much sf. The argument that at least some sf texts were justified in omitting women altogether was predicated on the notion that their ostensible subject matter – science and technology – were inherently masculine endeavours. Such views not only neatly sidestep the sociocultural relations of science and technology, but also serve to obscure the *active* reinforcement of the androcentric culture of the (Western) scientific 'world view'. As Brian Attebery notes: 'The master narrative of science has always been told in sexual terms. It represents knowledge, innovation, and even perception as masculine, while nature, the passive object of exploration, is described as feminine.'[2]

The narratives of 'Science' carry an implicit set of cultural assumptions about a whole series of relationships concerning subjectivity, knowledge, 'Nature' and gender, such that sf's central question 'what if?' ultimately cannot escape the analogous question 'what, then, becomes of us?' In what ways can we (re)imagine 'humanity'? Science fiction authors have employed a number of strategies to answer this question, in the process sometimes revealing, destabilizing or subverting normative understandings of gender. The earliest stages involved exposing the androcentric understanding that equates human with 'man', and making visible the repressed or absent feminine 'other' either through a denial of difference (the 'female man') or by a gynocentric re-valuing of the 'feminine'. Efforts to imagine a more equal gendered system may posit male and female as complementary halves which together equal 'humanity'; alternatively, the attempt to disrupt gendered binaries have taken the form of a number of 'androgynous' solutions: merging the binary into a singular 'gender' (the hermaphrodite); collapsing the binary by refusing gender categorization altogether; or positing a multiplicity of genders which subverts dualistic oppositions.

An examination of work which challenges traditional notions of gender needs to be contextualized within the broader field of 'androcentric' sf. Thus it is important to consider what representations and constructions of masculinity have been available and what implicit understandings of gender have thereby been implied. One very powerful image of masculinity in sf from the 1930s to 1950s was that of the 'super-man'. The superhuman qualities of such characters often lay in their intellectual and scientific superiority, rather than a more traditional masculine physicality. Such stories were indebted to Darwinian notions of evolution, and the highly gendered narrative of sexual selection. In Stanley Weinbaum's *The New Adam* (1939), Edmond Hall's superhuman powers are firmly located in terms of intellect, rather than in a hyper-masculinized body. Indeed, the depiction of his physical 'delicacy' complicates his masculinity, at times suggesting a 'coded' homosexuality. These are, indeed, narratives of the super-man whose vision of an improved 'humanity' derives from the evolution of certain traits specifically associated with the masculine. Despite – or perhaps because of – the strength of such narratives and metaphors, and the centrality of 'gender-coding' to the science/culture nexus, even androcentric sf highlights the way gender structures so many of our cultural 'stories'.

The subject of 'woman' was not, however, entirely absent from this masculinized arena; indeed, debates about the role of women and the representation of female characters in sf have been present from the genre's beginnings in the pulp magazines. Concerns about 'women in sf' developed from the 'sex in sf' question, which loomed large in the sf (un)consciousness from the late 1920s through the sexual liberation of the 1960s, to intersect with (and be partially absorbed by) feminist narratives from the 1970s to the present. The early debates concerning the appropriateness of 'sex' (read romance) in sf stories (or on the cover of the magazines in the form of scantily clad women) were intimately connected with notions about the place of women characters in sf, and cultural constructions of 'femininity' and 'masculinity'. The 'alien' could signify everything that was 'other' to the dominant audience of middle-class, young white Western males – including women, people of colour, other nationalities, classes and sexualities. The interactions between aliens and human men were often inherently, if covertly, sexual in nature. Further, in the name of keeping sf pure of 'puerile love interests', exclusionary tactics were pursued by male fans, authors and editors to situate women characters 'outside' the masculine domain of science and sf. The majority argued that sex had no place in the logical, scientific, 'cerebral' topos of sf, and, *ipso facto*, that there was no place for 'woman'.

There has, however, been a long tradition in sf where a certain 'female' character has had a central role – in stories where the traditional gendered hierarchies of society are overturned and where 'women rule'. These 'Woman Dominant' – or in the words of Joanna Russ, 'Battle of the Sexes' stories[3] – reveal a latent anxiety about changes and threats to the gendered order in a much more obvious fashion than the majority of sf. These texts confront anxieties over the potential 'feminine' challenge to gendered hierarchies and the 'heterosexual economy', which are threatened by images of self-sustaining matriarchal societies. And whilst they may at least hint at the vision of a more equal gendered social order, this possibility is undermined by figuring female desire for greater equality in terms of a (stereotypical) masculine drive for power and domination.

The biologically essentialist, gendered assumptions underpinning the narratives of science (and evolution) are clearly articulated in these stories, depicting matriarchies incapable of establishing a functioning 'scientifically' progressive society. Thomas Gardner's 'The Last Woman' (1932) tells of an all-male 'Science Civilization' where only one woman remains, and is ultimately executed. This potentially homosocial society reinforces a heterosexually based model of masculinity through use of an 'Elixir', whereby those 'energies that had been turned toward sex and the emotional side of life were released for thought and work'.[4] Not only women, but all symbolic images of the 'feminine' are eradicated through the removal of these distracting 'emotional' forces.

Not all battle of the sexes texts foreclosed the possibility of female rule – some early stories depicted successful matriarchies, whilst a number of later texts deconstruct the negative 'woman dominant' stories through ironic or satirical role reversals. Francis Stevens's 'Friend Island' (1918), presents a society where women are admitted to be the superior sex. Another unusual example was 'Via the Hewitt Ray', by Margaret F. Rupert (1930), in which Lucille Hewitt travels to another dimension where society is dominated by women with only a few 'breeding males'. What makes this story unusual is a reference to a 'reversed' system of prostitution, as men with 'physical beauty' are kept to satisfy women's 'biological urge[s]'. In Leslie Francis Stone's humorous 'The Conquest of Gola' (1931) a male invasion of a matriarchal planet is successfully resisted, primarily because the invaders cannot believe that the planet is ruled by women.

The work of C. L. Moore, one of the earliest and most successful female authors published in sf magazines, demonstrates other important developments in the treatment of gender. As well as her Amazon-like heroine, 'Jirel of Joiry' (from 1934), Moore offers an interesting approach to the female alien in 'Shambleau' (1933), which whilst ultimately depicting the medusa-like alien as a threat that must be contained, does emphasize the power of a 'female' sexuality, which at least temporarily 'feminizes' the 'hero' Northwest Smith by rendering him powerless and submissive. Most interesting in terms of gender is Moore's 1944 story 'No Woman Born', which offers remarkable insights into issues of embodiment, female beauty, power and what it means to be 'human', by uncoupling 'femininity' from the biologically female body. The cyborg Deirdre still possesses the feminine attributes of grace, beauty and her ability to dance, but through a wholly metallic body, which, as we come to realize, is endowed with 'hyper-masculine' qualities of super-human strength and agility. The perception of the male narrator, who worries about the 'fragility' of her 'glowing and radiant mind poised in metal', and her 'inhuman' appearance, is in tension with Deirdre's appreciation of the potentials and strengths of her new body.

The 1950s marked an important period in sf's engagement with sociocultural concerns, including a more engaged awareness of contemporary issues around sex, gender roles, race and ecology. The period from the late 1940s to the 1950s also saw the emergence and establishment of a number of important female sf writers, whose work often departed from traditional sf themes (such as Mildred Clingerman, Miriam Allen deFord, Margaret St Clair, Carol Emshwiller, Andre Norton, Kit Reed, Wilmar H. Shiras and Kate Wilhelm).[5] One text that is constantly valorized by critics as representing a watershed in sf's 'maturity' in its attitude to sex is Philip José Farmer's 'The Lovers' (1952), considered as one of the earliest to break sexual taboos and cited as evidence of sf's newly found progressiveness. It was left to later feminist critics to point out the misogyny of this graphic picture of miscegenation ending in the destruction of the *female* alien.[6]

The 1950s also saw a number of writers resolve the 'battle of the sexes' through some form of equality, including Robert Silverberg's 'Woman's World' (1957) and Frederik Pohl and Cyril Kornbluth's *Search the Sky* (1954). Best known of such works are Philip Wylie's *The Disappearance* (1951) and John Wyndham's 'Consider Her Ways' (1956). In *The Disappearance* women mysteriously vanish from men's lives, and vice versa. Although the male and female worlds are united at the end, women are shown to have dealt rather better with the separation than the men. However, the heterosexual economy is preserved, and only the inequalities of 'the sexes' are highlighted. 'Consider Her Ways', often considered a proto-feminist work, tells of a woman transported to a future matriarchal society arising after men had been wiped out by a virus. Much of the story centres around a stringent critique of the prescribed gendered roles for 1950s women. Yet, in many ways this matriarchy conforms to earlier examples, being modelled on a 'hive-like' society, with a total absence of sexual relations amongst the women.

Such role reversals engaged with gender to the extent that they parodied or criticized contemporary gendered norms through the familiar sf trope of 'defamiliarizing the familiar'. The other available option was to postulate a set of 'human behaviours' available to both men and women and depict female 'heroes' capably carrying out 'men's work'. Isaac Asimov's Robot series portrayed the female scientist Susan Calvin, who in a sense is masquerading as a 'female man'. However, Calvin's performance of masculine gender attributes ultimately compromises her identity – her 'cold nature', emotional isolation and adherence to rationality is apparently at odds with her 'natural' identity as a woman. More liberating examples of female characters are seen in the work of Robert Heinlein, who was one of the earliest authors to introduce considerations of sex and sexuality into sf. Unusually for his time, Heinlein routinely portrayed independent, competent and intelligent female characters, most notably in his juveniles such as *Have Spacesuit Will Travel* (1958), *Tunnel in the Sky* (1955) (which includes an African woman character) and *Podkayne of Mars* (1963). Ultimately, however, Heinlein's women are re-contained within a normative gendered order most often through their desire for male appreciation, remaining 'sexually dependent' whilst 'morally superior'.[7]

Heinlein's work also provides another example of the breadth of sf's engagement with gender issues, namely the complexity of representations of technology and masculinity. As technological development brings into question the boundaries of the organic, it can be seen to metaphorically threaten the embodied qualities of physical strength which inform social constructions of masculinity. Thus, 'technology' in sf can be read as both a signifier of masculinty, and also as a site of cultural anxieties about gender. In Heinlein's *Starship Troopers* (1959) the prosthetically enhanced troopers can be read as 'hyper-masculine', representing an 'aggressive overinflation of masculinity' in reponse to their hi-tech environment. In a manner foreshadowing the 'feminization' of cyberspace in later sf, the images of spaceships and launching tubes connote the feminine metaphors of pregnancy and childbirth: 'Being contained inside the ship and inside the suit, at the mercy of a woman at the controls, the marines' technologically-enhanced body becomes a site of great anxiety and ambiguity'.[8]

In the 1950s a number of female sf authors emerged who helped make women 'visible' in sf through a focus on female characters, or writing from what Merril termed 'the woman's point of view'.[9] Such woman-focused stories were castigated – both at the time and in later feminist critique – as 'sweet little domestic stories', 'wet-diaper' fiction or *'Ladies' Magazine fiction* – in which the sweet, gentle, intuitive little heroine solves an interstellar crisis by mending her slip or doing something equally domestic after her big, heroic husband has failed'.[10] Such a simplistic rendering however, does not consider the disruptive potential of locating the 'women's sphere' as central in a genre that privileged science, space travel or heroic quests. In Zenna Henderson's 'Subcommittee', an intergalactic war is prevented by the wife of a high official, who discovers the real nature of the alien's needs at a family picnic, when power politics and military intelligence has failed. Far from being a simplistic, essentialist celebration of feminine 'intuition', the story is 'revealing as a critique of power structures and the language of power and . . . as a study of gender'.[11] Shifting the focus to the social consequences of the 'masculinist' (public) sphere of technology, politics and the military is similarly disruptive. As author Connie Willis observes, Judith Merril's 'That Only a Mother' (1948) 'hardly classifies as a domestic tale. It's a story about radiation, infanticide, and desperate self-delusion that manages to be poignant and horrific at the same time.'[12]

In part due to the increased number of female writers in the field, and their introduction of more female characters, by the 1960s some texts began to move beyond merely rendering women 'visible', or claiming a limited equality based on denial of difference. Increasingly more complex characterizations are evident, with portrayals of women as fully 'human', rather than 'female men', or complementary adjuncts to, or reflections of, the masculine. Some sf writers began to construct societies in which human involvement was not constrained by the social mores predicated on biological sex. This was particularly evident in the work of those writers who envisioned a scientific culture which could accommodate – even welcome – knowledges based on a broader spectrum of human experience. Katherine MacLean was one of the earliest women writers to bring together 'hard sf' with intelligent female characters and an awareness of the foibles of cultural constraints attendant on such 'liberated' women. Similarly, Naomi Mitchison's *Memoirs of a Spacewoman* (1962) was unusually prescient in constructing a future society where the biological constraints of childbearing were totally disassociated from a woman's right to a fully 'human' array of choices and responsibilities – from career to parenthood. The spacefaring communications expert Mary casually reveals to us a 'future history' of science which takes for granted that there will be women – *and* women of colour – participating in all the sciences. Along with James Tiptree Jr and Alice Lightner, Mitchison's work was unusual for its concern with the intersection of both gender *and* race with scientific narratives.

From the 1960s on a number of sf texts helped shift the gender focus away from the 'Battle of the Sexes' to more egalitarian solutions. While still in dialogue with previous works, these texts offered more radical solutions by collapsing gendered roles onto one 'combined' sex, thus challenging the constraints of biological sex differences. Theodore Sturgeon's *Venus Plus X* (1960) postulates that equality can only be achieved through the removal of biological difference. In this future egalitarian and tolerant society the Ledom are 'biologically androgynous', sexually identical and can all give birth. Contemporary gender relations are compared unfavourably with that of the Ledom, in the process critiquing socially constructed notions of masculinity which rely on the identification of difference as a means of disempowering 'the other'.

In *The Left Hand of Darkness* (1969) Ursula Le Guin crystallized previous challenges to underlying gender assumptions with her 'thought experiment' of an androgynous society. The Gethenian inhabitants of the planet Winter are neuter except for certain periods of 'kemmer' when they can become either male or female: thus all Gethenians have the potential to both give birth *and* father a child. Le Guin directly confronts the question of socialised versus biological difference, as the human narrator, Genly Ai admits, 'It's extremely hard to separate the innate differences from the learned ones.'[13] In this society, 'humanity' is defined as a commonly accessible and shared set of values, attributes and behaviours tangibly separated from arbitrary and shifting notions of the self based only on a sexed embodiment. However, as Le Guin herself later admitted, her use of the masculine pronoun to refer to the Gethenians allows their society to be read as all-male: 'a safe trip into androgyny and back, from a conventionally male viewpoint'.[14]

The 1970s marks a high point in sf's engagement with gender with the publication of a significant group of texts which Russ would later classify as 'feminist utopias'. These self-consciously feminist works consistently challenge and disrupt the perceived 'naturalness' of gender, and locate the operation and proliferation of the more harmful effects of the gendered order deep within the political and cultural institutions of contemporary society. While each proposes different approaches to the problem of gender, the resulting fictive societies bear a remarkable number of similarities. Gender is seen (in most cases) to be 'socially produced', thus challenging taken-for-granted structures which reinforce gender binarisms. Extended families or communal life are presented as alternatives to the nuclear family, while parenting is shared amongst numerous 'mothers', who may be female or male. These societies also promote freedom of sexual expression, including homosexuality, in order to 'separate sexuality from questions of ownership, reproduction and social structure'.[15]

In Marge Piercy's *Woman on the Edge of Time*, Mattapoisett is a 'culturally androgynous' society, a paradigm of an egalitarian, ecologically sustainable world where artificial wombs are used so that no one gives birth but both men and women 'mother' (and breastfeed). Le Guin's *The Dispossessed* also argues for a world where biological sex no longer produces a gendered hierarchy; as one of her characters notes, 'A person chooses work according to interest, talent strength – what has the sex to do with that?'[16] Most of the other feminist sf 'utopias' disrupt gendered hierarchies by (re)constituting woman as human, in many cases by postulating a woman-only world, in order to provide women with full access to the range of experiences and emotions associated with humanity. Russ's 'When it Changed' and *The Female Man* represent in some ways the apogee of the engagement of sf and gender, with their devastating critique of female stereotypes and masculinist sf tropes, and deconstruction of the acceptable, liberal 'whole' woman towards a multiple, shifting postmodernist sense of female 'selfhood'. In the utopian world of Whileaway we see the most obvious, rigorous – and humorous – case for the argument that 'women' equals human – even when they are working, living, loving and reproducing without men. In Sally Miller Gearhart's *The Wanderground* (1980), Suzy McKee Charnas's *Motherlines* (1978) and Tiptree's 'Houston, Houston, Do You Read?' (1976), the equation of women as human can only be realized through the construction of a society where men are absent. As Charnas observed, without the constraints of ingrained assumptions about gender roles, her female characters had 'access to the entire range of human behaviour. They acted new roles appropriate to social relationships amongst a society of equals which allowed them to behave simply as human beings.'[17] Perhaps the most famed author to explore the ramifications of these ingrained gender roles was James Tiptree Jr. Celebrated in the mid-1970s as a 'masculine' writer, she was revealed in 1977 as Alice Sheldon. As both James Tiptree Jr, and her second pseudonym Raccoona

Sheldon, she was the writer of some of the most powerful critiques of traditional gender roles in this period, including 'The Women Men Don't See'
(1973) and 'The Screwfly Solution' (1977). In the first women choose aliens
over men; in the second aliens engineer a sex-violence link to lethal levels in
order to clear desirable real estate of pesky humans.

Rather than removing men, in works such as Delany's *Triton* (1976) the
notion of social manifestations of gender are multiple and diffused to the extent that they become meaningless, and all kinds of gender/sexual difference
are celebrated. On Triton, there are over forty 'sexes' in a societal structure
where bisexual, homosexual, heterosexual and celibate relationships are all
equally recognized and condoned. As in John Varley's *Steel Beach* (1992)
(and his other Eight World stories), sex changes, complete with full reproductive capabilities, are common. In these scenarios, the socially mediated
relation between sex and gender is dissolved into multiplicity and meaning-
lessness, as 'sex' becomes a referent, rather than a determinant of sexuality.
Another author who disrupts the gender binary in a similar way is Octavia
Butler (the first African-American woman to make a career writing sf) in
her Xenogenesis trilogy (1987–9). The alien Oankali have a third sex: the
ooloi who facilitate the Oankali's 'organic technology' of genetic exchange.
Butler's work always concerns the destructive effects of both race and gender;
in Xenogenesis radical change is required to construct a truly human(e)
society, requiring its characters to become other than human through mating
with Oankali ooloi.

The 1980s saw a move away from 'androgyny' to works which critiqued or
explored gender through dystopian visions, role reversals and worlds which
split men and women into separate societies. The re-emergence of sociobiol-
ogy was one discourse about gender that fed into the idea of the 1980s as a
period of conservatism and backlash, and texts such as Suzette Haden Elgin's
trilogy which began with *Native Tongue* (1984) and Margaret Atwood's *The
Handmaid's Tale* (1985) are conventionally read in terms of this conservative atmosphere (as could the 'role-reversal' of C. J. Cherryh's *The Pride of
Chanur*, 1982; Jayge Carr's *Leviathan's Deep*, 1979; and Cynthia Felice's
*Double Nocturne*, 1986). The separatist texts *Gate to Women's Country*
(1988) by Sheri S. Tepper and *The Shore of Women* (1986) by Pamela Sargent may be productively considered in the context of feminist critiques of
reproductive technologies: in both these texts artificial insemination is controlled by women, and rather than 'farming' ova, men are 'milked' for their
sperm. In Nicola Griffith's *Ammonite* (1993), a rare recent all-female world,
a virus has infected a planet's population and killed all the men. One of the
effects of the virus on the original inhabitants of Jeep is the ability to perceive and even influence their biochemistry, including developing a process

of 'gynogenesis', female control over a technology of reproduction. Reading such works as part of a feminist struggle over scientific narratives suggests at least some continuity with the 1970s works, rather than a 'failure' to live up to the revolutionary potential of the more overtly feminist utopias.

Another important locus of concerns about gender in 1980s sf – particularly in terms of masculinity – was cyberpunk. Described as the 'urban fantasies of white male folklore' the 'console cowboys' of this sub-genre enact a return to a 'purer' form of hard sf, apparently without cognizance of the impact of radical social movements such as feminism. Cyberpunk's representation of the body and human subjectivity recapitulate the old humanist dream of transcendence – here refigured as that of 'meat vs. mind'. Despite the potentially liberating promises of an escape from the body (and thus modernist notions of gendered subjectivity), and the presence of strong female characters, the dominance of the mind/body dualism in cyberpunk serves to reinforce the associated gender binaries. The only woman 'officially' associated with the cyberpunk movement, Pat Cadigan, offers a very different perspective which keeps in focus the gendered (and raced) nature of embodiment even in a virtual environment. *Synners* (1989), for example, critiques certain 'masculine' relations to technology, in particular the transcendental desire to escape the 'meat-prison'. Melissa Scott's *Trouble and her Friends* (1994), Mary Rosenblum's *Chimera* (1993), Maureen McHugh's *China Mountain Zhang* (1992) and Laura Mixon's *Glass Houses* (1992) all move beyond the heterosexism of cyberpunk and include lesbian, gay or bisexual characters, and confront the gendered issue of embodiment in a space that privileges the (masculinized) 'mind' over (feminized) 'body'.

Over the last couple of decades, increasingly nuanced explorations of gender are in evidence across a wide range of sf texts, for example, those which disrupt the conventionally 'masculinist' narratives of 'hard' sf and military sf. A number of authors have designed futures where 'science' is expanded to include areas considered 'unscientific' in Western technoculture. Communication – traditionally seen as a female attribute – operates as a 'science' in texts such as Bradley's Darkover novels (1962–2001), Sheri S. Tepper's *After Long Silence* (1987), Suzette Haden Elgin's *Native Tongue* (1984), Sheila Finch's *Triad* (1986) and Janet Kagan's *Hellspark* (1988).

The traditional male 'hero' at the heart of military space opera and future-war sf is also being rewritten in ways which challenges notions of masculinity. Lois McMaster Bujold's Vorkosigan series (1986 on) features the highly 'feminized' hero Miles Vorkosigan, whose abnormal physicality, avoidance of violence and relationships with women mark him as highly unconventional. Elizabeth Moon's Serrano series (1993–2001) plays with the masculine space of the military and 'the hunt' by placing women (and an elderly clutch of 'aunts') at the centre of political power. From a different perspective, Joe Haldeman's *Forever Peace* (1997) powerfully deconstructs notions of war and gender – and his own 1974 novel *The Forever War* – through a compelling examination of what would happen to humanity if it was incapable of violence.

From a twenty-first century perspective, the easily identifiable concerns of 1970s feminist sf texts have been absorbed into a much broader consideration of the intersections of gendered concerns with postcolonial theory, ecological politics and radical critiques of (Western) science. Both reflecting and encouraging such developments, in 1991 the James Tiptree, Jr Memorial Award was founded by Karen Joy Fowler and Pat Murphy, to be awarded to sf that 'expands or explores our understanding of gender'.[18] Authors as diverse as Raphael Carter, Theodore Roszak, James Patrick Kelly, Nancy Springer and Kim Stanley Robinson have been recognized by the award, providing an indication of the enormously rich and complex state of the engagement of sf and gender. Some of these 'Tiptree' texts eradicate gender altogether, such as Gwyneth Jones's White Queen trilogy, with her 'genderless' Aleutians, and Ian McDonald's *Sacrifice of Fools* (1996). Others, such as Melissa Scott's *Shadow Man* (1995), imagine multiple genders, or refuse gender through characters who are not identified as either male or female, including the narrators of Kelly Eskridge's 'And Salome Danced' (1994) and Emma Bull's *Bone Dance* (1991). The success of the Tiptree award clearly signals the appropriateness of the genre as a vehicle for exploring gender and humanity and 'unlearning' the strictures of cultural norms. Science fiction provides a space where writers can seriously address the challenge articulated by Karen Fowler: 'Just ask yourself, if we weren't taught to be women, what would we be? (Ask yourself this question even if you're a man, and don't cheat by changing the words).'[19]

## NOTES

1. My discussion is necessarily partial; there remains much critical work to be done on constructions of masculinity in sf for example, and I refer only briefly to the ground-breaking work of feminist sf writers as this subject is covered in the 'Feminism' chapter in this volume.

2. Brian Attebery, 'Science Fiction and the Gender of Knowledge', in Andy Sawyer and David Seed, eds., *Speaking Science Fiction* (Liverpool: Liverpool University Press, 2000), p. 134.

3. In Joanna Russ, 'Amor Vincit Foeminam', *Science-Fiction Studies* 7 (1980), pp. 2–15; see Justine Larbalestier, *The Battle of the Sexes in Science Fiction* (Middletown, CT: Wesleyan University Press, 2002), for detailed readings of this 'genre' and the stories discussed below.

4. Thomas S. Gardner, 'The Last Woman', in Sam Moskowitz, ed., *When Women Rule* (New York: Walker and Company, 1972), pp. 131–48.
5. See Pamela Sargent, ed., *Women of Wonder: The Classic Years* (New York: Harcourt Brace, 1995), for a sample of stories by many of these writers.
6. See, for example, Robin Roberts, *A New Species* (Urbana: Illinois University Press, 1993), p. 152. One contemporary critic who remained sceptical of this 'breakthrough' was Anthony Boucher; see his 'Sf Books: 1960' in Judith Merril (ed.), *The Best of Sci-Fi* (1961) (London: Mayflower, 1963), p. 379.
7. Farah Mendlesohn, 'Women in Science Fiction', *Foundation* 53 (Autumn 1991), p. 66.
8. Steffen Hantke, 'Surgical Strikes and Prosthetic Warriors', *Science-Fiction Studies* 25 (1998), p. 499.
9. Judith Merril, personal correspondence, cited in Justine Larbalestier and Helen Merrick, 'The Revolting Housewife', *Paradoxa* 18 (June 2003), pp. 136–56.
10. Joanna Russ, 'The Image of Women in Science Fiction' (1971), *Vertex* 1:6 (February 1974), p. 55.
11. Farah Mendlesohn, 'Gender, Power and Conflict Resolution', *Extrapolation* 35 (1994), pp. 120–9.
12. Connie Willis, 'Guest Editorial: The Women SF Doesn't See', *Asimov's Science Fiction Magazine* (October 1992), p. 8.
13. Ursula Le Guin, *The Left Hand of Darkness* (1969) (London: Granada, 1973), p. 200.
14. Ursula K. Le Guin, 'Is Gender Necessary? Redux', in her *Dancing at the Edge of the World: Thoughts on Words, Women, Places* (London, Paladin, 1992), p. 16.
15. Joanna Russ, 'Recent Feminist Utopias', in Marleen S. Barr, ed., *Future Females* (Bowling Green, OH: Bowling Green State University Popular Press, 1981), p. 76.
16. Le Guin, *The Dispossessed* (1974) (London: Grafton, 1975), p. 22.
17. Suzy McKee Charnas, 'A Woman Appeared' in Barr, ed., *Future Females*, pp. 106–7.
18. See the official website for the Award at http://www.tiptree.org.
19. Karen Joy Fowler, 'The Tiptree Award: A Personal History', *Wiscon 20 Souvenir Book* (Madison, WI: SF3, 1996), p. 109.

# 19

ELISABETH ANNE LEONARD

# Race and ethnicity in science fiction

Science fiction and the criticism of the genre have so far paid very little attention to the treatment of issues relating to race and ethnicity. The African-Caribbean writer Nalo Hopkinson says about her sf novel *Brown Girl in the Ring* (1998), 'I saw it as subverting the genre which speaks so much about the experience of being alienated, but contains so little written by alienated people themselves.'[1] Most English-language sf is written by whites. While some African-American writers produce work that has fantastic or magical elements, this work is not generally grouped with sf or fantasy; it is instead published as and treated by critics as African-American literature. The magical realist elements of Mexican, Native American or Indian subcontinent literatures are also not published or reviewed as speculative literature. Salman Rushdie's novel *Midnight's Children* (1980), for example, explores Indian independence and the tensions between Moslems and Hindus through the eyes of a boy who is one of a group of children born with powers such as telepathy, but it is not generally considered science fiction. Samuel R. Delany and other black authors, including Charles Saunders and Walter Mosley, have written about the racial issues connected to the field, ranging from the initial cold-shoulder treatment of Delany by racist old-guard white writers to the lack of a substantial black audience for the genre, but neither sf about race nor criticism of it have achieved the same prominence that works about gender issues have.[2]

Science fiction writers can use its imaginative possibilities to hypothesize worlds where existing social problems have been solved; they can also imagine a future where the problems have been magnified or extended into a grim dystopia. At the same time, however, they are bound and constructed by numerous other forces, including their own culture and experiences and their publisher's expectations and target audience. Being able to publish one's work in many ways comes out of a position of privilege, including both the education and the time for writing, and consequently those people who are oppressed the most are the ones least likely to be writing about it. Further, since racism often appears different to members of a minority than to members of a majority or dominant culture, what one white writer or reader perceives as a socially progressive work might be seen by a reader of colour as engaging with racist tropes or as an appropriation of the values and concerns of a minority culture. When sf writers, white or not, include racial issues in their fiction, they enter a territory bounded on one side by readers who feel that the work does not go far enough to address the social ills of the culture they write in and on the other by readers who think it goes too far.

By far the majority of sf deals with racial tension by ignoring it. In many books the characters' race is either not mentioned and probably assumed to be white or, if mentioned, is irrelevant to the events of the story and functions only as an additional descriptor, such as hair colour or height. Other sf assumes a world in which there has been substantial racial mingling and the characters all have ancestry of multiple races. These kinds of writing can be seen as an attempt to deal with racial issues by imagining a world where they are non-issues, where colour-blindness is the norm. This may be a conscious model for a future society, or a gesture to 'political correctness' by an author whose interests in the story lie elsewhere, but either motive avoids wrestling with the difficult questions of how a non-racist society comes into being and how members of minority cultures or ethnic groups preserve their culture. Nobel Laureate Toni Morrison sees many American texts as written in a response to an unarticulated black presence, as defining themselves by what they are not.[3] She further writes about the presence of people of colour as invisible to many writers and readers, just as it is invisible to much of the American population in general. Sheree R. Thomas expresses this same absence through the metaphor of 'dark matter': matter in the universe which cannot be observed directly but only deduced by its gravitational force. She views Africans and African-Americans as unseen but still affecting the world around them.[4] Even sf which does not explicitly delve into racial issues may still respond to them.

One recent example of this is Mike Resnick's book *A Miracle of Rare Design* (1994), which displaces the tension between Western culture and African culture on to a story line about humans and aliens. The book begins with a human, Xavier William Lennox, on the planet Grotomana, trying to observe the Grotomanans, known as Fireflies. The Fireflies have forbidden humans to have any access to their cities, so he is from the very beginning of the novel a transgressor. He sneaks into a religious ceremony, is caught and tortured, and left as a warning for other humans. While he is recovering from this event he is approached about a diplomatic mission back to Grotomana, the goal being to give the human Republic mining rights to diamonds. The exchange between Lennox and the representative of the Department of Alien Affairs, after he asks what happens if they refuse, is significant:

> 'Then the navy will move in with as much force as is required to pacify the natives and protect our mining operation.'
> '*Pacify*,' repeated Lennox, unable to keep the contempt from his voice. 'A polite euphemism for genocide.'[5]

While he violated the Fireflies' culture in order to observe their ritual, and while he thinks of them as 'primitive',[6] he does not approve of genocide.

Lennox later returns to the Firefly planet in a surgically altered body which is physiologically Grotoman. As a Firefly, he is mistreated by human soldiers, and remarks to their commander that 'If that's the way you treat unarmed Fireflies, it's no wonder they want you off the planet.'[7] He is beginning to understand the alien world-view through his biological transformation. Yet when he tells the commander that he took on the new body in order to prevent genocide, the commander remarks that he has 'done nothing to prevent the extermination of other alien races'.[8] The reason for Lennox's willingness to undergo such radical surgery is his curiosity about other cultures rather than any interest in what serves those cultures best.

This turns out to be the driving force of the character and the theme of the novel; Lennox undergoes repeated physical transformations and visits several other planets at the behest of the human Republic. However, the threat of genocide seems to only serve the purpose of providing an excuse for Lennox's cultural interference. The alien races are all portrayed as less civilized than humans, and no one ever asks if they have the right to keep humans from their planet or their resources. They are not, in other words, seen as equals with humans, just as Africans were not seen as equals by Europeans. Resnick's intent appears to be to show that his other races have abilities and capacities that are as special and important as any human, but this is undermined by Lennox's continual change, which is in many ways an appropriation of the African-American motif of 'passing'. Although Lennox's interest is in the cultural artefacts such as stories, religion, language and music of the different aliens he encounters, he is ultimately a colonizer. He takes what he wants from each culture and moves on to the next. The novel never steps outside the viewpoint of the dominant race or tries to imagine a solution to the problems of the encounters between two cultures; the encounters are only excuses for Lennox's next appropriation. The alien, Other, presence is shaped only by its relation to Lennox and not by itself. As much as Lennox becomes marginalized from human society, the novel evades any meaningful examination of marginalization and postcolonial conflict.

Resnick's novel is an example of how sf can respond to the history of Western and African cultural intersections, but it is silent about how the dominant culture is shaped by the minority culture. To further understand the problematic nature of such cultural shaping in sf, it is useful to look at sf that has dealt explicitly with racial relationships. One early story is 'The Comet' (1920), by the black writer W. E. B. Du Bois, better known for his writings about being black in early twentieth-century America. In this story, a black man named Jim, who has been sent into the dangerous lower vaults of a bank because a white man's life is too valuable for the risk, emerges to discover that all the people in New York appear to be dead as the result of the earth passing through the tail of a comet. The only other living person he finds is a white, upper-class young woman. Jim thinks that she would never have even looked at him previously and she realizes that she would never have imagined him as her rescuer because 'he dwelt in a world so far from hers, so infinitely far, that he seldom even entered her thought'.[9] But in the absence of other people as they search together for their families and other survivors she begins to see him as human. Later, however, her father arrives to rescue her. She thanks Jim and does not look at him as her father declares that he has always 'liked your people'[10] and gives him money, an act which classifies Jim as a servant and puts him back into the role of someone less than human.

In Du Bois's story, a thought experiment that investigates how much racial difference is constructed by society, racial difference is overcome only when Jim and the woman think themselves entirely alone in the world. As soon as other people enter, the old codes, rules and belief systems about race re-enter: African-Americans are not perceived as human by white Americans even while they are relied upon to do work that keeps society functioning, a view so entrenched in the culture that only a huge natural disaster can change it. Du Bois argues that racism lies in cultural practices as much or more than in individual beliefs.

One of the most notable examples of the exploration of race relations in sf is Ray Bradbury's short story 'Way In the Middle of the Air', part of *The Martian Chronicles* (1950), a book that replays issues of colonialism and race relations through the human invasion of and eventual settlement on Mars. 'Way In the Middle of the Air' specifically looks at African-Americans and white Americans and the way in which the whites define their existence through the lives of the blacks.

In the story, the blacks in the American south all leave for Mars. The main character, a white hardware-store proprietor named Samuel Teece, declares that the blacks 'should've given notice'. He and other white men sit on the porch of his hardware store and watch the 'slow, steady channel of darkness',[11] the blacks of the town leaving. They do not know who will do the jobs once taken by the black men and women. Teece tries to prevent two different blacks from leaving because of their obligations to him, but the debts of one is paid by other blacks and the work contract of another is taken over by a white on Teece's porch so the youth, Silly, can leave. Teece mocks him, asking if the rocket ships have the names of spirituals. Silly does not respond to his mockery at the time, but as he drives off out of earshot he shouts, 'What are you goin' to *do* nights, Mr. Teece?'[12] Teece thinks about the question and slowly realizes that Silly was asking him what he would do now that there is no one left to lynch. He has relied on blacks to be there not just to work for him but to be his victims. One might imagine that a racist white would be glad to see the blacks leave the world, but racism depends on the presence of those it hates. He and his fellow whites depend upon the blacks not just economically but also as a way to identify themselves by what they are not. Without a black presence, Teece has very little left of himself. Even though the story is chronologically set in the early twenty-first century, it is really the American south of the mid twentieth century that is depicted; Bradbury is writing not about the future but about his present.

Yet, even while the story unflinchingly depicts white racism, not just through lynching but through the characters' language and comments, one person saying, 'They make almost as good a money as a white man, but there they go', it does not fully show African-Americans as people, instead using stereotypes of African-American culture to reveal their absence. The blacks leaving are metaphorically transformed into a river, and silence replaces the sounds of song and laughter and 'pickaninnies rushing in clear water'. Left in the fields with the empty shacks are 'unfingerprinted' watermelons.[13] Bradbury uses sf effectively to portray white racism, but the story does not take the opportunity to reimagine a black culture independent of white perceptions. The story of the expansion of the African diaspora to Mars is never told.

For both Du Bois and Bradbury, sf provided a means to examine the simultaneous dependence on and contempt for black Americans by white Americans. What could not be imagined in a conventional, mainstream story can be described in sf, rendering the invisible visible, even if only for the duration of time it takes to read the story. In these stories, sf matters not for any predictive or imaginative aspects but for its capacity to reveal something about the era in which the stories were written. In exposing the racism of the world in which they were published, the stories subvert any comfortable escape from a white reader's own culture and beliefs and perhaps even create a momentary experience of readerly alienation.

Bradbury was not the only white writer to imagine black characters, however, and Robert A. Heinlein's novel *Farnham's Freehold* (1964) needs to be discussed alongside 'Way In the Middle of the Air'. Heinlein's novel is about a white family transported to a future in which America is ruled by blacks who practice slavery, polygamy and cannibalism. It was written and published during the early days of the American Civil Rights movement and appears to be a response to the changes happening to the American social order. In one significant exchange, a black character, Joseph, who had been a servant to the white family, says to the lead character, Hugh Farnham, '[H]ave you ever made a bus trip through Alabama? As a "nigger"?' When Hugh responds that he has not, Joseph says, 'Then shut up. You don't know what you are talking about.'[14] This suggests that Heinlein at some level understood how much black Americans were dehumanized and brutalized by white Americans in the south, but his depiction of a black civilization that relies on slavery and cannibalism continues the process of dehumanizing and seeing blacks as Other. He does not imagine a world where blacks and whites live together equally and freely but a world in which one has dominance over the other. Heinlein, who had non-white protagonists in some of his other fiction, clearly understood that racism needs to be addressed as a social issue. Yet in this book he was unable to see beyond the limits of his own experience and replace black absence with meaningful presence.

Cultures do not arise ahistorically, however, and the racial tensions in American society which are depicted in the works discussed above come in part out of the history of African enslavement. Science fiction can also be about the past, through alternate history or time-travel plots, and some latter twentieth-century novels make use of these devices specifically to write about racial issues and slavery. In Octavia Butler's novel *Kindred* (1979), a twentieth-century woman travels back to a Maryland plantation in the early nineteenth century; Orson Scott Card's novel *Pastwatch: The Redemption of Christopher Columbus* (1996) takes as its historical frame the European conquest of the Americas.

In *Kindred* the main character is a black woman named Dana who is drawn into the past of her distant ancestors whenever Rufus Weylin, the son of a plantation owner, is endangered. She knows from her family Bible that the white Rufus will grow up to father the daughter who is her several-times removed grandmother, and she speculates that she is being pulled back in time to keep her ancestry intact. One time she is accompanied by her white husband, Kevin Franklin, who is forced to pose as her owner and is stranded in the past for five years when she returns briefly to the twentieth century. The time travel has no technological explanation; Dana simply feels dizzy and is pulled back to Rufus by his need. Her returns to her era are precipitated by her own fear or mortal danger.

Butler's narrative also tells the history of Dana and Kevin's relationship, and she comments not only on the conditions of the past but the conditions of 1976 America. Other family members are unhappy about their marriage: Dana's uncle is disappointed because Kevin is white, and Kevin's sister surprises him with her bigotry. Dana's aunt would prefer that Dana marry a black man, but is pleased that if they have children they will be lighter-skinned blacks than Dana. What is more telling about twentieth-century views of race, however, is what happens to Dana and Kevin in the past.

After spending some time on the plantation, Kevin comments: '[T]his place isn't what I would have imagined. No overseer. No more work than the people can manage . . .'[15] He is becoming used to slavery. As a white, he does not see the things Dana does in the slave quarters, but he also does not look for them. He never thinks slavery is good, and when he is stranded he sees things that do show some of the conditions to be as bad or worse than he could have imagined, but his background cannot entirely offset the changes that come to him when he poses as a slave-owner. And Dana, in acting as a slave, becomes one. She persuades the slave woman Alice to go to Rufus's bed even though Alice hates him, and she continually forgives Rufus for his beatings and betrayals of her. She thinks, 'What had I done wrong? Why was I still slave to a man who had repaid me for saving his life by nearly killing me? Why had I taken yet another beating. And why . . . why was I so frightened now – frightened sick at the thought that sooner or later, I would have to run again?'[16] Her education, her knowledge of history, and her experiences in the twentieth century do not support or help her when she is faced with the actual conditions of slavery. The implication, echoing Du Bois, is that even for people who have put aside existing colour barriers in their own relationships and daily life, immersion in a racist system will recreate these barriers.

Racism in the past is dealt differently with Card's novel *Pastwatch*. Its characters come from many different ethnic backgrounds, and its plot is about an attempt to change history and Christopher Columbus's interactions with the native peoples that he encounters in the Caribbean and Americas. The novel begins in the twenty-third century with Tagiri, a woman who is 'as racially mixed as anyone else in the world these days',[17] observing her matrilineal African past through a device which allows people to watch events in past history. When she sees the child of one of the African women she watches captured and sold by an Arab slave-trader, she starts a project of watching the life of slaves throughout the world. Her research takes her to that of Hassan, who is watching the Carib and Arawak Indians in the

Caribbean prior to the arrival of the Spanish. When they watch together, they are seen by some of the people they watch and prayed to as gods to stop the enslavement.

Later research reveals that Christopher Columbus had intended to go on a crusade to stop the spread of Islam but was diverted instead to the search for the New World by the actions of other people from the future, a different future than Tagiri and Hassan's. A young Mexican man named Hunaphu Matamoro, engaging in the research of the pre-Columbian civilizations of South and Central America, realizes that this intervention, which led to slavery and colonialism in the Americas, occurred in order to prevent the conquest of Europe by the Tlaxcalans of Mesoamerica. Once Hunaphu has convinced others in the slavery project that the civilizations of the Americas were capable of this, he and two others, one being Diko, the daughter of Tagiri and Hassan and the other being Kemal Akyazi, a Turk who discovered the lost world of Atlantis, go into the past to perform another intervention, this time allowing Columbus to sail west but hoping to prevent the slavery and slaughter of the indigenous people by the multi-pronged approach of teaching Columbus to see non-whites as humans and stopping the Mesoamerican practice of human sacrifice.

Racial and ethnic issues are present throughout the novel, from Hunaphu's feeling of difference from his brothers because his father was Mayan when theirs was of Spanish descent to the representation of Muslims and Christians as still living in culturally different worlds. However, it is in the last portion of the novel, after Diko, Kemal and Hunaphu go back in time, that racial issues are most explicitly addressed. It is through the transformation of Columbus himself after Diko speaks with him on Haiti that Card does this. Columbus thinks,

> Until I spoke with *her*, I didn't question the right of white men to give commands to brown ones. Only since she poisoned my mind with her strange interpretation of Christianity did I start seeing the way the Indians quietly resist being treated like slaves ... Was it possible that God had brought him here, not to bring enlightenment to the heathen, but to learn it from them?[18]

The work that the black Diko does in speaking with the white Columbus allows him to begin seeing past colour differences, even past cultural differences, to an understanding that the Taino and other Caribbean tribes are as fully human as he is. The Spanish and the Taino begin to take on each other's language and customs. The intervention from the future strips Columbus of the assumptions and prejudices of his culture and upbringing, allowing him eventually to marry Diko and father a daughter who later becomes Queen of the new nation of Caribia. Colonialism and slavery are superseded by an independent and powerful new world empire which is equally matched with the Europeans, and racism is revealed as an ideology which can be altered by the introduction of a different world-view.

Card's novel is not entirely uncomplicated: the repeal of human sacrifice comes about in part through the substitution of a kind of Christianity. Hunaphu and Diko both in their own ways practise the imposition of one culture upon another in the work they do to organize and unify the peoples of the region. The introduction of a modified Christianity in the formation of a new nation is presumably a better choice than the alternatives presented, the historical enslavement and colonization of the new world or the hypothetical conquest of Europe by practitioners of human sacrifice, but it is still a shaping of one culture by another and a judgement of technologically advanced people about how to manipulate another society. Diko and the others cannot be sure that their intervention will not have repercussions into a future similar to those which came after the intervention which sent Columbus west instead of east. However, since the people who decide to send Diko and the others back in time to intervene are the ones whose present will be wiped out if they succeed, it is an intervention motivated by sacrifice and concern for others rather than personal gain.

*Pastwatch* is more hopeful than *Kindred*, if only because it shows how black people can influence white people and prevent slavery, whereas *Kindred* shows how slavery as a system grinds down and dehumanizes the people within it. Butler uses time travel and history together as a way to highlight the fragility of twentieth-century racial tolerance, while Card uses them to emphasize how people of different racial backgrounds can work together. This is presumably due in part to differences in Card's and Butler's own lives; it is easier to be hopeful about an end to oppression if one is not part of an oppressed group.[19] Despite these differences, however, both novels find ways for the voices of disenfranchised and alienated people to be heard, Butler by giving voice to a black woman and Card by foregrounding racism and oppression rather than ignoring it. They prod the readers to examine both their past and their present to think about what kind of future they want.

Other recent sf novels revolve around racial and cutural identity issues, suggesting that the genre is moving towards an opening up of its past insularity, parallel to what happened with women writers in the 1970s. Hopkinson's *Brown Girl in the Ring* (1998) recounts a Toronto where whites and middle- and upper-class people have abandoned the inner city to poverty, crime and a barter economy; the protagonist, Ti-Jeanne, uses African-Caribbean magic to fight the drug lord of the city. Kathleen Ann Goonan's *The Bones of*

*Time* (1996) draws on the beliefs and history of the Polynesian peoples who settled in Hawaii, and her characters come from the Asian-Hawaiian-white ethnic mix of the islands; her other novels about nanotechnology also include African-American and Caribbean characters. In *The Diamond Age* (1995), Neal Stephenson sets his future of nanotechnology in China and a world where people of all races and national origins have spread out across the globe into new tribes. Confucianism exists side by side with a neo-Victorian culture and an urban scenario of sophisticated weapons and lawlessness. Recent sf films and television shows have also been less homogeneously white; one episode of *Star Trek: Deep Space Nine* had the black Captain Sisko in an alternate world and personality where he wrote sf which he could not publish because no one believed that a black captain could exist.[20] Science fiction is a genre which is continually evolving, and as it encompasses a wider range of writers and readers it will reach a point where writing from or about a racial minority is neither subversive nor unusual but rather one of the traits which makes it a powerful literature of change.

## NOTES

1. Nalo Hopkinson, *Brown Girl in the Ring* (New York: Warner, 1998), n.p.
2. Their essays are collected together in Sheree Thomas, ed., *Dark Matter* (New York: Warner, 2000).
3. Toni Morrison, *Playing in the Dark* (New York: Vintage, 1993).
4. Thomas, *Dark Matter*, p. xii
5. Mike Resnick, *A Miracle of Rare Design: A Tragedy of Transcendence* (New York: Tor, 1994), pp. 51–2.
6. *Ibid.*, p. 22.
7. *Ibid.*, p. 110.
8. *Ibid.*, p. 112.
9. W. E. B. Du Bois, 'The Comet' (1920), reprinted in Thomas, *Dark Matter* pp. 5–18, at p. 9.
10. *Ibid.*, p. 17.
11. Ray Bradbury, *The Martian Chronicles* (New York: Doubleday, 1950), pp. 118, 117.
12. *Ibid.*, p. 127.
13. *Ibid.*, pp. 123, 129.
14. Robert A. Heinlein, *Farnham's Freehold* (1964) (New York: Signet, 1965), p. 208.
15. Octavia E. Butler, *Kindred* (1979) (Boston: Beacon, 1988), p. 100 (Butler's ellipsis).
16. *Ibid.*, p. 177.
17. Orson Scott Card, *Pastwatch: The Redemption of Christopher Columbus* (New York: Tor, 1996), p. 16.
18. *Ibid.*, p. 356.

19. Although, as a Mormon, Card might comment that the Mormons have their own founding stories of oppression. A factor in Card's treatment of early America may be Mormon traditions that the indigenous peoples of America were descended from the lost ten tribes of Israel.
20. 'Far Beyond the Stars', episode of *Star Trek: Deep Space Nine*; teleplay: Ira Steven Behr and Hans Beimler; story: Marc Scott Zicree (UPN, 1998).

# 20

### FARAH MENDLESOHN

# Religion and science fiction

The fascination of sf with faith and with ritual can be located in the geography of two strands of genre development. The first, scientific romance, bestowed upon sf a sense of grandeur and wonder at the cosmos and its works. From the scientific romance were drawn the great space operas of E. E. 'Doc' Smith, the spiritual journeys of David Lindsay (*A Voyage to Arcturus*, 1920) and the eschatological futurism of Olaf Stapledon. While the scientific romance did not support a religious interpretation of the world, it revelled in the immaterial and imparted to genre sf a desire for the transcendent; this vision of the future represented an attempt to peer into the heavens. The second, sf as it developed in the pulp magazines, leaned towards a much more material and ritualistic understanding of religion and, on the surface at least, this became the dominant mode of the sf encounter with religion.

Genre publishing began in the USA in the 1920s and much of what I describe in this chapter is consequent upon this specific cultural milieu. Most superficial accounts of the USA in this period adopt a particularist, northeastern approach in which America emerges into scientific and political rationalism at the beginning of the twentieth century. Yet most Americans remained deeply religious. From 1926 onwards, while court cases appeared to be ruling for ever greater secularization, legislation restricting the teaching of scientific knowledge and method quietly sneaked on to local statute books (this did not come to light until the curriculum reforms of the late 1950s, prompted by the Russian launch of Sputnik). By 1960, secularism, or at least a liberal interpretation of most faiths, provided an apparently hegemonic intellectual tradition in the USA. Consequent upon this, and stemming from the imperialist adventure-story model which much early genre fiction appropriated, the emerging sf world assumed it was the voice of a secularist future and treated religion with at best polite contempt: religion was essentially of the 'Other', the backward and the primitive, and its role in sf was either to be undermined or to indicate the level of civilization which any given alien race had achieved.

Three plots dominated the development of genre sf: the incredible invention, the future war and the fantastic journey. Of these three, it was primarily the last which offered possibilities for the exploration of religion and of faith. In the early magazines one of the commonest devices for 'strangeness' was to locate an otherwise rather ordinary adventure story in a forgotten or undiscovered land. These adventures frequently added mystical overtones through the facilitating device by which the protagonists were transported and reflected the growing interest of the Anglo-American middle classes in the value of other religious cultures as collectibles, and the increasing popularity of mysticism among this group. Spiritualism, while on the surface fundamentally alien to Christianity, experienced a resurgence in the 1920s alongside the rise of fundamentalism, although it was most popular among Anglicans and Episcopalians. In sf its greatest influence was felt in the scientific romance: *A Voyage to Arcturus* begins with a séance.

While these early stories are crucial to the emergence of sf they were at heart unconcerned with science or with futuristic speculation. By 1940 the fantastic had developed sufficiently to support two branches, and those tales more recognizable as fantasy (without any of the trappings of science), were hived off by Campbell into *Unknown*. While sf chose other-worldly locations and reached them by rocket ship, the belief that scientific Terrans were in competition with other gods persisted. The tradition of high-fantasy adventure, which influenced these tales, relied heavily on the exoticization of 'the Other' which displaced 'religion' on to the alternate culture and associated it almost entirely with 'the primitive'.

The focus on the exotic led to a concentration on ritual. Sf, like anthropology and religious studies, tends to focus in the first instance on practice rather than faith, which perhaps explains why, as Brian Stableford has pointed out, sf writers have chosen frequently to write about the crucifixion.[1] But significantly, the dynamic between the Reformation and Catholicism rested on a rejection of the link between ritual and faith, between ritual and meaning. Modernism, rooted in the same binary opposition, has extended the link: sf is full of stories in which superstition is defeated by explanation; the immaterial is tamed by manifestation. In Edgar Rice Burroughs's tales of Barsoom, John Carter, transported by a dreamlike act of will to a neo-Arabic Mars, meets and overthrows the, inevitably false because material, deity Issus.[2] Even a modern version of the trope, by a religious (Mormon) writer, exploits rather than disputes this materialism. In Orson Scott Card's *Speaker for the Dead* (1986) the alien pequeninos, or 'piggies', seem eminently rational and scientific until we discover that they have crucified a human anthropologist. The plot seems designed to follow the usual course, with the explanation justifying human rationalism. Instead, it becomes evidence that human mysticism, with notions of idealism, sacrifice and redemption, has served to obscure the pequeninos' scientific truth, that crucifixion triggers the biological change to their next life as a tree. It is human superstition that is mocked, but religion is not. Previous failed crucifixions of humans in this book take on the metaphor of sacrifice; the bonds between ritual and faith are reinforced by scientific rationalism. This particular scenario is common in other ways in sf: typically, any advanced alien which displays religious belief turns out to have merely encoded actual fact in ways which humans misunderstand. Heinlein uses this tactic for the Martians in *Stranger in a Strange Land* (1960); Judith Moffett rests an entire ecology on the principle in *Pennterra* (1987), where references to the planet as an *actant,* a presence which actively moves the plot along, prove literal.[3]

The association of religion with the uncivilized remained a common trope in the Golden Age of the 1940s and 1950s. One new twist was the use of religious belief and ritual as an indication of failure: tied to a common understanding of history as circular, sf writers increasingly saw religion as a point upon the curve through which humans, if separated from history and from civilization, would pass over and over again. Asimov's short story 'Nightfall' (1941) plunges a world into nightmare and superstition with its realization of the truth of its place in the universe, while in *Orphans of the Sky* (1963)[4] the inhabitants of Heinlein's colonizing spaceship resort to religion to explain an increasingly incomprehensible world. Post-holocaust fiction continually reprised this theme. Walter M. Miller Jr's *A Canticle for Leibowitz* (1960) is perhaps the most sophisticated of the sub-genre. Science is recreated as religious ritual in a devastated America, and it is the ossification of liturgy which ensures the survival of knowledge, but the association of religion with intellectual degradation remains intact. Most recently, Adam Roberts's novel *On* (2001) recycles this trope: an entire world has forgotten why it now lives on vertical shelves. Incapable of even the rudimentary science of the fifteenth century, the inhabitants have created a cod religious explanation. In this tradition, religion counterpoints not technology – although religious societies are often portrayed as anti-technology – but scientific thinking. Consequently, religion is seen less as a mode of thought and more as a lack of thought. This prejudice is reflected in the role which religion is permitted to play in world-building.

The materialistic utilitarianism of sf provides religion with a special role: to many authors, religion is the set dressing of alien theatres. While not all secularist cultures are considered advanced, it is usually a given that all advanced cultures are secularist; Iain M. Banks's Idarans (*Consider Phlebas,*

1987) are unusual in maintaining both advanced technology and a faith system which does not turn out to be a metaphoric description of their available material forms. But the indicative use of religion in world-building has been marred by laziness. For most, one religion would always be enough. *Star Trek*, with its one faith per planet, is perhaps the best known offender, but the problem is endemic: in Sheri S. Tepper's universe, for instance, there are many religions, but each planet is usually devoted to only one. In this area fantasy, with its cast of thousands and many hundreds of gods, shows a more developed sensibility than sf. The rare exceptions stand out: Edgar Rice Burroughs's Barsoom holds many cults all focused on a polytheistic pantheon (a reflection perhaps of early twentieth-century America's fascination with Hinduism), or Robert Heinlein's Venusians in *Space Cadet* (1948), who maintain at least two distinct faiths. The inhabitants of Gethen in Le Guin's *The Left Hand of Darkness* (1969) maintain a number of myth structures which are retold over the fireside to the alien diplomat, Genly Ai. All too often, the depiction of alien or foreign religion is with a broad brush: new swear words are invented (as on McCaffrey's Pern) or we are merely waved in the direction of 'the Gods'. Occasionally a marginal religion will be co-opted in order to make a point: Quakers become shorthand for pacifists and for a particular kind of community in Le Guin's 'The Eye of the Heron' (1980), Judith Moffett's *Pennterra* and Maureen McHugh's 'The Lincoln Train' (1995), but Le Guin does not seem to understand that pacifism is a long-term tactic, Judith Moffett's Quakers reach consensus in an implausibly brief period of time and Maureen McHugh's Quakers are unaware that their basic theology is a belief that there is God in everyone.

Judaism has held a special place in the genre. The cultural discourse of faith embodied in the Talmud has inclined Jewish thinkers towards reason, and to scientific rationalism. The subsequent enthusiasm for logic chopping has provided material for neat sf fables. Asimov's 'Silly Asses' (1958) exploits this tendency: the long-lived Rigellian race comment cynically on the prospects of a civilization that develops nuclear weapons before space travel, and Earth's name is removed from the book of civilized species, the rationalist equivalent of St Peter's list. Given that a disproportionate number of sf writers have been Jewish, it is unsurprising that some sf takes Jewishness as its theme. The stories in Jack Dann's anthology, *Wandering Stars* (1974), epitomize the sardonic influence of those who are often non-practising Jews, firmly attached to their religious culture.[5] In here, Robert Silverberg writes about a dybbuk finding itself in the body of an alien while William Tenn explores the problem of who and what is a Jew in a multi-species universe. However, because mainstream Judaism has tended to walk hand in hand with science and because ultra-orthodoxy remains the religion of a minority,

Judaism remains an attractive sideshow for most sf writers rather than a major concern. It differs from Islam which, in sf, has always been written about by outsiders, and without the same playfulness. The best recent treatment of Islam is probably in Jon Courtenay Grimwood's *Pashazade* (2001), and both Grimwood in *Effendi* (2002) and Kim Stanley Robinson in *The Years of Rice and Salt* (2002) have attempted to consider seriously the nature of Islamic fundamentalism within an Islamic context rather than merely as oppositional to the West.

The perhaps unexpected appearance of the missionary or the priest as a popular protagonist within sf owes its origins to anthropology, to the adventure novel and perhaps also to the popularity of the missionary movement in the late nineteenth and early twentieth centuries. Science fiction, like its close ally the utopia, depends in part on the figure of the outsider. The missionary takes his place alongside the policeman, the journalist, the merchant and the soldier as the archetypal outsider in an alien society: a personage licensed to ask questions in difficult circumstances. The missionary carries civilization and an authorial voice to challenge both the role of religion in a culture and its meaning for humans, but again the commonest trope is the missionary as destroyer of faith, however inadvertently. In Harry Harrison's 'The Streets of Ashkelon' (1965) it is precisely the missionary's attempt to bring a message of redemption that persuades the aliens to sin. While the punch-line of the story lies in their decision to crucify him in order to test his gospel of resurrection, the underlying message is the sinfulness of a faith that depends on the inculcation of superstition. James Blish's priest in *A Case of Conscience* (1958) justifies the destruction of world with his assertion that it can only be the devil's own creation. In Robert Presslie's 'Another Word for Man' (1958), the arrival of an alien on earth challenges and redeems the faith of a priest. He is forced to accept both the alien's personhood, and its status as a child of God when the alien, a medical missionary, gives its life to cure the priest's cancer. Even if the missionary is an alien, its function within sf remains to challenge and be challenged.

While Stableford argues that all of the above were manifestations of a post-nuclear interest in eschatology,[6] the evidence remains that in the post-war period the demonstrated legacies of religious prejudice mainly served to convince sf writers that they were correct in their general suspicion of religion in all its forms. For many authors, religion became essentially unAmerican, or at least marginal to the definition of an Earthman. Non-American writers producing for the American market also generally adopted this tone, although a British writer such as Clarke was able to create scientific wonder in the rigorous extension of religious ritual: in 'The Nine Billion Names of God' (1953) a computer completes the roll call of the names of God. The universe's purpose fulfilled, it closes down. Religious eschatology becomes a metaphor for the potential end time beckoned by the atom bomb. Clarke's other religiously inspired story, 'The Star' (1955), mourns that a planet died in the nova that formed the star over Bethlehem, and that coincidence is invested by religion with so much meaning. His third great religious work, the novel *Childhood's End* (1953), damns all religion as misguided, when at the end of the first section of the book our alien saviours turn out to be in the image of Lucifer, complete with horns and a tail. In all of these examples, the sf sense of wonder is distinguished from that of religious faith by its desire to find wonder in understanding.

Religion is repeatedly depicted as dangerous, diverting humans (and aliens) from the path of reason and true enlightenment. Robert Heinlein's novella, '"If This Goes On –"' (1940) portrays the majority as easily controlled by religious fanatics; Harry Harrison's 'The Streets of Ashkelon', already mentioned, assumes the Catholic missionary to be genuine in his belief, but it attacks the impact of superstition on a previously rational alien, and the focus of Christians on one particular, and horrific, part of the Christian story. The most extensive use of the missionary in recent sf has been by John Barnes, both ostentatiously, in *Sin of Origin* (1988), in which the universe is divided into spheres of religious influence, but also in his *Million Open Doors* sequence in which his ambassadors are peddling the religion of laissez-faire capitalism (a fair analogy, given that Marxism is one of the three religions in *Sin of Origin*). *Sin of Origin* depicts the impact of the Catholic Church as disruptive and traumatic. On a planet in which the three species live as a symbiotic trinity, the most disenfranchised are those who have survived bereavement. The message of rebirth into a new trinity is devastating to the social structure. The most telling point, however, is the unwillingness of the Church to take responsibility for what it has wrought. Handled by a believer, the result is different. In Mary Doria Russell's *The Sparrow* (1996) and *Children of God* (1998) the effect of religion on two intelligent species, one predator, one prey, overturns an entire ecosystem, and as with *Sin of Origin* the author is ambivalent about this outcome.

What strikes the reader when examining these texts as a body is the overriding message: that religion is not only dangerous and misleading, but that sentient beings are generally too weak-willed to reject it. However, many authors (whether they have believed it or not) have pandered to fannish beliefs that they, 'the mundanes', must be saved by us, the technocrats. A. E. Van Vogt expressed this fannish manifesto in his novel *Slan* (1940), and these ideas initially underpinned L. Ron Hubbard's 'self-awareness system', known first as Dianetics, and later as Scientology (recognized by the US government as a religion). Two authors who accept gullibility as natural to the human condition are William Tenn and James Tiptree Jr, both superlative short-story writers. In 'The Liberation of Earth' (1953) Tenn depicts our willingness to adopt any vaguely plausible myth as we are repeatedly 'liberated' by aliens with different ways of proving their connection with us. Tiptree's 'Help' (1968) posits the results if rival alien churches decided to convert us. Humans do not come out well in either story.

All of the above are in essence materialistic approaches to religion. For most sf authors, religion is functionalist. But religion also provides a discourse of power. The most impressive and the forefather of this tradition is perhaps Theodore Sturgeon's 'Microcosmic God' (1941). His protagonist succeeds in creating a microcosmic civilization, which he bullies and tortures to solve scientific and political problems. The story embodies both an assertion that *we* are god, and a challenge to the ethics of God's authority. Some authors have chosen to comment on the belief in God simply as the powerful *other*, Slonczewski most directly in *Brain Plague* (2000). Here the cultured micro-aliens must live in a negotiated harmony with their host: God is to be argued with, not obeyed blindly. In turn, writers such as Sheri Tepper and Dan Simmons have directly challenged the rights of divine authority. Tepper's Hobbes Land gods, depicted in *Raising the Stones* (1990), turn out in *Sideshow* (1992) to be a parasite, creating not holiness but empathy, which shapes action in ways that to the non-converted seems over-cooperative (even communist) and unambitious (a plot line previously used by *Star Trek*, in 'This Side of Paradise', 1967). Simmons is much more forceful. His *Hyperion* (1989) and *The Fall of Hyperion* (1990) posit a search for a god who is not worthy of worship and who turns out to be an alien parasite. Shaped by the story of Abraham's proposed sacrifice of Isaac, Simmons forces us to question the injustices perpetrated by God. In all these stories the relationship between humans and gods is symbiotic. Only Ken MacLeod, in *The Stone Canal* (1996) and *The Cassini Division* (1998), has emulated the ruthlessness of 'Microcosmic God'; anything that evolves faster, and thinks faster than us is competition, and the most brutal methods are acceptable to control or eradicate this threat. However godlike these beings may be, MacLeod insists that they have nothing to do with *religion*, because they manifest only an exaggeration of human abilities, what Vernor Vinge has termed 'weakly superhuman'.[7] Ironically, the discourse around this term and its companion term 'singularity' is itself eschatological in tone. Extropians (an ideological group with a strong presence on the net) are personally committed to, and argue for the near-future feasibility of, radical technological expansion of human lifespan, habitat, intelligence and emotional depth. Extropian believers (MacLeod is not), or those who believe in other forms of transhumanity, need only substitute 'apocalypse' for singularity, and 'rapture' for 'uploading' to become indistinguishable from any fundamentalist Christian in the USA.[8]

Not all sf writers have approached religion from a position of self-conscious materialism. The Second World War, the explosion of the atom bomb and the emergence of the counter-culture sponsored a more philosophical discourse in which faith rather than ritual became a matter of interest, and transcendence was incorporated into the range of human possibilities. One of the best-known novels of transcendence is Heinlein's *Stranger in a Strange Land* (1961), in which a rescued earth child, Michael Valentine Smith, brings back to earth the spiritual understandings of his Martian family. Although intended more sceptically, it became a bible for the counter-culture. By the 1970s, with the hippy movement in full swing, and later in tandem with the growing eco-movement of the 1980s, sf writers such as John Varley developed a broader notion of spirituality. Varley's 'The Persistence of Vision' (1978), set in a Deaf-Blind commune where communication is a function of touch, infused earlier understandings of religion as ritual with a sense of religion and sensory experience. Paganism also became both a source and theme for sf writers in the 1970s and 1980s, seeking to emphasize spirituality over ritual. As the new ecology movement came to the fore it left its imprint on sf's conceptualization of the spiritual world. The best examples of this are the novels of Richard Grant (*Saraband of Lost Time* (1985) and *Rumors of Spring* (1987)) which combine paganism with a waking nature as the trees take over the world to present humanity with both a threat and a challenge. Paganism's most noticeable influence, however, was in the realm of feminist sf. In the 1970s there was a wave of sf which envisaged feminist mother goddesses whose role was to ensure the power of women (Marion Zimmer Bradley's *The Ruins of Isis* (1978); Sheri Tepper's *The Gate to Women's Country* (1988)) or a beneficent nature, such as that found in Sally M. Gearhart's *The Wanderground* (1980), which envisaged a world in which animals died willingly to feed others. Elizabeth Hand's *Waking the Moon* (1995) was a welcome rejection of the more sentimental of these texts: in Hand's work nature is nasty and the mother goddess a demanding and cruel deity. The choice for the protagonists is between two cruel gods.

One consequence of this increasing interest in spirituality and Eastern religious traditions was a growing sensitivity to the depiction of alien religious practice: the best examples can be found in Octavia Butler's Xenogenesis series, Gwyneth Jones's Aleutian Trilogy and the work of C. J. Cherryh. This suggests that there may well be a link between intense consideration of alien culture and the rise of feminism, but there was no impact on the *diversity* of religious experience portrayed. The real impact was in the return to the themes propounded by Van Vogt of the super- or post-human. Extrasensory perception, increased intelligence and increased ethical awareness has, in sf, formed the basic elements in the process of transcendence, of becoming more than human. Olaf Stapledon's *Star Maker* (1937) contained the possibility that human evolution might one day dispense with the material, and since Stapledon, a number of authors have embraced the idea. A more ambivalent approach to transcendence is explored in John Clute's *Appleseed* (2001); absorption is to be resisted for it may result in the cold death of the universe.

The desire for transcendence contains within it a contempt for the merely human which other authors have challenged vigorously. Brian Stableford's Daedalus series (1976–9), in its rejection of every form of intellectual utopia, appears to make a claim for the preservation of humanity in its entirety. Uploading, the digitizing of human personalities, has been a popular solution to the longevity debate for some time, but inevitably provokes a debate about the nature of the soul and of the individual. Most recently, this debate has marked the work of both Banks and MacLeod. Banks's Culture novels and MacLeod's *The Cassini Division* can be read as an argument about the nature of personality. Iain M. Banks's Culture novels insist on the fundamental alienness of transcendence: it is those machines most divorced from their society which transcend, while MacLeod is bitterly opposed to the emergence of *any* alternative mode of progression other than the purely physical, and appears to be arguing against the proposition that we should evolve further. His characters revisit Sturgeon's civilization in a petri dish ('Microcosmic God') and its more recent reincarnation in virtual reality. MacLeod's Jovians are descendants of human uploads but their humanity is compromised. Humans reconstituted from the process of digitization in MacLeod's *The Stone Canal* question their uniqueness. In contrast, most citizens of the Culture cheerfully store back-up copies of themselves so that they may engage in high-risk sport. Similarly, in John Barnes's *A Million Open Doors* sequence, the only regret is for those who died before the technology was perfected.

Although it is not possible to create a clear chronology which traces the rise and fall of religious thinking in sf, by the 1980s there is clear evidence that sf writers acknowledged a new political order: the 1980s had witnessed a resurgence in the influence of Christian fundamentalism. It is important to understand that membership in the fundamentalist churches had risen steadily since the 1920s, but two developments brought this to the fore in the 1980s.[9] The first was pan-denominationalism: the massive levels of mobility among Americans combined with the rise of radio and TV churches broke down what had been rigid barriers between Methodists, Baptists and Pentecostalists.[10] By the 1980s churches were tending to align along liberal versus literalist understandings of the bible, and liberal versus conservative social attitudes. Fascinatingly, Jews and Muslims also began to co-operate with the Christian churches according to their literalist or conservative leanings.

The second factor was a realignment in fundamentalist theology. For much of the post-Civil War period, most Christian fundamentalists shared a common post-millennial belief that their presence on earth was a travail through which they must pass. Their religious efforts were to be focused on self-improvement, not world-improvement, the conversion of the individual rather than the salvation of the world. By the 1980s, however, liberal campaigners had forced the separation of church and state further than many committed Christians were willing for it to go, and whereas previously the doctrine of separation had been seen primarily as protecting the diversity of Christian denominations, by this stage it was viewed as an attempt to foist secularism upon a Christian nation. Supporting this sense of a Christian nation under siege was the rise of identity politics and the apparent collapse of the nation's sexual morality. From the mid-1970s onwards, conservative Christians began to take an increased interest in politics as politics moved away from the bread and butter issues, which they had regarded as none of their business, and towards the very moral issues central to theologies of personal redemption. In 1980 it seemed as if they had achieved their desires when Ronald Reagan was elected to the presidency on a conservative social and economic platform. While the Reagan presidency generally failed to create the revival in Christian morality which the religious Right sought, it did engender a sense of a nation divided between itself, with both sides feeling seriously under threat. Unsurprisingly, most sf writers chose to ally themselves with liberal individualism. Whereas Heinlein's "'If This Goes On – '" had stood very much alone before the 1960s, the 1980s and 1990s saw a wide range of sf hostile to the rise of fundamentalism. This work adopted a range of approaches: for many, it became necessary to challenge Christianity head-on, showing the power of other traditions. Paganism became an oppositional movement as the religious Right began to target fantasy fiction as *intrinsically* pagan (the earliest manifestation of this had been the attack on *The Wizard of Oz*; the most recent is that on *Buffy the Vampire Slayer* and *Harry Potter*). A number of writers responded with novels and short stories in which paganism defeats oppressive Christianity or revisioned an America in which witchcraft was taken seriously enough to persecute. Other sf writers simply envisaged what a world run by the religious Right might be like for the rest: Suzette Haden Elgin's *Native Tongue* (1984) focused on the experience of women in a fundamentalist America; John Whitbourn's *To Build Jerusalem* (1994) is a serious attempt to imagine a world in which the

Reformation failed; while David Weber's *For the Honor of the Queen* (1993) very convincingly depicted a colony settled by American fundamentalists. The election of President Clinton brought some relief to liberals (although Richard Grant's *In the Land of Winter* (1997), a tale of a pagan mother under attack by her community, makes the point that most of the battles were fought locally, in areas where the religious Right were politically dominant). But these narratives do not attempt to understand fundamentalism on its own terms. Two superb writers who attempt to get inside the skin of the religious Right are Terry Bisson and Ted Chiang. Bisson's 'The Old Rugged Cross' (2001), which depicts a near future in which, under the Freedom of Religion Act, convicts may select their own death. In this case the logic of religious rule requires a crucifixion; the story is bitter with salvation. Equally bitter is Chiang's 'Hell is the Absence of God' (2001), from the same collection.[11] Chiang's consideration of an ontological world in which the miraculous is a daily event directly challenges the comfortable assumptions of the religious Right that miracles are always *good* things; the passage of Angels has consequences and the absence of God is a very real threat. In contrast, Ken MacLeod succeeded in envisaging a plausible, balkanized Britain in which London might shelter a voluntarist fundamentalist city of Beulah, alongside the free city of Norlonto. Both are portrayed sympathetically: Jordan, the 'refugee' from Beulah, gets religion himself in *The Sky Road* (1999).

Finally, because the American mainstream is generally hostile to socialism, religion has been the main forum in which to question injustice without challenging the liberal hegemony of mainstream America, and this tradition has infected the genre. Barnes's missionary in *Sin of Origin* aims to bring an alien world into Christendom under their own terms rather than those of outsiders, although Barnes recognizes the ironies of cultural imperialism. A very few authors are inspired in this direction by their own religious beliefs, although religious faith is in itself unusual among writers in the genre. Mary Doria Russell, a Catholic convert to Judaism, sends a team of Jesuits plus one Sephardic Jew to a planet of sapient herbivores enslaved by carnivores, and the survivors introduce them to liberation theology (*The Sparrow* and *Children of God*). Orson Scott Card, a Mormon, posits Mormonism as the salvation of the world in the post-disaster novel *The Folk of the Fringe* (1989), and more interestingly created an entire new religion, that of the Speakers, in his *Speaker for the Dead*, who bring truth to memory. Judith Moffett, not herself a Quaker (and in fact originally from a fundamentalist Baptist family), uses the Quaker faith of her husband to create *Pennterra*, a colonization and first contact novel in which Quakers try to cope with a Gaian world and negotiate with non-Quaker settlers in ways that will provide justice for all. In a genre predicated on the thought experiment, theological discourse comes naturally. In a genre dedicated to world-building, recognizing the significance of faith has proven crucial in generating the critical density of the 'full' science fiction text.

## NOTES

1. Brian Stableford, 'Religion', in John Clute and Peter Nicholls, eds., *The Encyclopedia of Science Fiction* (London: Orbit, 1993), p. 1002.
2. Edgar Rice Burroughs, *The Gods of Mars* (Chicago: McClurg, 1918).
3. Brian Attebery, *Strategies of Fantasy* (Bloomington: Indiana University Press, 1992), p. 73.
4. This was a fix-up of two novellas, 'Universe' and 'Common Sense', both originally published in 1941.
5. Jack Dann, ed., *Wandering Stars: an Anthology of Jewish Fantasy and Science Fiction* (New York: Harper and Row, 1974).
6. Stableford, 'Religion', in Clute and Nicholls, *Encyclopedia*, pp. 1001–2.
7. Vernor Vinge, 'What is the singularity?' may be found at: http://www.ugcs. caltech.edu/~phoenix/vinge/vinge-sing.html, 1993.
8. Steve Allan Edwards, 'Mind Children', *21C:Scanning the Future*, 23 (1996), pp. 45–51.
9. Roger Finke and Rodney Starke, *The Churching of America* (New Brunswick, NJ: Rutgers University Press, 1992), p. 149.
10. See Joel A. Carpenter, *Revive Us Again* (New York: Oxford University Press, 1997).
11. P. N. Hayden, ed., *Starlight Three* (New York: Tor, 2001).

# FURTHER READING

*Reference works*

Barron, Neil, ed. *Anatomy of Wonder 4: A Critical Guide to Science Fiction* (New Providence, NJ: Bowker, 1995).

Bleiler, Everett F. *The Checklist of Science-Fiction and Supernatural Fiction* (Glen Rock, NJ: Firebell, 1978).

   *Science-Fiction: The Early Years* (Kent, OH: Kent State University Press, 1990) [annotated bibliography of English language sf to 1930].

   *Science-Fiction: The Gernsback Years* (Kent, OH: Kent State University Press, 1998) [annotated bibliography of sf magazines, 1926 to 1936].

Bleiler, Everett F., ed. *Science Fiction Writers. Critical Studies of the Major Authors from the Early Nineteenth Century to the Present Day* (New York: Scribner's, 1982).

Brown, Charles N. and Contento, William G., eds. *Science Fiction in Print – 1985: A Comprehensive Bibliography of Books and Short Fiction Published in the English Language* (Oakland, CA, 1986) [First of an annual publication, now available on-line at http://www.locusmag.com, and see there for details of a CD-ROM].

Clareson, Thomas D. *Science Fiction in America, 1870s–1930s. An Annotated Bibliography of Primary Sources* (Westport, CT: Greenwood, 1984).

Clute, John and Nicholls, Peter, eds. *The Encyclopedia of Science Fiction* (London: Orbit, 1993).

Contento, William G. *Index to Science Fiction Anthologies and Collections* (Boston: G. K. Hall, 1978). [A second volume, 1984, covers 1977–83; an on-line version is available at http://www.locusmag.com, and see there for details of a CD-ROM].

Currey, Lloyd W. ed. *Science Fiction and Fantasy Authors: A Bibliography of First Printings of Their Fiction and Selected Nonfiction* (Boston: G. K. Hall, 1979).

Day, Donald B. *Index to the Science Fiction Magazines, 1926–1950* (2nd edn, Boston: G. K. Hall, 1982).

Fischer, Dennis. *Science Fiction Film Directors 1895–1998* (New York: McFarland, 2000).

Garber, Eric and Paleo, Lyn. *Uranian Worlds: A Guide to Alternative Sexuality in Science Fiction, Fantasy and Horror* (2nd edn, Boston: G. K. Hall, 1990).

Guillemette, Aurel. *The Best in Science Fiction: Winners and Nominees for the Major Awards in Science Fiction* (Aldershot, Hants: Scolar Press, 1993).

Hardy, Phil. *The Aurum Film Encyclopedia Vol 2: Science Fiction* (London: Aurum, 1990).

*Locus: The Newspaper of the Science Fiction Field*, ed. Charles Brown, monthly [see http://www.locusmag.com].

Magill, Frank N., ed. *Survey of Science Fiction Literature* (5 vols.) (Englewood Cliffs, NJ: Salem, 1979).

Magill, Frank N., ed., with Tymn, Marshall B. *Survey of Science Fiction Literature. Bibliographical Supplement* (Englewood Cliffs, NJ: Salem, 1982).

Nicholls, Peter, ed. *The Encyclopedia of Science Fiction* (London: Granada, 1979).

Reginald, R. *Science Fiction and Fantasy Literature: A Checklist, 1700–1974, with Contemporary Science Fiction Authors II* (2 vols.) (Detroit, MI: Gale, 1979).

Tuck, Donald H., ed. *The Encyclopedia of Science Fiction and Fantasy. Volume 1: Who's Who, A-L* (Chicago: Advent, 1974); *Volume 2: Who's Who, M-Z* (Chicago: Advent, 1978); *Volume 3: Miscellaneous* (Chicago: Advent, 1982).

Tymn, Marshall B. and Ashley, Mike, eds. *Science Fiction, Fantasy, and Weird Magazines* (Westport, CT: Greenwood, 1985).

Watson, Noelle and Schellinger, Paul E., eds. *Twentieth-Century Science-Fiction Writers* (3rd edn, Chicago: St James, 1991).

Wolfe, Gary K. *Critical Terms for Science Fiction and Fantasy: A Glossary and Guide to Scholarship* (Westport, CT: Greenwood, 1986).

## 1. The history

Aldiss, Brian W. with David Wingrove. *Trillion Year Spree: The History of Science Fiction* (London: Gollancz, 1986).

Alkon, Paul K. *Science Fiction Before 1900: Imagination Discovers Technology* (New York: Twayne, 1994).

Armytage, W. H. G. *Yesterday's Tomorrows: A Historical Survey of Future Societies* (London: Routledge & Kegan Paul, 1968).

Ashley, Mike. *The Time Machines: The Story of the Science-Fiction Pulp Magazines from the Beginning to 1950. The History of the Science-Fiction Magazine Volume 1* (Liverpool: Liverpool University Press, 2000).

Atheling, William, Jr [James Blish]. *The Issue at Hand: Studies in Contemporary Magazine Science Fiction* (Chicago: Advent, 1973).

Berger, Albert. *The Magic That Works: John W. Campbell and the American Response to Technology* (San Bernardino, CA: Borgo, 1993).

Bretnor, Reginald, ed. *Modern Science Fiction: Its Meaning and Its Future* (New York: Coward McCann, 1953).

Carter, Paul A. *The Creation of Tomorrow: Fifty Years of Magazine Science Fiction* (New York: Columbia University Press, 1977).

Clarke, I. F. *The Pattern of Expectation: 1644–2001* (London: Cape, 1979).

*Voices Prophesying War: Future Wars 1763-3749* (2nd edn, Oxford: Oxford University Press, 1992).

Clute, John. *Look at the Evidence: Essays and Reviews* (Liverpool: Liverpool University Press, 1996).

Delany, Samuel R. *The Jewel-Hinged Jaw: Notes on the Language of Science Fiction* (1977; reprinted New York: Berkely Windhover, 1978).

*The American Shore: Meditations of a Tale of Science Fiction by Thomas M. Disch – Angouleme* (Elizabethtown, NY: Dragon Press, 1978).

Del Rey, Lester. *The World of Science Fiction: The History of a Subculture* (New York: Del Rey, 1977).

Disch, Thomas M. *The Dreams Our Stuff is Made of: How Science Fiction Conquered the World* (New York: Free Press, 1998).

Franklin, H. Bruce. *Robert A. Heinlein. America as Science Fiction* (New York: Oxford University Press, 1980).

*War Stars. The Superweapon and the American Imagination* (New York: Oxford University Press, 1988).

Greenland, Colin. *The Entropy Exhibition: Michael Moorcock and the British 'New Wave' in Science Fiction* (London: Routledge & Kegan Paul, 1983).

Hartwell, David G. *Age of Wonders: Exploring the World of Science Fiction* (New York: McGraw-Hill, 1984; 2nd edn, New York: Tor, 1996).

Huntington, John. *Rationalizing Genius: Ideological Strategies in the Classic American Science Fiction Short Story* (New Brunswick, NJ: Rutgers University Press, 1989).

Innerhofer, Roland. *Deutsche Science Fiction 1870–1914: Rekonstruktion und Analyse der Anfange einer Gattung* (Wien-Köln-Weimar: Böhlau, 1996).

James, Edward. *Science Fiction in the Twentieth Century* (Oxford: Oxford University Press, 1994).

Knight, Damon. *In Search of Wonder* (2nd edn, Chicago: Advent, 1967).

*The Futurians: The Story of the Science Fiction 'Family' of the 30's That Produced Today's Top SF Writers and Editors* (New York: John Day, 1977).

Kuhn, Annette, ed. *Alien Zone: Cultural Theory and Contemporary Science Fiction Cinema* (London: Verso 1990).

Landon, Brooks. *Aesthetics of Ambivalence: Rethinking Science Fiction Film in the Age of Electronic (Re)production* (Westport, CT: Greenwood, 1992).

*Science Fiction after 1900: From the Steam Man to the Stars* (New York: Twayne, 1997).

Lofficier, Jean-Marc and Lofficier, Randy. *French Science Fiction, Fantasy, Horror and Pulp Fiction* (Jefferson, NC: McFarland, 2000).

Malzberg, Barry. *The Engines of the Night: Science Fiction in the Eighties* (Garden City, NY: Doubleday, 1982).

Panshin, Alexei and Cory. *The World Beyond the Hill: Science Fiction and the Quest for Transcendence* (Los Angeles: Jeremy P. Tarcher, 1989).

Penley, Constance, *et al.*, eds. *Close Encounters: Film, Feminism and Science Fiction* (Minneapolis: University of Minnesota Press, 1991).

Pohl, Frederik. *The Way the Future Was: A Memoir*. New York: Ballantine, 1978.

Sobchak, Vivian. *Screening Space: The American Science Fiction Film* (New York: Ungar, 1987).

Stableford, Brian M. *Scientific Romance in Britain, 1890–1950* (London: Fourth Estate, 1985).

*The Sociology of Science Fiction* (San Bernardino, CA: Borgo, 1987).

'The Third Generation of Genre Science Fiction', *Science-Fiction Studies* 23 (1996), pp. 321–30.

Suvin, Darko. *Victorian Science Fiction in the UK: The Discourses of Knowledge and Power* (Boston: G. K. Hall, 1983).

Further reading

Telotte, J. P. *A Distant Technology: Science Fiction Film and the Machine Age* (Middletown, CT: Wesleyan University Press, 1999).
Telotte, J. P. *Science Fiction Film* (Cambridge: Cambridge University Press, 2001).
Warren, Bill. *Keep Watching the Skies! American Science Fiction Movies of the Fifties* (Jefferson, MO: McFarland, 1997).
Westfahl, Gary *The Mechanics of Wonder: The Creation of the Idea of Science Fiction* (Liverpool: Liverpool University Press, 1998).

## Critical approaches

Armitt, Lucie, ed. *Where No Man Has Gone Before: Women and Science Fiction* (London: Routledge, 1991).
Attebery, Brian. *Strategies of Fantasy* (Bloomington: Indiana University Press, 1992).
Barr, Marleen S. *Feminist Fabulation: Space/Postmodern Fiction* (Iowa City: Iowa University Press, 1992).
Barr, Marleen S., ed. *Future Females, The Next Generation: New Voices and Velocities in Feminist Science Fiction Criticism* (Boulder, CO: Rowman and Littlefield, 2000).
Broderick, Damien. *Reading by Starlight: Postmodern Science Fiction* (London: Routledge, 1995).
Bukatman, Scott. *Terminal Identity: The Virtual Subject in Postmodern Science Fiction* (Durham, NC: Duke University Press, 1993).
Burwell, Jennifer. *Notes on Nowhere: Feminism, Utopian Logic, and Social Transformation* (Minneapolis: University of Minnesota Press, 1997).
Cawelti, John E. *Adventure, Mystery, and Romance: Formula Stories as Art and Popular Culture* (Chicago: University of Chicago Press, 1976).
Cortiel, Jeanne. *Demand My Writing: Joanna Russ/Feminism/Science Fiction* (Liverpool: Liverpool University Press, 1999).
Curtain, Tyler. 'The "Sinister Fruitiness" of Machines: *Neuromancer*, Internet Sexuality, and the Turing Test', in E. K. Sedgwick, ed., *Novel Gazing: Queer Readings in Fiction* (Durham, NC: Duke University Press, 1997), pp. 128–48.
Donawerth, Jane L. *Frankenstein's Daughters: Women Writing Science Fiction* (Syracuse, NY: Syracuse University Press, 1997).
Donawerth, Jane L. and Kolmerten, Carol A., eds. *Utopian and Science Fiction by Women: Worlds of Difference* (Syracuse, NY: Syracuse University Press, 1994).
Franklin, H. Bruce. 'Star Trek in the Vietnam Era', *Science-Fiction Studies* 21:1 (March 1994), pp. 24–43.
'The Vietnam War as American SF and Fantasy', *Science-Fiction Studies* 17:3 (November 1990), pp. 341–59.
Freedman, Carl. *Critical Theory and Science Fiction* (Hanover, NH: Wesleyan University Press, 2000).
Gubar, Susan. 'C. L. Moore and the Conventions of Women's SF', *Science-Fiction Studies* 7 (March 1980), pp. 16–27.
Haraway, Donna. *Simians, Cyborgs, and Women. The Reinvention of Nature* (New York: Routledge, 1991).
'A Manifesto for Cyborgs: Science, Technology, and Socialist Feminism in the 1980s' [1985], reprinted in Elizabeth Weed, ed., *Coming to Terms: Feminism,*

*Theory, Politics* (New York: Routledge, 1989), pp. 173–204 (and in *Simians, Cyborgs and Women*).

Hayles, N. Katherine. *How We Became Posthuman: Virtual Bodies in Cybernetics, Literature and Informatics* (Chicago: University of Chicago Press, 1999).

Heller, Leonid. *De la science-fiction soviétique* (Geneva: L'Age d'homme, 1979).

Hollinger, Veronica. '(Re)Reading Queerly: Science Fiction, Feminism, and the Defamiliarization of Gender', *Science-Fiction Studies* 26 (1999), pp. 23–40.

Jameson, Fredric. 'Postmodernism, or the Cultural Logic of Late Capitalism', *New Left Review* (July/August 1984), pp. 53–94.

*Postmodernism, or The Cultural Logic of Late Capitalism* (Durham, NC: Duke University Press, 1991).

Kirkup, Gill, Janes, Linda, Woodward, Kathryn and Hoenden, Fiona, eds. *The Gendered Cyborg: A Reader* (London: Routledge, 2000).

Larbalestier, Justine. *The Battle of the Sexes in Science Fiction* (Middletown, CT: Wesleyan University Press, 2002).

Lefanu, Sarah. *In the Chinks of the World Machine: Feminism and Science Fiction* (London: The Women's Press, 1988) (in USA published as *Feminism and Science Fiction*, 1989).

Le Guin, Ursula K. *Dancing at the Edge of the World: Thoughts on Words, Women, Places* (New York: Grove, 1989).

Le Guin, Ursula K., ed. Susan Wood. *The Language of the Night: Essays on Fantasy and Science Fiction* (New York: Perigee, 1979).

McCaffery, Larry, ed. *Storming the Reality Studio: A Casebook of Postmodern Science Fiction* (Durham, NC: Duke University Press, 1991).

Marchesani, Joseph. 'Science Fiction and Fantasy', in C.J. Summers, ed., *The Gay and Lesbian Literary Heritage: A Reader's Companion to the Writers and Their Words, from Antiquity to the Present* (New York: Henry Holt, 1995), pp. 638–44.

Merrick, Helen. ' "Fantastic Dialogues": Critical Stories about Feminism and Science Fiction', in Andy Sawyer and David Seed, eds., *Speaking Science Fiction: Dialogues and Interpretations* (Liverpool: Liverpool University Press, 2000), pp. 52–68.

Merrick, Helen, and Williams Tess, eds. *Women of Other Worlds: Excursions through Science Fiction and Feminism* (Nedlands, WA: University of Western Australia Press, 1999).

Mohanraj, Mary Anne. 'Alternative Sexualities in Fantasy and SF Booklist' http://www.mamohanraj.com/balist.html.

Morton, Donald. 'Birth of the Cyberqueer', *Proceedings of the Modern Language Association* 110 (1995), pp. 369–81.

Moylan, Tom. *Demand the Impossible. Science Fiction and the Utopian Imagination* (London: Methuen, 1986).

Moylan, Tom. *Scraps of the Untainted Sky. Science Fiction, Utopia, Dystopia* (Boulder, CO: Westview, 2000).

Palumbo, Donald, ed. *Erotic Universe: Sexuality and Fantastic Literature* (Westport, CT: Greenwood, 1986).

Parrinder, Patrick. 'Revisiting Suvin's Poetics of Science Fiction', in Parrinder, ed. *Learning from Other Worlds* (Liverpool: Liverpool University Press, 2000), pp. 36–50.

Pearson, Wendy. 'Alien Cryptographies: The View from Queer', *Science-Fiction Studies* 26 (1999), pp. 1–22.

Penley, Constance, Lyon, Elisabeth, Spigel, Lynn and Bergstrom, Janet, eds. *Close Encounters: Film, Feminism, and Science Fiction* (Minneapolis: University of Minnesota Press, 1991).

Riemer, James D. 'Homosexuality in Science Fiction and Fantasy', in D. Palumbo, ed., *Erotic Universe: Sexuality and Fantastic Literature* (Westport, CT: Greenwood, 1986), pp. 145–61.

Rucker, Rudy, Wilson, Peter Lamborn and Wilson, Robert Anton, eds. *Semiotext(e): SF* (New York: Semiotext(e), 1999).

Russ, Joanna. 'Recent Feminist Utopias', in Marleen S. Barr, ed., *Future Females: A Critical Anthology* (Bowling Green, OH: Bowling Green State University Popular Press, 1981), pp. 71–85.

 *To Write Like a Woman: Essays in Feminism and Science Fiction* (Bloomington: Indiana University Press, 1995).

Sargent, Pamela, ed. *Women of Wonder: The Classic Years: Science Fiction by Women from the 1940s to the 1970s* (New York: Harcourt Brace, 1995).

 *Women of Wonder: The Contemporary Years: Science Fiction by Women from the 1970s to the 1990s* (New York: Harcourt Brace, 1995).

Sawyer, Andy and Seed, David, eds. *Speaking Science Fiction: Dialogues and Interpretations* (Liverpool: Liverpool University Press, 2000).

Scholes, Robert. *Structural Fabulation: An Essay on Fiction of the Future* (Notre Dame, IN: Notre Dame University Press, 1975).

Scholes, Robert and Rabkin, Eric. *Science Fiction: History, Science, Vision* (New York: Oxford University Press, 1977).

Slusser, George and Shippey, Tom, eds. *Fiction 2000: Cyberpunk and the Future of Narrative* (Athens, GA: University of Georgia Press, 1992).

Smith, Jeffrey D., ed. 'Symposium: Women in Science Fiction', *Khatru* 3 and 4 (November 1975), reprint ed. Jeanne Gomoll (Madison, WI: Corflu, 1993).

Suvin, Darko. *Metamorphoses of Science Fiction: On the Poetics and History of a Literary Genre* (New Haven, CT: Yale University Press, 1979).

Wolmark, Jenny. *Aliens and Others: Science Fiction, Feminism and Postmodernism* (Hemel Hempstead, Herts: Harvester Wheatsheaf, 1993; Iowa City: University of Iowa Press, 1994).

Wolmark, Jenny, ed. *Cybersexualities: A Reader on Feminist Theory, Cyborgs and Cyberspace* (Edinburgh: Edinburgh University Press, 1999).

### Sub-genres and themes

Attebery, Brian. *Decoding Gender in Science Fiction* (London and New York: Routledge, 2002).

Benford, Gregory. 'Imagining the Abyss': Preface to G. Benford and M. H. Greenberg, eds., *Hitler Victorious: Eleven Stories of the German Victory in World War II* (New York: Garland, 1986).

Bloch, Ernst. *The Principle of Hope* (Oxford: Blackwell, 1986).

Carpenter, Joel A. *Revive Us Again: the Reawakening of American Fundamentalism* (New York: Oxford University Press, 1997).

Chamberlain, Gordon B. 'Allohistory in Science Fiction': Afterword to C. G. Waugh and M. H. Greenberg, eds., *Alternative Histories: Eleven Stories of the World as It Might Have Been* (New York: Garland, 1986).

Clover, Carol J. *Men, Women and Chainsaws: Gender in the Modern Horror Film* (Princeton: Princeton University Press, 1992).

Cook, Diane. 'Yes Virginia, There's Always Been Women's Science Fiction ... Feminist Even', in Jenny and Russell Blackford *et al.*, eds., *Contrary Modes: Proceedings of the World Science Fiction Conference* (Melbourne: Aussiecon 2, 1985), pp. 133–45.

Cramer, Kathryn. 'Science Fiction and the Adventures of the Spherical Cow', *New York Review of Science Fiction* 1 (September 1988), pp. 1, 3–5.

Crick, Bernard. *In Defence of Politics* (London: Weidenfeld and Nicholson, 1962).

Delany, Samuel R. *Starboard Wine: More Notes on the Language of Science Fiction* (Pleasantville, NY: Dragon Press, 1984).

Ferguson, Niall. 'Virtual History: Towards a "Chaotic" Theory of the Past': Introduction to Ferguson, ed., *Virtual History: Alternatives and Counterfactuals* (London: Picador, 1997), pp. 1–90.

Ferns, Chris. *Narrating Utopia: Ideology, Gender, Form in Utopian Literature* (Liverpool: Liverpool University Press, 1999).

Finke, Roger and Starke, Rodney. *The Churching of America, 1776–1990* (New Brunswick, NJ: Rutgers University Press, 1992).

Fitting, Peter. 'So We All Became Mothers: New Roles For Men in Recent Utopian Fiction', *Science-Fiction Studies* 12 (1985), pp. 156–83.

Frank, Janrae, Stine, Jean and Ackerman, J., eds., *New Eves: Science Fiction About the Extraordinary Women of Today and Tomorrow* (Stamford, CT., Longmeadow, 1994).

Friedman, David. *The Machinery of Freedom* (New York: Harper and Row, 1973).

Goodwin, Barbara and Taylor, Keith. *The Politics of Utopia: A Study in Theory and Practice* (London: Hutchinson, 1982).

Hacker, Barton C. and Chamberlain, Gordon B. 'Pasts That Might Have Been, 11: A Revised Bibliography of Alternative History', in C. G. Waugh and M. H. Greenberg, eds., *Alternative Histories: Eleven Stories of the World as It Might Have Been* (New York: Garland, 1986).

Hantke, Steffen. 'Surgical Strikes and Prosthetic Warriors: The Soldier's Body in Contemporary Science Fiction', *Science-Fiction Studies* 25 (1998), pp. 495–509.

Hardesty, William H. 'Space Opera Without the Space: The Culture Novels of Iain M. Banks', in G. Westfahl, ed., *Space and Beyond: The Frontier Theme in Science Fiction* (Westport, CT: Greenwood, 2000), pp. 115–22.

Hartwell, David G. and Cramer, Kathryn, eds. *The Ascent of Wonder: The Evolution of Hard SF* (New York: Tor, 1994).

Hassler, Donald M. and Wilcox, Clyde, eds. *Political Science Fiction* (Columbia, SC: University of South Carolina Press, 1997).

Hellekson, Karen. *The Alternate History: Refiguring Historical Time* (Kent, OH: Kent State University Press, 2001).

James, Edward. 'Yellow, Black, Metal, and Tentacled: the Race Question in American Science Fiction', in P. J. Davies, ed., *Science Fiction, Social Conflict, and War* (Manchester: Manchester University Press, 1990), pp. 26–49.

'Even Worse, It Could Be Perfect': Aspects of the Undesirable Utopia in Modern Science Fiction', in G. Slusser *et al.*, eds., *Transformations of Utopia: Changing Views of the Perfect Society* (New York: AMS Press, 1999), pp. 215–28.

'A "Double-Dyed Distilled Detractor and Denigrator of Decency, Dignity and Decorum": Eric Frank Russell as Anarchist', *Anarchist Studies* 7 (1999), pp. 155–70.

Jones, Gwyneth. 'Metempsychosis of the Machine: Science Fiction in the Halls of Karma', *Science-Fiction Studies* 24 (1977), pp. 1–10.

*Deconstructing the Starships* (Liverpool: Liverpool University Press, 1999).

Kumar, Krishan. *Utopia and Anti-Utopia in Modern Times* (Oxford: Blackwell, 1987).

Leonard, Elisabeth Anne, ed. *Into Darkness Peering: Race and Color in the Fantastic* (Westport, CT: Greenwood, 1997).

Levitas, Ruth. *The Concept of Utopia* (London: Philip Allan, 1990).

Longhurst, Derek, ed. *Gender, Genre and Narrative Pleasure* (London: Unwin Hyman, 1989).

Malzberg, Barry N. 'The All-Time, Prime-Time, Take-Me-to-Your-Leader Science Fiction Plot', in Malzberg, *The Engines of the Night: Science Fiction in the Eighties* (1982) (New York: Bluejay, 1984), pp. 147–58.

May, Stephen. *Stardust and Ashes: Science Fiction in the Christian Perspective* (London: SPCK, 1998).

Mayo, Mohs, ed. *Other Worlds, Other Gods: Adventures in Religious Science Fiction* (New York: Doubleday, 1971).

McGuire, Patrick L. *Red Stars: Political Aspects of Soviet Science Fiction* (Ann Arbor, MI: UMI Research Press, 1985).

Mendlesohn, Farah. 'Women in Science Fiction: Six American Sf Writers Between 1960 and 1985', *Foundation* 53 (Autumn 1991), pp. 53–69.

'Gender, Power and Conflict Resolution: "Subcommittee" by Zenna Henderson', *Extrapolation* 35 (1994), pp. 120–9.

Mogen, David. *Wilderness Visions: The Western Theme in Science Fiction Literature* (2nd edn, San Bernardino, CA: Borgo Press, 1993).

Monk, Patricia. '"Not Just Cosmic Skullduggery": A Partial Reconsideration of Space Opera', *Extrapolation* 33 (1992), pp. 295–316.

Moorcock, Michael, 'Starship Stormtroopers', http://www.geocities.com/CapitolHill/Lobby/3998/Moorcock.html.

Morrison, Toni. *Playing in the Dark: Whiteness and the Literary Imagination* (1992) (New York: Vintage, 1993).

Nicholls, Peter, ed., with David Langford and Brian Stableford. *The Science in Science Fiction* (London: Joseph, 1982).

Omi, Michael. 'In Living Color: Race and American Culture', in I. Angus and S. Jhally, eds., *Cultural Politics in Contemporary America* (New York: Routledge, 1989), pp. 111–22.

Parkin-Speer, Diane. 'Almost a Feminist: Robert A. Heinlein', *Extrapolation* 36 (1995), pp. 113–25.

Rabkin, Eric. 'The Male Body in Science Fiction', *Michigan Quarterly Review* 33 (1994), pp. 203–17.

Ramsay, Robin. *Conspiracy Theories* (Harpenden: Pocket Essentials, 2000).

Reilly, Robert, ed. *The Transcendent Adventure: Studies of Religion in Science Fiction/Fantasy* (Westport, CT: Greenwood, 1985).

Roberts, Robin. *A New Species: Gender and Science in Science Fiction* (Urbana: Illinois University Press, 1993).

Russ, Joanna. '*Amor Vincit Foeminam*: The Battle of the Sexes in SF', *Science-Fiction Studies* 7 (1980), pp. 2–15.

Said, Edward. *Culture and Imperialism* (New York: Knopf, 1993).

Samuelson, David. 'A Softening of the Hard-SF Concept', *Science-Fiction Studies* 21 (1994), pp. 406–12.

Sanders, Joe L. 'Space Opera Reconsidered', *New York Review of Science Fiction* 82 (June 1995), pp. 1, 3–6.

Sands, Karen and Frank, Marietta. *Back in the Spaceship Again: Juvenile Science Fiction Series Since 1945* (Westport, CT: Greenwood, 1999).

Sargent, Lyman Tower. *British and American Utopian Literature, 1516–1985. An Annotated, Chronological Bibliography* (New York: Garland, 1988).

Segal, Howard P. *Technological Utopianism in American Culture* (Chicago: Chicago University Press, 1985).

Silverberg, Robert. 'Introduction', in M. H. Greenberg, ed., *The Way It Wasn't: Great Science Fiction Stories of Alternate History* (New York: Citadel Twilight-Carol, 1996), pp. vii–xii.

Slusser, George and Rabkin, Eric, eds. *Hard Science Fiction* (Carbondale: Southern Illinois University Press, 1986).

Stableford, Brian. 'The Last Chocolate Bar and the Majesty of Truth: Reflections on the Concept of "Hardness" in Science Fiction (Part 1)', *New York Review of Science Fiction* 71 (July 1994), pp. 1, 8–12 and 72 (Aug. 1994), pp. 10–16.

Thomas, Sheree, ed. *Dark Matter: A Century of Speculative Fiction from the African Diaspora* (New York: Warner, 2000).

Trotsky, Leon, Dewey, John and Novack, George, eds. *Their Morals and Ours: Marxist versus Liberal Views on Morality* (New York: Pathfinder, 1973).

*Uchronia: The Alternate History List*, ed. Robert B. Schmunk, http://www.uchronia.net/.

Westfahl, Gary. 'Beyond Logic and Literacy: The Strange Case of Space Opera', *Extrapolation* 35 (1994), pp. 176–88.

'Where No Market Has Gone Before: "The Science-Fiction Industry" and the *Star Trek* Industry', *Extrapolation* 37 (1996), pp. 291–301.

*Cosmic Engineers: A Study of Hard Science Fiction* (Westport, CT: Greenwood, 1996).

*Islands in the Sky: The Space Station Theme in Science Fiction Literature* (San Bernardino, CA: Borgo Press, 1996).

Westfahl, Gary, ed. *Space and Beyond: The Frontier Theme in Science Fiction* (Westport, CT: Greenwood, 2000).

Wolfe, Gary K., *The Known and the Unknown: The Iconography of Science Fiction* (Kent, OH: Kent State University Press, 1979).

Wolff, Robert Paul. *In Defense of Anarchism* (New York: Harper and Row, 1970).

Zaki, Hoda M. *Phoenix Renewed: The Survival and Mutation of Utopian Thought in North American Science Fiction, 1965–1982* (Mercer Island, WA: Starmont, 1988).

# INDEX

# Index

# Index

Index

Index

# Index

# CAMBRIDGE COMPANIONS TO LITERATURE

## CAMBRIDGE COMPANIONS TO CULTURE